Native
American Humor

NATIVE AMERICAN HUMOR

EDITED BY
JAMES R. ASWELL

ILLUSTRATED BY
LEO HERSHFIELD

HARPER & BROTHERS PUBLISHERS
NEW YORK AND LONDON

2-7

FIRST EDITION

A-W

Table of Contents

v

Editor's Foreword

THIS book rounds up some of the most telling examples of the American sense of humor during our age of great laughter—from Revolutionary times when its voice began to burst out clearly, through the turmoil of the Frontier and Civil War periods when it was at its most exuberant, to the 1890's when it was in danger of prattling itself into whimsy and commercial jokesmithing.

The collection is not an antiquarian study. Its only purpose is to entertain. All entries were chosen for ability to stand on their own feet as humor.

Included are sketches and tales by familiar humorists, ranging from Washington Irving to Bill Nye and Mark Twain. We are apt to think of these writers as mavericks rather than true representatives of a time which seems pretty stiff and declamatory, judged by the dreary halftones in textbooks, the lumpish, bird-bedropped public monuments, and most of the writing allowed to come down to us. Today, even such masters of fun-making as Josh Billings, John Phoenix, and Petroleum V. Nasby are little more than classroom hearsay. Equally hearty humorous creations—including Sut Lovingood, Sam Snaffles, and Simon Suggs, three characters which by right ought to be American classics—have been abandoned by the dozens to potters field. At best they are vaguely associated with gags of the stale "by cracky!" type.

For that we owe a grudge to the clique of New England literary gentlemen who appointed themselves custodians of our national culture. They were the ones who lowered the drape of starched respectability between their century and ours. It's high time to brush it aside and reclaim the laughter of a younger America for the delightful portion of our heritage that it is.

Some of the best writing of the period went, gratis, to newspapers and periodicals under pen names and anonymity. The authors were tramp printers, soldiers, reporters, preachers, doctors, editors, lawyers, politicians, merchants, swindlers, steamboat captains, actors, schoolmasters. They rubbed elbows daily with the vigorous life of their times and reported it with shrewdly humorous insight. In laughing at the hurlyburly of America, *they knowingly laughed at themselves as part and parcel of it.* That is the core of our native sense of humor.

Many of these unknown writers were gifted enough to have become major literary figures. But until 1846, when U.S. copyright regulations went into effect, it was next to impossible to make a living from writing in America. Editors loaded their magazines, gift annuals, and book lists with pirated stuff. Particularly they considered British publications fair game, and filched wholesale from them without so much as a thank-you. Pilferings back and forth across the sea continued to some extent until the international copyright agreement of 1891.

Meanwhile, the literary roost was ruled by those cultural backwoodsmen whose horizon was just about limited to the view from the steeple of the Old North Church. Drs. Holmes, Whittier, Emerson, and Longfellow proscribed realism, especially humorous realism, as vulgarity. They and their editorial followers held that the proper duty of writers was moral uplift, whether by essay, poesy, fiction, or breakfast table chitchat. On at least one occasion, they made Mark Twain himself writhe in humiliation like a worm in salt. By the latter part of the 19th Century, their censorship had a strong ally from outside. The portly and proper shadow of Victoria the Good, reaching across the English-speaking world, had become the substance of an age.

Put together as it has been, with an eye to the American sense of humor as such, the book contains amusing swatches from lives and writing that drop into no formal category of wit or humor. Liberties have been taken with the texts of many selections. To give the broadest possible cross-section in a limited space, it has been necessary to blue-pencil nearly every piece. Some have been cut to a third of their original leisurely length. In several cases that called for internal rearrangement. Some of the selections would have slowed modern reading because of elaborate misspelling. I haven't hesitated to reduce this to a minimum. In a handful of exceptions —notably the Petroleum V. Nasby sketch—translation would have spoiled the effect.

When an obscure topical point cropped up, it was eliminated unless it keyed organically into the piece. Then brief explanation was added in the author's style. If two or more versions of the same story occurred, the best features were combined. For example, *Frolic in the Knobs* has woven into it bits from five mountain shindig sketches by George Washington Harris. There has been considerable retitling. Selections have been arranged roughly in chronological order, with whatever deviations variety required. In gathering the anthology, I have read more than 400 books, the files of almost as many magazines and newspapers, and spot-checked literally thousands of others.

No one-volume collection can be exhaustive. Regretfully I have had to count out such entertaining things as the journals of Madam Sarah Kemble Knight and William Byrd of Westover, P. B. Shillaber's malaprop *Mrs. Partington*, and Charles Graham Halpine's *Private Miles O'Reilly*. The flavor of them can't be got from extracts. You need to read them in full. Other humorous writers of the period simply didn't amuse me. Among these were Freneau, Trumbull, Barlow, Halleck, Verplanck, Lowell, Hays, Asa Green, Willis Gaylord Clark, Kennedy, Cozzens, Goodrich, Lewis, Adams, Townsend, and most particularly Miss Marietta Holley who perpetrated the cornfed *Josiah Allen's Wife* series. Eugene Field's acid *Denver Tribune Primer* makes me laugh out loud. Not so with my publishers and my patient jury of friends. So out it went. The collection stops short of Mr. Dooley because he belongs to the modern school of American humor. Besides, he is liberally represented in other anthologies.

The foreword has been kept short. Readers interested in further detail will find tucked at the back of the book notes on as many of the writers as I have been able to track down.

JAMES R. ASWELL

Native
American Humor

☆

How to Receive a Challenge

HUGH HENRY BRACKENRIDGE

Major Valentine Jacko,
U. S. Army.
Sir,—

I have two objections to this duel matter.

The one is, lest I should hurt you; and the other is, lest you should hurt me.

I do not see any good it would do me to put a bullet through any part of your body. I could make no use of you when dead for any culinary purpose as I would a rabbit or a turkey. I am no cannibal to feed on the flesh of men. Why, then, shoot down a human creature of which I could make no use? A buffalo would be better meat. For though your flesh may be delicate and tender, yet it wants that firmness and consistency which takes and retains salt. At any rate, it would not be fit for long sea voyages. You might make a good barbecue, it is true, being of the nature of a racoon or an opossum, but people are not in the habit of barbecuing anything human now. As to your hide, it is not worth taking off, being little better than that of a year-old colt.

It would seem to me a strange thing to shoot at a man that would stand still to be shot at, inasmuch as I have heretofore been used to shoot at things flying or running or jumping. Were you on a tree now like a squirrel, endeavoring to hide yourself in the branches, or like a racoon that after much eyeing and spying, I observe at length in the crotch of a tall oak with boughs and leaves intervening, so that I could just get a sight of his hinderparts, I should think it pleasurable enough to take a shot at you. But, as it is, there is no skill or judgment requisite to discover or take you down.

As to myself, I do not much like to stand in the way of anything harmful. I am under apprehensions that you might hit me. That being the case, I think it most advisable to stay at a distance. If you want to try your pistols, take some object, a tree or a barn door, about my dimensions. If you hit that, send me word and I shall acknowledge that if I had been in the same place, you might also have hit me.

John Farrago
Late Captain, Pennsylvania Militia.

1796

Almanack Drolleries

ANONYMOUS

WHEN Sir William Johnson was appointed superintendent of Indian affairs, and went among the Mohawk, he was received and feasted by Hendrick, King of that nation, who speedily instructed him in the habits and customs of his people. He said that the Mohawk considered dreams as prophetic and that he trusted that the representative of His Majesty would conceive that any breach in that age-old custom would reflect unfortunately in respect to the regard the Mohawk felt for the subjects of Britain.

Sir William, cannily acknowledging that the British fully respected the usage of the country, Hendrick thus spoke:

"Last night I dreamed. I dreamed that the Great King would present me with a scarlet coat, of fine make, and ornamented with gold and silver."

"True for your dream," said Sir William Johnson. "Come you to me tomorrow, Hendrick." Which, he doing, he was given a beautiful coat, with scallops of gold braid and buttons of silver gilt.

Whereupon, after Hendrick had professed himself exceedingly pleased, Sir William said, "Last night, I, too, had a dream. I fancied, Hendrick, that you gave me deed and title to a parcel of 5,000 of the richest acres along the Mohawk River."

The following day Hendrick solemnly conveyed to Sir William a title to the aforesaid acres, and the Sovereign subsequently confirmed the deed. Then, the next day, Sir William, being after all an Irishman, said, "And what did you chance to dream last night, Hendrick?"

"My sleep was without dream," said the Mohawk.

"Come now, Hendrick," said Sir William. "You must have dreamed something."

"No," said the Mohawk. "That I did not. Sir William, never again shall I dream with you. You dream too big for an Indian."

A clergyman of Boston was offended in his dignity by a lad who passed him without doffing his hat.

"Do you know who I am, sir, that you pass me in that unmannerly way?" he said. "You are better fed than taught."

The lad, who was quite stout of build and ruddy, said, "May it be so, master. You only teaches me of Sundays, but I feed myself."

During the last election, a candidate visited a countryman in Pennsylvania, pressing for his vote, promising to turn out the party at present in power and to procure a new officialdom.

"Then I won't vote for you," said the farmer.

"Why not?" asked the candidate.

"I thought you were a champion of your country," said the farmer.

"So I am," said the candidate.

"So am I," said the farmer. "For that reason, I don't want to change administrations."

"That requires explanation," said the candidate, now wroth.

Said the countryman, "I know well, when I buy hogs lean, they eat like gluttons. But, when once they've got a little fat, they don't want half so much to keep 'em. So for that reason, I'm for sticking to the present set. They'll not devour half as much as the new one!"

Engraven on the headstones in the grave yards of New England are many wise and wry observations, of which the two following will serve as examples of an entire category:

> HERE LIE THE REMAINS OF SAMUEL E———,
> UNTIMELY JOINED TO HIS MAKER
> BY THE FALL OF A CHIMNEY
> IN A WINDSTORM.
> HE LEFT BEHIND, JANE, HIS COMELY YOUNG WIDOW,
> WHOSE ADDRESS IS 23 BEDFORD STREET,
> WHOSE DISPOSITION IS ONE
> WILLING TO BE COMFORTED.

And another:

> BENEATH THIS SILENT STONE IS LAID
> A NOISY, ANTIQUATED MAID,
> WHO, FROM HER CRADLE, TALKED TILL DEATH,
> AND NE'ER BEFORE WAS OUT OF BREATH.

WHITHER SHE'S GONE, WE CANNOT TELL,
FOR, IF SHE TALKS NOT, SHE'S IN HELL:
IF SHE'S IN HEAVEN, SHE'S THERE UNBLEST;
SHE HATES A PLACE OF REST.

If a book can't answer for itself to the public, it is of no sort of purpose for its author to do so.

Law are like cobwebs, which catch the small flies but are broken through by the large ones.

Modesty is a kind of fear that keeps a good man on the bottom.

Patience under misfortunes, is like opiates in a fever; tossing and tumbling only irritate the distemper.

Politics makes a man as crooked as a pack does a peddler; both teach a man to stoop.

Mix whisky and water, and you spoil two good things.

One day a gentleman was caught kissing a homely bar maid. When rallied by his friends, he said, "Thank God, I am not yet reduced to Brandy and Beauty to whet my appetite."

A somewhat illiterate gentleman in Virginia writes to a merchant in Richmond for a still of certain dimensions, and thus expresses himself: "Sir, I want a still maid that will work 36 gallants." We believe he meant gallons.

When Thomas Jefferson came to the Court at Paris as the new American Minister, he was introduced to a nobleman, who said, "Ah, yes. You replace Dr. Franklin, I believe."

"I succeed Dr. Franklin," Jefferson replied quickly. "No man can replace him."

1776-1821

Definition

PATRICK HENRY

GOVERNOR GILES, of Virginia, once addressed a note to Patrick Henry, demanding satisfaction:

"*Sir*: I understand that you have called me a 'bob-tail' politician. I wish to know if it be true; and if true, your meaning.

"Wm. B. Giles."

To which Patrick Henry replied:

"*Sir*: I do not recollect having called you a 'bob-tail' politician at any time, but think it probable I have. Not recollecting the time or occasion, I can't say what I did mean, but if you will tell me what you think I meant, I will say whether you are correct or not.

"Very respectfully,
"Patrick Henry."

1780

Battle of the Kegs

THE NEW JERSEY GAZETTE

Jan. 21, 1778—
Philadelphia has been entertained with a most astonishing instance of the activity, bravery, and military skill of the Royal Navy of Great Britain. The affair is somewhat particular, and deserves notice.

Some time last week, two boys observed a keg of singular construction floating in the river opposite to the city. They got into a small boat, and, attempting to take up the keg, it burst with a great explosion and blew up the unfortunate boys. Yesterday, several kegs of a like construction, made their appearance. An alarm was immediately spread through the city. Various reports prevailed, filling the city and the royal troops with consternation. Some reported that the kegs were filled with armed rebels, who were to issue forth in the dead of night, as the Grecians did of old from their wooden horse at the siege of Troy, and take the city by surprise; asserting that they had seen the points of rebel bayonets through the bungholes of the kegs.

Others said they were charged with combustibles, to be kindled by secret machinery, and, setting the whole Delaware in flames, were to consume all the shipping in the harbor. Whilst others asserted that they were constructed by art magic, would of themselves ascend the wharves in the night time, and roll all flaming through the streets of the city, destroying everything in their way.

Be that as it may, certain it is that the shipping in the harbor, and all the wharves in the city were fully manned.

The battle began. It was surprising to behold the incessant blaze that was kept up against the enemy, the kegs. Both officers and men exhibited the most unparalleled skill and bravery on the occasion, whilst the citizens stood gazing as solemn witnesses of their prowess.

From the *Roebuck* and other ships of war, whole broadsides were poured into the Delaware. In short, not a wandering ship, stick, or drift log but felt the vigor of the British arms. The action began about sunrise, and would have been completed with great success by noon, had not an old market woman, coming down the river with provisions, unfortunately let a small keg of butter fall overboard, which (as it was then ebb tide) floated down to the scene of action.

At sight of this unexpected reinforcement of the enemy, the battle was renewed with fresh fury. The firing was incessant till the evening closed the affair. The kegs were either totally demolished, or obliged to fly, as none of them have shown their heads since.

It is said His Excellency Lord Howe has dispatched a swift-sailing packet with an account of his victory to the court of London. In a word, Monday, the 5th of January, 1778, must ever be distinguished in history for the memorable BATTLE OF THE KEGS.

1778

Pithy Reply

Anonymous

A PERSON of the name of Palmer, who was a lieutenant in the new tory levies, was detected in the patriot camp at Peek's-kiln. He was seized and brought before the court-martial.

Intelligence of this reached Governor Tryon, who commanded the tory levies, and he penned a heated note to patriot General Putnam, representing as heinous the crime of trying a man commissioned by his majesty, and threatening vengeance in case he should be condemned and executed.

General Putnam wrote him the following reply:

"Sir,

"Nathan Palmer, a lieutenant in your king's service, was taken in my camp as a spy. He was tried as a spy. He was condemned as a spy. You may rest assured, sir, he shall be hanged as a spy.

"I have the honor to be &c.,

"Israel Putnam."

"P.S. Afternoon. He is hanged."

1796

9

Dr. Franklin

ANONYMOUS

SOME year since, as Dr. Franklin was travelling through New England, he, on a winter's evening, alighted at a tavern, and ordered his horse to be stabled. To the doctor's mortification, he found that only the public room in the house was accommodated with a fire, and that this was so engrossed by indolent countrymen that he could not approach it, shivering with bone-cold though he was.

"Landlord," said the doctor, "have you oysters?"

"Yes, Sir."

"Give my horse an half bushel of them."

"Sir! Oysters! Your *horse* an half bushel of oysters?"

"Yes, Sir. Give him the oysters."

The guest was obeyed; and as the discourse did not escape the attention of the countrymen, curiosity prompted them to repair to the stable to see in what manner the horse would eat the oysters?

But a few minutes, however, passed before the men returned, when the host exclaimed to Dr. Franklin, "*Sir, your horse won't eat the oysters.*"

"Will he *not*? Oh, then bring them here and roast them. They will answer for my supper," said the doctor, now comfortably seated by the fire.

Dr. Franklin, as agent for the Province of Pennsylvania, being in England at the time the Parliament passed the stampt-act for America, was freqently applied to by the Ministry for his opinion respecting the operation of the same. He assured them that the people of America would never consent to it.

The act was nevertheless passed, and the events shewed he had been right.

After the news of the destruction of the stampt paper had arrived in England, the Ministry again sent for the doctor, to consult with him, and concluded with the proposition, that if the Americans would engage to pay for the damage done in the destruction of the stampt paper, &c., the Parliament would repeal the act.

To this the doctor answered that it put him in mind of a Frenchman, who having heated a poker red hot, ran into the street, and addressing an Englishman he met there, said, "Hah, monsieur, voulez vous give me de plaisir et de satisfaction, and let me run dis poker only one foote up your backside?"

"What!" says the Englishman.

"Only to let me run dis poker one foote up your backside," says the Frenchman.

"Damn your soul!" says the Englishman.

"Well, den," says the Frenchman, pointing to about six inches of the poker, "only *so* far."

"No, no, damn your soul!" replies the Englishman. "What do you mean!"

"Well, den," says the Frenchman, "will you have de justice to pay me for de trouble and expence of heating de poker?"

Englishmen across the sea, said the doctor, would say to their lordships precisely what the other Englishman said to the Frenchman, "Be damned to you!"

A needy friend appealed to Dr. Franklin for aid whilst he was serving as American minister to the French. To which honest Benjamin replied:

Paris, April 22, 1784.

Dear ———,

I send you herewith a bill for ten *louis d'or*. I do not pretend to give such a sum, I only lend it to you. When you shall return to your country, you cannot fail of getting into some business that will in time enable you to pay all your debts. In that case, when you meet with another honest man in similar distress, you must pay me by lending this sum to him, enjoining him to discharge the debt by a like operation, when he shall be able, and shall meet with another such opportunity. I hope it may go thus through many hands before it meets a knave to stop its progress. This is a trick of mine for doing a great deal of good with a little money. I am not rich enough to afford much in good works, and so am obliged to be cunning and make the most of little.

Truly

Benj. Franklin.

1776-1784

Bring Back My Bonnie

IN 1784 a Boston paper printed the following advertisement:
RAN away from his wife and helpless family, on Friday last, John Spriggs, by trade a tailor, aged thirty-five, a wide mouth, zig-zag teeth, a nose of high-burned brick color, with a lofty bridge, swivel-eyed, and a scar (not an honorable one) on his left cheek. He primes and loads (that is takes snuff and tobacco); he is so loquacious that he tires every one in company, but himself. In order that he may entrap the sinner and the saint, he carries a Pack of Cards in one pocket, and the *Practice of Piety* in the other. He is a great liar, and can varnish falsehood with a great deal of art. Had on, when he went away, a three cocked hat, with a blue body coat, rather on the fade. He was seen in Bennington on Saturday last, disguised in a clean shirt.

1784

Humours of
Well-Fed Dominie Double-Chin

ANONYMOUS

PARSON T——, when about fulfilling his design of preaching to the Susquehanna Indians, applied to an opulent merchant for a small sum of money to enable him to prosecute his undertaking. "Why, what do you intend to do among the copper gentry?" says the merchant. "Prepare for them," says the Parson, "a place in the bosom of Abraham." "And do you imagine," says the merchant, "that father Abraham will thank you for filling his bosom with a pack of damned savages?"

A gentlewoman loved a doctor of physic and, to enjoy him, feigned herself sick. The doctor being sent for in all haste, went up and staid with her an hour. When he came down, her husband asked him how she did? "O," says he, "she has had two such *extreme* fits, that if you had seen one of them, it would have broke your heart."

A fat parson, who had long dozed over his sermons in his pulpit and his beer in his parlour, happened one Sunday, after a plentiful crop of tithes, to exert himself mightily. Deeply impressed by his own discourse, he, for the first time, acknowledged to his spouse at supper that he was somewhat choleric, but that hereafter he was resolved to practice what he preached. "But now, my jewel," says he, "let us refresh ourselves with a sip of the best." The obedient wife, ravished by his good humour, flew to the cellar. But, alas! The barrel was staved and quite empty, by some accident. What should she do? Returning with despair in her eyes, "My dear," she says, "what a sad accident has happened." "I am sorry," says the parson, "if anyone has met with misfortune. For my part, if it relate to me, I am resolved to bear it with Christian patience. But come, where's the beer?" "Alack-a-day! That is the very thing! How it happened, I cannot understand, but it is all swimming on the ground." The parson, flying into a violent passion, raved. "My life," says she, "do but reflect upon your sermon. Think of the patience of Job." "*Job!*" roared he. "Don't talk to me of Job's patience. *Job* never had a barrel of such beer!"

An arrogant Englishman passing through New-Jersey in a stage, entered into a lengthy detail in praise of the severity of British discipline, and observed as an instance, that two soldiers in Cornwallis' army were hung merely for robbing a hen-roost. A Jerseyman in company, said it was a pity this discipline had not been enforced among Lord Howe's men when they invaded New-Jersey. "Why so?" says the Englishman. "Because, sir," says the Jerseyman, "We should been happily rid of his lordship and his whole army together."

A young lady who had been lately married, and seeing her husband about to rise pretty early in the morning, says, "What, my dear? Are you getting up already? Pray lie a little longer and rest yourself." "No," replied he, "my dear, I must needs *get up* to rest myself."

Toasts Recommended

"Short shoes and long corns to the enemies of America."
"More friends and less need of them."
"May we kiss whom we please and please whom we kiss."
"Great men honest and honest men great."
"A head to earn and a heart to spend."

1795

The Indian Treaty Man

Hugh Henry Brackenridge

AT A certain inn on the Pennsylvania border, Captain Farrago was accosted by a stranger in the following manner:

"Captain," said he, "I have heard of a young man in your service who talks Irish. Now, sir, my business is that of an Indian treaty maker. I am on my way with a party of kings and half-kings to the Commissioners to hold a treaty. My king of the Kickapoos, who was a Welsh blacksmith, took sick by the way and is dead. I have heard of this lad of yours and wish to have him a while to supply the Welshman's place. The treaty-making will not last longer than a couple of weeks, and as the government will probably allow three or four thousand dollars for the treaty, it will be in our power to make it worth your while to spare your Irishman for that time."

"Your king of the Kickapoos?" said the Captain. "What does that mean?"

Said the stranger, "It is just this. You have heard of the Indian nations to the westward that occasionally make war on the frontier settlements. It has been the policy of government to treat with these and distribute goods. Commissioners are appointed for that purpose.

"Now, you are not to suppose that it is an easy matter to catch a real chief, and bring him from the woods. If, at some expense, one was brought, the goods and gifts would go to his use. It is much more profitable to hire substitutes and make chiefs of our own. And, as some unknown gibberish is necessary to pass for an Indian language, we generally make use of Welsh or Low Dutch or Irish. Here and there we pick up an ingenious fellow who can imitate a language by sounds of his own, but we prefer one who can speak a real tongue, and give more for him.

"We cannot afford you a great deal at this time for the use of your

15

man, because it is not a general treaty where twenty or thirty thousand dollars are appropriated by the Congress. It is an occasion, or what we call a running treaty, by way of holding fast friendship. The Commissioners will doubtless be glad to see us and procure from government an allowance for the treaty. For the more treaties, the more use for Commissioners. The business must be kept up, and treaties made, if there are none of themselves.

"My Piankasha and Choctaw chiefs are very good fellows. The one of them is a Scotch peddler that talks the Gaelic. The other has been some time in Canada and has a little broken Indian, I know not of what language. He has been of great service in teaching the rest some Indian customs and manners. I had the whole of them for the fortnight past learning war songs and dances and how to make responses at the treaty.

"If your man is tractable, I can make him a Kickapoo in about nine days. A breech-clout and leggins that I took off the blacksmith that died I have ready to put on him. He must have part of his head shaved and painted, with feathers on his crown. But the paint will wear off and the hair will grow in a short time, so that he can go about with you again."

"It is a very strange affair," said the Captain. "Is it possible that such deception can be practised in a new country? It astonishes me that the government does not detect such imposition.

"The government," said the Indian treaty man, "is at a great distance. It knows no more of Indians than a cow does of Greek. The Congress hears of wars and rumors of wars, and supports the executive in forming treaties. How is it possible for men who live remote from the scene of action to have adequate ideas of the nature of Indians or the transactions that are carried on in their behalf? Do you think that one-half of those savages that come to treat are real representatives of the nation? I speak of those particularly who come trading down to inland towns. I would not communicate these mysteries of our trade, were it not that I confide in your good sense, and have occasion for your servant."

"It is a mystery of iniquity!" said the Captain. "Do you suppose that I would countenance such a fraud upon the public?"

"I do not know," said the other. "It is a very common thing for men to speculate nowadays. If you will not, another will. A hundred dollars might as well be in your pocket as another man's. I will give you that for the use of your servant for a week or two, and say no more about it."

"It is a new idea to me entirely," said the Captain, "that Indian princes whom I have seen escorted down as such were no more than trumpery."

Said the Indian treaty man, "These things are now reduced to a system. It is so well known to those who engage in the traffic that we think nothing of it."

"How the devil," said the Captain, "do you get speeches made and interpret them so as to pass for truth?"

"That is an easy matter," said the other. "Indian speeches are nearly all alike. You have only to talk of burying hatchets, kindling fires, and brightening chains of friendship, with a demand at the latter end of rum to get drunk on."

"I much doubt," said the Captain, "if treaties that are carried on in earnest are of any great use."

"Of none at all," said the other, "especially as the practice of giving goods prevails. This is an inducement to fresh wars. This being the case, it can be no harm to make a farce of the whole matter; or rather a profit of it by such means as I have proposed to you, and have pursued myself."

"After all," said the Captain, "I cannot but consider it as a kind of contraband and illicit traffic. I must be excused from having any hand in it. I shall not betray your secret, but I shall not favor it. It would ill become me, whose object in riding about in this manner, is to impart just ideas on all subjects, to share in such ill-gotten gain."

The Indian treaty man, finding it in vain to say more, withdrew.

The Captain, apprehending that he might not yet drop his designs on the Irishman, but be tampering with him out of doors should he come across him, sent for Teague.

Teague, coming in, said the Captain to him, "Teague, I have discovered in you for some time past a great spirit of ambition which is, doubtless, commendable in a young person. I have checked it only in cases where there was real danger or apparent mischief.

"There is now an opportunity of advancing yourself, not so much in the way of honor as of profit. But profit brings honor, and, indeed, is the most substantial support of it. There has been a man here with me that carries on a trade with the Indians. He tells me that redheaded scalps are in great demand with them. If you could spare yours, he would give a good price for it. I do not well know what use they make of this article. Probably they dress it with the hairy side out, and make tobacco pouches for the chiefs when they meet in council. It saves dyeing. Besides the natural red hair of a man may be superior, in their estimation, to any color they can give by art.

"The taking off the scalp will not give much pain, it is so dexterously done with a crooked knife they have for that purpose. The mode of taking off the scalp is this: You lie down on your face. A warrior puts his feet upon your shoulders, collects your hair in his left hand, and drawing a circle with the knife in his left, makes the incision. With a sudden pull, he separates it from the scalp, giving in the meantime what is called the scalp yell. The thing is done in such an instant that the pain is scarcely felt.

"He offered me a hundred dollars if I would have it taken off for his use. He gave me directions, in the meantime, how to stretch it and dry it on a hoop. No! I told him it was a perquisite of your own, and you might dispose of it as you thought proper. If you choose to sell it, I have no objections, but the bargain should be of your own making, and the price such as should please yourself. It is probable that you may bring the price up by holding out a little. But I do not think it would be advisable to lose the bargain. A hundred dollars for a little hairy flesh is a great deal. You will trot a long time before you make that with me.

"He will be with you probably to propose the purchase. You will know him when you see him. He is a tall man with leggins on, and has several Indians with him, going to a treaty. He talked to me something of making you a king of the Kickapoos, after the scalp is off. But I would not count on that so much, because words are but wind, and promises easily broken. I would advise you to make sure of the money in the first place, and take chance for the rest."

I have seen among the prints of Hogarth some such expression of countenance as that of Teague at this instant. As soon as he could speak, he began to intimate his disinclination to the traffic. The hair of his scalp itself had risen in opposition to it.

"Will ye throw me into ridicule?" said he. "Am I to be thrown like a dog to the savages and have the flesh torn off my head to give to these wild beasts to make a knapsack to carry their praties and things in, for an hundred dollars or the like? It shall never be said that the hair of the O'Regans made moccasins for a wild Indian to trot upon. I would sooner throw up my own head, hair and all, than give it to these people to smoke with out of their long pipes!"

"If this be your determination," said the Captain, "it will behoove you to keep yourself somewhat close. While we remain at this public house, avoid any conversation with the chapman or his agents, should they come to tamper with you. For it is not improbable, while they are keeping you in talk, proposing to make you a Kickapoo chief and the like, they may snatch the scalp off your head, and you not be the wiser for it."

Teague thought the caution good, and resolving to abide by it, retired to the kitchen.

The maid at this time, happening to want a log of wood, requested Teague to cut it for her. Taking the ax, accordingly, and going out, he was busy chopping with his head down.

In the meantime, the Indian treaty man had returned with one in Indian dress, who was the chief of the Killinoos, or at least passed for such. He brought him as having some recruiting talents and might prevail with Teague to elope and join the company.

"I suppose," said the Indian treaty man, "you are the waiter of the Captain who lodges here at present?"

Teague, hearing a man speak, and lifting up his head, saw the leggins on the one and the Indian dress on the other. With a kind of involuntary effort, he threw the ax directly from him at the Killinoo. It missed him, but about an inch, and fell behind.

Teague, raising a shout of desperation, was fixed on the spot. His locomotive faculties were suspended. He could neither retreat nor advance, like one enchained or enchanted for the moment.

. The king of the Killinoos drew his tomahawk and prepared for battle.

The Captain, who was reading at the front window, hearing the shout, looked about and saw what was going on at the woodpile.

"Stop, villain!" he said to the king of the Killinoos. "You are not to take that scalp yet, however much you may value it. He will not take a hundred dollars for it, nor five hundred, though you make him a king of the Kickapoos or anything else. It is no trifling matter to have the ears slit in tatters and the nose run through with a bodkin, and a goose quill stuck across. So, you may go about your business—you will find no king of the Kickapoos here!"

Under the cover of this address of the Captain, Teague had retired to the kitchen and had ensconced himself behind the rampart of the maid.

The Indian treaty man and the Killinoo chief, finding the measure hopeless, withdrew, and turned their attention, it is to be supposed, to some other quarter to find a king of the Kickapoos, while the Captain, after paying his score at the inn, resumed his travels with Teague O'Regan.

1796

Jack and Gill
A Scholarly Commentary

JOSEPH DENNIE

AMONG critical writers, it is a common remark that the fashion of the times has often given a temporary reputation to performances of very little merit, and neglected those much more deserving of applause. I shall endeavor to introduce to the nation a work, which, though of considerable elegance, has been strangely overlooked by the generality of the world. It has, of late, fallen into disrepute, chiefly from the simplicity of its style, which in this age of luxurious refinement, is deemed only a secondary beauty, and from its being the favorite of the young.

I must acknowledge that at first I doubted in what class of poetry it should be arranged. Its extreme shortness, and its uncommon metre, seemed to degrade it into a ballad, but its interesting subject, its unity of plan, and above all, its having a beginning, middle, and an end, decide its claim to the epic rank.

The opening is singularly beautiful:

Jack and Gill

The first duty of the poet is to introduce his subject, and there is no part of poetry more difficult. Here our author is very happy: for instead of telling us, as an ordinary writer would have done, who were the ancestors of Jack and Gill, that the grandfather of Jack was a respectable farmer, that his mother kept a tavern at the sign of the Blue Bear; and that Gill's father was a Justice of the Peace, he introduces them to us at once in their proper persons.

I cannot help accounting it, too, as a circumstance honorable to the genius of the poet, that he does not in his opening call upon the Muse. This is an error into which Homer, and almost all the epic writers after him, have fallen; since by thus stating their case to the Muse, and desiring her to come to their assistance, they necessarily presuppose that she was absent, whereas there can be no surer sign of inspiration than for a muse to come unasked.

The personages being now seen, their situation is next to be discovered. Of this we are immediately informed in the subsequent line, when we are told:

> *Jack and Gill*
> *Went up a hill.*

Here the imagery is distinct, yet the description concise. The poet meant to inform us that two persons were going up a hill. Had the poet told us how the two heroes went up, whether in a cart or a wagon, and entered into the particulars which the subject involves, they would have been tedious, because superfluous.

These considerations may furnish us with the means of deciding a controversy, arising from a variation in the manuscripts; some of which have it *a* hill, and others *the* hill. As the description is in no other part local, I incline to the former reading. It has, indeed, been suggested that the hill here mentioned was Parnassus, and that the two persons are two poets, who, having overloaded Pegasus, the poor jaded creature was obliged to stop at the foot of the hill, whilst they ascended for water to recruit him. This interpretation, it is true, derives some countenance from the consideration that Jack and Gill were, in reality, as will appear in the course of the poem, going to draw water, and that there was on Parnassus such a place as Hippocrene, that is, a *horsepond,* at the top; but, on the whole, I think the text, as I have adopted it, to be the better reading.

Having ascertained the names and conditions of the parties, the reader naturally becomes inquisitive into their employment, and wishes to know whether their occupation is worthy of them.

> *Jack and Gill*
> *Went up a hill*
> *To fetch a bucket of water.*

Here we behold the plan gradually unfolding. We now discover their object, which we were before left to conjecture. Our acute author, instead of introducing a host of gods and goddesses, who might have impeded the journey of his heroes, by the intervention of the bucket, which is, as it ought to be, simple and conducive to the progress of the poem, has considerably improved on the ancient plan.

It has been objected that the employment of John and Gill is not sufficiently dignified for an epic poem; but, in answer to this, it must be remarked that it was the opinion of Socrates, and many other philosophers, that beauty should be estimated by utility, and surely the purpose of the heroes must have been beneficial. They ascended the rugged mountain to draw water, and drawing water is certainly more conducive to human happiness than drawing blood, as do the boasted heroes of the Iliad, or roving on the ocean and invading other men's property, as did the pious Aeneas.

Yes, they went to draw water. It might have been drawn for the purpose of culinary consumption; it might have been to quench the thirst of the harmless animals who relied upon them for support; it might have been to feed a sterile soil, and to revive the drooping plants, which they raised by their labors. Is not our author more judicious than Appollonius, who chooses for the heroes of his Argonautics a set of rascals, undertaking to steal a sheep skin? Do we not find the amiable Rebecca busy at the well? Does not one of the maidens in the Odyssey delight us by her diligence in the same situation?

But the descriptive part is now finished, and the author hastens to the catastrophe. At what part of the mountain the well was situated, what was the reason of the sad misfortune, or how the prudence of Jack forsook him, we are not informed, but so, alas! it happened:

> *Jack fell down—*

Unfortunate John, at the moment when he was nimbly, for aught we know, going up the hill, perhaps at the moment when his toils were to cease, he made an heedless step, his centre of gravity fell beyond his base, and he tumbled. Buoyed by hope, we suppose his affliction not quite remediless, that his fall is an accident to which the wayfarers of this life are daily liable, and we anticipate his immediate rise to resume his labors. But:

> *Jack fell down*
> *And broke his crown—*

Nothing now remains but to deplore the fate of the unhappy John. The mention of the *crown* has much perplexed the commentators. The learned Microphilus, in the 513th page of his *"Cursory Remarks"* on the poem, thinks he can find in it some illusion to the story of Alfred, who, he says, is known to have lived, during his concealment, in a mountainous country, and as he watched the cakes on the fire, might have been sent to bring water. But Microphilus' acute annotator, Vandergruten, has detected the fallacy of such a supposition, though he falls into an equal error in remarking that Jack might have carried a crown or a half crownpiece in his hand, which was fractured in the fall. My learned readers will doubtless agree with me in conjecturing that, as the crown is often used metaphorically for the head, and as that part is, or without any disparagement to the unfortunate sufferer, might have been, the heaviest, it was really his pericranium that sustained the damage.

Having seen the fate of John, we are anxious to know that of his companion. Alas!

And Gill came tumbling after.

Here the distress thickens on us. Unable to support the loss of his friend, he followed him, determined to share his disaster, and resolved that, as they had gone up together, they should not be separated as they came down.

In the midst of our afflictions, let us not, however, be unmindful of the poet's merit, which, on this occasion, is conspicuous. He evidently seems to have in view the excellent observation of Adam Smith, that our sympathy arises not from a view of the passion, but of the situation that excites it. Instead of unnecessary lamentation, he gives us the real state of the case; avoiding at the same time that minuteness of detail, which is so common among pathetic poets, and which, by dividing a passion and tearing it to rags, as Shakespeare says, destroys its force.

Of the bucket, we are told nothing, but it is probable that it fell with its supporters.

Let us conclude with a review of the poem's most prominent beauties. The subject is the *fall of man*. The heroes are men who did not commit a single fault, and whose misfortunes are to be imputed, not to indiscretion, but to destiny. The poet prudently clipped the wings of imagination, and repressed the extravagance of metaphorical decoration. All is simple, plain, consistent.

That part, too, without which poetry is useless sound, the moral, has not escaped the view of the poet. When we behold two young men, who but a short moment before stood up in all the pride of health, falling down a hill, how must we lament the instability of all things.

1801

Family Portraits from Cockloft Hall

WASHINGTON IRVING and JAMES KIRKE PAULDING

FROM time immemorial, it has been the rule of the Cocklofts to marry one of their own name. Every person of the least observation and experience must have observed that where this practice of marrying cousins and second cousins prevails in a family, every member in the course of a few generations becomes queer and original; as much distinguished from the common race as if he was of a different species. This has happened in our family, and particularly in that branch of it of which Mr. Christopher Cockloft, or, to do him justice, Mr. Christopher Cockloft, Esq., is the head.

Our family is of great antiquity, if there be any truth in the genealogical tree which hangs in my cousin's library. They trace their descent from a celebrated Roman knight, cousin to the progenitor of his majesty of Britain, who left his country on occasion of some disgust, and coming into Wales became a favorite of Prince Madoc, and accompanied that famous Argonaut in the voyage which ended in the discovery of America. I have sometimes ventured to doubt the authenticity of this portion of the annals, to the great vexation of Cousin Christopher who, though as orthodox as a bishop, would sooner give up the whole decalogue than lop off a single limb of the family tree.

II

COCKLOFT HALL is the country residence of the family, or rather the paternal mansion. It is pleasantly situated on the banks of the Passaic, a sweet pastoral stream; not so near New York as to invite an inundation of idle acquaintance, who come to lounge away an afternoon, nor so distant as to render it an absolute deed of charity or friendship to perform the journey.

It is one of the oldest habitations in the country, and was built by our grandfather, Lemuel Cockloft, to form, as the old gentleman expressed himself, "a snug retreat where he meant to sit himself down in his old days, and be comfortable for the rest of his life." He was at this time a few years over fourscore; but this was a common saying of his, with which he usually closed his airy speculations. One would have thought, from the long vista of years through which he contemplated many of his projects, that the old man had forgot the age of the patriarchs had long since gone by. He was for a considerable time in doubt on the question of roofing his house with shingles or slates; shingles would not last above thirty years! but they were cheaper than slates. He settled the matter by a kind of compromise, and determined to build with shingles first; "and when they are worn out," said the old gentleman triumphantly, " 'Twill be time enough to replace them with more durable materials."

But his contemplated improvements surpassed everything; and scarcely had he a roof over his head, when he discovered a thousand things to be arranged before he could "sit down comfortably." In the first place, every tree and bush on the place was cut down or grubbed up by the roots, because they were not placed to his mind; and a vast quantity of oaks, chestnuts, and elms set out in clumps, and rows, and labyrinths, which, he observed, in about five-and-twenty or thirty years at most would yield a very tolerable shade, and, moreover, would shut out all the surrounding country; for he was determined, he said, *"to have all his views on his own land and be beholden to no man for a prospect!"*

Another notion of the old gentleman was to blow up a bed of rocks for the purpose of having a fish pond, although the Passaic River ran at about one hundred yards distance from the house, and was well stored with fish; but there was nothing, he said, like having things to one's self.

So, on he went, and as his views enlarged, he *would* have a summer house built on the margin of the fish pond; he would have it surrounded with elms and willows; and he would have a cellar built under it for some incomprehensible reason, which remains a secret to this day. "In a few years," he observed, "it would be a delightful piece of wood and water, where he might ramble on a summer's noon, smoke his pipe, and enjoy himself in his old days."

Thrice honest old soul!—he died of an apoplexy in his ninetieth year.

Let no one ridicule the whim-whams of my grandfather. If—and of this there is no doubt, for wise men have said it—if life be but a dream, happy is he who can make the most of the illusion!

Though my grandfather is long since dead, the family has continued to glory in observing the golden rules of hospitality; which, according to the Cockloft principle, consists in giving a guest the freedom of the house, cramming him with beef and pudding, and, if possible, laying him under the table with prime port, claret, or London particular. The mansion appears to have been consecrated to the jolly god, and teems with monuments sacred to conviviality. Every chest of drawers, clothes-press, and cabinet is decorated with enormous China punch bowls, which Mrs. Christopher Cockloft has paraded with much ostentation, particularly in her favorite red damask bed chamber.

The Cocklofts especially pride themselves upon the possession of several family portraits, which exhibit as honest a set of square, portly, well-fed looking gentlemen and gentlewomen as ever grew and flourished under the pencil of a Dutch painter. Old Christopher, who is a complete genealogist, has a story to tell of each, and dilates with copious eloquence on the great services of the general in large sleeves, during the old French war; and on the piety of the lady in blue velvet, who so attentively peruses her book, and was once so celebrated for a beautiful arm.

In the grand parlor, the mantel-piece is decorated with little lacquered earthen shepherdesses; some of which are without toes, and others without noses; and the fire-place is garnished out with Dutch tiles, exhibiting a great variety of Scripture pieces, which my good soul of a cousin takes infinite delight in explaining. Poor Pindar Cockloft hates them as he does poison; for, while a younker, he was obliged by his mother to learn the history of a tile every Sunday morning before she would permit him to join his playmates. This was a terrible affair for Pindar, who, by the time he had learned the last, had forgotten the first, and was obliged to begin again. He assured me the other day, with a round college oath, that if the old house stood out till he inherited, he would have these tiles taken out, and ground into powder.

Cousin Christopher and his good wife have profound veneration for antique furniture; in consequence of which the old hall is furnished with old-fashioned bedsteads, with high testers; massy clothes-presses, standing most majestically on eagles' claws, and ornamented with a profusion of shining brass handles, clasps, and hinges; and around the grand parlor are solemnly arranged a set of high-backed, leather-bottomed, massy mahogany chairs that always remind me of the formal long-waisted belles, who flourished in stays and buckram. They are of such unwieldy proportions that it is quite a serious undertaking to gallant one of them across the room, and sometimes they make a most equivocal noise when you sit down in a hurry.

The propensity to save everything that bears the stamp of family antiquity has accumulated an abundance of trumpery and rubbish with which the hall is encumbered from the cellar to the garret. Every room, and closet, and corner is crammed with three-legged chairs, clocks without hands, swords without scabbards, cocked hats, broken candlesticks, and looking glasses with frames carved into fantastic shapes of feathered sheep, woolly birds, and other animals that have no names except in books of heraldry.

Several spirited attempts have been made by the Misses Cockloft to introduce modern furniture into the Hall, but with very indifferent success. Modern style has always been an object of great annoyance to honest Christopher, and is ever treated by him with sovereign contempt, as an upstart intruder. It is a common observation of his, that your old-fashioned, substantial furniture bespeaks the respectability of one's ancestors, and indicates that the family has been used to hold up its head for more than the present generation; whereas the fragile appendages of the modern style seem to be emblems of the mushroom gentility, and, to his mind, predicted that the family will molder away and vanish with its transient finery. The same whim makes him averse to having his house surrounded with poplars; which he stigmatizes as mere upstarts, just fit to ornament the shingle palaces of modern gentry, and characteristic of the establishments they decorate. Indeed, so far does he carry his veneration for antique trumpery, that he can scarcely see the dust brushed from its resting place on the old-fashioned testers, or a grey-bearded spider dislodged from its ancient inheritance, without groaning; and I once saw him in a transport of passion on Pindar's knocking down a moldering martin-coop with his tennis ball, which had been set up in the latter days of my grandfather.

In their attachment for everything that has remained long in the family, the Cocklofts are bigoted toward their old edifice, and I dare say would sooner have it crumble about their ears than abandon it. The consequence is, it has been so patched up and repaired that it has become as full of whims and oddities as its tenants; requires to be nursed and humored like a gouty old codger of an alderman, and reminds one of the famous ship in which a certain admiral circumnavigated the globe, which was so patched and timbered that at length not a particle of the original remained. Whenever the wind blows, the old mansion makes a most perilous groaning; and every storm is sure to make a day's work for the carpenter, who attends upon it as regularly as the family physician.

This predilection for everything that has long family attachment shows itself in every particular. The family carriage was made in the last French war, and the old horses were most indubitably foaled in Noah's ark. The domestics are all grown grey in the service of our house. We have a little, old, crusty, grey-headed negro, Caesar, who has lived through two or three generations of the Cocklofts, and of course has become a personage of no little importance in the household. He calls all the family by their Christian names, and is a complete Cockloft chronicle for the last seventy years.

There is scarce a little hamlet but has one of these weather-beaten wise-acres of negroes, who ranks among the great characters of the place. He is always resorted to as an oracle to resolve any question about the weather, shooting, fishing, farming, and horse-doctoring; and on such occasions will slouch his remnant of a hat on one side, fold his arms, roll his white eyes, and examine the sky, with a look as knowing as a magpie looking into a marrow bone. Such a knowing one is old Caesar, who acts as Cousin Cockloft's prime minister or grand vizier; assumes, when abroad, his master's style and title; to wit, Squire Cockloft; and is, in effect, absolute lord and ruler of the soil. To let my readers into a family secret, Cousin Christopher is notoriously henpecked by the old negro.

Caesar was a bosom friend and chosen playmate of Cousin Pindar and myself, when we were boys. Never were we so happy as when, stealing away on a holiday to the Hall, we ranged about the fields with him. He was particularly adroit in making our quail-traps and fishing rods; was always the ringleader in all the schemes of frolicsome mischief perpetrated by the urchins of the neighborhood; and considered himself on an equality with the best of us.

Many a summer evening do I remember when, huddled together on the steps of the Hall door, Caesar, with his stories of ghosts, goblins, and witches, would put us in a panic, and people every lane, and churchyard, and solitary wood with imaginary beings. In process of time, he became the constant attendant and Man Friday of Cousin Pindar, whenever he went a sparking among the rosy country girls of the neighboring farms; and brought up his rear at every rustic dance, when he would mingle in the sable group that always thronged the door of merriment; and it was enough to put to the rout a host of splenetic imps to see his mouth gradually dilate from ear to ear, with pride and exultation, at seeing how neatly Pindar footed it over the floor.

Caesar was likewise the chosen confidant and special agent of Pindar in all his love affairs, until, as his evil stars would have it, on his being intrusted with the delivery of a poetic billet-doux to one of his patron's sweethearts, he took an unlucky notion to send it to his own mistress, who, not being able to read, took it to her lady; and so the whole affair was blown. Pindar was universally roasted, and Caesar was discharged forever from his confidence.

Poor Caesar!—he has grown old, but he still remembers old times; and will, now and then, remind me of them as he lights me to my room, and lingers a little while to bid me good night. The honest, simple old creature has a warm corner in my heart. I don't see, for my part, why a body may not like a negro as well as a white man.

III

My COUSIN CHRISTOPHER enjoys unlimited authority in the mansion of his forefathers; he is truly what may be termed a hearty old blade; has a florid, sunshine countenance; and if you will only praise his wine and laugh at his long stories, himself and his house are heartily at your service. The first condition is, indeed, easily complied with. To tell the truth, his wine is excellent; but his stories are not of the best, and often repeated, are apt to create a disposition to yawn. When he enters upon one of his stories, it reminds me of Newark Causeway, where the traveller sees the end at a distance of several miles. To the great misfortune of all his acquaintances, Squire Cockloft can give the day and date, and name, and age, and circumstance with the most unfeeling precision. These, however, are but trivial foibles, forgotten, or remembered only with a kind of tender, respectful pity by those who know with what a rich, abundant harvest of kindness and generosity his heart is stored.

It would delight you to see with what social gladness he welcomes a visitor into his house; and the poorest man that enters his door never leaves without a cordial invitation to sit down and drink a glass of wine. By the honest farmers round his country-seat he is looked up to with love and reverence; they never pass him by without his inquiring after the welfare of their families, and receiving a cordial shake of his hand.

There are but two classes of people who are thrown out of the reach of his hospitality, and these are democrats, a prejudice partly owing to a little vivid spark of Toryism which burns in a secret corner of his heart; and Frenchmen; for he still cherishes the sad memory of my good Aunt Charity—who died of a Frenchman, as shall later be told.

The old gentleman considers it treason against the majesty of good breeding to speak to any visitor with his hat on; but the moment a democrat enters his door, he forthwith bids his man, Caesar, bring his hat, puts it on his head, and salutes the visitor with an appalling, "Well, sir, what do *you* want of me?"

He was a loyal subject of the Crown, had hardly recovered the shock of independence; and, though he does not care to own it, always does honor to His Majesty's birthday by inviting a few cavaliers, like himself, to dinner, and gracing his table with more than ordinary festivity. If by chance the Revolution is mentioned before him, my cousin shakes his head; and you may see, if you take good note, a lurking smile of contempt in the corner of his eye which marks a decided disapprobation of the sound. He once, in the fullness of his heart, observed to me *"that green peas were a month later than they were under the old government!"*

I remember a few months ago the old gentleman came home in quite a squall; kicked the poor mastiff out of his way, as he came through the hall; threw his hat on the table with most violent emphasis, and pulling out his box, took three huge pinches of snuff, and threw a fourth into the cat's eyes as he sat purring at the fireside. This was enough to set the body politic going; Mrs. Cockloft began "my dearing" it as fast as tongue could move; the young ladies took each a stand at an elbow of his chair; the servants came tumbling in; the mastiff put up an inquiring nose; and even Grimalkin, after he had cleaned his whiskers and finished sneezing, discovered indubitable signs of sympathy.

After the most affectionate inquiries on all sides, it turned out that my cousin, in crossing the street, had got his silk stockings bespattered with mud by a coach, which it seems, belonged to a dashing gentleman who had formerly supplied the family with hot rolls and muffins when they visited the city! Mrs. Cockloft thereupon turned up her eyes, and the young ladies their noses; and it would have edified a whole congregation to hear the conversation which took place concerning the insolence of upstarts, and the vulgarity of would-be gentlemen and ladies, who strive to emerge from low life by dashing about in carriages.

An object of the peculiar affection of Cousin Christopher is an old English cherry tree, which leans against the corner of the Hall; and whether the house supports it, or it supports the house, would be, I believe, a question of some difficulty to decide. It is held sacred by old Christopher because he planted it and reared it himself, and had once well-nigh broken his neck by a fall from one of its branches. This is one of his favorite stories, and there is reason to believe, that if the tree was out of the way, the old gentleman would forget the whole affair—which would be a great pity. The old tree has long since ceased bearing, and is exceedingly infirm; every tempest robs it of a limb; and one would suppose from the lamentations of Cousin Christopher on such occasions that he had lost one of his own. He often contemplates it in a half-melancholy, half-moralizing humor—"Together," he says, "we have flourished, and together we shall wither away; a few years, and both our heads shall be laid low, and, perhaps, my moldering bones may, one day, mingle with the dust of the tree I have planted."

At one time the old tree had obtruded a withered branch before Miss Barbara Cockloft's window, and she desired her father to order the gardener to saw it off. I shall never forget the old man's answer, and the look that accompanied it. "What," cried he, "lop off the limbs of my cherry tree in its old age? Why do you not cut off the grey locks of your poor old father?"

IV

As I have previously mentioned MRS. COCKLOFT, I might as well say a little more about her and my cousins, while I am in the humor.

She is a lady of wonderful nobility, a warm admirer of shining mahogany, clean hearths, and her husband; who she considers the wisest man in the world, bating the parson of our parish, who is her oracle on all occasions. She goes constantly to church every Sunday and Saint's-day; and inists upon it that no man is entitled to ascend a pulpit unless he has been ordained by a bishop. Nay, so far does she carry her orthodoxy that all the argument in the world will never persuade her that a Presbyterian or Baptist, or even a Calvinist, has any possible chance of going to heaven.

To sum up all her qualifications in the shortest possible way, Mrs. Cockloft is, in the true sense of the phrase, a good sort of woman.

The Misses Cockloft, whose pardon I crave for not having particularly introduced them before, are a pair of delectable damsels, who, having purloined and locked up the family Bible, pass for just what age they please to plead guilty to.

BARBARA, the eldest, has long since resigned the character of a belle, and adopted that staid, sober, demure, snuff-taking air becoming her years and discretion. She is a good-natured soul, whom I never saw in a passion but once, and that was occasioned by seeing an old favorite beau of hers kiss the hand of a blooming girl; and, in truth, she only got angry because, as she very properly said, "it was spoiling the child."

Her sister, MARGERY or MAGGIE as she is familiarly termed, seemed disposed to maintain her post as a belle, until a few months since; when accidentally hearing a gentleman observe that she broke very fast, she suddenly left off going to assembly, took a cat into high favor, and began to rail at the forward pertness of the young misses.

The young ladies are still visited by some half dozen of veteran beaux, who grew and flourished when the Misses Cockloft were quite children; but have been brushed rather rudely by the hand of time, who, to say the truth, can do almost anything but make people young. They are, notwithstanding, still warm candidates for female favor; look venerably tender, and repeat over and over the same honeyed speeches and sugared sentiments to the little belles that they poured so profusely into the ears of their mothers.

My Cousin PINDAR Cockloft is one of the family's most conspicuous members. He is now in his fifty-eighth year—is a bachelor, partly through chance, and an oddity of the first water. Half his life has been employed in writing odes, sonnets, epigrams, and elegies, which he seldom shows to anybody but myself after they are written; and all the old chests, drawers, and chair bottoms in the house teem with his productions.

In his younger days he figured as a dashing blade in the great world; and no young fellow of New York Town wore a longer pig tail, or carried more buckram in his skirts. From sixteen to thirty, he was continually in love, and during that period, to use his own words, he be-scribbled more paper than would serve the theatre for snow storms a whole season. Though he still loves the company of the ladies, he has never been known to exceed the bounds of courtesy in his intercourse with them; for, in his own rhyme:

"Though jogging down the hill of life,
"Without the comfort of a wife;
"And though I ne'er a helpmate chose,
"To stock my house and mend my hose;
"Still do I love the gentle sex,
"And still with cares my brain perplex,
"To keep the fair ones of the age
"Unsullied as the spotless page;
"All pure, all simple, all refined,
"The sweetest solace of mankind."

Pindar was the life and ornament of our family in town, until the epoch of the French Revolution, which sent so many unfortunate dancing masters from their country to polish and enlighten our hemisphere. This was a sad time for Pindar, who had taken a genuine Cockloft prejudice against everything French, ever since he was brought to death's door by a *ragout*. The Marseilles Hymn had much the same effect upon him that sharpening a knife on a dry whetstone has upon some people—it set his teeth chattering. He packed up his trunk, his old-fashioned writing desk, and his Chinese ink stand, and made a kind of growling retreat to Cockloft Hall, where he has resided ever since.

v

My AUNT CHARITY departed this life in the fifty-ninth year of her age, though she never grew older after twenty-five. In her teens she was, according to her own account, a celebrated beauty, though I never could meet with anybody that remembered when she was handsome. In the good old days that saw my aunt in the heydey of youth, a fine lady was a most formidable animal, and required to be approached with the same awe and devotion that a Tartar feels in the presence of his Grand Lama. If a gentleman offered to take her hand, except to help her into a carriage, or lead her into a drawing room, such frowns! such a rustling of brocade and taffeta! her very paste shoe buckles sparkled with indignation, and for a moment assumed the brilliancy of diamonds: in those days the person of a belle was sacred; it was unprofaned by the sacrilegious grasp of a stranger —simple souls!—they had not the waltz among them yet!

My good aunt prided herself on keeping up this buckram delicacy; and if she happened to be playing at the old fashioned game of forfeits, and was fined a kiss, it was always more trouble to get it than it was worth; for she made a most gallant defence, and never surrendered until she saw her adversary inclined to give over the attack. Once, when on a sleighing party, when they came to the Kissing Bridge, her swain attempted to levy contributions on Miss Charity Cockloft, who after squalling at a hideous rate, at length jumped out of the sleigh plump into a snow bank, where she stuck fast, until he came to her rescue. This Latonian feat cost her a rheumatism, from which she never thoroughly recovered.

It is rather singular that my aunt, though a great beauty, and an heiress withal, never got married. This much is certain, that for many years previous to her decease, she declined all attentions from the gentlemen, and contented herself with watching over the welfare of her fellow creatures. She was indeed observed to take a considerable lean toward Methodism, was frequent in her attendance at love feasts, read Whitefield and Wesley, and even went so far as to travel the distance of five-and-twenty miles to be present at a camp meeting.

This gave great offence to my Cousin Christopher, and his good lady, who, as I have already mentioned, are rigidly orthodox in the Established Church. Had my Aunt Charity not been of a most pacific disposition, her religious whim would have occasioned many a family altercation. She was indeed as good a soul as the Cockloft family ever boasted; a lady of unbounded loving-kindness, which extended to man, woman, and child. Was any acquaintance sick? In vain did the wind whistle and the storm beat; my aunt would waddle through mud and mire, over the whole section, but what she would visit them. She would sit by them for hours together with the most persevering patience, and tell a thousand melancholy stories of human misery, to keep up their spirits. The whole catalogue of *yerb* teas was at her fingers' ends, from formidable wormwood down to gentle balm; and she would descant by the hour on the healing qualities of hoarhound, catnip, and penny royal. Woe be to the patient that came under the benevolent hand of my Aunt Charity; he was sure, willy-nilly, to be drenched with a deluge of concoctions; and full many a time has my Cousin Christopher borne a twinge of pain in silence, through fear of being condemned to suffer the martyrdom of her materia medica.

But the truth must be told. With all her good qualities, my Aunt Charity was afflicted with one fault, extremely rare among her gentle sex —it was curiosity. How she came by it, I am at a loss to imagine, but it played the very vengeance with her and destroyed the comfort of her life. Having an invincible desire to know everybody's character, business, and mode of living, she took up her residence in town, and was forever prying into the affairs of her neighbors; and got a great deal of ill will from people toward whom she had the kindest disposition possible.

If any family on the opposite of the street gave a dinner, my aunt would mount her spectacles, and sit at the window until the company were all housed, merely that she might know who they were. If she heard a story about any of her acquaintance, she would, forthwith, set off, full sail, and never rest until, to use her usual expression, she had got "to the bottom of it;" which meant nothing more than telling it to everybody she knew.

I remember one night my Aunt Charity happened to hear a most precious story about one of her good friends, but unfortunately too late to give it immediate circulation. It made her absolutely miserable; and she hardly slept a wink all night, for fear her bosom friend, Mrs. Sipkins, should get the start of her in the morning. You must know there was always a contest between these two ladies, who should first give currency to the good-natured things said about everybody; and this unfortunate rivalship at length proved fatal to their long and ardent friendship. My aunt got up full two hours that morning before her usual time; put on her pompadour taffeta gown, and sallied forth to lament the misfortune of her dear friend. Would you believe it!—wherever she went, Mrs. Sipkins had anticipated her; and, instead of being listened to with uplifted hands and open-mouthed wonder, my unhappy aunt was obliged to sit quietly and listen to the whole affair, with numerous additions, alterations, and amendments! Now, this was too bad; it would have provoked Patience Grizzle or a saint. It was too much for my aunt, who kept her bed for three days afterward, with a cold; but I have no doubt it was owing to this affair of Mrs. Sipkins, to whom she would never be reconciled.

But I pass over the rest of my Aunt Charity's life, chequered with the various calamities, and misfortunes, and mortifications, incident to those worthy old gentlewomen who have the domestic cares of the whole community upon their minds. I hasten to relate the melancholy incident that hurried her out of existence in the full bloom of antiquated virginity.

In their frolicsome malice, the fates had ordained that a French boarding house, or *Pension Française*, as it was called, should be established directly opposite my aunt's residence. Cruel event!—it threw her into that alarming disorder denominated the fidgets; she did nothing but watch at the window day after day, but without becoming one whit the wiser at the end of a fortnight. She wondered why there was always such a scraping of fiddles in the parlor, and such a smell of onions from the kitchen; in short, neighbor Pension was continually uppermost in her thoughts, and incessantly on the outer edge of her tongue. This was, I believe, the first time she had ever failed "to get at the bottom of a thing;" and the disappointment cost her many a sleepless night, I warrant you. I have little doubt, however, that my aunt would have ferreted neighbor Pension out, could she have spoken or understood French; but in those times people in general could make themselves understood in plain English; and it was always a standing rule in the Cockloft family, which exists to this day, that not one of the females should learn French.

My Aunt Charity had lived for some time at her window in vain; when one day as she was keeping her usual look-out, and suffering all the pangs

of unsatisfied curiosity, she beheld a little, meagre, weazel-faced Frenchman, of the most forlorn, pitiful, and diminutive proportions, arrive at
neighbor Pension's door. He was dressed in white, with a little pinched-up
cocked hat; he seemed to shake in the wind, and every blast that went
over him whistled through his bones and threatened instant annihilation.
This embodied spirit of famine was followed by three carts, lumbered
with crazy trunks, chests, band boxes, bidets, medicine chests, parrots and
monkeys; and at his heels ran a yelping pack of little black-nosed pug
dogs.

This was the thing wanting to fill up the measure of my Aunt Charity's
affliction. She could not conceive, for the soul of her, who this mysterious
little apparition could be that made so great a display; what he could
possibly do with so much baggage, and particularly with his parrots
and monkeys; or how so small a carcass could have occasion for so
many trunks of clothes.

From the time of this fatal arrival, my poor aunt was in a quandary.
All her inquiries were fruitless; no one could expound the history of this
mysterious stranger. She never held up her head afterward—drooped
daily, took to her bed in a fortnight, and in one little month I saw her
quietly deposited in the family vault:—*dead of a Frenchman!* as the
family ever afterward said.

VI

The last time I saw my UNCLE JOHN was fifteen years ago, when I
paid him a visit at the old mansion. I found him reading a newspaper—
for it was election time, and he was always a warm Federalist; and had
made several converts to the true faith in his time; particularly one old
tenant of his who always, just before the election, became a violent anti-
Federalist in order that he might be convinced of his errors by my uncle,
who never failed to reward his conviction by some substantial benefit.

All his life Uncle John had been trying to get married, and always
thought himself on the point of accomplishing his wishes. His disappointments were not owing either to the deformity of his mind or person; for
in his youth he was reckoned handsome, and I myself can witness for
him that he had as kind a heart as ever was fashioned; neither were they
owing to his poverty—which sometimes stands in an honest man's way—
for he was born with the inheritance of a small estate which was sufficient
to establish his claim to the title of "one well to do in the world."

The truth is, my uncle had a prodigious antipathy to doing things in a

hurry. "A man should consider," said he to me once, "that he can always get a wife, but cannot always get rid of her. For my part, I am a young fellow, with the world before me"—he was about forty—"and am resolved to look sharp, weigh matters well, and know what's what before I marry. In short, I *don't intend to do the thing in a hurry, depend upon it!*"

On this whim he proceeded. He began with young girls and ended with widows. The girls he courted until they grew old maids, or married out of pure apprehension of incurring certain penalties hereafter; and the widows, not having quite as much patience, generally at the end of the year, while the good man thought himself in the highroad to success, married some harum-scarum young fellow who had not such an antipathy to doing things in a hurry.

My uncle would inevitably have sunk under these repeated disappointments—for he did not want sensibility—had he not hit upon a discovery that set all to rights at once. He consoled his vanity—for he was a little vain, and soothed his pride—which was his master passion—by telling his friends very significantly, while his eye would flash in triumph, "*that he might have had her.*"

His first love was the daughter of a neighboring gentleman farmer, who was reckoned the beauty of the whole world; a phrase by which the country people mean nothing more than the circle of their acquaintance, or that territory of land which is in sight of the smoke of their own hamlet. This young lady to whom he paid his addresses, in addition to her beauty, was highly accomplished. She had spent five or six months at a boarding school in town; where she learned to work pictures in satin and paint sheep that might be mistaken for wolves; to hold up her head, sit straight in her chair, and to think every species of useful attainment beneath her attention. The old mother was so enamoured of her daughter's accomplishments that she actually got framed a picture worked in satin by the young lady. It represented the tomb scene in Romeo and Juliet. Romeo was dressed in an orange-colored cloak, fastened round his neck with a large golden clasp; a white satin tamboured waistcoat, leather breeches, blue silk stockings, and white-topped boots. The amiable Juliet shone in a flame-colored gown, most gorgeously bespangled with silver stars, a high-crowned muslin cap that reached to the top of the tomb; on her feet she wore a pair of short-quartered, high-heeled shoes, and her waist was the exact facsimile of an inverted sugar loaf. The head of the noble Count Paris looked like a chimney-sweeper's brush that had lost its handle, and the cloak of the good Friar hung about him as gracefully as the armor of a rhinoceros.

With this accomplished young lady then did my Uncle John become deeply enamoured, and, as it was his first love, determined to bestir himself in an extraordinary manner. Once, at least, a fortnight, and generally on a Sunday evening, he would put on his leather breeches, for he was a great beau, mount his grey horse, Pepper, and ride over to see Miss Pamela, though she lived upward of a mile off, and he was obliged to pass close by a churchyard, which at least a hundred creditable persons would swear was haunted.

Miss Pamela could not be insensible to such proofs of attachment, and accordingly received him with considerable kindness; her mother always left the room when he came, and my uncle had as good as made a declaration, by saying one evening, very significantly, "that he believed that he should soon change his condition;" when, somehow or other, he began to think he was doing things in too great a hurry, and it was high time to consider: so he considered near a month about it, and there is no saying how much longer he might have spun the thread of his doubts had he not been roused from this state of indecision by the news that his mistress had married an attorney's apprentice, whom she had seen the Sunday before at church; where he had excited the applause of the whole congregation by the invincible gravity with which he had listened to a Dutch sermon.

My uncle only shrugged his shoulders, looked mysterious, and said, "Tut! I might have had her!"

The chamber in the Hall that was occupied by my honored Uncle John, exhibits many memorials which recall the solid excellence and amiable eccentricities of that gallant old lad. Over the mantel-piece hangs the portrait of a young lady dressed in a flaring, long-waisted, blue silk gown; be-flowered, and be-furbelowed, and be-cuffed in the most abundant manner. She holds in her hand a book, which she complaisantly neglects, to turn and smile on the spectator; in the other hand a flower, which I hope, for the honor of Dame Nature, was the sole production of the painter's imagination; and a little behind her is something tied to a blue riband, but whether a little dog, a monkey, or a pigeon, must be left to the judgement of future commentators.

This little damsel, tradition says, was my Uncle John's third flame; and he would infallibly have run away with her, could he have persuaded her into the measure; but at that time ladies were not so easily run away with as Columbine; and my uncle, failing in the point, took a lucky thought, and with great gallantry ran off with her picture, which he conveyed in triumph to Cockloft Hall, and hung up in his bed chamber as a monument of his enterprising spirit.

The old gentleman prided himself mightily on this chivalric manoeuvre; always chuckled and pulled up his stock when he contemplated the picture, and never related the exploit without winding up with—"I might, indeed, have carried off the original, had I chosen to dangle a little longer after her chariot wheels; but I always scorned to coax, my boy—always—'twas my way."

VII

Though our family is apparently small, yet like most establishments of the kind it does not want for honorary members. We are continually enlivened by the company of half a score of uncles, aunts, and cousins, in the fortieth remove, from all parts of the country, who profess a wonderful regard for Cousin Christopher, and overwhelm every member of his household, down to the cook in the kitchen, with their attentions.

We have for some weeks past been greeted with the company of two worthy old spinsters, who have come down to settle a lawsuit. They have done little else but retail stories of their village neighbors, knit stockings, and take snuff; the whole family are bewildered with churchyard tales of sheeted ghosts, white horses without heads and with large goggle eyes in their buttocks; and not one of the old servants dare budge an inch after dark without a numerous company at his heels.

My cousin's visitors, however, always return his hospitality with due gratitude, and now and then remind him of their fraternal regard, by a present of a pot of apple sweetmeats, or a barrel of sour cider at Christmas.

1807-1808

Tend to Your Part

Anonymous

THE Yankee schooner *Sally Ann*, under the command of Captain Spooner, was beating up the Connecticut River. Mr. Comstock, the mate, was at station forward. According to *his* notion of things, the schooner was getting a little too near certain flats along the larboard shore. So aft he goes to the Captain, with his hat cocked on one side, and says:

"Cap'n Spooner, you're getting a *leetle* too close to them flats. Hadn't you better go about?"

"Mr. Comstock," the Captain replied, "jest you go forard and tend to your part of the scunner, and I'll tend to mine."

In a high dudgeon, Mr. C. did go forward, and hallooed out to the crew, "Boys, see that mud-hook all clear for letting go!"

"Aye, aye, sir—all clear."

"Let go then!"

Down went the anchor, out rattled the chain, and the *Sally Ann* came luffing into the wind, and then brought up, all standing.

Mr. Comstock walked aft, touching his cap. He said to Captain Spooner, "*My* part is to anchor."

Early 1800's

Green Mountains Boy

ANONYMOUS

ON THE banks of the Hudson a bunch of village loafers were standing, seeing who could throw stones the farthest into the stream. A tall, rawboned, slabsided Yankee, and no mistake, came up and looked on. For awhile he said nothing, till a Yorker in a tight jacket began to try his wit on Jonathan.

"You can't beat that," said the Yorker, as he hurled a stone away out into the river.

"Maybe not," said Jonathan, "but up in Vermont in the Green Moun-tains, we have a pretty big river, considering, and t'other day I hove a man clear across it and he came down fair and square on the other side."

His auditors yelled in derision.

"Well, now, you may laugh," said Jonathan, "but I can do it again."

"Do what?" demanded the tight-jacketed Yorker quickly.

"I can take and heave you across that river yonder, just open and shut."

"Bet you ten dollars on it!"

"Done!" said the Yankee. Drawing forth a 10 note, he covered the Yorker's shinplaster. "Can you swim, feller?" he asked.

"Like a duck," says tight jacket.

Without further parley, the Vermonter seized the knowing Yorker stoutly by the nape of the neck and the basement of his pants, jerked him from his foothold, and dashed him heels over head into the Hudson. A shout ran through the crowd as he floundered in the cold water. He put back to the shore and scrambled up the bank.

"I'll take that ten-spot, if you please," said the shivering loafer, advanc-ing to the stake-holder. "You took us for greenhorns, eh? We'll show you how to do things down here in York."

"Well," said Jonathan, "I reckon you won't take no ten spot just yet, captain."

"Why? You lost the bet!"

"Not exactly. I didn't wager to do it the first time. Just said I could do it, and I tell you I can." And in spite of the loafer's utmost effort to escape him, he seized him by the scruff and seat and pitched him farther into the river than upon the first trial.

Again the Yorker floundered back through the icy water.

"Third time never fails," said the Yankee, stripping off his coat. "I can do it, I tell you!"

"Hold on!" said the victim.

"And I *will* do it, if I try till tomorrow morning," said Jonathan.

"I give it up!" shouted the sufferer between his teeth which now chattered like a mad badger's. "T-take the m-m-money!"

"Oh well, if that's the way it's done in York State," said the Vermonter, pocketing the money, and coolly turning away.

1820

Center Shot

ANONYMOUS

COWAN and Hoffman, Western hunters, were dead shots and each hotly jealous of the other's prowess. Setting out together one day after deer, they separated in the woods, taking opposite sides of a ridge.

Almost immediately, Hoffman heard Cowan's rifle fired off. He ran over to the spot, expecting to be obliged to help hang a deer. He found Cowan reloading but no deer carcass in sight. However, a startled calf was crashing off through the hazelnut bushes.

"Oh Lord!" Hoffman whooped with delight. "You didn't shoot at that *calf*, did you, hoss?"

"Supposing I did?" growled Cowan.

"Why'd you do a thing like that?"

"Took it for a deer."

"Don't look like you hit it."

"No—missed."

"How in the nation did that happen?"

"Wasn't just sure that it wasn't a calf."

"*That*," crowed Hoffman, "is what I call a pretty sorry hunter—to shoot at a calf for a deer, and miss it at that!"

"Don't be a fool," drawled Cowan, ramming home the charge in his rifle. "I shot at it just so as to hit it if it was a deer, and miss it if it was a calf."

1825

44

My First Visit to Portland

Seba Smith

IN THE fall of 1829, I took it into my head I'd go to Portland. I'd heard a good deal about Portland, what a fine place it was, and how the folks got rich there proper fast. I up and told father, and says:

"I am going to Portland, whether or no, and I'll see what this world is made of yet."

Father stared a little at first, and said he was afraid I would get lost; but when he see I was bent upon it, he give it up, and he stepped up to his chest and opened the till, and took out a dollar and gave it to me; and says he:

"Jack, this is all I can do for you. Go and lead an honest life, and I believe I shall hear good of you yet."

So I tackled up the old horse and packed in a load of axe-handles, and a few notions; and mother fried me some doughnuts and put 'em into a box, along with some cheese and sausages, and wrapped me up another shirt, for I told her I didn't know how long I should be gone.

Up at our place, we read the *Portland Courier*, so the first morning after I got in town I went to see the editor, for I knew from what I had seen in his paper that he was just the man to tell me which way to steer. And when I come to see him, I knew I was right. He took me by the hand, as kind as if he had been a brother, and says he:

"Mister," says he, "I'll do anything I can to assist you. Portland is a healthy, thriving place, and any man with a proper degree of enterprise may do well here. You must drive among the folks here just as though you were at home on the farm, among the cattle. Don't be afraid of any of them, but figure away, and, I dare say, you'll get into good business in a very little while."

"But," he says, "there's one thing you must be careful of. Don't get into the hands of those folks that trade up round Huckler's Row. There's some sharpers up there, if they get hold of you, would twist your eye-teeth out in five minutes."

Well, after he had give me all the good advice he could, I got breakfast; and then I walked all over the town to see what chance I could find to sell my axe-handles and things, and to get into business.

After I had walked about three or four hours, I come along towards the upper end of the town, where I found there were stores and shops of all sorts and sizes. And I met a feller, and says I:

"What place is this?"

"Why this," says he, "is Huckler's Row."

Well, then, says I to myself, I have a pesky good mind to go in and have a try with one of these chaps, and see if they can twist my eye-teeth out. If they can get the best end of a bargain out of me, they can do what there ain't no man in our place can do.

So in I goes into the best-looking store among 'em. And I see some biscuit lying on the shelf, and says I:

"Mister, how much do you ax apiece for them there biscuits?"

"A cent apiece," says he.

"Well," says I, "I shan't give you that, but if you've a mind to, I'll give you two cents for three of them, for I begin to feel a little as though I would like to take a bite."

"Well," says he, "I wouldn't sell 'em to anybody else so, but seeing it's you, I don't care if you take 'em."

I knew he lied, for he never see me before in his life. Well, he handed down the biscuits, and I took 'em and walked round the store a while to see what else he had to sell. At last, says I:

"Mister, have you any good cider?"

Says he, "Yes, as good as ever ye see."

"Well," says I, "what do you ax a glass for it?"

"Two cents," says he.

"Well," says I, "seems to me I feel more dry than I do hungry now. Ain't you a mind to take these here biscuits again, and give me a glass of cider?"

"I don't care if I do," says he.

So he took and laid 'em on the shelf again, and poured out a glass of cider. I took the cider and drinked it down, and to tell the truth, it was capital good cider. Then says I:

"I guess it's time for me to be a-going," and I stepped along towards the door.

But he says, "Stop, Mister. I believe you haven't paid me for the cider."

"Not paid you for the cider!" says I. "What do you mean by that? Didn't the biscuits I give you just come to the cider?"

"Oh, ah, right," says he.

So I started to go again, and says he:

"But, stop, Mister. You didn't pay me for the biscuits."

"What!" says I. "Do you mean to impose upon me? Do you think I'm going to pay you for the biscuits and let you keep 'em, too? Ain't they there now on your shelf? I guess, sir, you don't whittle me in that way!"

So I turned about and marched off, and left the feller staring and scratching his head, as though he was struck with a dunderment.

Howsomever, I didn't want to cheat him, only jest to show 'em it warn't so easy a matter to pull my eye-teeth out; so I called in next day, and paid him two cents.

1830

A Useful Coon Skin

David Crockett

I WILL just relate a little anecdote about myself which will show the people to the East how we manage election matters on the frontiers. It was when I first run for Congress.

Well, I started off to the Cross Roads, dressed in my hunting shirt, and my rifle on my shoulder. Many of our constituents had assembled there to get a taste of the candidates at orating. Job Snelling, a gander-shanked Yankee, who had been caught somewhere about Plymouth Bay and had been shipped to the West with a cargo of codfish and rum, erected a large shanty and set up shop for the occasion. A large posse of voters had assembled before I arrived. My opponent had already made considerable headway with his speechifying and his treating, when they spied me sauntering along.

"There comes Crockett!" cried one. "Let us hear the Colonel!" cried another. And so I mounted the stump that had been cut down for the occasion, and began to bushwhack in the most approved style.

I had not been up long before there was such an uproar in the crowd that I could not hear my own voice, and some of my constituents let me know that they could not listen to me on such a dry subject as the welfare of the nation until they had something to drink, and that I must treat them. Accordingly I jumped down from the rostrum, and led the way to the shanty, followed by my constituents, shouting. "Huzza for Crockett!" and "Crockett forever!"

When we entered the shanty Job was busy dealing out his rum in a style that showed he was making a good day's work of it. I called for a quart of the best, but the crooked critter returned no other answer than by pointing to a board over the bar, on which he had chalked in large letters, "Pay to-day and trust to-morrow." Ready money in the West, in

48

those times, was the shyest thing in all nature, and it was most particularly shy with me on that occasion.

The voters, seeing my predicament, fell off to the other side. I was left deserted and alone. I saw as plain as day that unless I got some rum speedily I should lose my election as sure as there are snakes in Virginny. So I walked away from the shanty, and not a voice shouted, "Huzza for Crockett!" Popularity sometimes depends on a very small matter indeed. In this particular it was worth a quart of New England rum, and no more.

Well, knowing that a crisis was at hand, I struck into the woods, with my rifle on my shoulder, my best friend in time of need. As good fortune would have it, I had not been out more than a quarter of an hour before I treed a fat coon, and in the pulling of a trigger he lay dead at the root of the tree. I soon whipped his hairy jacket off his back, and again bent my steps towards the shanty, and walked up to the bar. I threw down the coon skin upon the counter, and called for a quart. Job, though busy in dealing out rum, forgot to point at his chalked rules and regulations. He knew that a coon was as good a legal tender for a quart in the West as a New York shilling any day in the year.

My constituents now flocked about me, and cried, "Huzza for Crockett! Crockett forever!" Finding the tide had taken a turn, I told them several yarns to get them in a good humor. Having soon dispatched the value of the coon, I went out and mounted the stump without opposition, and a clear majority of the voters followed me to hear what I had to offer for the good of the nation. Before I was half through, one of my constituents moved that they would hear the balance of my speech after they had washed down the first part with some more of Job Snelling's extract of cornstalk and molasses. The question being put, it was carried unanimously. We adjourned to the shanty, and on the way I began to reckon that the fate of the nation pretty much depended upon my shooting another coon.

While standing at the bar, feeling sort of bashful while Job's rules and regulations stared me in the face, I cast down my eyes, and discovered one end of the coonskin sticking between the logs that supported the bar. Job had slung it there in the hurry of business. I gave it a sort of quick jerk, and it followed my hand as natural as if I had been the rightful owner. I slapped it on the counter. Job, little dreaming that he was barking up the wrong tree, shoved along another bottle, which my constituents quickly disposed of with great good humor, for some of them saw the trick. Then we withdrew to the rostrum to discuss the affairs of the nation.

I don't know how it was, but the voters soon became dry again. Nothing would do but we must adjourn to the shanty, and as luck would have it, the coonskin was still sticking between the logs, as if Job had flung it there on purpose to tempt me. I was not slow in raising it to the counter, the rum followed, of course, and I wish I may be shot if I didn't, before the day was over, get ten quarts for the same identical skin, and from a fellow, too, who in those parts was considered as sharp as a steel trap and as bright as a pewter button.

The way I got to the blind side of the Yankee merchant was pretty generally known before election day, and the result was that my opponent might as well have whistled jigs to a milestone as attempt to beat up for votes in that district. I beat him out and out, and there was scarce enough left of him, after the canvass was over, to make a small grease spot. He disappeared without even leaving a mark behind.

After the election was over, I sent Snelling the price of the rum, but took good care to keep the fact from the knowledge of my constituents. Job refused the money, and sent me word that it did him good to be taken in occasionally, as it served to brighten his ideas. But I afterwards learnt when he found out the trick that had been played upon him, he put all the rum I had ordered in his bill against my opponent, who, being elated with the speeches he had made on the affairs of the nation, could not descend to examine into the particulars of a bill of a vendor of rum in the small way.

1834

Soft Sawder

THOMAS CHANDLER HALIBURTON

HOW is it," said I to Sam Slick, "that you manage to sell such an immense number of clocks, which certainly can't be called necessary articles, among people with whom there seems to be so great a scarcity of money?"

Sam looked me in the face and said in a confidential tone, "Why, I don't care if I do tell you, for the market is glutted and I shall quit this circuit. It's done by a knowledge of soft sawder and human nature.

"Here is Deacon Flint's. I've got but one clock left and I guess I'll sell it to him."

At the gate of a most comfortable looking farmhouse stood Deacon Flint, a respectable old man who had understood the value of time better than most of his neighbors, to judge by the appearances of his place.

After the usual salutation, an invitation to alight was accepted by Sam. He said that he wished to take leave of Mrs. Flint before he left Colchester, Nova Scotia.

We had hardly entered the house before Sam, pointing to the view from the window, said, "If I was to tell them down in Connecticut that there was such a farm as this away Down East here in Nova Scotia, they wouldn't believe me. Why, there ain't such a location in all New England!" Sam praised the fine bottom land and admiringly said that the "water privilege" alone must be worth three or four thousand dollars— "twice as good as that Governor Case paid fifteen thousand dollars for. I wonder, Deacon, you don't put up a carding mill on it. The same works would carry a turning lathe, a shingle machine, a circular saw——"

"Too old," said the Deacon. "Too old for all these speculations."

"Old!" repeated Sam. "Not you! Why, you're worth half a dozen of the young men we see nowadays. You're young enough to——" Here

51

he said something in a lower tone of voice which I did not distinctly hear, but whatever it was, the Deacon was pleased. He smiled and said he did not think of such things now.

"But your beasts," the Deacon said. "Your beasts must be put in and have a feed."

As the old gentleman closed the door after him, Sam drew near to me and said in an undertone, "That's what I call soft sawder."

He was cut short by the entrance of Mrs. Flint.

"Just come to say goodbye, Mrs. Flint," he told her.

"What!" said she. "Have you sold all your clocks?"

"Yes, and very low, too. Money is scarce and I wished to close the concern. I'm wrong in saying *all*, for I have just one left. Neighbor Steel's wife asked to have the refusal of it but I guess I won't sell it. I had but two of them, this one and the feller of it that I sold to Governor Lincoln. General Green, the Secretary of State for Maine, said he'd give me fifty dollars for this here one. It has composition wheels and patent axles. It's a beautiful article, a real first chop, and no mistake, genuine superfine. But I guess I'll take it back. And, besides, Squire Hawk might think kind of hard that I didn't give him the offer."

"Dear me," said Mrs. Flint. "I should like to see it. Where is it?"

"Oh, it's in a chest of mine over the way at Tom Tape's store. I guess he can ship it on to Eastport."

"Just let's look at it," said Mrs. Flint. "That's a good man."

Sam Slick, willing to oblige, soon produced the clock, a gaudy, highly varnished trumpery affair. He placed it on the chimney piece, where its beauties were pointed out and duly appreciated by Mrs. Flint whose admiration was about ending in a proposal to buy when Deacon Flint returned from giving his directions about the care of the horses.

The Deacon praised the clock. He too thought it a handsome one. But the Deacon was a prudent man. He had a watch, he was sorry, but he had no occasion for a clock.

Sam said, "I guess you're in the wrong furrow this time, Deacon. It ain't for sale. And if it was, I reckon Neighbor Steel's wife would have it, for she gives me no peace about it."

Mrs. Flint said Mr. Steel had enough to do, poor man, to pay his interest without buying clocks for his wife.

"It's no concern of mine," said Sam, "what he has to do, as long as he pays me. But I guess I don't want to sell it. And, besides, it comes too high. That clock couldn't be made at Rhode Island under forty dollars."

Suddenly Sam started and said, "Why, it ain't possible!" He looked at his watch. "Why, as I'm alive, it's four o'clock, and if I ain't been two hours here! How on earth shall I reach River Philip tonight? I tell you what, Mrs. Flint. I'll leave the clock in your care until I return on my way to the States. I'll set it a-going and put it to the right time."

As soon as this operation was performed, he delivered the key to the Deacon, telling him to wind it up every Saturday night.

When we were mounted and on our way, Sam said, "That I call human nature. Now, that clock is sold for forty dollars. It cost me just six dollars and fifty cents. Mrs. Flint will never let Mrs. Steel have the refusal, nor will the Deacon learn until I call for the clock how hard it is to give up.

"We can do without any article of luxury we never had, but once we've had it, it's not in human nature to surrender it voluntarily. Of fifteen thousand sold by myself and my partners in this Province, twelve thousand were left in this manner. And only ten clocks were ever returned when we came back around."

Said Sam Slick, "You see, we trust to soft sawder to get the clocks *in* the house and to human nature that they never come *out* of it."

1834

The Hoss Swap

AUGUSTUS BALDWIN LONGSTREET

DURING the session of the Supreme Court in the Georgia village of ———, about three weeks ago, a young man was riding up and down the crowded principal street, spurring his horse to one group of citizens, then to another; then dashing off as if fleeing from danger; and, suddenly checking his horse, returned, first in a pace, then in a trot, and then in a canter. Tossing himself in every attitude which a man could assume on horseback, he fetched a whoop and swore that "he could out-swap any live man, woman, or child that ever walked these hills or that ever straddled hossflesh since the days of old daddy Adam.

"Did you ever see the Yaller Blossom from Jasper?" he shouted. "I'm the boy! The best man at a hoss swap that ever trod shoe leather!"

Old Peter Ketch, with his boy Ned at heel, stepped up and began thoroughly to survey the Yaller Blossom's horse with much apparent interest.

"Well, old coon," said the Blossom, "do you want to swap *hosses?*"

"Why, I don't know," said Old Pete. "I believe I have a beast I'll trade with you for that one, if you like him."

"Well, fetch your nag, my old cock. You're jist the lark I wanted to get hold of. I'm perhaps a leetle—jist a *leetle*—of the best man at a hoss swap that ever stole cracklings out of his mammy's fat-gourd! Where's your *hoss?*"

"I'll bring him presently. But I want to examine your hoss a little."

"Oh, look at him!" said the Blossom, alighting and hitting the horse a cut. "Bullet here is the best piece of hossflesh in the thirteen united universal worlds. There's no sort of mistake in little Bullet. He can pick up miles on his feet and fling 'em behind him as fast as the next man's hoss, I don't care where he comes from. And he can keep it up as long as the sun can shine without resting."

54

Little Bullet looked as if he understood it all, believed it, and was ready at any moment to verify it. He was a horse of goodly countenance, rather expressive of vigilance than fire. He had obviously suffered for corn, if you judge by ribs and hipbones, but he was as cheerful and happy as if he commanded all the corn cribs and fodder stacks in Georgia. His height was about twelve hands but, as his shape was somewhat that of the giraffe, his haunches stood much lower.

Bullet's tail, however, made amends for all his defects. From the root it dropped in a graceful festoon, then rose in a handsome curve, then resumed its first direction, then mounted suddenly upward like a cypress knee. The whole had a careless and bewitching inclination to the right. Bullet never stood still but always kept up a gentle fly-scaring movement of his limbs which was peculiarly fascinating.

"I tell you, man," said the Yaller Blossom, "Bullet's the best live hoss that ever trod the grit of Georgia! Bob Smart knows the hoss. Come here, Bob, and mount the hoss and show Bullet's motions."

Bob sprang on his back, with a fluttering noise of his lips, and away went Bullet, as if in a quarter race, with all his beauties spread in handsome style.

"Now fetch him back," said Blossom. Bullet turned and came in pretty much as he went out.

"Now trot him by." Bullet sidled to the right and left airily, and exhibited at least three varieties of trot in the short space of fifty yards.

"Make him pace," said the Yaller Blossom.

Bob commenced twitching the bridle and kicking at the same time. Bullet now struck out a gait of his own that certainly deserved a patent. It seemed to have derived its elements from the minuet, the jig, and the cotillion.

"Walk him," said Blossom.

Bullet was at home again, and he walked as if money was staked on him.

Peter Ketch had now sent his boy, Neddy, to bring up his horse, Kit. Neddy rode up on a well-formed sorrel of the middle size and in good order. Taken altogether, he threw Bullet entirely in the shade, though a glance would have satisfied anyone that Bullet had the decided advantage of him in the point of intellect.

"Why, man," said Blossom, "do you bring such a hoss as *that* to trade for Bullet? Oh, I see you've no notion of trading! Well, anyhow, let me look at him. Maybe he'll do to plow."

Old Ketch took hold of Kit's bridle close to the bit. "He ain't as *pretty* a hoss as Bullet, I know, but he'll do. Start 'em together for a hundred and fifty *mile* and if Kit ain't twenty mile ahead of him at the coming out, any man may take Kit for nothing. But he's a monstrous mean hoss, gentlemen. Any man can see that. He's the scariest hoss, too, you ever saw. He won't do to hunt on, nohow."

Turning to a gaping hillman, Ketch said, "Stranger, will you let Neddy have your rifle to shoot off him?" When the rifle was handed over, Ketch directed, "Lay the barrel between his ears, Neddy. Shoot at the knot in that stump."

Ned fired and hit the knot. Kit did not move a hair's breadth.

"Neddy," said Ketch, "take a couple of sticks and beat on that hogs-head at Kit's tail."

The boy did so, setting up a tremendous rattling, at which Bullet took fright, broke his bridle, and dashed off in grand style, and would have stopped all further negotiations by going home in disgust had not a bystander caught him and brought him back.

But Kit did not move.

"I tell you, gentlemen," said Peter Ketch, "he's the scariest hoss you ever saw! He ain't as gentle as Bullet but he won't do any harm if you watch him."

During all this, Blossom was looking him over with the nicest scrutiny. Having examined his frame and limbs, now he looked at his eyes. "He's got a curious look out of his eyes, old cock."

"Oh, yes, sir," said Ketch. "Jist as blind as a bat. Blind hosses always has clear eyes. Make a motion at his eyes, if you please, sir."

Blossom did so, and Kit threw up his head. Blossom repeated the experiment and Kit jerked back in considerable astonishment.

"Stone blind, you see, gentlemen," said Ketch. "But he's jist as good to travel of a dark night as if he had eyes."

"Blame my buttons," said Blossom, "if I like them eyes!"

"No," said Ketch, "nor me neither. I'd rather have 'em made of dia-monds."

Blossom had evidently made up his mind. "Well, old coon," he said, "make a pass at me."

"No," said Peter, "you made the banter. Now make your pass."

"Well, I'm never afraid to price my hosses. You must give me twenty-five dollars, boot."

"Oh, certainly! Say *fifty*, and my saddle and bridle thrown in. Here, Neddy, my son, take away Daddy's hoss."

"Well," said Blossom, "I've made my pass. Now you make yours."

Ketch said, "I'm for short talk in a hoss swap and always tell a gentleman at once what I aim to do. Give me ten dollars, boot."

Blossom swore absolutely and roundly that he never would give boot. There the parties stood for a long time. The bystanders began to taunt both of them. However, it was pretty well agreed that the old man had backed Blossom out.

At length Blossom swore he "never would be backed out after bantering a man. Jist to close the trade, I'll give three dollars boot." To this Peter Ketch agreed.

As he handed over the three dollars, Blossom said, "Now, I'm a man that, when he makes a bad trade, makes the most of it until he can make a better. I'm for no rues and after-claps."

"That's jist my way," said Ketch. "I never go to law to mend my bargains."

"Ah, you're the kind of boy I love to trade with," said the Yaller Blossom from Jasper. "Here's your hoss, old man. Take the saddle and bridle off him and I'll strip yours. But lift up the blanket easy from Bullet's back. He's a mighty tender-backed hoss."

The old man removed the saddle from Bullet but the blanket stuck fast. He tried to raise it but Bullet bowed himself, switched his tail, danced a little, and gave signs of biting.

"Don't hurt him, old man," said Blossom. "Take it off easy. I am perhaps a *leetle* of the best man at a hoss swap that ever catched an old coon!"

Ketch pulled at the blanket more and more roughly, and Bullet became more and more cavortish. When the blanket did come off, he had reached the kicking stage in good earnest.

Removal of the blanket disclosed a sore on Bullet's backbone that measured six full inches in length and four in breadth and had as many features as Bullet had motions.

The bystanders were sickened at the sight and some said that the brute who had ridden him in that plight deserved the halter. The prevailing feeling, however, was of mirth. The laugh became loud and general at the old man's expense, with the Yaller Blossom striking a pose and egging them on and enjoying every word of it.

Old Ketch said nothing. But his son Neddy couldn't grip his feelings so well. His eyes opened wider and wider from the first pull of the blanket. When the whole sore burst into view, astonishment and fright warped his face. He bore the cuts at his father as long as he could, then broke out,

"His back's mighty bad off, but dod-drot my soul if you've put it to Daddy as bad as you think you have."

Blossom slapped his leg and guffawed, "How so, bantam?"

"Old Kit's both blind *and* deaf, I'll be dod-drot if he ain't!"

"The devil he is!" said Blossom. "He jerked his head when I——"

"When I pinched him!" said Neddy. "He's stony blind and would jist as leave go against the house with you or in a ditch as anyhow. He can't *see* where he's a-going and he can't *hear* what you tell him to do. You go try him and see, Mister!"

"Neddy," said the old man, "you oughtn't to try and make people discontented with their things. Stranger, don't mind what the little boy says. If you can only get Kit rid of them little failings, you'll find him all kinds of a hoss. Come, Neddy, my son, let's be moving. The stranger seems to be getting snappish."

1835

Character of the Virginians

JOSEPH G. BALDWIN

PATRIOTISM with a Virginian is a noun personal. It is the Virginian himself, and something over. Virginianism is a sort of cocoa grass that has got into the soil and has so matted it over and so fibred through it that you may destroy the soil but you can't root out the grass. I makes no odds where the Virginian goes, he carries Virginia with him. He loves Virginia for herself and for himself, because she is Virginia and —everything else beside.

He never gets acclimated elsewhere. He may breathe in Alabama, but he lives in Virginia. The Virginian does not crow over the poor Carolinian, Tennessean, or Yankee. He does not reproach him with his misfortune of birthplace. He feels on the subject as a man of delicacy feels in alluding to a rope in the presence of a person, one of whose brothers "stood upon nothing and kicked at the United States." No, he thinks the affliction is enough without the triumph. He finds occasion to let the fact of his Virginia birth be known, and that bare mention is enough. It is fully able to protect and take care of itself. Like a ducal title, there is no need of saying more than to name it.

In politics the Virginian is learned much beyond what is written. He has heard a great deal of speaking on that prolific subject by one or two Randolphs and any number of Barbours. When two of opposite politics get together, it is amusing—if you have nothing else to do that day—to hear the discussion. I never heard a discussion in which old John Adams and Thomas Jefferson did not figure: As if an interminable dispute had been going on for so many generations between these two personages—as if the quarrel had begun before time, but was not to end with it. But the strangest part to me was that the dispute seemed to be going on without poor Adams having any defense or champion. It never waxed hotter than when both parties agreed in denouncing the man of Braintree as the worst of public sinners and the vilest of political heretics.

Directly or indirectly, Virginia has exerted an influence upon the national councils nearly as great as all the rest of the states combined. While Virginia has been talking for the benefit of the nation, the other— and less oratorically favored—states have been *doing* for their own bene- fit. Consequently, what she has gained in reputation, she has lost in wealth and material aids. Certainly the Virginia character has been less distinguished for its practical than its ornamental traits.

Eminently social and hospitable, kind, humane, and generous is the Virginian by nature and habit. He belongs to the gregarious, not to the solitary, division of animals. Society can only be kept up by grub and gab —something to eat and, if not something to talk about, talk. A Virginian can always get up a good dinner. He can also do his share in disposing of one after it is got up.

In petite manners—the little attentions of the table, the filling up of the chinks of the conversation with small fugitive observations, the supplying the hooks and eyes that keep the discourse going, the genial good humor which makes up in laughter what it wants in wit—in these, and in the science of getting through a picnic, or chowder party, or fish fry, the Vir- ginian is first, and there is no second.

Great is he, too, in mixing an apple toddy or mint julep where ice can be got for love or money. Every dish is a text. With accuracy and fulness he can discourse of horticulture, hunting, poultry, fishing—with a slight divergence in favor of fox-chasing and a detour towards horse racing now and then, and continual parentheses to recommend particular dishes or glasses. Oh! I tell you! If ever there was an interesting man, it is he. Others might be agreeable, but he was fascinating, irresistible, not-to-be- done-without.

In the fulness of time a new era set in, the era of credit without capital, and enterprise without honesty. The Age of Brass had succeeded the Arcadian Period—with the opening up of the Southwest to settlement— and speculation—a time when men got rich on the profits of what they owed instead of by saving part of their earnings and living at their own cost.

As the new Alabama and Mississippi country settled up, marvelous accounts went forth. Emigrants came flocking in. Every road leading to the new country was a vagrant stream of enterprise and adventure. Money, or the smutted rags that passed for money, was the only cheap thing to be had. Every crossroad and every avocation presented an opening through which fortune was seen in near perspective.

Credit was a matter of course. To refuse it—if the thing was ever done —were an insult for which a bowie-knife were not a too summary means of redress. The state banks issued their bills by the sheet, like a patent steam printing press. No other showing was asked of the applicant for a loan than an authentication of his great distress for money. Money had thus got to work on the principles of the charity hospital. If an overseer grew tired of supervising a plantation and felt a call to lay down his bull-whip for the yardstick, all he had to do was present himself to a banker, with a letter avouching his citizenship, and a clean shirt, and he was given a through ticket to speedy bankruptcy.

Prices rose like smoke. Lots in obscure villages sold at from thirty to forty dollars per acre—and considered dirt cheap, at that. In short, the country had got to be a full antetype of California, in all except the gold. Vulgarity, ignorance, fussy and arrogant pretension, rowdyism, bullying insolence ruled the hour. There was no restraining public opinion. The law was well-nigh powerless. Religion was scarcely heard of except as furnishing the oaths and technics of profanity. Larceny grew not only respectable but genteel. Swindling was raised to the dignity of the fine arts. The doggeries were in full blast, selling the meanest of whiskies. Gaming and horse racing were well-patronized. Occasionally the scene was diversified by a murder or two. Though they were perpetrated from behind a corner or behind the back of the deceased, whenever the accused chose to stand his trial, the murder was always found to be committed in self-defense, securing the homicide an honorable acquittal at the hands of his peers.

The same characteristics were visible in the professions. Men dropped down into their places as from the clouds. Nobody knew who or what they were, except as they claimed. Instead of taking to the highway and calling upon the wayfarer to stand and deliver, some unscrupulous horse doctor—that did not know a liver from a gizzard—would set up his sign as *Physician and Surgeon,* and draw his lancet on you, or fire at random a box of his pills into your bowels, with a vague chance of hitting some disease unknown to him, but with a better prospect of killing the patient. He charged some ten dollars a trial for his marksmanship.

Or a superannuated justice or constable from one of the older states was metamorphosed into a lawyer. Though he knew not the distinction between a fee tail and a female, he would undertake to construe, offhand, a will involving all the subtleties of uses and trusts.

But this state of things could not last forever. Society cannot always stand on its head with its heels in the air. The crash finally came, as if the ribs of nature broke and there was a scattering like the bursting of a thousand powder magazines.

But while the flush times lasted—the reign of humbug and wholesale insanity—many Virginians came to the Southwest, for the yearning for wealth is a catching disease. Superior to many of the settlers in elegance of manners and general intelligence, it was the weakness of the Virginian to imagine he was superior, too, in the essential art of making his way in a new country. What a mistake that was!

In the old country, a Virginian starting on a capital of a plantation and fifty or sixty negroes, might reasonably calculate, by the aid of a usurer and the occasional sale of a negro or two, to hold on, without declared insolvency, until a green old age. His estate melted like an estate in chancery, under the gradual thaw of expenses. But in this new, fast country, it went by the sheer cost of living or by a galloping consumption by ruinous investment.

All the habits of the Virginian's life, his tastes, his associations, his education—everything: the trustingness of his disposition, his want of business qualifications, his sanguine temper, all that was Virginian in him—made him fore-ordained prey. Where the keenest speculator in lands and crops was bit, what chance had he? But how could he believe it? How could he believe that the stuttering, grammarless Georgian could beat him in a land trade? If he made a bad bargain, how could he expect to get rid of it? He had never heard of the elaborate machinery of ingenious chicane, such as feigning bankruptcy, fraudulent conveyances, making over his property to his wife.

He lived freely, for it was a liberal time, and it was not for a Virginian to be behind others in hospitality and liberality. He required credit, and of course had to stand security in return. When the crash came, he fell an easy victim. Virginians in the new country broke by neighborhoods. They usually endorsed notes for each other, and when one fell—like the child's play of putting blocks on end at equal distances—all fell. Each got broke to pay security on another's note, and yet few were able to pay their own debts. So powerless were they in those times that they reminded you of an oyster, both shells torn off, lying on the beach, with the seagulls screaming over them. The only question was, which should gobble them up?

There was one consolation. If the Virginian involved himself like a fool, he suffered himself to be sold out like a gentleman. When his card house of visionary projects came tumbling down about his ears, the next question was, "Where am I to go?"

Many of them, having lost all by eating and drinking, sought justice from meat and drink, which might at least support them in poverty. Accordingly, they kept tavern and made barter of hospitality a business, the only disagreeable part of which was receiving the money. And while I confess I never knew a Virginian out of the State to keep a bad tavern, I never knew one to draw a solvent breath from the time he opened house until death or the sheriff closed it.

Others got to be not exactly overseers but some nameless thing for some more fortunate Virginian who had escaped the wreck. The well-to-do Virginian got his former boon companion to live with him on board or other wages, in such relation that the friend was not often found at table at the dinings given to the neighbors. He got to be called Mr. Flournoy, instead of Bob, and slept in an outhouse in the yard.

Some of the younger scions who had received academical or collegiate educations heroically led the Forlorn Hope of the battle of life, the corps of pedagogues of country schools—*academies*, I beg pardon for not saying. For, under Virginia economy, every crossroad log cabin where boys were flogged from B-a-k-e-r to Constantinople grew into the dignity of a sort of runt college. The teacher vainly endeavored to hide the meanness of the calling beneath the sonorous sobriquet of Professor.

Divers others of the emigrant Virginians simply vanished, but what became of them I never knew. Those who had fathers, uncles, aunts, or other like resorts in Virginia limped back, with feathers moulted and crestfallen, carrying their fortune—six bits in money and the balance in experience.

1853

Two Penn State Pungents

ANONYMOUS

SOME time ago there lived in Pennsylvania a gentleman of indolent habits, who made a business in the winter season of visiting his friends extensively. After wearing out his welcome in his own immediate vicinity last winter, he thought he would visit an old Quaker friend, some twenty miles distant, who had been a school-fellow of his. On his arrival, he was cordially received by the Quaker, he thinking his visitor had taken much pains to come so far to see him. He treated his friend with great attention and politeness for several days, but as he did not see any signs of his leaving, he became uneasy, but bore it with patience till the morning of the eighth day, when he said to him:

"My friend, I am afraid thee will never visit me again."

"Oh, yes, I shall," said the visitor. "I have enjoyed my visit very much. I shall certainly come again."

"Nay," said the Quaker, "I think thee will never visit me again."

"What makes you think I will not come again?" asked the visitor.

"If thee does never *leave*," said the Quaker, "how can thee come again?"

The visitor left.

"I say, Squire, what'll you take for that there dog of yours?" said a Yankee peddler to an old Dutch farmer, in the neighborhood of Lancaster. "He ain't a very good-looking dog, but what was you calculating he'd fetch?"

"Ah," responded the Dutchman, "that dog isn't worth nothing, most. He is not worth you to buy him.".

"Guess two dollars about would git him, wouldn't it? I'll give you that for him."

"Yaas, he isn't worth that."

"Well, I'll take him," said the peddler.

"Stop," said the Dutchman. "About that dog is one thing I cannot sell."

"Oh, take off his collar," said the peddler. "I don't want that."

"His collar isn't," said the Dutchman. "He a poor dog is, but something he has I cannot sell."

By now the Yankee was irritated. "Well, what in the nation is it, then?"

The Dutchman lighted his pipe and smiled. "Sell I cannot," he said, "the wag of that dog's tail when I home from the fields come in."

1830's

The Trumpet Sounds

ANONYMOUS

ON A Saturday afternoon preceding the opening of a back-woods camp meeting where he was to preach, Lorenzo Dow, the somber Savanarola of Methodism, was jogging along on his bony horse when he noticed a stout little Negro boy skipping along with a small tin horn in his hands, giving it a playful blast every few paces.

Dow reined his horse, saying, "My son, can you really blow that horn?"

"Yes, sir," replied the boy. "I kin toot right good when I gits in behind it."

"Let me hear you, my son."

So the boy inflated his velvet cheeks and made the woods resound.

"Good enough," said Dow. "Do you, my son, know a tall, lone pine tree skirting the camp grounds at Sharon?"

"Yes, sir, I does, very well, master."

Lorenzo then put his hand in his pocket, and pulling out a silver dollar, showed it to the boy, and told him what he must do to earn it. The boy was highly delighted and promised punctuality, with secrecy.

On the Sabbath, a large meeting assembled at Sharon to hear the famous Lorenzo Dow: serious old men and their wives, wild boys and their sweethearts, almost all on horseback, sometimes by twos and threes, besides Negroes from a great distance on foot, for they love anything that has a laugh attached to it, and they knew that Lorenzo was good for a joke, even if it did hit hard.

Dow selected a rather brimstone text, and made the application as strong as possible, but he only forced his way slowly among the health-ful, honest-hearted people, who were hard to frighten. He enumerated

67

the enormity of the vices he thought to prevail, but they were so used to them that the words slid over them like water over a duck's back.

At length, he boldly described in the plainest kind of language the appearances and character of "the last great day," and what would be their condition when that day came.

"Suppose," exclaimed the preacher suddenly, and then paused—"that this day!" He saw that some of the women became a little fidgety, and nudged the men into silence and attention. "Suppose," repeated he, elevating his voice, "that this day Gabriel should blow his trump!"

At this moment, the little Negro from the top of the lofty pine blew a loud and clamorous blast. The audience was overwhelmed. The women shrieked. The men rose in great surprise. The horses tied round the camp neighed, reared, and kicked, while the terrified negroes changed their complexion to a dull purple color. Never was alarm, surprise, and astonishment more promptly exhibited.

Lorenzo Dow looked with grave but pleased attention upon the successful result of his experiment, until the first clamor had subsided, and some discovered the character of the artificial angel and were about to apply a little hickory after the pine.

But this suggestion was arrested by the loud and solemn tones of the preacher, who, looking very firmly into the faces of his disturbed audience, as he leaned over them to continue his discourse, said:

"And now, if a little Negro boy, with a tin horn, on the top of a pine bush, can make you feel so—*how will you feel when the day of doom does come!*"

1849

The Great Charter Contest in Gotham

Cornelius Mathews

THERE is a particular time in the city of New York, when ragamuffins and vagabonds take a sudden rise in respectability; when the uncombed locks of a wharf rat are looked upon with as much veneration as if they belonged to Apollo in his brightest moments of inspiration. At this singular and peculiar period, all the higher classes, by a wonderful readiness and felicity of condescension, step down from their pedestals and smilingly meet the vulgar gentry.

About this time, gloves go out of repute, and an astonishing shaking of dirty fists takes place all over the metropolis. Happy, golden time! Reader, if you chance not to comprehend this sweet condition of things, be informed that a Charter Election comes on next month!

The charter contest of the year eighteen hundred and —, is, perhaps, the fiercest on record in the chronicles of New York. Several minor skirmishes took place with regard to aldermen, assessors, and constables, but the main brunt and heat of the engagement fell upon the election of a Mayor to preside over the destinies of the metropolis.

It seemed from the grounds on which it was fought, to be the old battle of patrician and plebeian. On the one side, the candidate was Herbert Hickock, Esquire, a wholesale auctioneer and tolerably good Latin Scholar; a gentleman who sallied forth every morning at nine o'clock from a fashionable residence in Broadway, dressed in a neat and gentlemanly suit of black, an immaculate pair of gloves, large white ruffles in his bosom, and a dapper cane in his hand.

Opposed to him as a candidate for the Mayoralty was a retired shoemaker, affectionately known as Bill Snivel. He was particularly celebrated

69

for the amount of unclean garments he was able to array about his person, a rusty, swaggering hat, and a rugged style of English.

The great principles upon which the warfare was waged were on the one hand, that tidy apparel is an indisputable evidence of a foul and corrupt code of principles; and on the other, that to be poor and unclean denotes a total deprivation of the reasoning faculties.

At the approach of a New York election, it is truly astonishing how great a curiosity springs up as to the personal habits of the gentlemen presented on either side as candidates. The most excruciating anxiety appears to seize the community to learn certain little biographical incidents as to the birth, parentage, morals, and everyday details of his life.

Also, as everyone knows, the advent of an election creates a general and clamorous demand for full-grown young men of twenty-one years of age. To meet this demand, a surprising cultivation of beards took place among the Hickock youth who happened to want a few days or months of that golden period.

Furthermore, a large number of Bill Snivel voters in the upper wards of the city were forced to repair for the benefit of their health to the more southern and genial latitudes of the first, second, and third wards. Hickock men in those Hickock-favoring wards emigrated to the northern wards. Pleasant aquatic excursions, too, were undertaken by certain gentlemen of the Bill Snivel tinge of politics (whose proper domicils were at Hartford and Haverstraw), and they came sailing down the North and East Rivers in all kinds of craft, on visits to their metropolitan brethren, and dropped their compliments in the shape of small folded papers in square green boxes with a slit in the top.

The Bill Snivel and the Hickock meetings, each had some particular oratorical favorite. In one, a slim man was in the habit of exhibiting a long sallow face at eight o'clock every evening, between a tall pair of sperm candles and solemnly declaring that—the country was ruined and that he was obliged to pay twelve and a half cents a pound for liver! At the Bill Snivel meetings, a short, stout man, with an immense bony fist, was accustomed to appear on a high platform—and announce that "the people was on its legs again"; and that "the Democracy was carrying the country before it," which was a profound postulate meaning—the Democracy was carrying the Democracy before it—they constituting the country at all times, and the country at all times constituting the Democracy.

In the meantime, Committeemen of all sorts and descriptions are at work in rooms of every variety of wall and dimension. The whole city is covered with handbills, caricatures, manifestoes, exposures, pointed facts, neat little scraps of personal history, and various other pages of diverting political literature. Swarms cluster about the polls. Banners stream from windows, cords, and housetops. A little man rides about on the box of an enormous wagon, blowing a large brass trumpet, and waving a white linen flag with a catching inscription—and he labors at the trumpet till he blows his face out of shape and his hat off his head, and waves the flag till it seems to be a signal of distress.

Scouring Committees beat furiously through the wards in every direction. Diving like sharks into cellars, they bring up as it were between their teeth, wretched scarecrow creatures who stare about them, when introduced to daylight, as if it were as great novelty to them as roast beef. Ascending into garrets, like mounting hawks, they bear down in their clutches trembling old men who have vegetated in those dry, airy elevations apparently during a whole century.

Prominent among the bustling busy-bodies of the hour is Fahrenheit Flapdragon, member of the Hickock General Committee, the Hickock Vigilance Ward Committee, the Wharf Committee, the Advertising Committee, the Committee on Flags and Decorations, the Committee on Tarbarrels and Tinderboxes, one of the Grand Committee on Drinking Gin Slings and Cigar Smoking, and member of the Committee on Noise and Applause. By dint of energetic maneuvering, Flapdragon had likewise succeeded in being appointed Chairman of the Committee on Chairs and Benches. The deciding vote he had himself judiciously cast in his own favor.

The little man, of a truth, was so tossed and driven about by his various self-imposed duties in the committee rooms, streets, and along the wharves, that he came well-nigh going stark mad. During the day, he hurried up and down the streets, from poll to poll, bearing tidings from one to the other—distributing tickets—cheering on the little boys to shout, and placing big men in the passages to stop the ingress of Bill Snivel voters.

At night, what with drinking gin slings and brandy and water at the bar to encourage the vagabonds that stood looking wistfully on—talking red hot Hickock politics to groups of four, five, and six—and bawling applause at the different public meetings he attended—he presented at the close of the day's services such a personal appearance that anyone might have supposed he had stayed in an oven till the turning point between red and brown arrived, and then jumped out and walked home with the utmost possible velocity to keep up his color. There are seventeen wards in the city, and every ward has its Fahrenheit Flapdragon.

While these busy little Committee men are bustling and hurrying about, parties of voters are constantly arriving on foot, in coaches, barouches, open wagons, and omnibuses, accompanied by some electioneering friend who brings them up to the polls. Every hour the knots about the door swell, until they fill the street.

In the interior of the building, meanwhile, a somewhat different scene presents itself. Behind a counter, on three wooden stools, three men are perched with a green box planted in front of the one in the center, and an officer with a staff at either end. The small piece of green furniture thus guarded is the ballot box, and all sorts of humanity are every moment arriving and depositing their votes. Besides the officers, three fierce looking men stand around the box and challenge in the most determined manner every suspicious person of the opposite politics.

"I challenge this man's vote," says one, as a ragged young fellow with a dirty face and strong odor of brandy approaches. "I don't believe he is entitled to vote."

"Yes he is," replied another. "I know him—he's a good citizen. But you may swear him, if you choose."

At this, the vagabond is pushed up to the counter by one of his political friends. His hat is knocked off by an officer. The chief inspector presents an open Bible, at which the vagabond stares as if it were a stale codfish instead of the gospels. A second friend raises his hand for him, and places it on the book. The chief inspector is about to swear him, when the Hickock challenger cries out, "Ask him if he understands the nature of an oath?"

"What's an oath?" asks the inspector solemnly.

"Damn your eyes!" hiccups the young Bill Snivel voter.

"Take him out!" shouts the inspector, and the officers in attendance, each picking up a portion of his coat collar, hurry him away through a back door into the street, and dismiss him with a hearty punch of their staves in the small of his back.

The battle by no means ceases at the going down of the sun. For there is in each ward a meeting in some small room in the second story of a public house, where about one hundred and fifty miscellaneous human beings are entertained by sundry young attorneys and other spouters, practising the English language and exercising the force of their lungs. At these meetings, you will be sure to meet with certain stereotyped faces—which are always there, always with the same smiling expression—and looking as if they were part of the wainscoting or lively pieces of furniture, fixed there by the landlord to please his guests:

The smiling gentlemen are office seekers. In the corner, sitting on a table, you may observe a large, puffed-out man with red cheeks. He is anxious to obtain the appointment of beer-gauger under the corporation. Standing up by the fireplace is a man with a dingy face and shivering person, who wishes to be city weigher of coal, talking to a tall fellow who stoops in the shoulder like a buzzard, with a prying nose and eye, and a face as hard and round as a paving stone, who is making interest for re-appointment as a street inspector. There is also another, with brown, tanned countenance, patriotically lamenting the decline of the good old Revolutionary spirit—who wants the office of leather inspector.

The most prominent man at these meetings is the orator Bog, a person whose reputation shoots up into a wonderful growth during the three days of election, while his declamation is fresh, but suddenly withers away when the heat of the conflict has cooled. His eloquence is the peculiar offspring of those sunny little republican hot beds, ward meetings.

He has just described the city as "split like a young eel from nose to tail by the diabolical and cruel knife of these modern Catalines," the aldermen of the city—they having recently run a street through it north and south.

"These are the men," he exclaims with an awful smile on his countenance, "these are the men that dare insult the Democracy by appearing in public—like goslings—yes, like goslings!—with such articles as these on their legs!" Thrusting a pair of tongs, heretofore dexterously concealed under the skirts of his coat, into his hat, which stood upon the table before him, he drew out a pair of fine silk stockings and swung them triumphantly above the heads of the mob, which screamed and clamored with huge delight at the spectacle.

"And such articles as these!" Bog shouted, producing from the hat a shirt about small enough for a yearling infant, with enormous green ruffles about large enough for a Patagonian.

"Look at it!" cried Bog, throwing it to one of the mob.

"Smell of it!" cried Bog.

Several lusty vagabonds came near going into fits, when orator Bog facetiously, though gravely, stopped his nose with his thumb and finger, and remarked, "I think someone has brought a skunk into the room!"

The last hour of the last day of the Great Charter Contest has arrived. Every carman, every merchant's clerk, every Negro with a freehold, every stevedore, every lamp-lighter, every street-sweeper, every vagrant, every vagabond has cast his vote. Garret, cellar, sailor's boarding house, shed, stable, sloop, steamboat, and dockyard, have been ransacked, and not a human being on the great island of Manhattan has escaped the clutch of the Scouring and District Committees of the two great contending parties.

At this critical moment, and as the sun began to look horizontally over the chimney-tops with a broad face, two persons were prowling and prying along the wharf on the East River, like a brace of inquisitive snipe.

At the selfsame moment the eyes of both alighted on an object floating in the water; at the selfsame moment both sprang forward with a boat-hook in his hand and fastened on the object at either end. It was dragged on shore, and proved to be the body of a man in a fragmentary blue coat, roofless hat, and corduroy pantaloons.

"I claim him," said one of the boathook gentlemen, a member of the Seventh Ward Hickock Wharf Committee. "I saw him first! He's our voter by all that's fair!"

"He wants a jug-full of being yours, my lad," retorted the other, a member of the Bill Snivel Wharf Committee. "He's too good a Christian to be yours, for don't you see he's just been baptized?"

By this time, a mob had gathered about the disputants, who stood hold-ing the rescued body, each by a leg.

"Why, you fools!" cried a medical student, pushing his professional nose through the throng. "You'll give the man apoplexy if you hold him that way just half a minute longer!"

In a trice, after, a second medical student arrived, and hearing what the other said, exclaimed, "It's the best thing you can do—hold him just as he is, or he's sure to get the dropsy."

The mob, however, interfered—the man was laid on his back—and one of the medical students (who favored the Hickock politics) taking hold of one wrist—and the other (who advocated Bill Snivel) seizing the other, they commenced chafing his temples and rubbing the palms of his hands.

Meantime, the Wharf Committeemen felt inclined to renew the dis-pute as to their claim on the body of the half-drowned loafer, but by advice of the medical gentlemen, the claim was referred to be settled by the man's own lips, whenever he should recover the use of them.

The medical students chafed and rubbed, and every minute leaned down to the ear of the drowned body, as if to catch some favorable gnosis.

"Hurrah for Hickock!" shouted the man, opening his eyes just as one of the medical students had withdrawn his mouth from his ear. The Hickock portion of the crowd gave three cheers.

"Hurrah for Bill Snivel!" shouted the resuscitated loafer, as the other medical student applied his lips to his ear.

The loafer was now raised upon his legs, and marshalled like some great hero between the medical students and the two members of the Wharf Committees, and borne towards the polls, having each hand alternately supplied by the Hickock people and the Bill Snivel with the tickets of the respective parties. They arrived at the door of the election room, with the body of this important and disputed voter, just one minute after sundown, and finding this thus to be of no value—since the polls had closed—united in applying their feet to his flanks and kicking him out of the building.

In two or three days the votes of the city were duly canvassed, and it was found that they stood for Bill Snivel 13,000; for Herbert Hickock, 13,303—scattering 20. Three hundred and three Bill Snivel voters having, in consequence of their limited knowledge of orthography and politics, voted for Bill Snivel for constable, Herbert Hickock, Esq., was therefore declared duly elected Mayor of the city and county of New York.

1838

Mississippi Politics, Yankee-Style

ANONYMOUS

As SERGEANT S. PRENTISS rose to leadership in the law and among the Whigs in Mississippi, he made bitter enemies. Unable to make any headway against such a spellbinder, as a last resort the Democrats planned to put him down by recourse to the "laws of honor." It was presumed that Prentiss, a Yankee, born in Portland, Maine, would not fight. If he refused, he would be disgraced in the eyes of the Mississippi land-owners and conservatives, and his overwhelming influence over them lost. A wretched creature who lived in Vicksburg, who, though once respectable, had lost everything but a certain physical courage, was selected to presume an insult and send a challenge.

Upon receiving the message, Prentiss at once comprehended the plot. He was expected to bear the degradation not only of backing down, but the additional mortification of doing it before a man socially beneath contempt.

The following morning, Prentiss made up a bundle, with a letter neatly tied on the outside, and by the hands of his servant sent it to the challenger.

The principal and his friends were confounded at such a proceeding. "Certainly," said they, "Mr. Prentiss must be profoundly ignorant of the laws of honor, else he would not send an answer to a challenge by the hands of a nigger!" But the reading of the note explained:

"Mr. ———, I have received your challenge to mortal combat; before I can accept it, I insist that you shall have at least one quality of a gentleman, *viz.*, be habited in a clean shirt, which desirable article I send you by the honest bearer of this note. Thus strengthened in your social position by a single quality that makes you worthy of my notice, I will then proceed to arrange further preliminaries."

It is useless to say that the duel did not take place.

J. F. H. CLAIBORNE

On the opposite side of the political fence was another Yankee, Franklin E. Plummer, a native of Massachusetts, who beat the piney woods of Mississippi for the votes of what Prentiss would have called "the unwashed Democracy." Among Plummer's shrewdly calculated electioneering tactics were professions of complete ignorance of book-learning, obligingly holding calves away from cows at milking time, and helping backwoods mothers pick red bugs from their babies.

During one campaign for the Democratic primary, Plummer ran against the late Powhattan Ellis who was, in turn, Circuit Judge, United States District Judge, Senator in Congress, and Minister to Mexico. Though always a straight-out Democrat, Judge Ellis was aristocratic in his tastes, habits, and appearance; very dignified, precise, and dressy. In the course of the canvass, when fording a flooded creek, Judge Ellis lost his portmanteau, a circumstance which Plummer immediately learned.

In the next issue of the Monticello paper, Plummer had this advertisement published:

"*Lost by Hon. Powhattan Ellis*, in crossing Tallahala, the following articles: 6 lawn handkerchiefs; 6 cambric shirts; 2 cambric nightshirts; 1 night cap; 1 pr. stays; 4 pr. silk stockings; hair-brush, flesh-brush, nailbrush, clothes-brush, razors and dressing glass, pomatum, perfume, &c., &c."

That advertisement killed the Judge east of Pearl River. Such a sample of swelled head effeminancy and Natchez dandyism was not wanted in the piney woods.

1880

Indian Sign

ANONYMOUS

SHORTLY after my father had settled the family on the Ohio," said the first man born west of the Alleghanies, "my mother went to fetch water from a stream a little way outside the stockade.

"Lifting her head, after dipping the water, she saw an Indian in war paint close beside her. He raised a whoop, and she instantly fled like a deer. Being young and active, she gained the shelter of the stockade, within which she fell exhausted.

"Some time after that, I was ushered into life. The reddish darkness of my complexion was always referred to the fact of my mother having been frightened and followed by an Indian."

"And a mighty natural mode of accounting for it," said the man seated next him. "But, may I ask, did you ever hear your poor mother say whether the Indian overtook her or not?"

1830's

Training Day

H. H. RILEY

IN THE New England village where I was reared, militia training days—which, according to law, took place once a year—were affairs of great military spirit. I can recollect the names of scores of generals, colonels, majors, captains, and even corporals. Yes, corporals! Just any man couldn't be a corporal in those days. Why, bless your soul! There was General Peabody and General Jones and Major Goodwin and Major Boles, and any quantity of colonels.

On Training Day nobody worked. The village was upside down. 'Seventy-six was in command and martial law declared.

Major Boles I recollect when in the active discharge of his duty. He always grew serious as the great militia muster drew on. He went away off by himself where he could be alone with the spirits of his forefathers. He burnished up his sword, shook out the dust from his regimentals, warned his children to stand out of the way, and looked ferociously at his wife. He knew he was *Major* Boles, and he knew every other respectable man knew it.

But Major-General Peabody was the greatest general *I* ever saw. When a boy, I looked upon him as a very bloodthirsty man. Nothing would have induced me to go near him. He was a little fellow in stature, had a hard round paunch that looked like an iron pot, and short, thick legs. His face was freckled and his hair gray. He wore two massive epaulets and an old Revolutionary cap shaped like the moon in its first quarter, from which a white and red feather curved over his left ear. He had a sword, and *such* a sword! Nobody dared touch it, for it was the *General's* sword!

Training Day usually opened with a boom from the field-piece at sunrise that shook the hills. About ten in the morning, the soldiers began to pour in from all quarters. Drums and fifes, and muskets and rifles filed along in confusion—ambitious companies in uniform and common militia out according to law.

Uncle Joe Billings, who had played the bass drum for more than twenty years, gravely marched along all by himself, his drum slung around his neck, his head erect, his step firm, pushing along to headquarters at the measured beat of his own music, now and then cutting a flourish with his right hand for the amusement of the children who were capering around him.

Knots of militiamen gathered around the tavern and made a circle for the music to practice, preparatory to the great come-off. Then came the good old Continental tunes that were full of fight, played by old fifers and drummers who had been through the wars. They were men who made a solemn and earnest thing of martial music.

The captains and colonels and generals did not mix with the common soldiers on Training Day. No! Nor speak to them. Rank meant something. They felt as though they were out in a war. They kept themselves covered from the public gaze in a secluded corner of the tavern and were waited upon with great respect by those of inferior grade. Sometimes a guard was stationed at the door to prevent a crowd upon their dignity. Occasionally, one of them would bustle out among the rank and file on some momentous duty, fairly blazing with gold and silver, lace and feathers. But there never was an instance of one of these characters recognizing even his own brother while in military costume.

About eleven o'clock the solemn roll of the drums was heard. Loud voices of command followed. Swords flashed and feathers danced in the organization of the companies. Then came the training, real training, a mile down the street, a mile back again, a perfect roar of music, and flags flying, and horses prancing. What was rain or dust or mud with such an army? They marched straight through it. The sweat poured down but the army moved on for hours and hours in its terrible march.

The great sight of the day, however, was the Major-General and his staff. I mean, of course, Major-General Peabody.

They were not seen until about three o'clock in the afternoon, it being customary for them to withdraw from public observation the day prior to the muster. When the army was drawn up in the field for inspection, there was usually a pause for an hour, a pause deeply impressive. We never knew exactly where the General and his staff were concealed. Some said they were housed in one place, some in another.

Upon the discharge of the cannon, they burst upon us, glittering like the sun. They came cantering down the road with perfect fury in a cloud of dust, followed by a score of boys on a sharp run to keep up.

General Peabody and his staff always rushed headlong into the field, without looking to the left or to the right. I recollect that on one occasion he demolished an applecart and absolutely turned everything topsyturvy, besides creating great consternation among the bystanders. It did not disturb him.

Passing the ruins of the applecart and entering within the guarded lines, he halted and took a survey of his troops. The music saluted him. The companies waved their flags. He rode a little nearer, rose in his stirrups, jerked out his sword, and, looking ferociously, cried out, "*Shoulder arms!*"

This cry was repeated by the subordinate officers.

After awhile, the privates, one after another, lazily lifted their pieces to their shoulders.

The General was in the act of rising again and was drawing in his breath for a command of thunder, when his horse wheeled at the report of a musket that went off in the lines and came near upsetting him, feathers and all. He fell into the arms of one of his aides and very soon righted himself.

Striking his horse across the rump, he cut a great many flourishes on the field to the astonishment of the lookers-on. He then rushed through the orders of the day like a madman. He was manifestly utterly fearless of consequences.

I hope my readers are satisfied that Major-General Peabody was a great military character. I recollect, when a boy, that I heard him say that he was very sure *he* would be the last man to run in a fight, that he was afraid to trust himself in a battle, for he never could lay down his sword until the last enemy was massacred.

The old man was laid under the turf one autumn afternoon many years ago, but his prowess is not forgotten to this day. His son, Colonel Asher Peabody, who inherited his father's spirit, erected a stately monument over his remains. It was covered with drums and fifes and swords and waving banners and big-mouthed guns, intermixed with texts of Scripture, the virtues of the deceased, admonitions to the living, and so forth.

This monument was always as terrific to me as the General himself. In my boyish days I always contemplated it from a distance, not knowing but that it might blow up a piece of juvenile impertinence, like myself, on the spot.   1854

Lilly Davy and Ole Goliah

BAYNARD RUST HALL

It BEGUN to look like trouble twixt de chilluns of Israel and de Philistines. Dem heathen Philistines dey want to ketch King Saul and his folks for to make dem slaves, so dey comes down to pick a quorl and begins a-totin off all dey corn.

Dat stick in King Saul's gizzard, and he up and says, sezee, "I'm not gwine to be used up dat away by dem uncircumcized heathen, and let dem tote off our folkses' corn to chuck to dey hogs. So, Jonathan, we'll drum up and *in*list some soldiers and try dem a battle."

And den King Saul and his soldiers dey goes up, and de heathen Philistines dey comes down, and dey makes war.

De Philistines had dey army up dar on a mountain. King Saul had his'n camped out over across a branch, and it was chuck full of sling rock all along de bottom.

King Saul and his soldiers was pepper-hot for to fight when he first *in*list dem, but when dey gits up to de Philistines, dey cool off mighty quick. Kaze why? Kaze a great big, ugly old giant he comes a-rampin out in front of de Philistines like a half-starved lion seekin to devour. He come a-tearin out to git some of King Saul's soldiers to fight a duel.

Well, King Saul he says to Jonathan and de other big officers, "I ain't gwine to fight dat great big feller!" And atter dat, dey ups and says, "We ain't gwine fight him, nuther. He's all kivered with sheet-iron and his head's up so high we must stand a-hossback to reach him!"

Den King Saul he got down in de jaw, and he turn and ax if somebody wouldn't hunt up a soldier dat would fight de giant, and he'd give him his daughter for wife and make him de king's son-in-law. And den one ole man, dey call him Abner, he come up and say to Saul so:

"Please, your majesty, sir, I kin git a young feller to fight him." And he tells how David had jist rid up in his carriage and left it wid de man what tends de hosses—and how he heared David a-quorlin wid his brothers and a-wantin to fight de giant.

Den King Saul he feel mighty glad, and he made dem bring David up, and King Saul he begin talkin so, and David answer so:

"What's your name, little feller?"

"I was chrissen Davy."

"Who's your father?"

"Dey call him Jesse."

"What you foller for a livin?"

"I tend my father's sheep."

"What you come atter? Ain't you afeared of dat great ugly giant up dar, lilly David?"

"I come to see atter my other brothers, and bring dem some cheese and mutton and some clean shirts and trousers and have de other ones washed. And when I come, I hear ole Goliah a-hollerin out for somebody to fight a duel wid him, and den all de soldiers run away to dey tents. I'm not gwine to run away. If King Saul wants somebody for to fight de giant, I'll fight him for him."

"I mighty feared, lilly Davy, you too leetle."

"I kin lick him, King Saul. One day I gits asleep ahind a rock, and out comes a lion and a bar and begins a-totin off a lamb. And when I heared dem roarin and pawing bout, I run atter dem and ketch up, and I kill dem both widout no gun nor sword, and I bring back my poor lamb. I kin lick old Goliah, I tell you, please your majesty, sir."

Den King Saul he glad, and he pat him on de head and call him "lilly Davy," and wants him to put on his own armor made of brass and sheet-iron, but David say he trust to his sling. And den he goes out to fight de ole giant.

So ole Goliah, when he see David a-comin, he holler out so, and Davy he say back so:

"What you come for, lilly Jew?"

"You'll find out mighty quick. I come to fight you a duel."

"Huhh! huhh! haw! Think I gwine fight purty lilly baby? I want King Saul or Abner, or a big soldier man."

"Hold your jaw—I'll make you laugh tother side directly, ole grizzle-guzzle. I'm man enough for de biggest giant Philistine."

"Go way, poor lilly boy! Go home, baby, to your mother, and git a sugar plum. I don't want to kill no lilly boy."

"Come on! Don't be afeared! Don't run away! I'll ketch you and lick you!"

"You leetle rascal! I'll cuss you by all de gods—I'll cut out your sassy tongue—I'll break your blackguard jaw—I'll rip you up and give you to de dogs and crows—!"

"Don't cuss so, ole Golly! I sposed you wanted to fight so come on wid your ole iron-pot hat on!"

"You nasty leetle rascal, I'll come and kill you dead as chopped sassidge meat!"

De ole giant he so mad he jist jumpin. Lilly Davy stood his ground and let him come. Ole Goliah come a-bustin across de branch, a-wavin his sword and throwin up de water tree-top high. Lilly Davy reach down a git a sling rock bout de size of ole Goliah's fingernail. He slip it in de sling and commenced twirling it round his head.

"You brushin de flies, lilly baby?" hollers de big giant. "Well, brush dem good, kaze dey's de last you gwine have de chance to brush at!"

"It's a big fly I'm brushin," said David. "And here's de brush!"

Wid dat, lilly Davy he let fly his pebble, and seemed like people heared a bee in de air.

Ole Goliah was hauling back his sword to chop lilly Davy split from his hat to de fork of his britches when de bee-sound went *plunk* like somebody takin a tap on a melon to see is it ripe. De giant look like he aim to slap at a sting on de side of his head. But den he seem like he loses intrust kaze he gittin so sleepy and so tired. He let his big ole sword drap ahind him and he jist flop de other way, kee-*rash!* slop down on his face.

Den King Saul and all de folkses dey holler, "Hurraw for lilly Davy!" and de heathen Philistines dey run off up de mountain, kaze dey didn't want to be round lilly David when de bottoms was full of sling-rock. And dat's how de big corn-stealin ended.

1854

The Hoosier

DAN MARBLE

WHEN I passed over from Cleveland to Cincinnati the last time in a stage, we had a good team, spanking horses, a fine coach, and one of them *drivers* you read of. There was nine "insiders," and I don't believe there ever was a stage full of Christians ever started before, so chuck full of music.

There was a beautiful young lady going to one of the Cincinnati academies. Next to her sat a peddler; wedging him in was a dandy blackleg, with jewelry and chains round about his breast and neck enough to hang him. There was myself and an old gentleman, with large spectacles, gold-headed cane, and a jolly soldering-iron looking nose. By him was a circus rider, and a cross old woman came next, and whose look would have given any reasonable man the double-breasted blues before breakfast. Alongside of her was a real backwoods preacher, with the biggest and ugliest mouth ever got up since the flood. He was flanked by an Indiana Hoosier, "going down to Orleans to get an Army contract to supply the forces then in Mexico with beef."

We rolled along for some time; nobody seemed inclined to open. The old aunty sat bolt upright, looking crab apples at the Hoosier and preacher. The young lady dropped the green curtain of her bonnet over her pretty face, and leaned back in her seat to nod and dream over japonicas, pantalettes, and poetry. The old gentleman, proprietor of the nose, looked out at the corduroy and swashes. The gambler fell off into a doze, and the circus covey followed suit, leaving the preacher and me face to face and saying nothing to nobody. The Hoosier stuck his head out the window and criticised the cattle we now and then passed. I was wishing somebody would give the conversation a start, when Indiana made a break—

"This Ohio ain't no great stock country," says he to the old gentleman with the cane.

"No, sir," says the old gentleman. "There's very little grazing here, and the range is pretty much wore out."

Then there was nothing said again for some time. By and by the Hoosier opened again—

"It's the damnedest place for simon-trees and turkey buzzards I ever did see!"

The old gentleman with the cane didn't say nothing, and the preacher gave a long groan. The young lady smiled through her veil, and the old lady snapped her eyes and looked sideways at the speaker.

"Don't make much beef here, I reckon," says the Hoosier.

"No," says the old gentleman.

"Well, I don't see how in hell they all manage to get along in a country where there ain't no ranges and they don't make no beef. A man ain't considered worth a cuss in Indiana that hasn't got his brand on a hundred head."

"Yours is a great beef country, I believe," says the old gentleman.

"Well, sir, it ain't anything else. A man that's got sense enough to follow his own cow bell with us ain't in no danger of starving. I'm going down to Orleans to see if I can't git a contract out of Uncle Sam to feed the boys that's been licking them Mexicans so bad. I suppose you've seed them lies that's been in the papers about the Indiana boys at Buena Vista?"

"I've read some accounts of the battle," says the old gentleman, "that didn't give a very flattering account of the conduct of some of our troops."

With that, the Indiana man went into a full explanation of the affair, and getting warmed up as he went along, began to swear like he'd been through a dozen campaigns himself. The old preacher listened to him, with evident signs of displeasure, twisting and groaning till he couldn't stand it any longer.

"My friend," says he, "you must excuse me, but your conversation would be a great deal more interesting—and I'm sure would please the company much better—if you wouldn't swear so terribly. It's very wrong to swear, and I hope you will have respect for our feelings, if you ain't no respect for your Maker's."

The Hoosier shut his mouth right in the middle of what he was saying, while his face got fiery red.

"I know," says the preacher, "that a great many people swear without thinking, and some people don't believe the Bible."

And then he went on to preach a regular sermon against swearing and to quote Scriptures like he had the whole Bible by heart. He undertook to prove the Scriptures were true, and told us all about the miracles and prophecies and their fulfillment. The Hoosier listened, without ever opening his head.

"I've just heard of a gentleman," says the preacher, "that's been to the Holy Land, and went over the Bible country. It's astonishing what wonderful things he has seen. He was at Sodom and Gomorrow and seen the place where Lot's wife fell."

"Ah!" says the old gentleman with the cane.

"Yes," says the preacher, "he went to the very spot. What's the remarkable thing of all, he seen the pillar of salt she was turned into!"

"Is it possible!" says the old gentleman.

"Yes, sir, he seen the salt standing there to this day."

"What!" says the Hoosier. "Real, genuwine, good salt?"

"Yes, sir, a pillar of salt, just as it was when that wicked woman was punished for her disobedience!"

The Hoosier, with an expression of countenance that plainly told that his mind was powerfully convicted of an important fact, asked, "Right out in the open air?"

"Yes. Standing right in the open field where she fell."

"Well, sir," says the Hoosier, "all I've got to say is, *if she'd dropped in Indiana, the cattle would have licked her up before sundown!*"

1840

Proof

ALBERT PIKE

AN EMINENT member of the Arkansas bar, in an action for slander brought by a female client of his against one Thomas Williams, who uttered some injurious imputations against her virgin purity, thus broke forth, "Who is this Tom Williams, gentlemen of the jury, that comes riding out of the Cherokee Nation on the suburbs of posterity? He knocked at my client's door in the middle of the night, and she refused to get up and let him in. Wasn't that proof of her virginity?"

1840

Fox Grapes

William Tappan Thompson

JEST sich another scrape as I got in tother day has never
been heard of—or my name hain't Majer Jones, that's all.

It was last Sunday, and Miss Mary Stallins and Miss Carline and
Miss Kesiah and all of the Stallineses were at church, and when it was
out, I rid up alongside of Miss Mary and 'lowed I'd see her home. She's
the darlinest gal in Georgia, and I begun to feel mighty good.

But before we got out of sight of the church, thar was a whole gang of
fellers and a heap more young ladies come ridin up and reinin in and
prancin and cavertin about so nobody could tell who was riding with
which. They was all jabberin and talkin and laughin, as if they'd been
to a corn-shuckin instead of a meetin-house.

Of course Cousin Pete was thar on Uncle Josh's old white-eyed hoss.
Here lately he'd been cuttin a few too many fond capers near Miss Mary
to suit me, and the way he tumbled the big words about was astonishin.
I didn't say much, but rid close to Miss Mary, so Cousin Pete couldn't
shine much thar.

Well, we all got to Miss Stallinses', without any particler accident
happenin, though I expected any minute to see some of 'em heisted
right in the mud the way they kept whippin one another's hosses and
playin all manner of pranks with each other. When we got thar the whole
crowd stopped and somebody proposed a walk down to the branch to git
some grapes. All hands was agreed cept Old Miss Stallins, who said, it
bein Sabbath, the gals better stay home and read the Bible. But you know
it ain't any use to talk about religion to young gals when they ain't sick
nor sorry about nothin. So, away we went, but I tuck good care to git
alongside of Miss Mary and thar I stuck till we got down to the branch
whar the grapes were.

Wild grapes was jist gittin good, and I never seed a pretty young lady yet that didn't like somethin sour. Thar's lots of fox grapes all round the plantation but the best ones is down on the branch.

Cousin Pete and Ben Biers and all the fellers fell to gittin grapes for their ladies, but they all had their Sunday fixins on and was afraid to go into the brush much.

"Oh, my! What pretty grapes is on that tree!" says Miss Mary, lookin up halfway to the top of the great big gum-tree that stood right over the water, and her pretty bright eyes sparklin like dewdrops in the sunshine. "Oh," says she, "I wish I had some!"

Cousin Pete had been tryin to make himself very poplar with Miss Mary, but he didn't seem to care about them high grapes more'n some that was lower down. All the gals had got their eyes on them high grapes.

"Them grapes is like the young ladies," says Cousin Pete.

"Why is they like the gals?" asked Miss Kesiah.

"I reckon it's cause they's hard to git!" says Bill Wilson.

"No," says Tom Stallins, "it's cause they's more trouble to git than they's worth."

"Ain't you shamed, Brother Tom!" says Miss Carline.

"What do you think, Majer?" says Miss Mary, and she give me one of them witchin side-looks of hers that almost made me jump right out of my boots.

"Why," says I, "I think they's like the young ladies cause they's sour grapes to them as can't git 'em."

"Yes, Majer," says she, "but you know they can git 'em that has the the prowess to *win* 'em!" And then she give me a look that made me feel prouder than I ever did afore in my life. "And *you* can git 'em if you try, Majer. I know you can!"

When she said that last part, I seed Cousin Pete's lip sort of drap. My heart like to knock the buttons off my jacket, and I do believe I'd had them grapes if I'd had to dig the tree up by the roots. My hat went off quicker than a flash, and up the old sweet-gum I went like a cat squirrel.

"Don't fall, Majer," says Miss Mary. When she said that, I swar I like to let go, it made me feel so interestin. I wasn't no time gittin to the very tiptop branch and the first thing I done was to cut off the largest bunch and throw it right down to Miss Mary's feet.

"Thank you, Majer, thank you," says she.

"Throw me some, Majer," says Miss Carline.

"And me, too"—"And me, too"—"Thank you, Majer"—"Throw me some, Majer"—"Ain't Majer Jones kind?"—"It takes *him* to climb a tree," says all the gals.

"He's good as a coon," says Ben Biers.

"I can beat him anytime," says Tom Stallins.

"No y-o-u can't, Brother Tom, no sich thing!" says Miss Mary, poutin out her pretty lips at him.

By this time I had give 'em more grapes than they could all eat, and carry home, to boot. If I had jest come down then, I'd come out first rate. You know, that's the nice point—to know when to stop. Thar is sich a thing as bein a leetle *too* smart. That's jest whar I missed the figure.

I was standin on one vine right over the branch, with my hands hold of one over my head, and thinks I to myself, how it would 'stonish 'em all now to see me skin the cat! My spunk was up and, thinks I, I'll jest show 'em what I can do. So up I pulls my feet and twisted 'em round through my arms over backwards, and was lettin my body down tother side foremost, when they all hollered out:

"Oh, look at Majer Jones! Oh, see what he's a-doin!"

"Oh, I'm so afraid!" says Miss Mary.

That made me want to do my best, so I let myself down slow and easy, and I begun to feel with my feet for the vine below.

"Oh, my gracious!" says Miss Kesiah. "See how he *is* twisted his arms round!"

Somehow, I couldn't find the vine. My arms begun to hurt, but I didn't say nothin.

"A l-e-e-t-l-e further forward, Majer," says Tom Stallins.

"No—more to the right," says Ben Biers.

The gals were all lookin, and didn't know what to say. I kept tryin to touch both ways, but cuss a vine was thar. Then I tried to git back again, but I couldn't raise myself, somehow, and I begun to feel monstrous dizzy. The water below looked sort of yaller and green and had sparks of fire runnin all through it, and my eyes begun to feel so tight, I thought they would bust.

They was all hollerin somethin down below, but I couldn't hear nothin but a terrible roarin sound, and the first thing I knowed, somethin tuck me right under the chin, and before I had time to breathe, *kersplash* I went, right in the cold water, more'n six foot deep. I got my mouth chock full of muddy water, and how upon earth I got out without

drowndin I can't see, for I was almost dead before I drapt, and when I come down, I hit somethin that like to broke my jawbone, and skinned my nose a sight to behold.

When I waded out, the gals were all screamin for life, and Miss Mary was pale as her pocket-handkerchief.

"Oh, I'm so glad you ain't hurt no worse, Majer!" says she. "I thought you was killed."

But, Lord! She didn't begin to know how bad I was hurt. I sot down on a log a little, and the fellers all come round laughin like they was most tickled to death.

Tom Stallins says, "Warn't I right, Majer? Ain't they more trouble to git than they's worth after you's got 'em?"

I didn't say nothin to *him* because he's Miss Mary's brother. But Cousin Pete come up with his fine riggins on, a-laughin like a great long-legged fool, as he is. Says he, "Ain't you shamed to cut sich antics as that! I'd have more sense. Jest look at your nose—*ain't* you got yourself in a nice fix with your smartness!"

The gals was gittin ready to go home. Miss Mary was lookin monstrous serious when Cousin Pete says, "Don't you think he looks like a drownded rat, Miss Mary?"

"I think he looks as good, like he is, as you do any time!" says she, lookin as mad as she could.

Pete sort of looked a little sheepish, and turned round and tried to laugh. "I wouldn't take no sich duckin as that," says he, "not for all the sour grapes and sour gals in Georgia!"

Thinks I, "That's sort of personally insultin to Miss Mary," and I seed her face grow sort of red.

"You wouldn't, wouldn't you?" I says, and with that I jest tuck hold of the gentleman and pitched him neck and heels into the branch.

When he got out, he 'lowed he'd settle with me some other time when thar wasn't no ladies along to take my part. That's the way Cousin Pete settles all his accounts—some other time.

Tom Stallins tuck his sisters home, and the rest of the fellers went along, but Cousin Pete and I didn't show ourselves no more that day. I hain't seed him since, but thar's been all sorts of a muss between Mother and Aunt Mahaly about that Sunday business. I don't think I'll ever skin the cat agin.

1840

Declaration of Independence

ANONYMOUS

WEARIED of the sloppy service tendered them by an inn on the route of the Circuit Court, a parcel of North Carolina lawyers, in the 1840's, thus memorialized the proprietor:

When, in the course of human events, it becomes necessary for a half-hungry, half-fed, imposed-on set of men to dissolve the bonds of landlord and boarder, a decent respect for the opinions of mankind requires that they should declare the causes which have impelled them to separation.

We hold these truths to be self-evident: That all men are created with mouths and stomachs; and they are endowed by their creator with certain inalienable rights; among which is, that no man shall be compelled to starve out of mere compliance to a landlord; and that every man has a right to wet his whistle with the best going.

The history of the present landlord of the White Lion is a history of repeated insults, exactions, and injuries, all having in direct object the establishment of absolute tyranny over their stomachs and throats. To prove this, let facts be submitted to a candid world.

He has refused to keep any thing to drink but mean, bald-faced whiskey.

He has refused to set upon his table for dinner any thing but turnip soup, with a little tough beef and sourcrout, which are not wholesome and necessary for the public good.

He has refused to let his only servant, Blink-Eyed Joe, put more than six grains of coffee to one gallon of water.

He has turned loose a multitude of mosquitoes to assail us in the peaceful hours of the night and eat our substance.

He has kept up, in our beds and bedsteads, standing armies of merciless savages, with their scalping knives and tomahawks, whose rule of warfare is undistinguished destruction.

He has excited domestic insurrection among us by taking bitters before breakfast and making his wife and servant do the same before dinner, whereby there is often the deuce to pay.

He has waged cruel war against nature herself, by feeding our horses with broomstraw, and carrying them off to drink where swine refused to wallow.

He has protected One-Eyed Joe in his villainy, in the robbery of our jugs, by pretending to give him a mock trial, after sharing with him the spoil.

He has cut off the trade from foreign Port, and brought in his own bald-faced whiskey, when we had sent him to buy better liquor abroad; and with a perfidy scarcely paralleled in the most barbarous ages, he has been known to drink our foreign spirits, and fill up our bottles with his own dire potions.

He has imposed taxes upon us to an enormous amount, without our consent, and without any rule but his own arbitrary will and pleasure.

A landlord whose character is thus marked by every act which may define a tyrant and a master is unfit to keep a boarding house for Cherokee Indians.

Nor have we been wanting in our attention to Mrs. B. and Miss Sally. We have appealed to their native justice and magnanimity. We have conjured them to alter a state of things which would inevitably interrupt our connexion and correspondence. They, too, have been deaf to the voice of justice. We, therefore, are constrained to hold all three of these parties alike inimical to our well-being, and regardless of our comfort.

We, therefore, make this solemn declaration of our final separation from our former landlord, and cast our defiance in his teeth.

1840's

My First Call in the Swamp

HENRY CLAY LEWIS (Madison Tensas)

"COME quick, Mass Doctor! Ole Missis got a fit!"
From the appearance of the crop-eared mule the Negro messenger
bestrode, he had ridden in great haste. He obviously belonged to some
small planter living in the swamp section of my new practice.

"Ole Missis got a fit," he repeated. "I spect she's monstrous low. As I
come by de lot, I hear Mass Bill holler to Mass Bob and tell him, after he
got done knocking de horns off de young bull, to come in de house and
see his granmammy die."

Ordering a servant to catch my horse, I began to prepare for the ride,
my first professional call in the Louisiana swamp, where I had determined
to begin my first practice. I questioned the Negro as to the nature of the
disease, the age of the patient, and other circumstances of the case that
might enable me to carry suitable medicines along.

"You say your mistress has fits? Does she have them often?"

"Not as I knows, Mass Doctor. But I did hear her say dat when she use
to live in Georgy she was monstrous nervous-like in de full of de moon."

"How old is your mistress? Do you know, boy?"

"How ole? Why, Mass Doctor, she git a pension from de Revolution
War. Ole Missis ole, for a fact!"

"Anything happened lately that could have given your mistress the fit?"

"Nothing, Mass Doctor, dat I knows of, cept day before yesterday night
Ole Missis private jug give out and she told one of de boys to go in de
smokehouse and draw it full agin, but de fool chile stuck de light too near
de barrel and de whiskey caught fire and de smokehouse burn down."

"Your old mistress has been without her whiskey, then, for two days?"

"Yes, Mass Doctor."

I had learned enough about the case to give me a suspicion of the disease. Knowing how much depended on the success with which I treated my first cases, I took on a serious and reflective air. Labeling a bottle of brandy *Arkansas Fitifuge*, I slipped it in my saddlebag and we set off.

When we reached the log house, my horse reeking with sweat from the haste with which we had traversed the muddy roads, I introduced myself—as I had never seen one of the family before or they me—as Doctor Tensas, and asked to see the patient.

From the countenances of the assembled old women in the room I saw that they were disappointed in the appearance of the new doctor and that my unstriking and youthful visage was working against me. In fact, as I approached the bed, which was surrounded with old women, I heard one crone remark under her breath, "Blessed Jesus! Is *that* a doctor? Why, his face's as smooth as an egg shell and my son John pears a heap older than him, and *he's* only been pupped eighteen years. Gracious knows!"

Paying no attention to her, but determined to show her that I knew a thing or two, even though beard and whiskers I had none, I commenced examining the patient. I was surprised at the example of longevity in that insalubrious climate that the old woman presented. Her hair was whiter than the inside of a persimmon seed and the skin of her face resembled a piece of corrugated and smoky parchment, cleaving tightly to the bones, bringing out all their prominences and showing the course of the arteries and veins beneath. Her mouth was partly open and I saw not the vestige of a tooth.

She would lie very quietly in a dull, comatose condition for a few moments and then, giving a loud cry, attempt to rub her stomach against the rafters of the cabin, mumbling out something about "Whiskey spilt! . . . smokehouse ruint! . . . General Andy Jackson fit the Injuns!" It required the united strength of several of the women to keep her on the bed.

The examination verified my suspicion as to the nature of the disease, *sub-hysteria* and *quasi delirium tremens*, amalgamated through loss of her usual beverage—a not very flattering diagnosis. I had too much knowledge of human nature to give the least intimation to the females of my real opinion. I had been told by an old practicioner of medicine, "If you wish to ruin yourself in the estimation of your female patients, hint that the disease they are laboring under is connected with hysterics." If the mere intimation of hysteria produced such an effect, what would a positive diagnosis that it was not only hysterics but a touch of drunken mania? I had not the courage to calculate upon such a subject but hastily dismissed it.

Pronouncing that she had *fits*, sure enough, I commenced the treatment. Brandy and opium were the remedies indicated. I administered them freely at half-hour intervals, with marked benefit.

At last, she fell into a gentle slumber. As I heard her quiet breathing and saw the regular rise and fall of her bosom, I felt happier by the bedside of that old drunken woman in that obscure swamp than if the many voices of the city were shouting praise to my name.

It was now past midnight. Up to this time, I had not moved from the bedside and began to get wearied. I could with safety transfer her care to one of the old dames. I determined to do so and try and obtain some sleep.

The house consisted of a double-pen log cabin, of small dimensions, with a passage the full depth of the house running between the pens. As sleep was absolutely required for the patient and the old dames gathered around the fire discoursing of the marvels of their individual experiences with disease bid fair to wake the patient, I appealed that we should go to the other room. The old ladies agreed, as they were all dying to have a talk with the young doctor.

The men of the family had adjourned to the fodder house to pass the night, so the old women and I had the whole room to ourselves. In despite of my hints of being very tired and sleepy and "I wish I hadn't such a long ride to take tomorrow," they commenced their attacks in earnest by opening a tremendous battery of small talk and queries on me. They were only extracting from me the performance of one of the prescribed duties of the country physician, performed by him from time immemorial.

The doctor of a country settlement was then a very important character in the community. Traveling about from house to house, he became the repository of all the news, scandal, and secrets of the neighborhood, which he was expected to retail out as required for the moral edification of the females of his beat. Consequently, his coming was an event of great and exciting interest to womankind generally.

It is a trite observation "that when you have rendered yourself popular with the wife, you are insured of the patronage of the husband." Apply it to the whole sex of women and it still holds good. Married or single, they hold the men up. So, on a rawhide-bottomed chair I sat in that log cabin in front of a cheerful fire—for, though spring, the nights were sufficiently cool to render a fire pleasant—the apex of a pyramid of old women who stretched in two rows, three on each side, down to the jambs of the chimney.

There was Mrs. Pechum and Mrs. Stivers and Mrs. Linsey, on one side, and Mrs. Dims—who, unfortunately, as she informed me, had had her nose bit off by a wild hog—and Mrs. Ripson and Mrs. Tillot, on the other. Six old women with case-hardened tongues, and only one poor humble Swamp Doctor to talk to them all. Fearful odds!

What marvelous stories I told them about things I had seen and what wonderful recitals they gave me in turn. How first I addressed my attention to one side of the pyramid and then bestowed an equal intensity upon the other. How learnedly we discoursed upon herbs and comfrey tea and sweet gum salve. How readily we all acquiesced upon the broken-nosed lady's remark, "Bless Jesus, we must all die when our time comes." And what a general smile—which I am certain had it not been for the nearness of the invalid would have amounted to a laugh—went round the pyramid when Mrs. Pechum, who talked through her nose, snuffled out a witticism of her youngest son when he was a babe, in which the point of the joke lay in *bite* or *right* or *fight* or some word of some such sound, but which the imperfection of her pronunciation somewhat obscured. How intently we all listened to Mrs. Stivers' ghost story; what upholding of hands and lap-dropping of knitting and exclamations of fear, horror, and admiration, and "Blessed Master!" and "Lordy Gracious!" and "Well, did you ever!" and "You don't say so!" and "Dear heart do tell!" What a universal sigh was heaved when the beautiful maid that was haunted by the ghost was found drowned in a large churn of buttermilk that her mother had set away for market. And how we debated whether the hives were catching or not and were perfectly unanimous in the conclusion that Sheep Saffron was wonderful truck for doctoring.

Suddenly one of those small screech owls so common in the South and West gave forth his discordant cry from a tree near the house.

Instantly every voice was hushed. All the lower jaws of the old women dropped. Every eye was dilated till the whites looked like a circle of cream around a black bean. Every forefinger was raised to command attention and every head gave a commiserative shake, moderating gradually to a solemn settling.

After a considerable pause, Mrs. Ripson broke the silence. "Poor creature! She's gone, Doctor. The fitifuge can't cure her. She's knit her last pair of socks. Blessed Master! The *screech owl* is hollered and she's bound to die, certain!"

"Certain!" every female voice moaned and every head nodded to the melancholy decision.

I broke my usual rule, never to acknowledge ignorance upon any matter to ladies, and asked Mrs. Ripson to enlighten me.

Never shall I forget the mingled look of astonishment and contempt that the old lady cast upon me as she replied, "How does screech owls hollering make sick people die? Blessed Master! You a doctor and ask such a question! Why, I never set up with a sick body and heard a screech owl holler or a dog howl or a scratching agin the wall but what they died. If they didn't then, they did before long. Which proves the sign were true. Blessed Master! What weak creatures we are, after all! I recollect when I lived down in Buncombe County, North Carliny—Miss Dims, you knowed Miss Plyser what lived down to Zion Spring?"

Mrs. Dims, the noseless lady, snuffled out that she did, as well as one of her own children, as the families were familiar and saw a heap of one another.

"Well," said Mrs. Ripson, "Miss Plyser were taken awful sick after eating a bait of cold fried collards. I always told her cold fried collards wasn't good for her delicate constitution but the poor creature loved them and wouldn't take my advice, and it would have been a great deal better for her if she had, for she might have been a-setting here tonight, for her husband said if circumstances hadn't altered his determination he didn't know but what he would like to take a look at them Louisiana bottoms where all you have to do to clear the land is to cut down all the trees and wait for the next overflow to wash them off—but, perhaps, she wouldn't, neither, for, after all, he didn't come and, you know, she couldn't come without him, excepting she done like Eliza Johnson's middle daughter, Prinsanna, who left her husband in the State of Georgy and come to Louisiana and got married to another man—the pizen varmint to do such as that, and her own lawful husband, for I know that he borrered a dollar of my Sister Jane's husband to pay for the license and the eatables for the crowd—but, Blessed Master, where *am* I talking to!

"Well, as I said, Miss Plyser made herself monstrous sick eating cold fried collards. When I got where she was, they had sent for the doctor. Shortly after I come, he come. The first thing he asked for after he got in the house was for a handful of red pepper pods. It were a fine season for pepper and other garden truck, and when he got them he took a handful of lobelia and mixt the pepper pods with it and poured hot boiling water over it and made a strong decoction.

"Just as it was got ready, but before it was give, I heared a screech owl holler on the gable end of the cabin. I said then, as I say now, that it was a sign and a forerunner that she were going to die. But the doctor, in spite of my persuadements, give her a tin cup of pepper and lobelia. I knowed it was no use. The screech owl had hollered. She were called for. And just to think of a nice young woman like her, with the prettiest pair of twins in the world, and as much alike as two peas, only one had black hair and light eyes and the other had black eyes and light hair, being carried to the grave by cold fried collards! But the Lord is in the heavens and he knows.

"Well, the first dose he give her didn't affect much. Then he commenced steaming her, and then the sweat begun to come out, and she went right down and begun to sink. Blessed Master, it were too late. The screech owl had hollered. The Lord be merciful to her soul! But I said from the first she would die.

"Doctor, we'd better see how Miss Jimsey is. The screech owl is hollered and she must go, though all the doctors of a king was here. Poor creature, she has lived a long time, and I expect her Lord and Master wants her."

To the somewhat disappointment of the dames, I thought, we found the invalid still buried in a profound slumber. Her regular, placid breathing indicated that the proper functions of the system were being restored. I softly felt her pulse and it, too, showed improvement.

Leaving the room, we returned to the other cabin. I informed the family that she was much better. If she did not have a return of the spasms by morning, and rested undisturbed in the meantime, she would get well. But I saw that the superstition had too deep a hold on their minds for my opinion to receive their sanction.

An incredulous shake of the head was my only reply, except for the owl enthusiast. "Doctor, you're mistaken, certain!" she said. "The screech owl is hollered. She is bound to die. It's a sure sign and can't fail."

It would require a ponderous tome to contain all that passed in conversation during our vigil that night. Morning broke, and I went softly in to see if my patient still slept. The noise I made in crossing the rough floor aroused her. As I reached the bedside, she half-raised herself up. To my great astonishment, she accosted me in her perfect senses.

"I suppose, young man, you're a doctor, ain't you?"

I assured her that her surmise was correct and pressed her to cease talking and compose herself. She would not do it, however, and demanded to see the medicine I was giving her.

I produced the Arkansas Fitifuge. As it was near the time that she should take a dose, I poured one out and gave it to her.

Receiving it at first with evident disgust, with great reluctance she forced herself to drink a small quantity. I saw pleasure and surprise light up her countenance. She drank a little—looked at me—took another sip—and then, as if to test it by the other senses, applied it to her nose. All the results were satisfactory, and she drank it to the dregs without a murmur.

"It's monstrous pleasant truck," she said. "What did you say was the name of it?"

"Arkansas Fitifuge, madam, one of the best medicaments for spasmodic diseases that I have ever used. You were in fits last night when I arrived but, you see, the medicine is effecting a cure. You are now out of danger, although extreme quietude is highly necessary."

"Doctor," she said, "Will you give me a leetle more? I declare, it's pleasant. Doctor, I'm mighty nervous generally. Don't you think I'd better take it pretty often through the day? If they'd sent for you sooner, I wouldn't been half as bad off. But thank the Lord you have proved capable, sent to me in the hour of need, and I won't complain but trust in a merciful Saviour."

The lady of screech owl memory now crowded forward and asked, "How do you feel now, Sister Jimsey? Do you think you're looking up this morning?"

"Oh, Sister Ripson, thank the Lord, I do feel a power better this morning. I think in the course of a day or two I will be able to get about again."

"Well, Merciful Master, wonders will never stop! Last night I thought sure you couldn't stand it till morning. Specially after I heared the screech owl holler! 'Tis a miracle, sure, or else this is the wonderfulest doctor in creation!"

"Did the screech owl holler more than once, Sister Ripson?"

"No, he only screeched once. If he'd hollered the second time, I'd defied all the doctors in the created world to cure you. The thing would have been unpossible!"

Now, the aforesaid screech owl had actually screeched twice, but I was unwilling to disturb the old lady. So I directed the fitifuge to be given at regular intervals through the day. Then, amidst the blessings of the patient, the congratulations of the family for the wonderful cure and their assurances of future patronage, I took my departure for home.

As I left, I heard the same old lady who had underrated me at my entrance ejaculate, "Well, bless the Lord I didn't die last year of the yaller janders, or I'd never lived to see with my own eyes a doctor who could cure a body after the screech owl hollered!"   1843

Unrehearsed Stage Effect

SOL SMITH

PIZARRO was one of our most popular stock plays. My brother Lem's *Rolla* in this play was his best tragic character. When dressed for the part, he looked every inch an Indian chief.

At Columbus, Georgia, we produced this tragedy with real Indians for the Peruvian army. The effect was very striking, but there were some unrehearsed effects not set down in the bills.

I had bargained with a chief for twenty-four Creek Indians (to furnish their own bows, arrows, and tomahawks) at 50 cents each and a glass of whiskey. Unfortunately, the whiskey was paid and drank in advance, causing a great degree of exhilaration among our new supers. They were ranged at the back of the theater building in an open lot during the first act. On the commencement of the second, they were marshaled into the back door and posted upon the stage behind the scenes.

The entrance of the character Rolla was the cue for a shout by the company, carpenters and scene-shifters. The Indians, supposing their time had come, raised such a yell as I am sure had never before been heard inside a theater. This outburst being quelled, the scene between Alonzo, Cora, and the Peruvian chief proceeded to its termination uninterrupted. But when the scene changed to the Temple of the Sun, disclosing the troops of Rolla (the Creeks) drawn up on each side of the stage in battle array, the plaudits of the audience were met by whoops and yells that might be, and no doubt were, heard a mile off.

Order being partially restored, Rolla addressed his army and was greeted with another series of yells and shouts, even louder than those that had preceded.

Now came my turn to take part in the unique performance. As High Priest of the Sun and followed by half a dozen virgins and as many priests, with measured step timed to slow music, I emerged from behind the scenes and with solemn march perambulated the stage. In dumb show, I called down a blessing on the swords of King Ataliba and General Rolla and, in the usual impressive style, looking up into the front gallery, commenced the Invocation to the Sun.

Before the time for the joining in of the chorus, I found I was not entirely alone in my singing. A humming sound, at first low and mournful and rising gradually to *forte*, greeted my ear. And when our chorus *did* join in the strain, it was quite overpowered by the rising storm issuing from the stentorian lungs of the savages. In short, *the Indians were preparing for battle* by executing the Creek War Song and Dance!

To attempt stopping them we found would be a vain task. So, after a moment or two of hesitation, the virgins made a precipitate retreat to their dressing rooms where they carefully locked themselves in. The King, Rolla, and the High Priest stood their ground and were compelled to submit to the new order of things. The Indians kept up their song and war dance for full half an hour, performing the most extraordinary feats ever exhibited on a stage, in their excitement scalping King Ataliba by snatching off his wig, demolishing the altar, and burning up the Sun.

As for Lem and I, under the circumstances we thought it better to join in with them. We danced until the perspiration fairly rolled from our bodies in large streams, the savages all the time flourishing their tomahawks and knives around our heads and performing other little playful antics.

At last, to put an end to a scene that was becoming more and more tiresome, someone gave an order to drop the curtain. However, this stroke of policy did not stop the ceremonies. They proceeded without intermission until the savages had finished their song and dance. When each received his promised half-dollar, they consented to leave the house. Our play went on without them.

Next night the same troupe came to the theater and wanted to assist in the performance of Macbeth but I most positively declined their aid.

1845

Politics Makes Bedfellows

Henry S. Foote

When Judge Harris was riding the circuit in Simpson County, he put up at an inn in Westville on a bright Sunday evening. He asked to be shown to his room, and proceeded to it. He found a gentleman and a lady in it, and returning, asked to be shown to another. Some little delay occurred before this was done, and when he reached the second room, he found that also occupied.

Judge Harris came back to the bar and indignantly addressed the host, "Pray, sir, are you keeping a bawdy house? I found the first room already in possession of a man and a woman—the latter of whom I understand to be your wife—lying upon the bed. On opening the door of the second room, I found the same woman lying on the bed there, but attended by another man. I wish to know what all this means?"

"My dear Judge," said the tavern-keeper, "it's not possible for me to say a single word about the matter at present. You see, I am a candidate for constable here, and very hard run for votes. The election will come off tomorrow, after which I promise you there shall be no similar cause for complaint."

1878

Taking the Census

JOHNSON J. HOOPER

THE Census Law for 1840 called for the collection of statistical information concerning the resources and industry of the country, over and above the counting of noses. The popular impression, that a tremendous tax would soon follow the minute investigation of the private affairs of the people, caused the census taker to be viewed in no better light than that of a tax-gatherer. In some portions of the country, the excitement against the officers—who were known as the *"chicken men"*—made it almost dangerous for them to proceed with the business of taking the census. Bitter were the taunts, threats, and abuse which they received on all hands, but most particularly from the old women of the country. The dear old souls could not bear to be catechised about the produce of their looms, poultry yards, and dairies.

We speak from experience, and feelingly, on this subject: For it so happened that the U.S. Marshal of the Southern District of Alabama, arming us with the proper quantity of blanks, sent us to count the noses of all the men, women, and children, and chickens resident upon those nine hundred square miles of rough country which constitute the County of Tallapoosa.

Children shouted, "Yonder goes the chicken man!" Men said, "Yes, damn him, he'll be after the taxes soon!" The old women threatened to set the dogs on us, while the young women observed "they didn't know what a man wanted to be so perticlar about gals' ages for, without he was going a-courting."

We rode up one day to the residence of a widow rather past the prime of life—just that period at which nature supplies most abundantly the oil which lubricates the hinges of the female tongue—and, hitching to the fence, walked to the house.

"Good morning, madam," said we, in our usual bland and somewhat insinuating manner.

"Morning," said the widow gruffly.

Drawing our blanks from their case, we proceeded, "I am the man, madam, that takes the census, and——"

"The mischief you are!" said the old termagant. "Yes, I've hearn of you. Parson Williams told me you was coming, and I told him jist what I tell you, that I'd set the dogs on ye!

"Here, Bull! Here, Pomp!"

Two wolfish curs responded, by coming to the door, smelling at our feet with a slight growl, and then laid down on the steps.

"Now," continued the old she-savage, "them's the severest dogs in this country. Last week Bill Stonecker's two-year-old steer jumped my yard fence. Bull and Pomp tuck him by the throat, and they killed him afore my boys could break 'em loose, to save the world!"

"Yes, ma'am," said we, meekly. "Bull and Pomp seem to be mighty fine dogs."

"You may well say that. What I tell 'em to do, they do. If I was to sic 'em on your old hoss yonder, they'd eat him up afore you could say Jack Roberson. And it's jist what I shall do, if ye try to pry into my concerns! They're none of your business, nor Van Buren's neither, I reckon! Oh, old Van Buren! I wish I had you here, you old rascal! I'd show you what! I'd—I'd make Bull and Pomp show you how to be sending men to take down what little stuff people's got, jist to tax it, when it's taxed enough already!"

All this time we were perspiring through fear of the fierce guardians of the widow's portal. At length, when she paused, we remarked that as she was determined not to answer questions about the produce of the farm, we would just set down the age, sex, and complexion of each member of her family.

"No sich thing—you'll do no sich thing!" said she. "I've got five in family, and that's all you'll git from me. Old Van Buren must have a heap to do, the dratted old villain, to send you to take down how old my children is! I've got five in family, and they are all between five and a hundred year old. They are all a plaguey sight whiter than you, and whether they are *he* or *she* is none of your concerns."

We told her we would report her to the U.S. Marshal and she would be fined, but it only augmented her wrath.

"Yes! Send your Marshal, or your Mr. Van Buren here, if you're bad off

to! Let 'em come! Let Mr. Van Buren come! Oh, I wish he *would* come!"
—and her nostrils dilated and her eyes gleamed. "I'd cut his head off!"

"That might kill him," we ventured, by way of a joke.

"Kill him! Oh, if I had him by the *ears*, I reckon *I* would kill him! A
pretty feller, to be eating his vittles out of gold spoons that poor people's
taxed for, and raising an army to git him made king of Ameriky! The
outdacious, nasty, stinking old scamp!"

She paused a moment, and then resumed, "And now, mister, jist put
down what I tell you on that paper. Don't be sending no lies to Washington City. Jist put down 'Judy Tompkins, *ageable* woman, and four children?"

And, perforce, that is how the entry had to be made in the census of
1840.

Our next encounter was with an old lady who lived nearby and *seemed*
more than anxious to help us with our undertaking.

Striding into the house and taking out our papers, we said, "Taking
the census, Ma'am."

"Ah! Well! Bless your soul, honey, take a seat. Now do! Are you the
gentleman that Mr. Van Buren has sent out? I wonder! Well, good Lord
look down, how *was* Mr. Van Buren and family when you seed him?"

We explained that we had never seen the President, didn't know him
from a side of sole leather, and that we had been written to, to take the
census.

"Well, now, *that* agin! Lord love your soul! Well, I suppose thar's
mighty little here to take down. Times is hard, God's will be done, but
looks like people can't git their jist rights in this country. The law is all
for the rich and none for the poor——"

Here we interposed that we wished to take down the number of the
old lady's family, and the produce raised by her last year, and be off.
After a good deal of trouble, we got through with the descriptions of the
members of her family and the statistical table as far as the article *cloth*.

"How many yards of cotton cloth did you weave in 1840, ma'am?"

"Well, now! The Lord have mercy! Less see! You know Sally Higgins
that used to live in the Smith Settlement? Poor thing, her daddy druv her
off on the count of her having a little-un, poor creature. Poor gal, she
couldn't help it, I dare say. Well, Sally she come to stay along with me
when the old man druv her away, and she was a powerful good hand to
weave, and I *did* think she'd help me a power. Well, after she'd been here
awhile, her baby it tuck sick, and old Miss Stringer she undertuck to help

it—she's a powerful good hand, Old Miss Stringer, on yerbs, and sich like. Well, the Lord look down from above! She made a sort of tea, as I was a-saying, and she give it to Sally's baby, but it got worse—the poor creature —and she give it tea, and she *give* it tea, and looked like the more she give it tea, the more——"

I said, "My dear madam, I am in a hurry. Please tell me how many yards of cotton cloth you wove in 1840? I want to get through with you and go on."

"Well, well, the Lord-a-mercy! Who'd a-thought you'd a-been so snappish! Well, as *I* was a-saying—the baby got worse, and old Miss Stringer, she kept a-giving it the yerb tea twell at last the child it looked like it *would* die, anyhow. And bout the time the child was at its worst, old Daddy Sykes he come along, and he said if we'd git some nightshed berries and stew 'em with a little cream and some hog's lard—now, old Daddy Sykes is a mighty fine old man, and when my boys had that case in court, he give 'em a heap of mighty good counsel in that case. 'Boys,' says he, 'I'll tell you what you do. You go and——' "

"In God's name," said we, "tell about your cloth, and let the sick child and Miss Stringer, Daddy Sykes, the boys, and the lawsuit go to the——"

"Gracious bless your dear soul! Don't git aggravated. I was jist a-telling you how it come I didn't weave no cloth last year."

"Oh, well. You didn't weave *any* cloth last year. We'll go on to the next article."

"Yes. You see, the child it begun to swell and turn *yaller*, and it kept a-walling its eyes and a-moaning, and I knowed——"

"Never mind about the child. Just tell me the value of the poultry you raised last year."

"Oh, well—yes—the chickens, you mean. Why, the Lord love your poor soul, I reckon you never in your born days seen a poor creature have the luck I did. Looks like we shall never have good luck agin, for ever since the boys got into that lawsuit in court——"

"Never mind the lawsuit! Let's hear about the chickens, if you please."

"God bless you, honey, the *owls* destroyed in and about the best half that I did raise. Every blessed night the Lord sent, they'd come and set on the comb of the house and *hoo-hoo-hoo*, and one night, perticlar, I remember, I had jist got up to git the nightshed salve to rub Sally Higginses' ailing little gal with——"

"Well, well, what was the value of what you *did* raise?"

"The Lord above look down! They got so bad—the owls did—that they tuck the old hens as well as young chickens. The night I was a-telling you bout, I hearn something *squall! squall!* And I says, 'I bet that's old Speck that nasty owl's got.' For I seen her go to roost with her chickens, up in the plum tree, agin the smokehouse. So I went to whar old Miss Stringer was a-sleeping, and says I, 'Miss Stringer! *Oh* Miss Stringer! Sure's you're born, that stinking owl's got old Speck out of the plum tree.' Well, old Miss Stringer she turned over 'pon her side like, and says she, 'What did you say, Miss Stokes?' And says I——"

We began to get very tired, and signified the same to the old lady, and begged she should answer directly and without any circumlocution.

"The Lord love your dear heart, honey, I'm a-telling you as fast as I can. The owls they got worse *and* worse, after they'd swept old Speck and all her gang, and they went to work on t'others.

"Well, Bryant—that's one of my boys—he 'lowed he'd shoot the pestersome critters—and so one night after that, we hearn one holler, and Bryant he tuck the old musket and went out and, sure enough, there was *owley*—as *he* thought—a-setting on the comb of the house. So he blazed away and down come—what on *earth did* come down, do you reckon, when Bryant fired?"

"The owl, I suppose."

"No sich a thing, no sich! The owl *warn't thar!* 'Twas my old house cat come a-tumbling down, a-spitting, sputtering, and a-scratching, and the fur a-flying every time she jumped, like you'd a-busted a feather bed open! Bryant he said the way he come to shoot the cat instead of the owl, he seed something white——"

"For heaven's sake, Mrs. Stokes, give me the value of your poultry, or say you will not. Do one thing or the other."

"Oh, well, dear love your soul, I reckon I had last year night about the same as I've got this."

"Then tell me how many dollars worth you have now, and the thing's settled."

"I'll let you see for yourself," said Mrs. Stokes, and taking an ear of corn out of a crack between the logs of the cabin and shelling off a handful, she commenced scattering the grain on the floor, all the while screaming:

"Chick, chick, chick—chick-ee—chick-ee—chick-ee—ee!"

Here they came, roosters and hens, pullets and little chicks—crowing, cackling, chirping; flying and fluttering over beds, chairs, and tables; alighting on the old woman's head and shoulders, fluttering against her sides, pecking at her hands, and creating a din and confusion altogether indescribable.

The old lady seemed delighted, thus to exhibit her feathered stock, and would occasionally exclaim, "A nice passel, ain't they? A *nice* passel!" But she never would say what they were worth. No persuasion could bring her to the point, and our papers at Washington contain no estimate of the value of Mrs. Stokes' poultry, though, as she said herself, she had a mighty nice passel!

1841

Never Bet the Devil Your Head

EDGAR ALLAN POE

IT IS not my design to vituperate my friend, Toby Dammit. He was a sad dog, it is true, but he himself was not to blame for his vices. They grew out of a personal defect in his mother. She did her best in the way of flogging him while an infant—for duties, to her well-regulated mind, were always pleasures, and babies, like tough steaks, are invariably the better for beating.

But—poor woman! She had the misfortune to be left-handed, and a child flogged left-handedly had better be left unflogged. The world revolves from right to left. It will not do to whip a baby from left to right. If each blow in the proper direction drives an evil propensity out, it follows that every thump in an opposite direction knocks its quota of wickedness in.

Thus it was that no matter how often and severely he was cuffed, Toby Dammit grew worse and worse. At six months of age, I caught him gnawing a pack of cards. At seven months he was in the consistent habit of catching and kissing the female babies. So he went on, increasing in iniquity until I went down on my knees, and, uplifting my voice, made prophecy of his ruin.

Perhaps the worst of all his vices was a propensity for cursing and swearing, and for backing his profane assertions with bets. He could scarcely utter a sentence without interlarding it with propositions to gamble. However, I will do my friend the justice to say that with him the thing was a mere formula—nothing more—imaginative phrases wherewith to round off a sentence. No one ever thought of taking him up.

For poverty was another vice which the peculiar deficiency of Dammit's mother had entailed upon her son. He was detestably poor. This was the reason, no doubt, that his expressions about *betting* seldom took a pecuniary turn. I will not be bound to say that I ever heard him make use of such a figure of speech as "I'll bet you a dollar." It was usually "I'll bet you what you please," or "I'll bet you a trifle," or else, more significantly still, "I'll bet the Devil my head."

This latter form seemed to please him best—perhaps because it involved the least risk. His head was small, and thus his loss would have been small, too. In the end, he abandoned all other forms of wager, and gave himself up to, "I'll bet the Devil my head," with a pertinacity and exclusiveness of devotion that displeased not less than it surprised me. I am always displeased by circumstances for which I cannot account. Mysteries force a man to think, and so injure his health.

One fine day, having strolled out together, arm in arm, our route led us in the direction of a river. There was a bridge, and we resolved to cross it. It was roofed over by way of protection from the weather; and the archway, having but few windows, was uncomfortably dark. At length, having passed nearly across the bridge, we approached the end of the footway, when our progress was impeded by a turnstile of some height. Through this I made my way quietly, pushing it around as usual.

But this would not serve the turn of Toby Dammit. He insisted upon leaping the stile, and said he would cut a pigeon-wing over it in the air. Now this, conscientiously speaking, I did not think he could do. I therefore told him in so many words that he was a braggadocio, and could not do what he said.

He straightway offered to bet the Devil his head that he could.

I was about to reply, when I heard close at my elbow an ejaculation, "Ahem!" I started and looked about me in surprise. My glance fell into a nook of the framework of the bridge, and upon the figure of a little lame old gentleman of venerable aspect. Nothing could be more reverend than his whole appearance, for he not only had on a full suit of black, but his shirt was perfectly clean, and the collar turned very neatly down over a white cravat, while his hair was parted in front like a girl's. His hands were clasped pensively together over his stomach and his two eyes were carefully and piously rolled up into the top of his head.

I perceived that he wore a black silk apron over his small clothes. This was a thing I thought very odd. Before I had time to make any remark, however, he interrupted me with a second "Ahem!"

To this observation I was not immediately prepared to reply. The fact is, remarks of this laconic nature are nearly unanswerable. I am not ashamed to say, therefore, that I turned to Mr. Dammit for assistance.

"Dammit," I said, "what are you about? Don't you hear? The gentleman says 'Ahem!' "

If I had shot Mr. D. through and through with a bomb, or knocked him in the head with a copy of the *Poets and Poetry of America*, he could scarcely have been more discomfited than by those simple words. "You don't say so?" he gasped at length. "Are you quite sure he said *that*? Well, at all events, I am in for it now, and many as well put a bold face on the matter. Here goes then—*ahem!*"

At this, the little old gentleman seemed pleased, God only knows why. He left his station at the nook of the bridge, limped forward with a gracious air, took Dammit by the hand, and shook it cordially, looking all the while straight up in his face with an air of the most unadulterated benignity.

"I am quite sure you will win, Dammit," said he, "but we are obliged to have a trial, you know, for the sake of mere form."

With a deep sigh, my friend took off his coat. The old gentleman now took him by the arm and led him more into the shade of the covered bridge—a few paces back from the turnstile.

"My good fellow," said the little old gentleman in black, "I make it a point of conscience to allow you this much run. Wait here till I take my place by the stile, so that I may see whether you go over it handsomely, and don't omit any flourishes of the pigeon wing."

Here he took his position by the stile, looked up—and I thought—smiled very slightly, then tightened the strings of his apron, saying: "One—two—three—and away!"

Punctually at the word "away" my friend set off in a strong gallop. I saw him run nimbly and spring grandly from the floor of the bridge, cutting the most awful flourishes with his legs as he went up. I saw him high in the air, pigeon-winging it to admiration just over the top of the stile; and, of course, I thought it an unusually singular thing that he did not *continue* to go over.

But the whole leap was the affair of a moment, and before I had a chance to make any profound reflections, down came Mr. Dammit on the flat of his back, *on the same side of the stile from which he had started.* At the same instant I saw the old gentleman limping off at top speed, having caught and wrapped up in his apron something that fell heavily into it from the darkness of the arch just over the turnstile.

At all this I was much astonished, but I had no leisure to think, for Mr. Dammit lay particularly still, and I concluded that his feelings had been hurt, and that he stood in need of my assistance. I hurried up to him and found that he had received what might be termed a serious injury. The truth is, he had been deprived of his head, which, after a close search, I could not find anywhere. A thought struck me, and I threw open an adjacent window of the covered bridge, when the sad truth flashed upon me at once. About five feet just above the top of the turnstile and crossing the arch of the footpath so as to constitute a brace, there extended a great iron bar. With the edge of this brace it appeared evident that the neck of my unfortunate friend had come precisely in contact.

He did not long survive his terrible loss. I bedewed his grave with my tears, worked a bar sinister on his family escutcheon, and for the general expenses of his funeral sent in my very moderate bill. When payment was refused it, I had Mr. Dammit dug up at once, and sold him for dog's meat.

1841

Turned Tables

ANONYMOUS

ALTHOUGH in his will he was to free his own slaves, the fiery and eccentric John Randolph, of Roanoke, was well-known to detest free negroes. Apparently the freeman—one of the blackest hue— who served him when he took his dinners privately in his parlor while staying at one of New York's most elegant hotels, was fully aware of Randolph's attitude.

At any rate, when the man had served the soup, the Virginia statesman snarled: "Leave the room."

The negro bowed, but took his station behind Randolph's chair.

"Fellow!" thundered Randolph. "Leave the room, I say!"

"Excuse me, sah," said the negro. He drew himself up stiffly and met with a cold eye that of the master of repartee and invective under whose aspish tongue in Congress even the redoubtable Clay and Webster had cowered. "Excuse me, sah, but I must stay. *De management holds me sponsible fo de silver.*"

1841

Mike Hooter's Tall Bar Story

WILLIAM HALL

IT'S no use talking bout your Polar Bar and Grizzly Bar, and all that sort of varment. They ain't nowhere, for the big black customer down in our neck of the woods, in the Yazoo Bottoms, beats 'em all holler. They come as nigh being human critters as anything I ever see that don't talk. Why, if you was to hear anybody else tell about the bar fights I've had, you wouldn't believe 'em. And if I wasn't a preacher and couldn't never lie none, I'd keep my fly-trap shut till the day of judgment.

I've hearn folks say as how bars can't think like other human critters. What a lie! You tell *me* one of 'em don't know when you've got a gun and when you ain't? Just wait a minute, and my private opinion is, when you've hearn me through, you'll talk t'other side of your mouth.

You see, one day long time ago, I made a pointment with Ike Hamberlin to go out in the bottoms next Sunday to seek whom we couldn't kill a bar. You know, bacon was scarce and so was money, and them fellers down in Mechanicsburg wouldn't sell on "tick," so we had to depend on the varments for a living.

Well, Ike Hamberlin thought he'd be kind of smart and beat Old Preach (that's what them Cole boys used to call me), so as soon as day-crack, he hollered up his puppies and *put!* I spied what he was about, for I hearn him laughing to one of his niggers the night before—so I told my gal Sal to fill my private tickler full of the old raw still-juice, and then fixed up and tramped on after him, but didn't take none of my dogs.

Ike hadn't got far into the cane-thicks before his dogs they begin to whine and turn up the hair on their backs. And, by-and-by, they all tucked tail and sort of sidled back to where he was standing.

"Sick him!" says Ike, but the critters wouldn't hunt a lick. I soon discovered what was the matter, for I calculated them curs of hisn wasn't worth shucks in a bar fight—so I knowed there was bar about.

Well, Ike he coaxed the dogs, and the more he coaxed, the more they wouldn't go, and when he found coaxing wouldn't do, then he scolded and called them some of the hardest names ever you hearn (such as son-of-a-bitch, and such like), but the critters wouldn't budge a peg. When he found they wouldn't hunt nohow he could fix it, he begin a-cussing. He didn't know I was there. If he had a-suspicioned it, he'd no more swore that he'd a-dared to kiss my Sal on a washing day. You see, both of us belonged to the same church, and Ike was class leader.

The dogs they sidled back, and Ike he cussed, and I lay down and rolled and laughed sort of easy to myself, till I was so full I thought I'd bust my boiler. I never see anything so funny in all my life! There I was laying down behind a log, fit to split, and there was the dogs with their tails the wrong end down, and there was Ike a-raring and a-pitching— a-ripping and a-tearing—and a-cussing worse than a steamboat captain. I tell you, it fairly made my hair stand on end. I never see a customer so riled before in all my born days——

—Yes I did, too, once—only once. It was that feller Arch Cooley that used to oversee for old Ben Roach. Didn't you know that hoss-fly? He's a few! Well, *he* is. Jewhilliken! How he could whip a nigger! And swear! Whew! I tell *you*, all the sailors and French parrots in Orleans ain't a patching on him. I hearn him let hisself out one day, and I pledge my word he cussed enough to send twenty preachers right kerlumpus into hell! And what was worse, it was all bout nothing, for he warn't mad a wrinkle. But all that ain't neither here nor there.

As I was saying before, the dogs they smelt bar sign and wouldn't budge a peg, and after Ike had almost cussed the bark offn a dogwood sapling he was standing by, he lent his old flintlock rifle up against it, and then he peeled off his old blanket coat and laid her down, too.

I discovered mischief was a-coming, for I never *see* a critter show wrathy like Ike did. Toreckly, I see him walk down to the creek bottom, bout fifty yards from where his gun was, and then he began picking up rocks and slinging 'em at the dogs! Didn't he link it into 'em! It minded me of David whaling Goliah, it did! If you'd a-seen him and hearn them puppies holler, you'd a-thought he'd a-knocked the hind-sights offn every bitches' son of 'em!

But that ain't the fun yet. While Ike was a-lamming the dogs, I hearn a crackling in the cane, and I looked up, and there was one of the eternalest, wholloping bars coming through the cane and kerslosh over the creek, and he stopped right plumb smack up against where Ike's gun was.

Toreckly he took hold of Ike's old shooter, and I thought I see him tinkering bout the lock and kind of whistling and blowing over it. I was astonished, I tell you, but I kept low and dark, and in about a minute Ike got done licking the dogs and went to get his gun.

Jeeminy, criminy! If you'd only been where I was! I *do* think Ike was the maddest man that ever stuck an ax into a tree, for his hair stood right straight up and his eyes glared like two dogwood blossoms.

But the bar didn't seem to care shucks for him. He just sot the old rifle back against the sapling and walked off on his hind legs just like any human.

Then I says to myself, "Mister Bar," says I, "the place where you're a-standing ain't exactly healthy. If you don't wabble off from there pretty soon, Missis Bar will be a widder!"

With that, Ike grabbed up the old rifle and took most particular aim at the bar—and, by hokey, the gun only snapped!

"Now," says I, "Mister Bar, go it, or he'll make bacon of you!"

But the varment didn't wink. He just stood still as a post, with the thumb of his right paw on the end of his smeller, and wiggling his t'other fingers.

All this time, Ike he stood there like a fool, a-snapping and a-snapping the old rifle at the bar, and the bar he looking kind of queer-like, out of the corner of his eye, and sort of laughing at him.

Toreckly I see Ike take down the old shooter, and kind of examine the lock, and when he done that, he laid her on his shoulder and shook his fist at the bar, and walked towards home, and the bar he shook his fist at Ike and went into the cane-brake, and then I run off.

Why, you see, the long and short of it is, that the bars in our neck of the woods, down in the Yazoo Bottoms, has something of the human in 'em, and this feller knowed as much about a gun as I do' bout preaching. So when Ike was licking the dogs, this bar he just blowed all the powder out of the pan of the flintlock, and to make it safe, he took the flint, too— and that's why he stood there so cool and let Ike snap away at him.

1843

An Unfortunate Race

SOL SMITH

BETWEEN Caleba Swamp and Line Creek we saw a crowd gathered near a drinking house, most of them seated and smoking. We stopped to see what was the matter. There had been a quarter-mile race for a gallon of whiskey. One man had ridden into a corner of the log groggery at full speed, and now lay with a gash in his throat which might have let out a thousand lives. I asked if a doctor had been sent for, and the drawled reply was that the man was past doctoring, as good as dead.

"Has he a wife and children?" asked I.

"No children that I know on," said a female sitting on the ground a few paces from the dying man, smoking her pipe.

"Do you know his wife?" I asked. "Has she been informed of his untimely end?"

"Do I *know* her? Well, I reckon you ain't acquainted about these parts. I'm the widder."

"*You*, madam! *You* the wife of the man who has been so untimely cut off?"

"Yes, and what about it? Untimely cut off? His throat's been cut, that's all, by the sharp end of that log, but as for it being untimely, it's as well now as any time. *He warn't of much account, nohow.* But," she sighed, "it *was* an unfortunate race—poor man, he lost the whiskey."

1845

Frolic in the Knobs

George Washington Harris

TALK of your bar hunts and your deer hunts and knottin tigers' tails through the bungholes of barrels and cock fightin and all that, but if a reglar-built frolic at Jo Spragginses' in the Knobs of Old Knox County don't beat 'em all blind for fun, then I'm no judge of fun. I said fun and I say it agin—from a kiss that cracks like a wagon whip to a fight that rouses up all outdoors! And as for laughin, why they *invented* it, and the last laugh on earth will be heard at a Knob dance about three in the mornin!

Let me tell you about the motions I made at Jo Spragginses' a few days ago. Jo lives in a log house whar he gives a frolic once in three weeks in plowin time, and one every Saturday night the balance of the year. He asks two bits for what corn-juice you can suck and he throws the gals in free, and a bed in the hay if you git too hot to locomote. The supper is made up by the fellers. Every one fetches somethin—some a lick of meal, some a middlin of bacon, some a hen, some a possum, some a grab of taters or a pocketful of peas or dried apples, and some only fetches a good appetite and a skin chock full of particlar deviltry.

By sundown the gals come a-pourin out of the woods for the frolic like ants out of an old log when t'other end's afire. They looked jist as fine as silk, fixed up in all kinds of fancy doins, from broad-striped homespun to the sunflower calico. If one had a silk gown, she'd be too smart to wear it to Jo Spragginses', for if she did, she'd go home in her petticoat tail for certain. The homespun gals would tear it off'n her quicker than winkin.

Well, the sun had about set before I got the cows fed and had my pony saddled, but an owl couldn't have catched a rat before I was in sight of Jo's with my gal Jule Sawyers up behind me, a-huggin mighty tight. The yard and house was full of fellers and gals—the numbers nigh onto even, too—jist a few more boys than gals. That made it more excitin, for it give the gals a chance to kick and squeal without runnin any risk of not gittin kissed at all, and it give reasonable grounds for a few scrimmages among the he's. Any fool knows that kissin and fightin is the pepper and salt of all social gatherins.

My Jule she bounced off jist like a bag of wool rolls and I hitched the pony to a saplin that warn't skinned, so he'd git a craw full of good fresh bark before mornin. I give Jule a kiss, and in we walked.

"Hey! Hurray!" said the boys.

The gals was a-floppin on the beds, gigglin, whisperin, and a-ticklin one another while the boys pranced around and showed off. "My gracious!" the gals said. "If it ain't Sugartail Harlan and Jule Sawyers! Well, I know we'll have a reel now!"

Boys and gals commenced a-millin about, makin a powerful various racket, with a heap of yellin, sich as: "Hurray! Go it while you're young! Every man praise his country! Clear the ring! Whar's that air crock of baldfaced drinkin likker and that gourd of honey to sweeten it with? Miss Spraggins, drive out them dratted towheaded brats of yours! Give room!"

The old woman was busy cookin at the fireplace, a-singin:

> *"Daddy killed the blind bull,*
> *"Human nater, human nater!*
> *"Mammy fried a pan full,*
> *"Sop and tater, sop and tater!"*

Miss Spraggins left off and turned and combed the sweat from her brows and flang it, and she said, "You, Bill Jones, quit smashin that air cat's tail!"

"Let her keep her tail clear of my ant-killers!" Bill yelled back

She'd no more'n turned back to her cookin than she squealed when she were slapped onto her rear, but Jake Snyder said, "Cook on, old woman. Don't mind me—but you stooped so fair!"

Then Jake he said, "Hey, Suze Thompson, come here and let me pin your dress behind. Your back looks exactly like a blaze on a white oak."

"My back ain't nothin to you, Mister Smarty," said Suze, with her face a-lookin like a full cross twixt a gridiron and a steel trap.

But the frolic was fixin to begin and everybody was yellin at the old fiddler, "Give us *Forked Deer*, old fiddle-teaser! Gather your gals for a breakdown! Give us *Natchez-under-the-Hill!* No, give us *Rocky Mountain* or *Miss McCloud!*"

Some feller sings out, "*Miss McCloud* be damned, and *Rocky Moun-*

tain, too! Jist give us, 'She wouldn't, and she couldn't, and she didn't come at all!' "

"Give old fiddler a drink," said somebody. "Give him a flask, and every time he stops, repeat the dose."

"Thar!" said the old fiddler. "That's it. Now, make or break! Go it!" And if I know what goin it *is*, we *did* go it, while he played his three-stringed fiddle with a grasshopper jerk.

The first reel was called the Leather Shoe Dance and t'other the Barfoot Reel. Had to split 'em up that way because the dancin would turn into fightin before the first set got off the floor if you mixed 'em. The shoes would scronch the bar toes in dancin, and right then and thar they'd mix for a fight. Me and Jule Sawyers we danced in the one I named last.

Well, we danced and hurrawed till about midnight. Then Miss Spraggins tuck a roastin ear out'n her mouth and scraped off the loose grains and silks from her chin, and sung out, "Stop that thar dancin and come and git your supper!"

It was set in the yard on a table made of forked branches driv in the ground and planks out of the stable-loft, with sheets for tablecloths and a big fire of fat lightwood to see by. One feller helt his head back and lined out the hymn:

> *"The martins builds in boxes,*
> *"The foxes dens in holes,*
> *"The serpents crawls in rockses,*
> *"The earth's the home of moles,*
> *"Cock-a-doodle-do, it's movin,*
> *"And dram time's come agin!"*

So we had kissed and danced, and now we drunk ourselves into a perfect thrashin-machine appetite. The vittles hid themselves in an alarmin manner.

Jo Spraggins sung out, "Knives is scarce, so give what thar is to the gals and let the balance use their paws. Paws was invented before knives, anyhow. Now, gents, jist walk into the fat of the land. I'm sort of afeared the honey won't last till daybreak, but the likker will. Let the gals have the honey. You men drink yours and run and kiss the gals for sweetenin."

When eatin and drinkin was spoke of, an old Hardshell preacher come a-walkin in out of nowhar in the dark, with his mouth mortised into his face in a shape like a mule's hoof, heels down. He was a-sighin and a-groanin and a-shakin his head, and lookin like he had the bellyache. He couldn't have looked more solemncoly if his mammy had died that mornin owin him two dollars and a half. Like all Hardshells, he was dead agin women and lovely sounds and motions and dancin and cussin and kissin.

The whiskey part of the frolic he had nothin agin. I *knowed* that, for every time he rolled his eyes towards the barrel he'd lick his lips sort of sloppy-like, jist as if he'd been dippin his bill into chicken gravy and were a-tryin to save the stray draps that hung outside his face.

Jo Spraggins now come up, and Hardshell told him he'd come to stay all night, if he suited all round. "Certainly, oh yes, and welcome!" said Jo.

I sort of edged up aside him and, says I, "Mister, will you have a few draps?"

He blowed an awful sigh, and says he, "This is a wicked and a perverse generation of vipers, young man." He groaned and shuck his head, and sent one look of his eyes towards the whiskey.

I went and fotch him a big slug into a gourd. That shovel-shaped under-lip of his jist fell outwards like the fallin door of a coal stove, and he upsot the gourd inside of his teeth. I seed the mark of the truck a-goin down his throat jist like a snake travelin through a wet sausage gut. He smelt into the gourd a good long smell, turned up his eyes, and said, "Barm of life."

After that, me and Jule we tuck a notion and went around the house into a chimbly corner, and thar was two fellers thar, one of 'em a she, a-whisperin. We went to tother corner, and thar was two more. Then we went to the stable, and heared whisperin thar—it might been rats a-runnin in the straw. Them out-of-the-way spots was so crowded that we started back inside the house whar, as we thought, the dance was a-fixin to commence agin.

But the groanin old Hardshell rascal had done got the dancin stopped. He'd tuck the fiddle away from the fiddler and were a-holdin it by the neck with one hand and a-makin gestures with the bow in t'other. He was mounted onto a cheer, exhortin 'em about their sins, with the dancin sins at the head, wearin sunflower calico ones next, and then come their smaller sins, sich as riding behind fellers on the same hoss, whisperin out of doors, and a-winking behind turkey-tail fans and hankerchers. The *he* sins, of the small sort, was a-wearin of store-clothes, smellin of cinnamon oil, and a-totin striped sugar candy in their pockets to turn the minds of the weak gals.

The womenfolks was backed up in bunches, in the corners and agin the beds, with their fingers in their mouths. The he-fellers all looked like they'd most as leave fight as not, if they knowed how to start the thing, when in bounced Jo Spraggins.

He looked like a catamount, jist a-grittin his teeth like he was chompin eggshells. One jump and he stood in front of old Hardshell. He said, "You durned, incompassable old waterdog! You cussed hypocritical, ungrateful old musrat! *You* hell-fire, divin, splatterin, pond-makin, iron-jacketed old son of a mud-turkle! Git off'n that cheer!"

As he said that, he loaned the parson a most tremendous whack, and I seed his shoe soles a-goin up each side of Jo's fist, and the little musicianer a-snatchin his fiddle and bow in midair. It was a lick, that if it'd been a kick, a four-year-old mule would have been powerful proud of it. The old Shell lit onto this all-fours, and jist went a-scootin into outer darkness. But nobody noticed him any more, for that busted it. The fightin become general.

Oh hush! It makes my mouth water now to think what a beautiful row we had. One feller from Cady's Cove knocked a hole in the bottom of a fryin pan over Dan Turner's head and left it a-hangin round his neck, the handle-a-flyin about like a long queue, and thar it hung till Jane Thurman cut it off next day with a coldchisel. Another feller got knocked into a meal barrel. He was as mealy as an Irish tater and as hot as hoss radish. And two fellers fought out of the door, down the hill, and into the creek, and thar ended it in a quiet way, all alone.

As the couples come in from out of doors, a-lookin sort of sneakin and pale, one at least out of every pair got jumped on by somebody. Maybe a gal would kiver a comin-in gal, another gal would go for the hair and skin of the comin-in he-feller. Then, agin, the fist of a he would meet another comin-in he right twixt the eyes, and so on till the thing got to be durnedably mixed up and lively.

Well, a perfect mule from Stock Creek hit me a wipe with Old Miss Spragginses' churn. He made kindlin wood of it, and I lit onto him. We *had* it, head-and-tails, for a very long time, all over the house. But the truth must come out and shame my kin. *He warped me nice.* So, jist to save his time, I hollered calf-rope. The lickin he give me made me sort of uneasy and hostile-like. It woke my wolf wide awake. I begun to look about for a man I could lick, and no mistake.

The little fiddler come scrougin past, holdin his fiddle up over his head to keep it in tune, for the fightin was gittin tolerably brisk.

"You're the one," thinks I. And jist I grabbed Old Miss Spragginses' dough tray and split it plumb open over his head. He rotted down, right thar, and I paddled his t'other end with one of the pieces. While I was mollifyin my feelins in that way, his gal slipped up behind me and fotch me a rake with the iron pothooks from the fireplace.

Jule Sawyers was thar and jist annexed to her right off. And a mighty nice fight it was! Jule carried enough hair from her head to make a sofa, and striped and checked her face like a partridge-net hung on a white fence. She hollered for her fiddler but, oh pshaw! He couldn't do her a bit of good. He was too busy rubbin first his broken head and then his blisters at t'other end. So when I thought Jule had give her plenty, I pulled her off and put her in a good humor by given her about as many kisses as would cover a barn door.

I needed a drink, so I started for the creek. The first thing I saw was more stars with my eyes shut than I ever did with 'em open. I looked around.

It was the fiddler's big brother.

I knowed what it meant. So we locked horns without a word, thar all alone, and I do think we fought an hour. At last some fellers heared the jolts, and they come and dug us out, for we had fought into a hole whar a big pine stump had burnt out. Thar we was, up to our girths, a-peggin away, face to face, and no dodgin.

Well, it's now sixteen days since that fight and frolic at Jo Spragginses', and last night Jule picked gravels out of my knees as big as squirrel-shot. Luck rather run agin me that night, for I didn't lick anybody but the fiddler—and had three fights. But Jule licked her gal, and that's some comfort. I suppose a feller can't always win.

After the fight, we made friends all around, except the fiddler—he's hot yit—and danced and likkered at the tail of every reel till sunup, when them that was sober enough went home and them that was wounded stayed whar they fell. I was in the list of the wounded, but could have got away if my pony hadn't chewed bark clean through that saplin I'd hitched him to and gone home without a partin word.

So Sugartail and Jule had to ride shank's mare, and a right peart four-legged nag she is. She was weak in two of her legs, but t'other two—oh, my stars and possum dogs! They make a man swaller tobacker jist to look at 'em, and feel sort of like a June bug was a-crawlin up his trousers and the waistband too tight for it to git out.

I'm a-goin to marry Jule, I swear I am! We'll set square into house-keepin, and I'll stick to her till thar's enough white frost in hell to kill snapbeans.   1846

The Shifty Man

JOHNSON J. HOOPER

IT IS not often that the living worthy furnishes a theme for the biographer's pen. The pious task of commemorating the acts and depicting the character of the great and good is generally, and properly, deferred until they are past blushing or swearing. But no rule is without an exception. There are cases and persons in which and to whom the general rule cannot be considered to apply.

Take, by way of illustration, the case of a candidate for office. His life up to the time when his reluctant acquiescence to the wishes of his friends was wrung from him, MUST be written. It is an absolute political necessity. His enemies *will* know enough to attack. His friends *must* know enough to defend. Thus, Jackson, Van Buren, Clay, and Polk have each a biography published while they live. Nay, the thing has been carried further. In the first of each "Life" there is found a lithograph of the subject of the pages to follow. Not only are the moral and intellectual endowments of the candidate heralded to the world of voters; but an attempt is made to create an idea of his *physique*. By this means, all the country has in its mind's eye an image of a little gentleman with a round, oily face—sleek, able pate, delicate whiskers, and foxy smile, which they call Martin Van Buren. And future generations of naughty children who will persist in sitting up when they should be a-bed, will be frightened to their cribs by the lithograph of "Major General Andrew Jackson," which their mamas will declare to be a faithful representation of the Evil One—an atrocious slander, by the bye, on the potent and comparatively well-favored prince of the infernal world.

What we have said in the preceding paragraphs was to prepare our readers for the fact that we intend to furnish for their instruction a few incidents—for we are far too modest to attempt a connected memoir—

in the life of the renowned SIMON SUGGS, of Tallapoosa. Since Suggs thinks it more than probable that he will "come before the people of Tallapoosa for election" in the course of a year or two, we are bound in honor to furnish the Suggs party with such information respecting him, as will enable them to vindicate his character whenever and wherever it may be attacked by the ruthless and polluted tongues of his enemies.

It is necessary that we should describe Suggs so that all who have never yet seen him may be able to recognize him immediately whenever it shall be their good fortune to be inducted into his presence.

His head is somewhat large and thinly covered with coarse, silver-white hair. Beneath thin brows, a pair of eyes with light-gray pupils and variegated whites dance and twinkle with the utmost appearance of candor. In the neighborhood of these eyes is a long, low nose, singularly pointed and rubicund, where it overhangs the mouth. But the mouth is Suggs' greatest feature, and measures about four inches horizontally. Dipping below this, a sharp chin thrusts under his bristly, iron-gray beard. All these facial beauties are supported by a long and skinny, but muscular neck, inserted after the ordinary fashion in the upper part of a frame, lithe, long, and sinewy, and clad in Kentucky jeans, a trifle worn. Add to this, that our friend is about fifty years old, and seems to indurate as he advances in years, and our readers will have as accurate an idea of the personal appearance of Simon Suggs as we are able to give them.

The moral and intellectual qualities which, with the physical proportions, make up the entire entity of Suggs, may be readily described. His whole ethical system lies snugly in his favorite aphorism—"IT IS GOOD TO BE SHIFTY IN A NEW COUNTRY"—which means that it is right and proper that one should live as merrily and comfortably as possible at the expense of anyone but one's-self.

So, in the year 1832, Simon Suggs was settled on public land on the Tallapoosa River in Alabama, with a pretty large family, considerable experience, but without funds. Some might have termed Simon Suggs a common squatter, but had they asked, the proud reply would have been forthcoming: "I am a speculator, sir!"

It may seem odd that a man without a dollar should be a speculator, even in the newly opened Creek Country of Alabama. To some, speculation may seem inseparably connected with capital. Business requiring actual cash outlay, Simon regarded as only fit for purse-proud clodheads. *Any* fool could speculate if he had money. But to make profits without a cent in one's pocket—*that* required judgment, discretion, ingenuity. . . .

Simon Attends a Camp Meeting

As Simon sat one day, ruminating upon the unpleasant condition of his finances, Mrs. Suggs informed him that "the sugar and coffee was nigh about out, and that there was not a dozen joints and middlins all put together in the smoke house."

Suggs bounced up on the instant, exclaiming, "Damn it! *Somebody* must suffer!"

Exactly what he meant by these words must be left to the commentators. It is enough for us that we shall give all the facts in this connection. Having uttered the exclamation, Suggs drew on his famous old green-blanket overcoat, and ordered his horse, and within five minutes was on his way to a camp meeting, then in full blast on Sandy Creek, twenty miles distant.

When he arrived there, he found the hollow square of the encampment filled with people, listening to the midday sermon and its exhortations. A half-dozen preachers were dispensing the word; the one in the pulpit, a meek-faced old man, of great simplicity and benevolence. His voice was weak and cracked, notwithstanding which, he contrived to make himself heard occasionally above the din of the exhorting, the singing, and the shouting which were going on around him.

The other preachers were walking to and fro among the mourners— a host of whom occupied the seat set apart for their especial use—or made personal appeals to the mere spectators. The excitement was intense. Men and women rolled about on the ground, or lay sobbing or shouting in promiscuous heaps. More than all, the Negroes sang and screamed and prayed. Several, under the influence of what is technically called "the jerks," were plunging and pitching with convulsive energy. The great object of all seemed to be to see who could make the greatest noise.

"Bless my old soul!" screamed the preacher in the pulpit, "if yonder ain't a squad in that corner that we ain't got one out of yet! It'll never do!"—raising his voice—"You must come out of that! Brother Fant, fetch up that youngster in the blue coat! I see the Lord's a-workin upon him! Fetch him along—Glory!—yes!—hold to him!"

"Keep the thing warm!" roared a man of stout mould and florid countenance, who was exhorting a bevy of young women among whom he was lavishing caresses. "Keep the thing warm, brethren!—Come to the Lord, honey!" he added as he vigorously hugged one of the damsels he sought to save.

"Oh, I've got him!" said another in exulting tones, as he led up a gawky youth among the mourners. "I've got him—he tried to git off, but—ha, Lord!"—shaking his head as much as to say, it took a smart fellow to escape him— "Ha, Lord!"—and he wiped the perspiration from his face with one hand, and with the other patted his neophyte on the shoulder—"He couldn't do it! No! Then he tried to argy with me—but bless the Lord!—he couldn't do that neither! Ha! Lord! I tuck him, first in the Old Testament—bless the Lord!—and I argyed him all through Kings—then I throwed him into Proverbs—and from that, here we had it up and down, clear down to the New Testament, and then I begun to see it work him!—then we got into Matthew, and from Matthew right straight along to Acts; and *thar* I throwed him! Y-e-s L-o-r-d and h-e-r-e he is! Now g-i-t down thar!"—assuming the nasal twang and high pitch which are, in some parts, considered the perfection of the rhetorical art—"and s-e-e if the L-o-r-d won't do somethin f-o-r you!" Having thus deposited his charge among the mourners, he started out, summarily to convert another soul.

"Gl-o-*ree!*" yelled a huge, greasy woman, as in a fit of the jerks she threw herself convulsively from her feet and fell like a thousand bricks across a diminutive old man in a little round hat, who was squeaking consolation to one of the mourners.

"Good Lord have mercy!" screamed the little man earnestly and un-affectedly, as he strove to crawl from under the mass that was crushing him.

In another part of the square, a dozen old women were singing. They were in a state of absolute ecstasy, as their shrill pipes gave forth:

> "I rode on the sky,
> "Quite ondestified, I,
> "And the moon it was under my feet!"

Near these last stood a delicate woman in that hysterical condition in which the nerves are incontrollable, and which is termed the "holy laugh." A hideous grin distorted her mouth, and was accompanied with a maniac's chuckle; while every muscle and nerve of her face twitched and jerked in horrible spasms.

Amid all this confusion and excitement, Suggs stood unmoved. He viewed the whole affair as a grand deception—a sort of "opposite line" running against his own—and looked on with a sort of professional jealousy.

Sometimes he would mutter running comment upon what passed before him.

"Well, now," said he, as he observed the full-faced brother who was officiating among the women, "that thar feller takes *my* eye! Thar he's been this half hour, a-figurin amongst them gals, and's never said the first word to nobody else. Wonder what's the reason these here preachers never hugs up the old ugly women? Never seed one of 'em do it in my life— the spirit never moves 'em that way! It's nature, though. The women, *they* never flock round one of the old dried-up brethren—bet two to one old Splinter-Legs thar"—nodding at one of the ministers—"won't git a chance to say turkey to a good-lookin gal today! Well, I judge if I was a preacher, I'd save the prettiest souls first, myself."

While Suggs was in the middle of this conversation with himself, he caught the attention of the preacher in the pulpit, who inferring from an indescribable something in his appearance that he was a person of some consequence, immediately determined to add him at once to the church, and to that end began a vigorous, direct personal attack.

"Brethren!" he exclaimed, "I see yonder a man that's a sinner! I *know* he's a sinner! *Thar* he stands!"—pointing at Simon—"a miserable old critter, with his head a-blossomin for the grave! A few more short years, and d-o-w-n he'll go to perdition, lessen the Lord have mer-cy on him! Come up here, you old hoary-headed sinner, a-n-d git down on your knees, a-n-d put up your cry for the Lord to snatch you from the bottom-less pit! You're ripe for the devil—you're b-o-u-n-d for hell, and the Lord only knows what will become of you!"

"Damn it," thought Suggs, "*if* I only had you down in the creek swamp for a minute or so, *I'd* show you who's *old*! *I'd* alter your tune *mighty* sudden, you sassy old deceitful rascal!" But he judiciously held his tongue.

The attention of many having been directed to Simon Suggs by the preacher, he was soon surrounded by numerous well-meaning and, doubtless, very pious persons, each of whom seemed bent on the applica-tion of his own particular recipe for the salvation of souls.

For a long time Suggs stood silent, or answered the incessant stream of exhortation only with a sneer; but at length his countenance began to give token of inward emotion. First his eyelids twitched—then his upper lip quivered—next a transparent drop formed on one of his eye-lashes, and a similar one on the tip of his nose—and, at last, a sudden bursting of air from nose and mouth told that Simon Suggs was over-powered by his emotions. At the moment of the explosion, he made a feint as if to rush from the crowd, but he was in experienced hands, who well knew that the battle was more than half won.

"Hold to him!" said one. "It's a-workin in him as strong as a Dick hoss!"

"Pour it into him," said another. "It'll all come right directly."

"That's the way I love to see 'em do," said a third. "When you begin to draw the water from their eyes, tain't goin to be long afore you'll have 'em on their knees!"

And so they clung to Suggs manfully, and half-dragged, half-led him to the mourners' bench; by which he threw himself down, altogether un-manned, and bathed in tears. Great was the rejoicing of the brethren, as they sang, shouted, and prayed around him—for by this time it had come to be generally known that the "convicted" old man was Simon Suggs, the very chief of sinners in all that region.

Suggs remained grovelling in the dust during the usual time and gave vent to even more than the requisite number of sobs, groans, and heart-piercing cries. At length, when the proper time had arrived, he bounced up, and with a face radiant with joy, commenced a series of vaultings and tumblings which laid in the shade all previous performances of the sort at that camp meeting. The brethren were in ecstasies at this demonstrative evidence of completion of the work; and whenever Suggs shouted, "Gloree!" at the top of his lungs, every one of them shouted it back until the woods rang with echoes.

The effervescence having partially subsided, Suggs was put upon his pins to relate his experience, which he did somewhat in this style—first brushing the tear drops from his eyes and giving the end of his nose a preparatory wring with his fingers:

"Friends," he said, "it don't take long to curry a short hoss, accordin to the old sayin, and I'll give you the particlars of the way I was brought to knowledge"—here Simon wiped his eyes, brushed the tip of his nose, and snuffled a little—"in less'n no time."

"Praise the Lord!" cried a bystander.

"You see, I come here full of romancin and devilment, and just to make game of all the perceedins. Well, sure enough, I done so for sometime—"

"Dear soul alive! *don't* he talk sweet!" cried an old lady in black silk—"Where's John Dobbs? You, Sukey!"—screaming at a Negro woman on the other side of the square—"if you don't hunt up your Mass John in a minute and have him here to listen to this experience, I'll tuck you up when I git home and give you a hundred and fifty lashes, madam! —see if I don't! Blessed Lord!"—referring to Simon's relation—"ain't it a *precious* discourse!"

"I was just a-thinkin how I should turn it all into ridicule, when they begun to come round me and talk. Long at first, I didn't mind it, but after a little, that brother"—pointing to the reverend gentleman who had so successfully carried the unbeliever through the Old and New Testament, and who, Simon was convinced, was the big dog of the tanyard— "that brother spoke a word that struck me clean to the heart, and run all over me like fire in dry grass—"

"I-I-I can bring em!" cried the preacher alluded to, in a tone of exultation. "Lord, thou knows if thy servant can't stir 'em up, nobody else needn't try—but the glory ain't mine! I'm a poor wor-r-um of the dust," he added, with ill-managed modesty.

"And so from that, I felt something a-pullin me inside—"

"Grace! Grace! Nothin but grace!" exclaimed one, meaning that grace had been operating on Suggs' gastric region.

"And then," continued Suggs, "I wanted to git off, but they helt me, and bimeby I felt so miserable, I had to go yonder"—pointing to the mourners' seat—"and when I lay down thar it got worse and worse, and peared like somethin was a-mashin down on my back—"

"That was his load of sin!" said one of the brethren. "Never mind, it'll tumble off presently, see if it don't!" And he shook his head professionally and knowingly.

"And it kept a-gittin heavier and heavier, until it looked like it might be a four year old steer, or a big pine log, or somethin of that sort—"

"Glory to my soul!" shouted Mrs. Dobbs. "It's the sweetest talk I ever hearn! You, Sukey! Ain't you got John yit? Never mind, my lady, I'll settle with you!" Sukey quailed before the finger which her mistress shook at her.

"And after awhile," Suggs went on, "peared like I fell into a trance, like, and I seed—"

"Now we'll git the good of it!" cried one of the sanctified.

"And I seed the biggest, longest, rip-roarinest, blackest, scaliest—" Suggs paused, wiped his brow, and ejaculated, "Oh, L-o-r-d!"

"Sarpent! Warn't?" asked one of the preachers.

"No, not a sarpent," replied Suggs, blowing his nose.

"Do tell us what it was, soul alive!—where is John?" said Mrs. Dobbs.

"Alligator!" said Suggs.

"Alligator!" repeated every woman present, and screamed for very life.

Mrs. Dobbs' nerves were so shaken by the announcement, that after repeating the horrible word, she screamed to Sukey, "You, Sukey, I say, you, Su-ke-e-y! If you let John come a-nigh this way where the dreadful alliga—pshaw! What am I thinkin bout? Twarn't nothin but a vision!"

"Well," said Suggs in continuation, "the alligator kept a-comin and a-comin towards me, with his great jaws a-gapin open like a ten-foot pair of tailor's shears—"

"Oh! Oh! Oh! Gracious above!" cried the women.

"SATAN!" was the laconic comment of the oldest preacher present, who thus informed the congregation that it was the devil which attacked Suggs in the shape of an alligator.

"And then I concluded the jig was up, without I could block his game some way, for I seed his idee was to snap off my head—"

The women screamed again.

"So I fixed myself just like I was perfectly willin for him to take my head and rather he'd do it as not"—here the women shuddered perceptibly —"and so I helt my head straight out"—Suggs illustrated by elongating his neck—"and when he come up and was a-goin to *shut down* on it, I just pitched in a big rock which choked him to death, and that minute I felt the weight slide off, and I had the best feelins anybody ever had!"

"Didn't I *tell* you so? Didn't I *tell* you so!" asked the brother who had predicted the off-tumbling of the load of sin. "Ha, Lord, fool *who*! I've been *all* along thar! and I know every inch of the road just as good as I do the road home!"—and then he turned round and round, and looked at all, to receive a silent tribute to his superior penetration.

Suggs was now the lion of the day. Nobody could pray so well, or exhort so movingly as Brother Suggs. Nor did his natural modesty prevent the proper performance of appropriate exercises. With the Reverend Bela Bugg (him to whom, under providence, he ascribed his conversion), he was a most especial favorite. They walked, sang, and prayed together for hours.

"Come, come up! Thar's room for all!" cried Brother Bugg, in his evening exhortation. "Come to the seat, and if you won't pray yourselves, let *me* pray for you!"

"Yes!" said Simon, by way of assisting his friend. "It's a game that all can win at! Ante up, ante up, boys—friends I mean—don't back out!"

"Thar ain't a sinner here," said Bugg, "no matter if his soul's black as midnight, but what thar's room for him!"

"No matter what kind of hand you've got," added Simon in the fullness of his benevolence, "take stock! Here am *I*, the whiskey'dest and blindest of sinners—have spent my whole life in the service of the devil—

have come in on *nary* pair and won a *pile!*" And Suggs' face beamed with holy pleasure.

And thus Simon continued, until the services were concluded, to assist in adding to the number at the mourners' bench; and up to the hour of retiring, he exhibited such enthusiasm in the cause that he was unanimously voted the most efficient addition the church had made during the meeting.

The next morning, when the preacher of the day first entered the pulpit, he announced that Brother Simon Suggs, mourning over his past iniquities, and desirous of going to work in the cause as speedily as possible, would take up a collection to found a church in his own neighborhood, at which he hoped to make himself useful as soon as he could prepare himself for the ministry, which the preacher didn't doubt would be in a very few weeks, as Brother Suggs was "a man of mighty good judgment and of great discourse." The funds were to be collected by Brother Suggs, and held in trust by Brother Bela Bugg, who was the financial officer of the circuit, until some arrangement could be made to build a suitable church house.

"Yes, brethren," said Suggs, rising to his feet, "I want to start a little association close to me, and I want you all to help. I'm mighty poor myself, as poor as any of you—don't leave, brethren"—observing that several of the well-to-do were about to go off—"don't leave. If you ain't able to afford anything, just give us your blessin, and it'll all be the same."

This insinuation did the business, and the sensitive individuals reseated themselves.

"It's mighty little of this world's goods I've got," resumed Suggs, pulling off his hat and holding it before him, "but I'll bury *that* in the cause, anyhow," and he deposited his last five dollar bill in the hat.

There was a murmur of approbation at Suggs' liberality throughout the assembly.

Suggs now commenced collecting, and very prudently attacked first the gentlemen who had shown a disposition to escape. These, to exculpate themselves from anything like poverty, contributed handsomely.

"Look here, brethren," said Simon, displaying the bank notes thus received, "Brother Snooks has drapped a five with me, and Brother Snodgrass a ten! Of course, it ain't expected *that you that ain't as well off as them* will give as much. Let every one give accordin to their means."

This was another chain shot that raked as it went. Who so low as not to be able to contribute as much as Snooks and Snodgrass?

"Here's all the *small* money I've got about me," said a burly fellow, ostentatiously handing to Suggs, over the heads of half a dozen, a ten dollar bill.

"That's what I call mannanimous!" exclaimed Simon. "That's the way every rich man should do!"

These examples were followed, more or less closely, by almost all present, and a very handsome sum was collected in a very short time.

The Reverend Mr. Bugg, as soon as he observed that our hero had obtained all that was to be had at that time, went to him and inquired what amount had been collected? Suggs replied that it was still uncounted, but that it couldn't be much under a hundred.

"Well, Brother Suggs, you'd better count it and turn it over to me now. I'm goin to leave presently."

"No!" said Suggs. "Can't do it!"

"Why? What's the matter?" inquired Bugg.

"It's got to be *prayed over*, first!" said Simon, a heavenly smile illuminating his whole face.

"Well," said Bugg, "less go one side and do it."

"No!" said Simon solemnly.

Mr. Bugg gave him an inquiring look.

"You see that creek swamp?" asked Suggs. "I'm a-goin down in *thar!* I'm a-goin to lay this money down *so*"—showing how he would place it on the ground—"and I'm a-goin to git on these here knees"—slapping the right one—"and I'm n-e-v-e-r a-goin to quit the grit till I feel it's got the blessin! And nobody ain't got to be thar a-gittin down on their poor old achin knees but me!"

Mr. Bugg greatly admired Suggs' fervent piety, and bidding him godspeed, turned off.

Suggs struck for the swamp sure enough, where his horse was already hitched.

"If them feller's ain't done to a cracklin," he muttered to himself as he mounted, "*I'll* never bet on two pair again! They're peart at the snap game themselves, but they're badly lewed this hitch! Well! Live and let live is a good old motto, and my sentiments exactly!"

And giving the spur to his horse, off he cantered.

Simon Fights the Tiger

Reader, did you ever encounter the TIGER? Not the bounding creature of the woods, with deadly fang and claw, that preys upon blood and muscle—but the stealthier and more ferocious animal that ranges amid the busy haunts of men—which feeds upon coin and bank notes—whose spots, more attractive than those of its namesake of the forest, dazzle and lure, like the brilliantly varying hues of the charmer snake, the more intensely and irresistibly, the longer they are looked upon—the thing, in short, of pasteboard and ivory, mother-of-pearl and mahogany—the FARO BANK!

Almost every man has his idiosyncrisy—his pet and peculiar opinion on some particular subject. Simon Suggs has his, and he clings to it with a pertinacity that defies alike the suggestions of reason and the demonstrations of experience. Simon believes that he can *whip* the Tiger in a fair fight. He has always believed it; he *will* always believe it.

After one of his more successful speculations, Simon Suggs made his way to Tuscaloosa for what he was certain would be the final vanquishment of the Tiger. Indeed, he scarcely allowed himself time to bolt the excellent supper served him at Duffie's before he outsallied to engage the adversary.

In the street, he suffered not himself to be beguiled into a moment's loitering by the strange sights displayed in the blaze of lamplight from stores, groggeries, and the like. The music of a fine amateur band preparing for a serenade was no music to him. In short, so eager was he to give battle that he hurried along, with the long stride of the backwoods, hardly turning his head, seemingly in a turkey-dream. But Suggs is an observant man and notes with much accuracy whatever comes before him, all the while a body would suppose him to be asleep.

Passing a well-lit bookseller's shop, he mused, "Hell and scissors! Whoever seed the like of the books. Ain't thar a pile! Well, mother wit can best book learnin at *any* game. There's Squire Hadenskelt, up home—he's got two cartloads of law books, though, and here's the very man that knocked a fifty out of him once at short cards, before a right smart active sheep could flop his tail one time, and can do it again, whenever he gits over his shyness.

"Yes," mused Suggs, as he loped along, "human nature and the human family is *my* books. And I've never seed many but what I could hold my own with. Let me git one of these book-learned fellers over a bottle of old corn and a handful of cards, and I'm apt to git what he knows and, in a general way, give *him* a wrinkle into the bargain! Books ain't fitten for nothin but just to give to children a-goin to school to keep them out of mischief. As Old Jedediah used to say, 'Book learnin spoils a man if he's got mother wit, and if he ain't got that, it don't do him no good'."

Thus Simon at last reached Clare's Saloon. Passing into the bar room,

he stood a moment looking around to find the way to go to the Faro
Banks. In a corner, he discovered a stairway above which was burning
a lurid red lamp. Waiting for no other indication, he strode up the stairs.
At the landing above, he found a door, closed and locked. But light
came through the keyhole and the sharp rattling of dice and jingling of
coin could be heard beyond the door.

Simon knocked.

"Hello!" said somebody within.

"Hello, yourself!" said Suggs.

"What do you want?" said the voice.

"A game."

"What's the name?" said the voice.

"Cash," said Simon.

"He'll do," said another voice in the room. "Let Cash in."

The door was opened and Simon entered, half blinded by the sudden
burst of light which streamed from the chandeliers and lamps and was re-
flected in every direction by the mirrors almost walling the room. In the
center of the room was a small bar. Here stood a pockmarked clerk who
sold to the company costly wines and liquors. Disposed at regular intervals
around the room were tables for the various games played, all thronged
with eager customers and covered with heavy piles of doubloons, dollars,
and banknotes. Most in the room were well dressed; there was very little
noise but very deep playing.

As Simon Suggs entered, he made his bow and saluted the company, "Good evenin, Gentlemen!"

No one acknowledged their pleasure at seeing him or seemed to notice
him at all; he therefore repeated, "I say, *good evenin*, Gentlemen!"

There was only a slight laugh from some of the company. Suggs
began to feel a little awkward, standing up before so many strangers, well
dressed strangers at that, and he in his worn Kentucky jeans. While he
was hesitating as to what he must do next, he overheard a young man
standing a few feet from him half-whispering to another.

"Jim," said the young man, "I bet that's your uncle, General Witherspoon!—hasn't he been expected here for several days with a large drove of
hogs?"

"By Jupiter!" said the other young man. "It could be, though I'm not
certain. I haven't seen him since I was a little fellow. What makes you
think it's him? You never saw him."

"No, but he suits the description given of your uncle very well— You know, white hair, red eyes, big mouth, and so forth. Does you uncle gamble?"

"They say he does. But my mother, who is his own sister, knows hardly any more about him than the rest of the world. We've only seen him once in fifteen years."

Simon continued surveying the establishment, with a concentrated look of slight deafness, as if, particularly, he had not heard the slightest syllable of the young men's low-voiced conversation.

Looking steadfastly at Simon, the second young man murmured, "I'm damned if I don't believe it's he! He's as rich as mud and a jovial old cock of a bachelor—I must claim kin with him."

Simon had no reasonable objection to being believed to be General Witherspoon, the rich hog drover from Kentucky; in fact, he determined that if he was not respected as General Witherspoon for the remainder of the evening, it should be somebody else's fault, not his. In a few moments, indeed, it was whispered through the company that the red-eyed man with the white hair was the wealthy field officer who drove swine to increase his fortune. Simon thought he discovered a very considerable improvement in the way of politeness on the part of all present.

Sauntering up to the Faro bank with the intention of betting, with the spirit and liberality which General Witherspoon would have displayed, he called for, "Twenty-five dollar checks, and that pretty tolerable damned quick!"

The dealer handed him the red checks and he piled them upon the Ten.

"Grind on!" said Simon.

A card or two was dealt, and the keeper, with a bow, handed Simon twenty more red checks.

"Deal away," said Simon, heaping the additional checks on the same card.

Again the cards flew from the little box, and again Simon won.

Several were now overlooking the game. Among the rest was the young man who was so happy as to be the nephew of General Witherspoon.

"The old codger has nerve!" said one.

"And money, too, from the way he bets," said another.

"To be sure he has," said a third. "That's the rich hog drover from Kentucky."

By this time Simon had won seven hundred dollars but he was not at all disposed to discontinue. Now he thought was the golden moment in which to press his luck, the moment to flay this high-flown establishment.

As he won the fifth consecutive bet, Suggs remarked, "*That* brings the fat in great flecks as big as my arm. It's 'Horray, Brother John, every shot a turkey!' as the boy said. Here goes again." And he staked his winnings and the original stake on the Jack.

"General," said a bystander, "I wouldn't stake so much on a single card!"

"*You* wouldn't," said Simon, turning round and eyeing him, "because *you* never toted a pile of that size."

The obtrusive onlooker shrank back under the rebuke, and the crowd voted Simon not only a man of spunk but a man of wit.

Just then the Jack won, and Suggs was better off by fifteen hundred dollars than when he had entered the saloon.

"That's better," he said. "Just the least grain in the world better than drivin hogs from Kaintucky and sellin them for cents a pound."

The nephew of General Witherspoon was now confident that Suggs was his uncle. He pushed up to him, smiling broadly, with: "Don't you know me, Uncle?" at the same time extending his hand.

Suggs drew himself up with considerable dignity and said that he did not know the young man.

"Don't you know me, Uncle? Why, I'm James Peyton, your sister's son. She has been expecting you for several days."

"All very well, Mr. Jeemes Peyton, but this little world of ours is tolerably full of rascally impostors. Gentlemen of my—that is to say, you see—men that have got somethin is apt to be took in. So it stands a man in hand to be a little particlar. Just you better answer me a forward question or two," said Simon, subjecting Mr. Peyton to a test which, if applied to himself, would have blown him sky-high.

"Oh, he's genuine," said several of the crowd.

"Hold on, Gentlemen. This young man might want to borrer money of me."

Mr. Peyton protested against any such supposition.

"Oh, well," said Suggs, "I might want to borrer money of *you*, and—"

Mr. Peyton signified his willingness to lend his uncle the last dollar in his pocket book.

"Very good, very good," grunted Suggs, "but I happen to be a little *notiony* about such matters. It ain't *every* man I'd borrer from. Before I handle a man's money in the way of borrerin, in the first place I must know him to be a gentleman. In the second place, he must be my friend.

In the third place, I must think he's both able and willin to afford the accommodation."

Mr. Suggs paused and looked around to receive the applause which he knew must be elicited by such magnanimity. The applause *did* come. And the crowd thought, while they gave it, how difficult and desirable a thing it would be to lend money to General Thomas Witherspoon, the rich hog drover.

Simon now resumed his examination of Mr. Peyton. He asked, "What's your mother's first name?"

"Sarah," said Mr. Peyton meekly.

"Right—so far. How many children has she?"

"Two. Myself and Brother Tom."

"Right again. Tom, Gentle*men*," he added, turning to the crowd and venturing a shrewd guess, "Tom, Gentle*men*, were named after me. Warn't he, sir?" he said to Mr. Peyton sternly.

"He was, sir. His name is Thomas Witherspoon Peyton."

Suggs bobbed his head to the company, and the crowd decided that the General was a devilish sharp old cock. And the crowd wasn't very far out of the way.

Simon was not acting in this matter without an object. He intended to make a bold play for a small fortune. He knew that, in the attempt, it was quite possible that he should lose the money he had won, in which case it would be convenient to have the credit of General Witherspoon to cover his retreat.

"Gentle*men*," he said to the crowd, with whom he had become vastly popular, "your attention, one moment, *if* you please!"

The company accorded him its most respectful and obsequious attention.

"Come here, Jeemes."

Mr. James Peyton approached to within eighteen inches of his new-found uncle, who raised his hands above the young man's head in the most impressive manner.

"One and all, Gentle*men*," said he, "I call on you to witness this here young man is my proper, genuwine nephew, my Sister Sarah's son—and wish him respected as such. Jeemes, hug your old uncle!"

Young Mr. James Payton and Simon Suggs then embraced. Several of the bystanders smiled, but most of them accounted it a solemn and affecting sight. One, who had been making a revolving circuit to the bar all the while, wept and expressed the opinion that nothing so soul-moving had ever before taken place in the City of Tuscaloosa. As for Simon, he managed to dab at his eyes and screw his knuckles against them so briskly that the real tears pumped up and rolled down his face.

Wiping the tears away with a flourish, Simon renewed his engagement with the Tiger. But luck seemed to have deserted him in a pet.

"There goes a dozen damned fine fat hogs," said he as the bank won a bet of two hundred dollars.

He shifted about, from card to card, but the bank won always. At last he returned to the Ten, upon which he bet five hundred dollars. "Now I'll wool you," he said.

"Next time," said the dealer, as he threw the winning card on his own pile.

"That makes my hogs squeal," said Suggs, and everybody admired the fine nerve of the hog drover.

In half an hour, Suggs was as flat as tape. Not a dollar remained of his winnings or his original stake. He asked, "Could a body bet a few mighty fine bacon hogs against money at this table?"

The dealer declared that he would be happy to accommodate the General upon his word of honor.

It was not long before Suggs had bet off a very considerable number of very fine hogs in General Thomas Witherspoon's uncommonly fine drove. He began to feel, too, as if a meeting with the veritable drover, already due in Tuscaloosa, might not be entirely agreeable. He began, therefore, to entertain serious notions of leaving in the stage that night. Honor demanded, however, that he should settle to the satisfaction of the dealer.

Accordingly, he called, "Jeemes!"

Mr. Peyton responded very promptly to the call.

"Now," said Simon, "Jeemes, I'm a little behind to this gentleman here and I'm obliged to go to Greensboro in tonight's stage on account of seeing if I can engage pork thar. Now, if I shouldn't be here when my hogs come in, do *you*, Jeemes, take this gentleman to wherever the boys puts them up and let him pick thirty of the finest in the drove. You *hear*, Jeemes?"

James promised to attend to the delivery of the hogs.

"Is that satisfactory?" asked Simon.

"Perfectly," said the dealer. "Let's take a drink."

Before Suggs went up to the bar, he patted James upon the shoulder and intimated that he desired to speak to him privately. Mr. Peyton was highly delighted at this mark of his uncle's confidence and turned his head to see whether the company noted it. Having observed that they did, he accompanied his uncle to an unoccupied part of the saloon.

"Jeemes," said Suggs thoughtfully, "has your mother—bought—her—her—pork yet?"

James said she had not.

"Well, Jeemes, when my drove comes in, do you go down and pick her out ten of the best!"

Mr. Peyton made his grateful acknowledgements for his uncle's generosity, and they started back toward the crowd. But Simon halted him after a couple of steps.

"I'd like to forgot," he said. "Have you as much as a couple of hundred by you, Jeemes, that I could use till I git back from Greensboro?"

Mr. Peyton was very sorry he hadn't more than fifty dollars about him. His uncle could take that, however—as he did, forthwith—and he would jump about and get the balance in ten minutes.

"Don't do it, if it's any trouble at all, Jeemes."

But Mr. James Peyton was determined that he would raise the wind for his rich bachelor uncle, let the trouble be what it might, and in a few minutes he returned and handed Suggs the desired amount.

"Much obliged to you, Jeemes. I'll remember you for this." Which, from the mouth of General Thomas Witherspoon, could mean but one thing.

Suggs took a glass of spirits with his friend, the Faro bank dealer, whom he assured he considered the "smartest and cleverest feller out of the State of Kaintucky." Then he said he wished to retire, but just as he was leaving, it was suggested in his hearing that an oyster supper would be no inappropriate way of testifying his joy at meeting his obliging nephew and so many true-hearted friends.

"Ah, Gentlemen," he said, "the old hog drover's broke now, or he'd be proud to treat to somethin of the sort. They've knocked the leaf-fat out of him tonight, in wads as big as mattock handles." He watched the bar keeper out of the corner of his left eye.

"Anything this house affords is at the disposal of General Witherspoon," said the genial and pockmarked worthy.

"Well, well!" said Simon. "You're all so accommodatin that I must stand it, I suppose, though I oughtn't to be so extravagant."

"Take the crowd, sir?" said the pockmarked bar clerk.

"Certain," said Simon.

"How much champagne, General?"

"Oh, I reckon we can make out with a couple of cases," said Suggs.

There was a considerable ringing of bells for a brief space. Then a door which Simon hadn't seen before was thrown open and the company ushered into a handsome supping apartment. Seated at the board, Suggs outshone himself. To this day, some of the *bon mots* which escaped him on that occasion are remembered and repeated.

At length, after the proper quantity of champagne and oysters had been swallowed, one young gentleman arose and remarked that he had a sentiment to propose.

"I give you, Gentlemen," said he "the health of General Witherspoon! Long may he live and often may he visit our city and partake of its hospitalities!"

Thunder rolls of applause followed this toast. Suggs, as in duty bound, got up from his chair to respond.

"Gentle*men!*" said he. "Gentle*men*, I'm devilish glad to see you all and much obliged to you, besides. You are the finest people I ever was amongst and treat me a damned sight better than they do at home!"—Which was a fact. "However, I'm a poor hand to speak, but here's wishin luck to you all. And if I forget you," he said, seeming to blunder in his speech, "I'm damned if you ever forget me!"

Again there was a mixed noise of human voices, plates, knives and forks, glasses, and fine bottles, and then the company voted to disperse, all agreeing on the noble-hearted qualities of General Thomas Witherspoon.

As Simon and James Peyton passed out, the bar keeper handed the former a slip of paper containing such items as:

27 dozen of oysters	$27.00
2 cases of Champagne	$36.00

It made a grand total of sixty-three dollars.

Suggs nodded to Mr. Peyton and observed, "You'll attend to this?"

James Peyton declared his entire willingness to do so, and the pair walked out and bent their way to the stage office where the Greensboro coach was already drawn up. Simon wouldn't wake the hotel keeper to get his saddlebags, because, he said, he would probably return in a day or two.

"Jeemes," he said, as he held the young man's hand, "Jeemes, has your mother bought her pork yet?"

"No, sir," said Peyton. "You know you told me to take *ten* of your hogs. Don't you recollect?"

"Don't do that," said Simon sternly.

Peyton stood aghast. "Why, sir?" he asked.

"Take *TWENTY!*" said Suggs. And, wringing the hand he held, he bounced into the coach and was whirled away.

1846

Somebody in My Bed

ANONYMOUS

As I continued, the Captain's interest in my story mounted. His eyes bulged as I recounted how, when I returned to my room at the tavern, through some mistake a strange girl had been given my room and was soundly asleep on what should have been my bed.

"I gazed at her," said I, "and thought I had never witnessed anything more beautiful. From underneath a little night cap, rivalling the snow in whiteness, fell a stray ringlet over a neck and shoulders of alabaster."

"Well?" said the Captain, giving his chair a hitch.

"Never did I look upon a bust more perfectly formed. I took hold of the coverlet and softly pulled it down."

"Well!" said the Captain, betraying excitement.

"To her waist—" said I.

"Well!" said the Captain, dropping his newspaper.

"She had on a nightdress, buttoned up before—but softly I opened the first two buttons."

"Well!!!" said the Captain, wrought to the highest pitch.

"Then," said I, "ye gods! What a sight to gaze upon! Words fail! Just then——"

"WELL!!!" said the Captain, hitching his chair right and left, and squirting his tobacco juice against the stove so that it fairly sizzled.

"Then," I said, "I thought I was taking a mean advantage of her, so I went and slept in another room."

"It's a lie!" shouted the Captain, jumping up and kicking over his chair. "IT'S A LIE!"

1840's

147

The Finishing-Up Country

THOMAS BANGS THORPE

A STEAMBOAT on the Mississippi, in making its regular trips, carries between places varying from one to two thousand miles apart. As these boats advertise to land passengers and freight at "all intermediate landings," the heterogeneous character of the passengers can scarcely be imagined by one who has never seen it with his own eyes. Starting from New Orleans in one of these boats, you will find yourself associated with everything from the wealthy Southern planter and a venerable bishop, to desperate gamblers, peddlers of tin-ware from New England, land speculators and honest farmers, and a great variety of men from upriver sections—Wolverines, Suckers, Hoosiers, Buckeyes, and Corncrackers, besides a plentiful sprinkling of the half-horse, half-alligator species peculiar to the margins of the Old Mississippi.

One of the latter I encountered on one occasion when I took passage from New Orleans on board the *Invincible*. I had settled in the cabin to read the latest newspaper, while the mixed company around me were launched in conversation, when we were startled by a loud Indian whoop, uttered in the social hall, that part of the cabin fitted off for a bar. Then there was a loud rooster crowing, and the hero of these windy accomplishments thrust his head into the cabin and hallooed out:

"Hurrah for the Big Bar of Arkansaw!"

All conversation dropped in the cabin. In the midst of surprise, the Big Bar walked in. Clad in rough homespun clothing, dyed a dingy brown from the steepings of butternut bark, he was tall and big of bone, with clay-colored, leathery skin, and a mass of lank, oily black locks over his knobby face—a face rather Indian-looking than otherwise. Obviously he had been taking more than several horns of baldfaced ruin at the bar, and

148

was in a genial mood. He took a chair, put his feet on the stove, and looking back over his shoulder, passed the general and familiar salute of:

"Strangers, how are you?" He then expressed himself as being as much at home as if he had been at "the Forks of Cypress Creek, and perhaps a little more so."

Some of the gentlemen, at this familiarity from a backcountry squatter, looked a little angry, and some astonished. But in a moment every face was eased in a smile. Something about the Big Bar won the heart on sight.

He had been to New Orleans, on some concern of his. He hadn't particularly cared for the great city and vowed he never intended making another visit "in a crow's life." Possibly he had been taken in on some deal with the clever city merchants. Certainly, as he said, he had more than once been called "green."

"That's no matter," he said. "*They* are the *real* know-nothings. They are as green as a pumpkin vine. Why, they couldn't in farming, I bet, raise a crop of turnips. And as for shooting, they'd miss a barn if the door was swinging."

After rambling on with some more of the same, he puzzled about what the New Orleans gentlemen called game. "Birds and such they call game. Why, strangers, if you asked me how we got our *meat* at home, I'd give you a list of varments that would make a caravan, beginning with the bar and ending with the wildcat. That's meat, though—not game. Game, indeed! A bird is too trifling. I never shot at but one. I'd never forgiven myself for that if it'd weighed less than forty pounds. I wouldn't draw a rifle on anything less than that—and when I meet with another wild turkey of that weight, I'll drop him."

"A wild turkey weighing forty pounds?" exclaimed twenty voices in the cabin at once.

"Yes, strangers, and wasn't he a whopper?"

"Where did all that happen?" asked a cynical-looking Hoosier.

"Happen! Happened in Arkansaw. Where else could it have happened but in the creation state, the finishing-up country—a state where the soil runs down to the center of the earth and the government gives you a title to every inch of it. And its airs! Why, stranger, just breathe Arkansaw air and it will make you snort like a horse. It's a state without a fault, it is!"

"Excepting mosquitoes!" exclaimed the Hoosier.

"Well, stranger, excepting them. For it is a fact that they are rather enormous and do push themselves in somewhat troublesome. But, stranger, they never stick twice in the same place. Give them a fair chance for a few months and you will get as much above noticing them as a alligator. Mosquitoes is nature and I never find fault with her. If they are large, Arkansaw is large, her varments are large, her trees are large, her rivers are large. A small mosquito would be of no more use in Arkansaw than preaching in a cane-brake."

This argument used the Hoosier up, and the Arkansawyer started on a new track to explain how numerous bear were in his diggings, where he represented them to be "about as plenty as blackberries, and a little plenti-fuller."

A timid little man inquired if the bear in Arkansaw ever attacked the settlers in numbers?

"No," said our hero, warming up to the subject. "No, stranger, for you see it ain't the nature of bar to go in droves, but they squander about in pairs and singles. And then, the way I hunt them—the old black rascals know the crack of my gun as well as they know a pig's squealing.

"That gun of mine is a perfect *epidemic among bar*. If not watched closely, it will go off as quick on a warm scent as my dog Bowie-knife will. Whew! Why, that dog thinks the world is full of bar, he finds them so easy. It's lucky he don't talk as well as think. For, with his natural modesty, if he should suddenly learn how much he is above all other dogs in the universe, he would be astonished to death in two minutes.

"Strangers, that dog knows a bar's way as well as a horse-jockey knows a woman's. He always barks at the right time, bites at the exact place, and whips without getting a scratch. I never could tell whether he was made expressly to hunt bar, or whether bar was made expressly for him to hunt. Anyhow, I believe they were ordained to go together."

"What season of the year do your hunts take place?" inquired a gentle-man.

"The season for bar hunting, stranger," said the man of Arkansaw, "is generally all the year round, and the hunts take place about as regular. I read that varments have their fat season and their lean season. That is not the case in Arkansaw. Feeding as they do on the spontaneous productions of the soil, they have one continued fat season the year round—though in winter, critters is rather more *greasy* than in summer, I admit.

"For that reason, Arkansaw bar *run* in warm weather, but in winter—which is the fat season in other places—here they only *waddle*. Fat, fat! It's the enemy to speed, it tames everything that has plenty of it. Run an Arkansaw bar in his fat condition, and the way it improves the critter for eating is amazing. It sort of mixes the oil up with the meat till you can't tell t'other from which. I've done this often.

"I recollect one purty morning in particular. I put an old he-fellow on the stretch, and considering the weight he carried, he run well. But the dogs soon tired him down, and when I came up with him, wasn't he in a beautiful sweat! And then to see his tongue sticking out of his mouth a foot, and his sides sinking and opening like a bellows, and his cheeks so fat he couldn't look cross! In this fix, I blazed at him. Pitch me naked in a briar patch, if the steam didn't spout out of that bullet hole ten foot in a straight line! I have no doubt, if that bar had kept on two miles further, his insides would have been stewed. And I expect to meet with a varment yet, of extra bottom, who will run himself into a skinful of bar's grease, ready for use."

"Whereabouts are these bears so abundant?" inquired the gentleman, with increasing interest.

"Why, stranger, in the neighborhood of my settlement, one of the purtiest places on Old Mississippi—a perfect location, and no mistake. It's a place had some defects until the river made the cut-off at Shirttail Bend, and that remedied the evil. It brought my cabin on the edge of the river—a great advantage, I tell you. You can now roll a barrel of whiskey into my yard in high water from a boat, as easy as falling off a log. It's a great improvement. Taking it by hand in a jug overland, as I used to do, *evaporated* it too fast, and it became expensive.

"Stranger, just stop with me a month or two, or a year, if you like, and you will appreciate the place. I can give you plenty to eat. Besides hog and hominy, you can have bar ham and bar sausages, and a mattress of bar skins to sleep on, and a wildcat skin, pulled off whole, stuffed with corn shucks, for a pillow. That bed would put you to sleep if you had rheumatics in every joint of your body. I call that bed a *quietus*.

"Then look at my land—the government hasn't got another such piece to dispose of. Such timber and such bottom land! I once planted in those diggings a few potatoes and beets. They took a fine start, and about that time I went to Old Kentucky on business. Didn't hear from them growing things in three months, when I stumbled on a fellow that had stopped at my place with an idea of buying me out.

" 'How did you like things?' said I.

" 'Purty well,' said he. 'The cabin is convenient and the timber land is good. But the bottom land ain't worth the first red cent.'

" 'Why?' said I.

" 'Because it's full of cedar stumps and Indian mounds,' said he. 'It can't be cleared.'

" 'Lord!' said I. 'Them cedar stumps is beets and them Indian mounds is tater hills.'

"You see, the crop was overgrown in my absence. The soil in Arkansaw is *too* rich. Planting in Arkansaw can be dangerous.

"I had a good-sized sow killed in that same bottom land. The old thief stole an ear of corn and took it down where she slept at night to eat. Well, she left a grain or two on the ground, and lay down on them. Before morning the corn shot up, and the percussion killed her dead.

"So, I don't plant any more in that rich Arkansaw land. Nature intended Arkansaw for a hunting ground, and I don't go against nature."

Hoosiers, Buckeyes, Suckers, Corncrackers, gentlemen, merchants, and thieves of all descriptions, within and without the Law—none had the temerity to gainsay the climactic pronouncement of the man from the finishing-up country. There was nothing else *to* be said.

1850's

Shaking Hands

Edward Everett

THERE are few things of more common occurrence than shaking hands. Yet I do not recollect that much has been written on the subject.

Among the ancients, I have been unable to find any distinct mention of *shaking hands*. They joined but did not shake them. Although I find frequently such phrases as *jungere dextras hospitio,* I do not recollect to have met with that of *agitare dextras*. I am inclined to think that the practice grew up in the age of chivalry when the cumbrous iron mail in which the knights were cased prevented their embracing and when, with fingers clothed in steel, the simple touch or joining of fingers would have been but cold welcome. A prolonged junction was a natural result to express cordiality. As it would have been awkward to keep the hands unemployed in this position, a gentle agitation or shaking might have been naturally introduced.

How long the practice may have remained in this rudimental stage, it is impossible in the silence of history to say. There is nothing enabling us to trace the progress of the art into the forms in which it now exists among us. I shall pass immediately to the enumeration of these forms.

1. The *pump-handle* shake is the first that deserves notice. It is executed by taking your friend's hand and working it up and down through an arc of fifty degrees for about a minute and a half. To have its true nature, force, and distinctive character, this shake should be performed with a fair, steady motion. No attempt should be made to give it grace, and still less vivacity. The few instances in which the latter has been tried have universally resulted in dislocating the shoulder of the person on whom it has been attempted. On the contrary, persons who are partial to the *pump-handle* shake should be at some pains to give it an equable, tranquil

movement, which should on no account be continued after perspiration on the part of your friend has commenced.

2. The *pendulum* shake may be mentioned next, as being somewhat similar in character, but moving, as the name indicates, in a horizontal direction. It is executed by sweeping your hand horizontally toward your friend's and, after the junction is effected, rowing with it from one side to the other, according to the pleasure of the parties. The only caution in its use, which needs particularly to be given, is not to insist on performing it in a plane strictly parallel with the horizon when you meet a person who has been educated to the *pump-handle* shake. I had two uncles, both estimable men, one of whom had been brought up in the *pump-handle* shake, and the other had brought home the *pendulum shake* from a foreign voyage. They met, joined hands, and attempted to put them in motion. They were neither of them feeble men. One endeavored to pump and the other to paddle. Their faces reddened, the drops stood on their foreheads. It was at last a pleasing illustration of the doctrine of the adjustment of forces to see their hands slanting into an exact diagonal—in which line they ever afterward shook. But it was plain to see there was no cordiality in it, as is usually the case with compromises.

3. The *tourniquet* shake derives its name from the instruments made use of by surgeons to stop the circulation of the blood in a limb about to be amputated. It is performed by clasping the hand of your friend as far as you can in your own and then contracting the muscles of your thumb, fingers, and palm to produce the proper degree of pressure. Particular care ought to be taken, if your own hand is as hard and big as a frying pan and that of your friend as small and soft as a young maiden's, not to make use of the *tourniquet* shake to the degree that will force the small bones of the wrist out of place. A hearty young friend of mine who had pursued the study of geology and acquired an unusual hardness and strength of hand and wrist by the use of the hammer, on returning from a scientific excursion, gave his gouty uncle the *tourniquet* shake with such severity that my young friend had the satisfaction of being disinherited as soon as the uncle got well enough to hold a pen.

4. The *cordial grapple* is a shake of some interest. It is a hearty, boisterous agitation of your friend's hand, accompanied with moderate pressure and loud, cheerful exclamations of welcome. It is an excellent traveling shake and well adapted to make friends.

5. The *grievous touch* is opposed to the *cordial grapple*. It is a pensive

junction followed by a mild, subsultory motion, a cast-down look, and an inarticulate inquiry after your friend's health.

6. The *prude major* and *prude minor* are nearly monopolized by ladies. They cannot be accurately described but are constantly noticed in practice. They never extend beyond the fingers and the *prude major* allows you to touch even them only down to the second joint. The *prude minor* gives you the whole of the forefinger.

I might go through a long list of the *grip-royal,* the *sawmill* shake, and the shake with *malice aforethought,* but these are only combinations of the three fundamental forms already described as the *pump-handle,* the *pendulum,* and the *tourniquet.* In like manner, the *loving pat,* the *reach romantic,* and the *sentimental clasp* may be reduced in their main movements to various combinations of the last three types given in the list.

I should trouble you with a few remarks in conclusion on the mode of shaking hands as an indication of character, but through my study window I see a friend coming up the avenue. He is addicted to the *pump-handle.* I dare not tire my wrist by further writing.

1850

Whar Joe Went To

Anonymous

WIDOW Harris, the hostess of the Sign of the Buck tavern, was sitting on her porch stringing dried slips of pumpkin when she saw a traveller on horseback approaching. "I do believe that's Bill Meriweather," said she. "It's about time for him and Joe to come round agin a-buyin shoats. But whar's Joe? Whar on earth is Joe?"

Now, she was about the most *searching* old lady in the whole of southern Kentucky, and she was a-tremble with curiosity when Mr. Meriweather rode up and she called out, "How do you do, Bill Meriweather?"

"Lively," said he, dismounting. "How do you come on yourself, old woman?"

"Pretty well, Bill—but whar's Joe?"

Up to this time, Mr. Meriweather had been as pleasant and jovial a looking Green River man as you might find in a week's ride. But no sooner did the old lady fire her question—and he knew from experience that she would not let up till she pried loose a detailed answer—no sooner did she put her breathless, "Whar's Joe?" than he gave her an imploring look of despair, dropped on the porch bench beside her, let his head fall into his open palms, and uttered a great sigh.

"Merciful heavens! What can the matter be?" exclaimed the old lady, now thoroughly excited. "Is thar anything the matter with Joe?"

Mr. Meriweather could only shake his head, moaning, "Poor Joe! Poor Joe!"

"Whar *is* Joe?" said the widow, now beside herself. "Is he sick?"

"Oh-h no," said the brother faintly.

Was Joe dead, the Lord ha' mercy on our sinful souls? Had he gone to Orleans or Californy? *Whar* was Joe?

At each query Mr. Meriweather groaned and shook his head.

"Then," said the old lady tartly, "*do* tell a body what's become of him!"

"Well, you see, Mrs. Harris," replied Mr. Meriweather, interrupting his narrative with sighs and groans, "Joe and I went up early in the spring to get a flatboat load of rock from Boone County to put up the foundation of the new house we're a-building, for there ain't any rock down in them rich soily bottoms in our parts. Well, we managed to get our boat loaded and started home.

"You never did see anything rain like it did that first day. We didn't have any shelter on the flat, so when we tied up at sundown we raised a rousing big fire on the bank and cooked some grub. Well, I'd eaten a matter of two pounds of sidemeat and half of a possum, and was a-setting on a log smoking and a-talking to Brother Joe. He was standing chock up agin the fire, with his back to it, a-drying out. You recollect, Mrs. Harris, what a dressy sort of chap Joe was?"

"Lord ha' mercy, yes! He was a fine little feller."

"Well, Brother Joe was always fond of brass buttons on his coat and the flaringest kind of red neckerchers, and this time he had on a pair of buckskin breeches, with straps under his boots to hold them down tight. So when I was a-talking to him of the prospects of the next day, all of a sudden I thought the little feller was a-growing uncommon tall—till I diskivered that the buckskin breeches, that were as wet as a young rooster in a spring rain, were beginning to smoke and draw up, kind of, and were a-lifting Brother Joe off the ground.

" 'Brother Joe,' says I, 'you're a-going up.'

" 'Brother,' says he, 'I ain't a-doing anything else.'

"And he scrunched down mighty hard, but it warn't of any use, for before long he was a matter of some fifteen foot up in the air."

"Merciful powers!" gasped Widow Harris.

" 'Brother Joe,' says I.

" 'I'm here,' says he.

" 'Catch hold of the top of that blackjack oak,' says I.

"And he sort of leaned over and grabbed the sapling like as maybe you've seed a squirrel haul in an elm switch of a June morning. But it warn't of any use, Mrs. Harris, if you'll believe me, for it gradually begun to give way at the roots, and before he'd got five foot higher, it just split out of the ground as easy as you'd pull a spring raddish.

" 'Brother Joe,' says I.

" 'I'm a-listening,' says he.

" 'Cut the straps to them buckskin breeches,' says I, for I seed it was his last chance.

"He looked sort of reproachful at me. The dressy little chap hated to spoil his new breeches, but after awhile he outs with his jack-knife, and leaning over sideways, made a rip at the strap across the sole of his left boot. There was a considerable degree of crackling for a second or two, then a crash, sort of like as if a load of cord wood had broke down, as that left breeches leg snapped up to where it wanted to shrink to, and the first thing I knowed t'*other* leg shot up like, and started him—and the last I seed of Brother Joe, he was *whirling round like a four-spoked wheel with the rim off, away down close toward sundown!*"

1850

Fare You Well, Joe Clark

ANONYMOUS

H<small>E WAS</small> the fondest man of a bird, Joe Clark was, you ever see. No man in North Carolina fancied the birds more than Joe did. From the time he was a little feller, paddling round in the dust before his pa's cabin, as naked as a jaybird, he fancied all flying things. He thought wings was the wonder of this world.

Any time, he'd leave off suckling of his mammy, or eating stripe candy, or hoeing the corn to watch a flock of parakeets, or put his head back and foller the turkey buzzard, drifting so high and free up yonder as slow as thought.

"I'd druther be a bird," he says, "and make gay in the cool air than be a royal king with a crown of gold." Anybody had them sort of druthers was plentiful tuck with the birds.

It may be he had bird-nature borned into him. People, the old folks that knowed him, said he even favored a bird, his looks did. They said he was a small-made feller, with a little picky way of walking about, and eyes as bright as a field-sparrer's, and a way of holding his head to one side, observing—and sort of spurts of straw-colored hair sticking out round his head like the feathers of a nestling.

After his mammy and his pa was tuck off, Joe he never was caught at any useful work no more. The little old cabin and the three or four acres went to wreck and ruin, and the weeds and grass rolled over everything. Generally you could find Joe Clark, night or day, rambling round studying of the birds. In daytime it was the flocking pigeons, hawks, the sassy jays or the old scamp crows, and the small change of the other day-flyers like chickadees, sapsuckers, mocking birds, and so forth. At night when the moon was riding over the world, he liked to perch hisself onto a high limb where he could keep a look-out for owls and whippoorwills, night hawks, and them lost-sounding killdees. Never could just seem to fill up on the birds, Joe couldn't.

Seemed to Joe Clark that flying was the topmost of all the gifts the Lord had fetch on for His created things.

Preacher Milroy said, when Joe one Sunday backed him into a Scriptural corner, he said, "I am a learned man in the testaments. His name be praised! He has give the sons of old Daddy Adam dominion over the lands of the earth and the waters of the briny deep."

"But," says Joe Clark, "it don't exactly look to me like we are in as good favor before the throne as the birds."

The preacher he throwed up his palms and he said, "Study sin, young man. Sin is more profitable to study, for His ways are surely not our'n. The Devil puts questions in our mouth. Do you flip cards, my son? Do you tread the wicked mazy dance? Do you covet your neighbor's handmaiden and his ox?"

"No, sir," says Joe, "but I'd admire to know why folks can't fly round in the air like the birds?"

"We are but poor worms in the dust," says the preacher, "and all flesh is grass. It's no use frittering your wits away in vain envy of the birds of passage. There is wings prepared for the deserving in the great hereafter. If 'twas intended for us to fly in the flesh, it stands to reason our arms'd be feathered out with pinions like unto the eagle. There is some things here below, son, as we wasn't meant to poke into."

It didn't rightly look like anybody'd be as mulish as to fly into the face of them sort of reverend facts. But just then nobody was minding Joe Clark, because everybody, nigh about, was hit by two fevers.

One was the gold fever. Everybody was powerful tuck with California. It was said, the word passed round, that out there gold just bust out of the dirt. If a feller was to stump his toe and fall flat on his face, they said, when he got up, all he had to do was brush his whiskers and enough gold dust sifted out to buy a rich little valley farm.

Men got in a terrible sweat to put out for California, and them that could, they went. Them that their women wouldn't let 'em go, caught the other fever, the gambling complaint. They couldn't set still hardly, they got so unrestless. Even the steadiest kind of family men'd sneak off to the crossroads and fall into pitching dollars with the gambling, drinking set.

The chiefest feller to hang out round the crossroads was Joe Clark. Looked like he'd gone into the business of watching dollar-pitching instead of the birds. Watching was all, too. He never had even a half-dime to pitch.

The way to pitch dollars is, you draw a line in the dust, then measure off eighteen paces and make another line. That's where you toe up and pitch at the first line. The feller who his dollar is nighest the line takes all.

Well, sir, it got so there was a scrap every time dollars was pitched, almost. Each time the men crowded up to measure whose dollar was nighest, somebody's dollar was missing. Didn't matter, though, how sharp everybody looked to see if any feller stooped and snatched, nobody done so, but a dollar, and sometimes two dollars, was missing.

It sounded like a bewitchment, till some boy he happened to notice Joe Clark before the pitching commenced. Joe was hid behind a tree. He was putting a ball of the stickiest stuff on earth on each heel of his boots, mashing it down. It was tar, is what—tar from good old North Carolina pine trees, the best tar of all for putting on your boots and walking among silver dollars.

The fellers laid hands on Joe Clark and it looked bad for him. He never said a word, but there was a man there, he was venerable in years and hog-rich, and he said, "Boys, let's not make no haste here. We all know as Joe Clark is bird-brained. His mind goes kind of counter-clockwise. More than that, this prank of his'n has made me laugh, and things on this world being like they are, I disremember if I've ever laughed out loud since forty years now."

One of the drinking set he up and said money was money, and he couldn't spare the dollars Joe Clark had walked off with, stuck to his heels. He says all the signs pointed to a cowhiding.

But the old man held up his hand and laughed two or three times so everybody could see he was laughing. He says he'd always heard it called the Tar Heel State, but though he carried more years than anybody there, he'd never heard why. When anybody had asked him, he'd have to own he didn't know. Now, says he, he could give a good answer, when somebody pried into why North Carolina is the Tar Heel State.

"It's worth a hatful of silver to me," he says. "You all boys just please to turn Joe here aloose, and, as I'm a rich man, I'll make up everybody's losses, including the claims of the rogues that lost nothing, providing they're reasonable. I've got money to throw to the birds, if the birds isn't too greedy."

The fellers dropped off Joe, then and there, and he made tracks. He never showed up again at a dollar-pitching no more. Fact is, the two dollars he got away with that day was just exactly enough to round out the sum of money he figured he needed.

Next time anybody saw him, he was coming from town, beat out and tired. He was rolling a hogshead of tar he'd bought with his money, and it was uphill work.

Preacher Milroy was walking along, keeping to the shade and fanning hisself with his hat.

"I do declare," he says, "if it ain't Joe Clark. Praise be to his name, Joe, what on earth are you doing out in the heat of the day like you are, rolling that hogshead of tar up the side of the mountain?"

"I'm going to California," says Joe, straining away at the barrel.

"Ah, yes, blessed be His mercy," says the preacher. "So many is tearing off to them parts these days. Going to California. But it looks like a tar barrel."

"Yes, sir, it does," says Joe. "It's just the way tar barrels looks."

The preacher he sort of fell into step with Joe, and he says, "Now, let's see if we can't pull ourself together, Joe. May His grace shower upon us, I thought I heard you say going to California."

"Yes, sir, preacher, that's where I'm headed."

"Going to sell tar to the wicked miners, heaven look down?"

"No, sir," says Joe, sweating away and pushing. "Not that I know of."

"Mercy on a sinful world, son. Then what are you fixing to do with all this tar you are pushing up the side of the mountain?"

"Well," says Joe, "I'm going to fly to California. It'll be quicker."

Preacher Milroy he commenced helping Joe heave away at the hogshead of tar. "Is that a clear fact?" he says. "Well, now, grant us vision. Going to fly to California. To be sure, to be sure. You're *going to what?*"

"Fly."

"Will wonders never cease, are you back onto the birds again, Joe? I thought I'd settled that novelty plumb out of your silly head, son. You don't mean to begin to tell me, poor boy, that you aim to fly to California on some bird with a big hogshead of Carolina tar on your back?"

"No, sir. With my own wings. I've already fixed up some frames, so now all I need is to get me enough feathers and stick 'em on the wing-frames which I have made, with the sort of tar that won't come unstuck, and let 'em set, and then start out into flying. I mean to put out long before the snow flies, because a man can fly better if he's not hindered with any cold weather fixings."

The preacher he stopped pushing at the barrel. He set down squat in the middle of the road, holding his hat over his head to shade it.

"Joe Clark, son," he says, "from time unto time, the uncharitable has spoke of you as bird-brained. I know you can't be all that bird-brained. Therefore, Joe, as the Everlasting sees me, all of this is something I happen to be dreaming, because I must have been knocked down of the heat and the summer sun. So, by your leave, I'll just be going on home now. It's easy to see I'm noway in my right mind."

When the preacher made it home, he tuck to his bed and got his wife to draw the blinds and keep wet cloths on his head and let him smell camphor, and never said a word to nobody.

A few days after, it having come on a rain and a freshening wind, he felt it was safe for him to get out of doors again, and he went up on the mountain to see after Joe. For that good old man of God wasn't noways satisfied. He'd never been told of any heat-dream like unto the one he'd had. It had left his hands, where he'd had a dream of helping out Joe to push the hogshead, all gummed up with tar that his wife had to scrub off with turpentime.

Up on the mountain he met up with Joe, where he was hid among the weeds and the saplings that had thrived right up against the back door of what dry rot had left standing of the cabin. Joe was setting on the ground beside of two monstrous great wings of wood and weaved straw, with leather sleeves on 'em. Joe was dabbing of hot tar on them wings, and just as careful as a woman piecing a quilt, he was arranging the feathers of birds in place.

"How do you come on, preacher?" says Joe. "Like you can see, I'm most done with my wings here, even if I am running sort of scarce of feathers just now. I need a various few more of 'em, and then I'm on my way."

Preacher Milroy he never said a word, not one frazzling word. He just spun hisself round like a child's top, and he tucked his head low, and felt his way down the mountain like a blind man lost from his bearings. He never told nobody about what he thought he'd seen or what he figgered he'd heard Joe Clark say, the preacher didn't, till nigh a week after. He wasn't just sure in his mind whether all this was so, or some terror his own mind had cooked up to tempt him to the Devil. He was a man which he had so many times warned the people against tale-carrying.

But everybody begun to get stirred up. There was commotions among poultry. Something was chasing their ducks, hens, and geese of nights. One morning the preacher missed his own big old gobbler. He hunted high and low, and never found him till he craned his neck over a big log. There crouched the old gobbler, low against the ground, ashamed to come out into the open because his handsome tail-feathers he used for strutting had been snatched out bald.

Well, Preacher Milroy got up in the pulpit with a heavy heart the next Sunday. Though he said he grieved to do it, he made the people plain as to who was out plucking their fowls and why he was doing it.

"Nor that ain't all," an old granny woman got up and says in meeting. "My eyes is dim, but I can see some things. Yesterday, forenoon, I was out on the mountain, gathering of my yerbs and doctorments, being as my stocks is running low because it has been so much summer complaint and bold hives this season. I worked up the ridge, gathering and putting away, when right on the point of the ridge I see something I never heard of before."

"Say on, Sister Mayberry," says the preacher.

Says old Mrs. Mayberry, shaking her head and shooting up her eyes, "It was poor little old Joe Clark, him I delivered into this sad world of troubles, no other! He was up nigh to the top of that dead granddaddy of an old he-balsam, astraddle there, and hammering away like a pecker-wood starved.

"When I up and says, lawful mercy on this living earth, Joe? he says he was just putting up of his platform. When I says, awful day of judgment, was he aiming to stand up there on the tip of the world and preach to the birds? he says no, he was fixing hisself a handy place where, poor boy, he could slip his wings onto his arms and put out for California.

" 'You watch a turkey buzzard, granny,' says he to me, down where I was standing with my head turned up. 'You observe any of them heavy kind of birds like I have been doing since I can remember. They're neat in the air, but get 'em on the ground, then what? Comes time to wing it, and they are punished to pull off. A turkey buzzard or even a king eagle, they hobble round till they find theirself some little rise in the ground to leap off'n.

" 'Well, Granny, I've figgered it all out,' he says, never leaving off his hammering a minute. 'I'm heap heavier than any turkey buzzard I ever met. I need me a real high place like this plank platform I've just about fin-ished nailing here on this tall limb of the old he-balsam, if I aim to get a good start migrating to California like I'm going to do tomorrow morning. I'll wave down below at your house tomorrow when I pass over, Mrs. Mayberry. So watch out for me.'

"As truth is my witness," says the granny, "them was the very words the poor little feller spoke to me."

Preacher Milroy broke up meeting for everybody to take out for the mountain to head off Joe from dashing his pitiful self onto the rocks.

The preacher he was fat, but not that broke of his wind that he didn't run over all but the leanest and spryest stripling boys. He tore along, praying, and crying aloud what a sin and a shame it was nobody had tuck no steps till now to save that orphanless boy from his wild self.

Oh, what a scrambling, such tears! up that mountainside, till the preacher who was way apast the most nimblest, he shouted to the others that prayers is always answered.

"Look up yonder!" says he. "It's Joe on his he-balsam. He isn't jumped yet that I can see."

Well, sir, sure enough, there Joe he stood up on that platform he'd made. He was on the edge of his platform, fanning the air easy and slow with his monstrous wings like an old hen does to cool herself off.

Then the preacher made a trumpet of his hands, and he shouted up into the air where Joe was teetering, "Don't you never do it! Joe Clark, I knowed your daddy and your mammy before you was ever thought of. So just you set down where you are on that platform up in that high old he-balsam tree like I tell you till help gets a chance to climb up that tree to you."

Joe up there flipped one of his wings up to his ear. "Can't hear exactly what you say!" he yells down, with his voice high and thin. "But it does my heart good to look down there on the side of the mountain and see all my friends and neighbors all foregathering for to fare me well. Even if you do look like bugs, I thank you!"

"Hold fast there, my Joe!" shouts the preacher. "Rest easy till we climb up nigh enough to talk it over with you."

"Much oblige!" Joe yells back. "I wish you fare you well, also."

Then the preacher and all the good people, they give down on their knees and raised a prayer to the heavens, for Joe they see was on his toe-tips with his wings working faster and faster, till he lent out into the gulf of empty air. They let out one big groan and popped their hand over their eyes, while Preacher Milroy said rest and peace to his bird-brained, poor little soul.

That's the way it generally is. People won't listen to reason when they see it. There's my second daughter's husband, he that come up here from

Casual County. Last week he was laying in of his winter's wood, and I says to him, "Elijah, you are going to need half that much again."

"Why so, old man?" he says.

"Boy," I says, "it's going to be a mean winter. All season I've been noticing the signs. The white-faced hornets is building their nests," I says, "a good three or four foot off the ground, so as to get high enough on the weed-stalks to clear the coming snow. Then, you look at the hickernuts. Their hulls is thick, and squirrels is furred like a feather bed——"

But Elijah just throwed up his head and laughed at an old man like me. *Who? Joe Clark?*

Why, nothing could happened to him but what did happen. There couldn't be no two ways about it. No man could have studied and worked on it as hard as Joe done and not fly. *He flew to California, of course.*

The next word anybody in North Carolina ever heard of him was the rumor gold was so rich in California that a man could just up and walk through another feller's claim and pick up a little fortune on his boots.

What with the wear and tear of getting there, I guess Joe Clark needed hisself a new pair of wings.

1870's

Up to the Lord

JOHNSON J. HOOPER

IT CAME to pass that Brother Crump, a leading Hardshell Baptist, during the liveliest period of the cotton season, drove to Wetumpka and disposed of his crop of ten bales at the very fair price of 12½ cents per pound. It was more than Brother Crump expected, and as the world was easy with him, he determined to invest, and did actually invest, a portion of the proceeds in a barrel of whiskey, paying therefor at the rate of precisely two pounds of middling cotton for one gallon of ditto whiskey.

Of course, it was norated in the settlement that Old Man Crump had bought a whole barrel, and after a few weeks people began to observe that his nose grew redder and his eye more moist.

Sore troubled was Brother Noel, a fellow Hardshell and intimate of Brother Crump. So one morning he stepped over to Brother Crump's and found the old man in a half doze on his little porch.

As soon as he was aware of the presence of his neighbor, Brother Crump asked, "Won't you take a dram?"

"Why, yes, I'm not agin a dram when a body wants it."

Brother Crump got his bottle, and the friends took a dram apiece.

"Don't you think, Brother Noel," said Crump, "that spirits is a blessing?"

"Y-e-s!" responded Noel. "Spirits is a blessing, but according to my notion, it's a blessing that some of us abuses."

"Well, now, Brother Noel, *who* do you think abuses the blessing?"

"Well, it's hard to say—but people talk—and don't you think *you* drink too much, Brother Crump?"

"It's hard to say—it's hard to say," returned Crump. "Sometimes I've thought I *was* drinking too much. Then, agin, I'd think *maybe not.* What is man? A weak *worm* of the dust! What the Lord saith, that shall be done! So I left it to the Lord, Brother Noel, to say whether I was going too far in spirits. I put the whole responsibility on him. I prayed to him, if I was drinking too much, to *take away my appetite for spirits.*"

Here Brother Noel groaned piteously, and asked, "What *then*, Brother Crump?"

"And," replied Crump, "I've prayed that prayer three times, and——— HE HAIN'T DONE IT!"

1851

Going to Bed Before a Young Lady

Attributed to Stephen A. Douglas

As I was saying, ten years ago, Judge Stephen A. Douglas, of Illinois, was a beardless youth of twenty years of age, freshly come amongst the people of the Sucker State, with an air about him suspiciously redolent of Yankeeland. He had come on business. A political fortune was to be made, and no time lost. He was about launching on the sea of popular favour, and he commenced a general survey the day he arrived. He soon made himself District Attorney, member of the Legislature, Register of the U. S. Land Office, Secretary of State, and Judge of the Supreme Court.

"How do you adapt yourself," said I, "Judge, to the people? How did you 'naturalize' yourself, as it were?"

"Oh, nothing easier; you see I like it. It's democratic. But it did come awkward at first. You know I am, or rather was, bashful to rather a painful degree. Well, now, nine-tenths of my constituents despise luxuries, and have no such thing as a second room in their houses. In beating up votes, I live with my constituents, eat with my constituents, drink with them, lodge with them, pray with them, laugh, hunt, dance and work with them; I eat their corn dodgers and fried bacon, and sleep two in a bed with them. Among my first acquaintances were the L——s, down under the Bluffs. Fine fellows, the L——s,—by the way, I am sure of five votes there. Well, you perceive, I had to live there: and I did live there. But, sir, I was frightened the first night I slept there. I own it; yes, sir, I acknowledge the corn. An ice in August is something: but I was done to an icicle; had periodical chills for ten days. Did you ever see a Venus in linsey-woolsey?"

"No!"

"Then you shall see Serena L——s. They call her the 'White Plover'; seventeen:—plump as a pigeon, and smooth as a persimmon. How the devil, said I to myself, soliloquizing the first night I slept there, am I to go to bed before this young lady? I do believe my heart was topsyturvied, for the idea of pulling off my boots before the girl was death. And as to doffing my other fixtures, I would sooner have my leg taken off with a wood-saw. The crisis was tremendous. It was nearly midnight, and the family had been hours in bed. Miss Serena alone remained. Bright as the sun, the merry minx talked on. It was portentously obvious to me at last, that she had determined to outsit me. By repeated spasmodic efforts, my coat, waistcoat, cravat, boots and socks were brought off. During the process, my beautiful neighbor talked to me with unaverted eyes, and with that peculiar kind of placidity employed by painters to embody their idea of the virgin. I dumped myself down in a chair, in a cold perspiration. A distressing thought occurred to me. Does not the damsel stand on a point of local etiquette? It may be the fashion of these people to see strangers in bed before retiring themselves. May I not have kept those beautiful eyes open, from ignorance of what these people deem good breeding? Neither the lady's eyes nor tongue had indeed betrayed fatigue. Those large jet eyes seemed to dilate and grow brighter as the blaze of the wood fire died away; but doubtless this was from kind consideration for the strange wakefulness of her guest. The thing was clear. I determined to retire, and without delay. I arose with firmness, unloosed my suspenders, and in a voice not altogether steady, said:

" 'Miss Serena, I think I will retire.'

" 'Certainly, sir,' she quietly observed. 'You will lodge there, sir'; inclining her beautiful head towards a bed standing a few yards from where she was sitting. I proceeded to uncase; entrenching myself behind a chair the while, fondly imagining the position offered some security. It is simply plain to a man in his senses, that a chair of the fashion of the one I had thrown between myself and 'the enemy,' as a military man would say, offered almost no security at all. No more, in fact, than standing up behind a ladder—nothing in the way of the artillery of bright eyes, as a poet would say, sweeping one down by platoons. Then I had a dead open space of ten feet between me and the bed; a sort of Bridge of Lodi passage which I was forced to make, exposed to a cruel raking fire fore and aft. Although I say it, who should not say it, an emergency never arose for which I had not a resource. I had one for this. The plan was the work of a moment, I de——"

"Ah! I see, you stormed the battery and s—"

"Bah! don't interrupt me. No; I determined, by a bold ruse de guerre, to throw her attention out of the window, clear the perilous passage, and fortify myself under the counterpane before she recovered her surprise. The plan failed. You see I am a small man, physically speaking. Body, limbs, and head, setting up business on one hundred and seven and a half pounds, all told, of flesh, blood, and bones, cannot, individually or collectively, set up any very ostentatious pretensions. I believe the young lady must have been settling in her mind some philosophical point on that head. Perhaps her sense of justice wished to assure itself of a perfectly fair distribution of the respective motives. Perhaps she did not feel easy until she knew that a kind Providence had not added to general poverty individual wrong. Certain it was, she seemed rather pleased with her speculations; for when I arose from a stooping posture finally, wholly disencumbered of cloth, I noticed mischievous shadows playing about the corners of her mouth. It was the moment I had determined to direct her eye to some astonishing circumstance out of the window. But the young lady spoke at the critical moment.

" 'Mr. Douglas,' she observed, 'you have got a mighty small chance of legs there.'

"Men seldom have any notice of their own powers. I never made any pretensions to skill in ground and lofty tumbling; but it is strictly true, I cleared, at one bound, the open space, planted myself on the centre of the bed, and was buried in the blankets in a twinkling."

"I congratulate you, my boy," said I, poising a cube of the crimson core of the melon on the point of my knife; "a lucky escape truly! But was the young lady modest?"

"Modest, sir!—there is not in Illinois a more modest, or more sensible girl. It's habit—all habit. I think nothing of it now. Why, it's only last week I was at a fine wedding party, and a large and fine assembly of both sexes lodged in the same room, with only three feet or so of neutral territory between them."

"You astonish me, Mr. Douglas."

"Fact, sir, upon my honour. You see these people are the very soul of hospitality, and never allow a fine social party to turn out at twelve o'clock at night to go long distances home. All that is more cleverly managed here. An Illinois bed has a power of elongation or expansion perfectly enigmatical to strangers. One bed four feet wide, will, on occasion, flank one whole side of the house, and is called a field-bed, and large parties will range themselves on opposite sides of the house as economically as candles in a box."

1851

Sloshin About

ANONYMOUS

IN PIKE COUNTY there was a trial for a general row. A witness testified that one Saltonstall "jest kept sloshin about." As the remark was frequently repeated, Saltonstall's lawyer said:

"Come, witness, say over again what it was that Mr. Saltonstall had to do with the affair."

"Saltonstall? Why, I've told you several times. The rest of em clinched and paired off, but Saltonstall jest kept sloshin about."

"We want to know what that is," said the lawyer, quite testily. "It isn't exactly legal evidence in the shape you put it. Tell us what you mean by *sloshin about?*"

"Well," answered the witness, very deliberately, "I'll try. You see, John Brewer and Sykes, they clinched an fought. That's in the legal form, ain't it?"

"Oh yes, go on."

"Abney an Blackman then pitched into one another, an Blackman bit off a piece of Abney's lip. That's legal, too, ain't it?"

"Proceed."

"Well, Simpson an Bill Stones an Murray was all together on the ground, a-bitin, gougin, an a-kickin each other. That's legal, too, is it?"

"Very—but go on."

"And Saltonstall made it his business to walk backward an forward through the crowd, with a big stick in his hand, an knock down every loose man in the crowd as fast as he come to em. And *that's* what I call *sloshin about!*"

1850's

A Sleep-Walking Incident

ANONYMOUS

WHEN I was a youngster many years ago, I was sent into the upper mountain counties of this State of Tennessee, on a trip of business, which I contrived to make a trip of pleasure. Night had overtaken me some miles short of my intended stopping place. I hailed the first house I came to, a square cabin with but one apartment, which served as "parlor, hall, kitchen, and all." I asked if I could obtain shelter for myself and horse?

A stout, iron-looking little old man answered the summons. After resting his arms and chin on the gate for some seconds, he said, rather deliberately, that he "didn't exactly know, seeing as how his house was small and he had company, but seeing as how I was a benighted boy, he reckoned I might just light."

I did so, and found the house full of girls. First, there was the old woman, all tidiness and check apron, then three blooming daughters, all shyness and blushing, a married daughter and her yearling child (these were the "company" alluded to,) and then there was that everlasting, long-legged, ubiquitous eighteen-year-old boy who is to be seen at all houses in the country, with that tight roundabout, strained across his shoulder blades, and given to mixed socks and low-quartered shoes. His name was Tewalt, and I shall never forget the service he rendered me in my hour of great peril.

Supper passed off, during which and the interval preceding bedtime, I was subjected to categorical examination on matters in general, and my business in particular, the old lady acting as principal inquisitor, prompted in giggling whispers by the girls, while the married daughter nursed her yearling and tried to look matronly. Meanwhile, I counted the beds, three, all in a row across the back of the house. I counted noses and found an awful disproportion between them and the beds.

174

But just as I was getting desperate, the old lady peremptorily ordered Tewalt off to bed, then with the help of the girls made another bed into a gigantic shakedown before the fire. She managed to increase its dimensions prodigiously until it attained at least the size of an ordinary onion bed. This encampment before the fire was for the benefit of the girls, married and single, rank and file, baby and all. Thus was safely disposed of my horrid suspicion that I might have to sleep spoon-fashion with perhaps three, and the fat baby at the foot. Tewalt and I were to share one bed, the old folks the one remaining.

The old lady, considerate old soul, hung a quilt over two chairs as a kind of battery for me to undress behind, and cautioning the girls in an undertone not to look, told me I might go to bed as soon as I liked. I obeyed, and in spite of the stray eye-shots fired at me from the fireplace, and the smothered giggles, got safely to bed and was soon asleep.

. The first thing I remembered, I felt someone inflicting furious digs in my side. It struck my dreaming mind that it was Tewalt. This awoke me, and I still found the pinching going on, about 120 to the minute.

"Hello, old fellow!" says I. "That'll do. What in the name of the lunatic asylum do you want?"

"It ain't no *old* feller, an you may thank gracious goodness it ain't. But you better just git right up an mosey, afore I *call* the old feller!"

This was spoken close to one of my ears in a good round whisper. A suppressed sort of giggling sounded in the other ear. I ventured to raise my head a fraction and saw the fire was not in the place it had occupied when I went to bed. Had Tewalt turned my bed round? I listened, and the old clock had moved to another point of the compass and was boxing away. The old man's snoring, too, like the clock and fire, had changed its quarters. Well, what was the matter? Was I tight? No, I had drank nothing. Was I crazy? No, for I was fully aware of everything, save that my ideas of relative position had become confoundedly mystified.

"I say," whispered the voice in my ear, "cuss your sassy little picture, are you a-goin to leave before I call dad? For he'll fix you in a minute, an us gals couldn't save your scalp if we wanted to, little hoss."

The awful truth flashed on my mind! I had gone sleep-walking and got into bed with the girls, and would soon be a lost boy!

But my presence of mind came to my aid, so I replied to this whispered tirade by giving a heavy groaning sort of snore, and turning over from my tormentor, I reconnoitered my location by throwing out first an arm and then a leg.

The arm lit across the heaving warm breast of somebody with considerable energy, for quick as light it was seized, and no rocket ever flew with more of a vim that it did from its soft resting place, and lit smack across the face of my pinching friend, the married daughter, who was unmasked by this move of her sister, for in its descent it chanced also to hit the yearling a wipe in the neighborhood of its nose. Such a yell as followed, such a series of yells, I never before heard. My leg, I suppose, also lit upon forbidden ground, for it followed the arm, and then came a wicked sort of dig in my side, inflicted by a naked elbow.

Well, after calculating the probable location of my own bed, I made one bound which cleared me of the enemy's camp, and I lit alongside Tewalt.

"Durn your carcass," says he, "you wanted to sleep *warm*, did you, so you just goes atween the gals! They *warmed* ye, didn't they?"

A running fire of conversation was kept up between the shakedown and the old folks' bed for some time, but as it was not of a very complimentary nature, so far as I was concerned, I will not inflict upon the reader what both pained and scared me. After rolling about in a rather perturbed state of mind, I fell asleep, and was awoke by the old lady to come to breakfast. Tewalt was gone, I knew not where. The shakedown had vanished. Things looked tidy and clean.

When we set up to breakfast, the girls blushed, the married one looked serious, the old lady seemed pious, and the old man looked devilish. You may guess how I relished my breakfast. Not a word did I say, and the old lady's disposition of the previous evening to ask questions seemed to have vanished.

The meal over, I asked the old man the amount of my bill?

"I don't charge ye a cent!" This was said in a tone and manner that I neither liked nor understood.

My horse was at the gate, with Tewalt holding the bridle. I turned round to bid the girls good morning, and there they were, holding up the mantleboard with their foreheads, and seemed to be in tears. This mystified me more than ever. The old man had taken down an old blacksnakish looking rifle, and was changing the priming. Shakily I inquired if he was going to hunt?

"Y-a-s," he drawled out. "I'm a-goin to kill a mink that's been among my pullets."

Well, I didn't like *that*, either, so, without more ceremony, I started to the horse. As I left the door, I heard one of the girls (a sweet, blue-eyed damsel she was, too,) the one who had converted my arm into a projectile with such dire effect the night before, say, "Oh, daddy, now, don't! Poor little feller! Don't, daddy, don't!"

The old scoundrel growled a reply which I did not hear, and followed me.

When I reached my horse and mounted, Tewalt, who stood on the off side of the horse, drew from the leg of his breeches a long, keen hickory, and stealthily gave it to me, saying, "Don't hold it so dad'll see it. When you git the word, just give that horse of yourn hot darnation about his tail, or maybe you won't ride long if ye don't."

He was cut short by the approach of the old *he*, rifle in hand.

"Now, sir," says he, "ye come here benighted, didn't ye?"

"Yes, sir," said I submissively.

"I took ye in like a gentleman didn't I? I fed your hoss on the best I had, didn't I? I give ye a good bed to sleep on, didn't I? Ye got your breakfast, didn't ye? My boy and gals treated ye like a gentleman, didn't they?"

I nodded.

"Well, I've refused your money, hain't I?"

"Yes, sir, but I wish you would—"

"Stop! That ain't the pint. *But this is the pint!*" And the fire simmered in his eyes like molten iron in glass globes. "Ye've eat my bread—your hoss eat my corn—ye smoked my pipe—ye had my bed, an all for nothin— AND ye wanted to circumvent, not one, but all my gals, married and single, *at one bite!* Damn your snakish little gizzard! I never violate the laws of hospitality at this house nor on my land. Ye see that cross fence down *thar*."

It was about one hundred and fifty yards off. I barely nodded my head. In looking, my eye caught the form of Tewalt, and the girl with the blue eyes, behind the stable, busily enacting a piece of pantomime, evidently for my benefit. Tewalt gave an imaginary horse an awful imaginary thrashing, leaning forward, and stealing a look over his shoulder as if he expected to see the devil. The girl took very deliberate aim at him with a cornstalk, and then poked him between the shoulder blades with it in no slight manner.

"Well," the old *he* was saying, "when I give ye the word, ye may start, but if ye start too soon, I'm damned if I won't spile your hide on my own ground, and I don't want to do that. When ye start, so do I. When I git to that fence—it's the line to my property—then we're clear off my ground. *That's when I'm a-goin to shoot ye!* I'll only spile ye with two holes, one behind, t'other before. An ye can't say I hurt ye on my land."

He began to hitch up his breeches with his disengaged hand, and I began gently plying my horse on the off side with my heel and the hickory, to stir him up a little. I had ridden in a few quarter races in my time, and was pretty well up to the dodge. The old villain asked between his set teeth, "Are ye ready?" I shouted, "Go!" And away we went.

My hickory now rained a cloudburst of licks on the horse. It streaked for the fence. I ventured a quick look over my shoulder. The old *he* was running after us like the devil beating tan bark. He foamed at the mouth until it adorned each corner like a pair of whiskers made of whipped eggs. He was running *some*, I tell *you!*

My horse, perfectly astounded at the unusual treatment, fairly flew. The panels of the fence looked like a continuous stripe along the road, and the wind whistled a jig in my ears.

Spang! Whizzz-phit! The ball had sped, and it had missed. I saw it tear the bark from a hickory a few yards ahead. How fresh and warm the blood rushed back around my heart! I felt safe and mischievous, and began to rein up my horse. I wheeled him in the road. There stood the old he, leaning on the muzzle of his rifle, as if in a brown study.

I shouted, "Hello, old cock! You have good vittles, and a fine family of gals in particular, but I'd not give a button for your gun or your temper. Tell the gals goodbye, and the same to you, you old scatter-gun. You can't shoot for sour owl bait!"

He began to reload furiously, so I whistled to my horse and left those parts forever. I have often wondered what he did to Tewalt for smuggling the hickory switch which enabled me to tell this story.

1851

Uncle Josey and the Sheriff

T. A. BURKE

MANY persons in the County of Hall, State of Georgia, recollect Uncle Joseph, who used to visit the county site regularly on General Muster Days and Court Week. Josey Johnson loved his dram and was apt, when he got among the boys in town, to take more than he could conveniently carry. His inseparable companion on all occasions was a black pony, who rejoiced in the name of "General Jackson."

One day while court was in session in the little village of Gainesville, the attention of the judge and bar was attracted by a rather unusual noise at the door. Looking up, His Honor discovered General Jackson and Uncle Josey deliberately entering the Hall of Justice. This, owing to the fact that the floor of the court house was nearly on a level with the ground, was not difficult.

"Mr. Sheriff," said the judge, "see who is creating such a disturbance in this court."

"It's only Uncle Josey and Ginral Jackson, Judge," said the intruder, with a drunken grin. "Jest me and the Ginral come to see how you and the boys is gittin along."

"Mr. Sheriff," said the judge, totally regardless of the friendly interest manifested in his own and the lawyers' behalf by Uncle Josey—"Mr. Sheriff, please collect a fine of ten dolllars from Uncle Josey and the General, for contempt of court."

"Look-a-here, Judge, old feller," said Uncle Josey, as he stroked the General's mane, "you don't mean to say it, now do ye? We hain't had that much money in a coon's age."

"Very well, then, Mr. Sheriff," said the judge, "in default of the payment of the fine, you will convey the body of Joseph Johnson to the county jail, there to be retained for the space of twenty-four hours."

"Now, Judge," said Uncle Josey, "you hain't in right down good earnest, is ye? Uncle Josey ain't never been put in that there boardin house yit, which he don't want to be neither."

"The sheriff will do his duty immediately," was the judge's stern reply.

Accordingly, Uncle Josey and the General were marched off toward the county prison, which stood in a retired part of the village. Arriving at the door, the prisoner was commanded by the sheriff, "Light, Uncle Josey."

"Look-a-here, Jess, hossfly, you ain't a-gwine to put your Uncle Josey in there, is ye?"

"Bliged to do it, Uncle Josey," replied the sheriff. "If I don't, the Old Man will give me thunder when I go back. I hate it powerful, but I must do it."

"But, Jess, couldn't you manage to let the old man git away? Nobody to see ye. Now do, Jess! You know how I fit for ye in the last election, when you run along of Jim Smith, what like to beat ye for sheriff, which he would a-done it, if it hadn't been for your Uncle Josey's influence."

"I know that, Uncle Josey, but there ain't no chance. My oath is very pointed against allowin anybody to escape. So you must go in."

"I tell ye what it is, Jess. I'm afeared to go in there. It looks too dark and dismal."

"There ain't nothin in there to hurt you, Uncle Josey."

"Yes, there is, Jess. You can't fool me that-a-way. I know there is somethin in there to ketch the old man."

"No there ain't. I pledge you my honor there ain't."

"Well, Jess, if there hain't, you jest go in and see, and show Uncle Josey you hain't afeared."

"Certainly. I ain't afeared to go in."

Saying which, the sheriff opened the door, leaving the key in the lock. "Now, Uncle Josey, what did I tell you? I knowed there warn't nothin in here," he called.

"Maybe there hain't where you are standin, but jest less see you go up into that dark place, in the corner."

"Well, Uncle Josey, I'll satisfy you there ain't nothin there, either," and he walked toward the dark corner. As he did so, the old man closed the door and locked it.

"Hello there!" yelled the officer. "None of your tricks, Uncle Josey! This is carryin the joke a damned sight too far!"

"Joke? I hain't a-jokin, Jess. Never was more in earnest in my life. There hain't nothin in there to hurt you, though, that's one consolation.

Jest hold on a little while and I'll send some of the boys down to let ye out."

Before the sheriff could recover from his astonishment, the pony and his master were out of hearing.

Uncle Josey stopped at the grocery, took a drink, again mounted the General, and called the keeper of the grocery to him—at the same time drawing the key of the jail from his pocket. He said:

"Here, Jeemes, take this here key, and if the Old Man or any of them boys up there at the court house asks after Jess Runion, the sheriff, jest ye give 'em this key and my compliments, and tell 'em Jess is safe. Ketch 'em takin in old Uncle Josey, will ye? Git up, Ginral, these here boys won't do to trust. So we'll go into the country where people is honest if they *is* poor!"

1851

My First Appearance at the Bar

JOSEPH G. BALDWIN

SOME twenty years ago, shortly after I obtained license to practice law, a client called at my office to retain my service in a suit for slander. The case stands on record, *Stephen O. Higginbotham vs. Caleb Swink*. The aforesaid Caleb, greatly envying the happy state and condition of said Stephen," a butcher who, "until the grievances," etc. "never had been suspected of the crime of hog-stealing," etc., said "in the hearing and presence of one Samuel Eads and other good and worthy citizens," of and concerning the plaintiff, "you" (the said Stephen meaning) "are a noted hog-thief and stole more hogs than all the wagons in town could haul off in a week on a turnpike road."

The way I came to be employed was this:

Higginbotham had retained Frank Glendye, a great brick in damage cases, to bring the suit. Glendye had prepared the papers and got the case on the pleadings. But while the case was getting ready, Frank was suddenly taken dangerously drunk, and I was hurriedly called on to take his place.

The defendant, a well-to-do farmer, was represented by Caesar Kasm, an old-time lawyer, the race of which is fortunately now extinct. He was about sixty-five, of stout build and something less than six feet in height. He dressed in the old-fashioned fair-topped boots, ruffled shirt, buff vest, and hair a grizzly grey, roached up flat and stiff in front, and hanging in a queue behind, tied with an eel skin.

Old Kasm's face was round and florid, and his bearing decidedly soldierly. His features, especially the mouth, turned down at the corners like a bull dog's, and his nose perked up with unutterable scorn. The eyes were of a bluish grey, all light and no heat. In his bailisk gaze virtue herself looked like something sneaking and contemptible. His smiles had a frost-bitten air, as if they had lain out overnight. One felt less at ease under those frozen smiles than under any one else's frowns. He was close-shaven and powdered every morning, and except for a few scattering grains of snuff which fell between his nose and his gold snuff box, a speck of dirt was never seen about his carefully preserved person.

The faculty he chiefly employed in court was a talent for vituperation. He had cultivated it as a science, which was like putting guano on the Mississippi Bottoms, the natural fertility of his mind for it was so great. He poured out, not vials, but demijohns of vituperation, snarling at counsel, witness, and judge alike.

That morning, on getting to the courthouse, I found that my case was set first on the docket. Looking around, I saw old Kasm, with his green bag and half a library of old books on the bar before him. The old fellow gave me a look of malicious pleasure—like that of a hungry tiger from his lair, cast upon an unsuspecting calf browsing near him.

I tried to put on a bold face, though my heart was running down like a jackscrew under a heavy wagon. My conscience—and in those early days I had not practised it away—was not quite easy. I couldn't help feeling that it was hardly honest to be leading my client where he was sure to be peppered.

The judge took up the docket. "Special case—Higginbotham vs. Swink: Slander. Mr. Baldwin for pl'ff—Mr. Kasm for def't."

I had the witness called up, posted my client behind me in the bar, and put the case to the jury. The defendant pleaded justification, and Not Guilty. I got along pretty well, I thought, on the proofs.

The cross-examination by old Kasm—though he quibbled, misconstrued, objected, and bullied mightily—didn't seem to hurt me anything. The judge was a clever sort of man and didn't like Kasm much. When old Kasm had got the statements of the witness in a fog, the judge took the examination himself.

I had a strong case. The plaintiff's injury from Caleb Swink's slanderous remarks was shown by the facts that:

The Masons had refused to admit him to fellowship until he could clear up these charges.

The Methodist Church, of which he was a class leader, had required him to have the charges judicially settled.

Charges of hog-stealing had been reiterated by the defendant, with increased bitterness and aggravated insult. The defendant had declared that he meant to run the plaintiff off and buy his land at his (the defendant's) own price. He often repeated his slanders in public, and once at the church door.

The defendant's testimony was weak. Some of his witnesses spoke of having heard hogs squeal late at night at the plaintiff's slaughter house, and something of hogs having been stolen in the neighborhood. This was about all of the proof.

The plaintiff, my client Higginbotham, laid his damages at $10,000.

I rose to address the jury, for by this time a good deal of my trepidation had worn off. I might have made a pretty good *out* of it, if I had thrown myself upon the merits of the case, acknowledged modestly my own inexperience, plainly stated the evidence and the law, and let it go at that.

But the evil genius that presides over bantling lawyers would have it otherwise. The citizens of the town and country had gathered in great numbers, and I could not miss such an opportunity for display.

I started in, so I thought, in pretty good style. As I went on, however, my fancy got the better of my judgment. Poetry and declamation were succeeded by pathos and fiery invective.

Shakspere suffered. "He who steals my purse steals trash," etc. I spoke of the sufferings of my poor client, almost broken-hearted beneath the weight of the terrible persecutions of his enemy. Growing bolder, I turned on old Kasm. I congratulated the jury that they had penetrated the fact that here the genius of slander had found an appropriate defender in the genius of chicane and malignity. I complimented the jury on their patience—on their intelligence. I spoke of the public expectation —of the thundering plaudits that would welcome the righteous verdict that the jury would render. I wound up by declaring that I had never known a case of slander so aggravated in all the course of my practice at the bar.

Much more I said that happily has now escaped me.

When I concluded, Sam Hicks, a tailor friend of mine, and one or two other friends, gave out a faint sign of applause—but not enough to make any impression.

The jury were a plain, matter-of-fact looking set of fellows. I did not note, or probably know, a fact or two about them which I found out afterward.

Old Kasm had held his head down while I was speaking. I entertained the hope that I had cowed him. But when he raised up his face of brass and I saw the iciness of his eyes, I saw the very devil was to pay. His queue stuck out behind and shook itself stiffly like a buffalo bull's when he is about making a savage and fatal plunge.

With an affectation of indifference, I watched old Kasm rise. He took a glass of water, with his hand trembling a little. He took a pinch of snuff and led off in a voice slow and measured, but slightly—*very* slightly—tremulous. By a strong, and obvious, effort, he seemed to recover his composure.

He commenced by saying that he had been some years in the practice. He would not say he was an *old* man. That would be in bad taste, perhaps. The young gentleman who had just closed his remarkable speech, harangue, poetic effusion, or whatever it might be called—if indeed any name could be safely given to it—the young gentleman evidently did not think he was an old man, for he could hardly have been guilty of such rank indecency as to have treated age with such disrespect—he would not say, with such insufferable impertinence . . .

"And yet," he continued, "I am of age enough to recollect the day of his birth—and then I was in full practice in this courthouse. I confess, though, gentlemen, that I *am* old enough to remember when a youth's first appearance at the bar was not signalized by impertinence toward his seniors—when public opinion did not think that flatulent bombast and florid trash, picked out of fifth-rate romances and namby-pamby rhymes, redeemed the upstart sauciness of a raw popinjay toward the experienced members of the profession he disgraced.

"And yet, this ranting youth may be right. I am not old in that sense which disables me from defending myself, and *that* this young gentleman shall right well know before I have done with him.

"First, let me retort to this youth, that he is a worthy advocate of his butcher client. For when we heard his vehement roaring, we might have supposed his client had brought his most unruly bull-calf into court to defend him, had not the roaring soon convinced us that the animal was of the species more remarkable for the length of its ears than even the power of its lungs.

"Perhaps the young gentleman has taken his retainer and contracted for butchering my client on the same terms as his client contracts in his line—that is, on shares. At any rate, the butcher, Higginbotham, who seems to be pretty well up to the business of *saving other people's bacon*, seems rather easily satisfied in his choice of the means to save his own. I trust, however, whatever was the contract, that the young gentleman will make his equally worthy client stand up to it. I should like that, on one occasion, it might be said that the excellent butcher *was made to pay for his swine.*

"I find it difficult, gentlemen, to reply to any part of the young man's effusion, except his argument, which is the smallest part of it, and next to his pathos, the most amusing. His figures of speech are, some of them, quite good, and have so been considered for the last thousand years. However, they have become so commonplace by constant use that they tire hearers nearly as much as his original phrasings. Indeed, it was never hard to tell when the gentleman recurred to his own ideas. He is like a catbird—the only intolerable discord she makes being her own notes—though she gets on well enough as long as she copies and cobbles the songs of other warblers.

"But, gentlemen, if this young orator's argument was amusing, what shall I say of his pathos? Such a face—so woe-begone, so whimpering! There was something exquisite in his picture of the woes, the wasting grief, of his client, the butcher Higginbotham, mourning—as Rachel mourned for her children—for his character, *because it was not.*

"Gentlemen, look at Higginbotham!

"Why, he weighs twelve stone *now*! He has three inches of fat on his ribs this minute! He would make as many links of sausage as any hog that ever squealed at midnight in his slaughter pen, and has lard enough in him to cook it all! If this man has 'wasted to a shadow,' as the young gentleman claims, why didn't he show himself, when in flesh, at the last fair beside the Kentucky ox? That were a more honest way of making a living than stealing hogs!

"But Butcher Higginbotham is pining in grief. Like the poetic youth, his learned counsel, may I be permitted to quote Shakspere? It may be that this tender-hearted, sensitive butcher was lean before, and like Falstaff, throws the blame of his fat on sorrow and sighing, 'which has puffed him up like a bladder!'"

(Here my client, Higginbotham, got up and left the courtroom in disgust.)

"There," said old Kasm, pointing at Higginbotham's retreating back—"There, gentlemen, he goes, 'larding the green earth as he walks along!' Poor Hig! Stuffed like one of his own blood puddings with a dropsical grief which nothing short of ten thousand dollars of Swink's money can cure.

"And now, gentlemen, I come to the blood-and-thunder part of this young gentleman's harangue. If any part of his rigmarole was windier than any other part, this was it. He turned himself into a small cascade, making a great deal of noise to make a great deal of froth—tumbling, roaring, foaming. The shallower it ran, all the noisier it seemed. He fretted and knitted his brows. He beat the air and he vociferated, always emphasizing the meaningless passages most loudly. He puffed, swelled out, and blowed off, until he seemed like a new bellows, all brass and wind. He mouthed it, as stage players ranting out fustian in a barn theater, (mimicking)—'Who steals my purse, steals trash.' (I don't deny that.) ' 'Tis something,' (query?)' 'nothing,' (exactly.) ' 'Tis mine; 'twas his, and has been slave to thousands—but he who filches me from my good name, robs me of that which not enricheth him,' (not in the least.) 'but makes me poor indeed.' (Just so, but whether poorer than when he parted with the encumbrance is another matter.)

"But the young gentleman refers to his youth. He ought not to reproach us of our maturer age in that indirect way. No one would have suspected him of youth, or youth of him, if he had not told it. Indeed, from hearing him speak, we were prepared to give him credit for *any length of ears*. But does not the youth remember that Grotius, the peerless Dutch jurist, was only seventeen when he was in full practice, and that he was Attorney General when he was twenty-two? And what is this greater light to Grotius? Not the burning of my smokehouse to the conflagration of Moscow!

And yet, young Grotius here tells us in the next breath that he never knew such slander in the course of his practice. Wonderful, indeed! seeing that his practice has all been done within the last six hours. Why, to hear him talk, you would suppose that he was an old Continental lawyer, grown grey in the service. H-i-s p-r-a-c-t-i-c-e! Why, he is just in his legal swaddling clothes! His PRACTICE! I don't wonder he can't see the absurdity of such talk!

"He talked, too, of the *public* expectations, and all that sort of demagogism. I observed no evidence of any great popular demonstration in his favor, unless it be a tailor I saw stamping his feet, but whether that was because he had sat cross-legged so long he wanted exercise, or was rejoicing because out of fees from this trial he had prospect of payment for an old account, the young gentleman can possibly tell better than I can."

(Here Hicks, my tailor friend, left the courtroom.)

"But," said old Kasm, "I suppose the young gentleman meant to frighten *you* into a verdict by intimating that the mob, frenzied by his eloquence, would tear you to pieces if you gave a verdict for the defendant. It is like the equally eloquent barrister out West who, concluding a case, said:

" 'Gentlemen, my client is as innocent of stealing that cotton as the sun at noonday. And, if you give the verdict agin him, his brother, Sam Ketchins, next Muster Day, will maul every mother's son of you.'

"I hope the sheriff will see to his duty and keep the crowd from you, gentlemen, if you should give us a verdict!

"But, gentlemen, I am tired of winnowing the chaff. It is all froth, all wind, all bubble."

Kasm left me here for a time, and turned upon my client. Poor Higginbotham caught it thick and heavy. Old Kasm wooled him and then skinned him. Hig never skinned a beef so thoroughly. Kasm put together all the facts about the witnesses' hearing the hogs squealing at night, and the losses of pigs in the neighborhood. He perverted the testimony and supplied omissions, until you would suppose, on hearing him, that it had been fully proved that poor Hig had stolen all the meat he had ever sold in market.

He then came back to me with renewed appetite. He said he would conclude by paying his valedictory respects to his juvenile friend, as this was the last time he ever expected to have the pleasure of meeting him.

"That poetic young gentleman has said that by your verdict against his client you would blight forever Higginbotham's reputation and that of his family—that you would bend down the spirit of his manly son and dim the radiance of his blooming daughter's beauty. Very pretty, upon my word! But, gentlemen, not so fine—not so poetical by half as a precious morceau of poetry which adorns the columns of the village newspaper, bearing the initials J.G.B. I must beg to read it, not for the instruction of the young gentleman—he has already seen it—but for the entertainment of the jury. It is addressed to R.B., a young lady of this place. Here it goes."

Judge my horror when I saw him take a newspaper from his pocket, and, pulling down his spectacles, begin to read off in a stage-actor style some verses I had written for Rose Bell's album.

Rose had been worrying me for some time to write her something. To get rid of her importunities, I had scribbled off a few lines and copied them in the volume. Rose, the little fool, took them for something very clever (she never had more than a thimbleful of brains in her doll-baby head)—and was so tickled with them that she got her brother Bill, then about fourteen, to take them to the printing office. Bill threw them under the door. The printer, as big a fool as either, not only published them, but, in his infernal kindness, puffed them in some critical commendation of his own, referred to "the gifted author" as "one of the most promising younger members of our bar."

The fun by this time grew fast and furious. The country people, who had about as much sympathy for a young town lawyer, badgered by an older one, as for a young cub beset by curs; and who had about as much idea or respect for poetry as for witchcraft, joined in the mirth with great glee. They crowded around old Kasm, and stamped and roared as at a circus.

The judge and sheriff in vain tried to keep order. Indeed, his honor smiled out loud once or twice, and to cover his retreat, pretended to cough, and fined the sheriff five dollars for not keeping silence in the court. Even the old clerk, whose immemorial pen behind his right ear had worn the hair from that side of his head, and who hadn't smiled in court for twenty years, and boasted that Patrick Henry couldn't disturb him in making up an entry, actually turned his chair from the desk and *put down* his pen.

Old Kasm went on reading and commenting by turns. I forget what the ineffable trash was, but I do know I couldn't stand it any longer. I fled. The last thing I heard was old Kasm calling me back, amidst the shouts of the audience.

The next information I received of the case was in a letter that came to me at Natchez, my new residence, from Hicks, about a month afterwards. He told me that the jury had given a verdict for defendant, but before the court had adjourned, Frank Glendye had got sober and moved for a new trial on the ground that the verdict was against evidence, and that the plaintiff had not had justice "by reason of the incompetency of his counsel, and the abandonment of the cause." Higginbotham got a new trial and won damages to the tune of $2,000, and Swink was in for the $500 costs, besides.

Later I heard that old Kasm had died of an apoplectic fit in the court-house while abusing an old preacher who testified against him in a case. Though I was not mentioned in his will, he had left me something to remember him by. Bright be the bloom and sweet the fragrance of the thistles on his grave!

1853

Law on the Frontier

Samuel A. Hammett

WHAT a time there is in a county town when the court's a-settin. All the rogues is there for some reason or nother. Some because they're sent for and has to come—some to swear outdacious lies to clear their friends or to stock the jury—and a pile of 'em to play faro and poker. There's more mischief, gamblin, and drinkin a-goin on while the court's a-holdin than in a whole year besides.

I've seen some tall things at them gatherins. I remember a young lawyer comin to Opelousas to set up, just as court was comin on. He hung his shingle out to let people know he were up for all the courts, although he expected to do the reglar quantity of starvin which the young ones has to go through with. And so he was real took aback when a lanky, squint-eyed lookin critter walked into the office, without knockin, and opened with:

"Hello, stranger, howdy. You're one of them lawyer fellers, ain't you?"

"Why, yes, sir, that's my profession. Happy to do anything in my line for yourself or friends."

"Yes, sir-e-e. That's what I calculated. You see, Squire, I've got into a right smart difficulty, and me and my friends has been havin a talk about it. We allowed our old pack of lawyers warn't worth shucks, and as we hearn tell of a stranger just havin arrove, we reckoned I'd best give him a try."

"Much obliged, sir. Bein a newcomer, I have nothin else on my hands, and can give my whole time to your business."

"Well, stranger, all I want you to do is make a speech for me half an hour long, and here's a fifty dollar bill. All I want is the speech, and don't disremember it must last half an hour, and nothing shorter."

"Really, sir, you're very liberal. Very liberal indeed! But what is the case?"

"Oh, nothin particlar, only I happened to kill one of my own beeves that some thievin critter had set his brand on afore it was a yearlin. You don't need no items nor witnesses. You just be to court tomorrow mornin at nine. Good day."

This was all the lawyer got out of the chap—though, bein his first case, he was mighty anxious to know all about it so he could do somethin uncommon smart in the defense. He looked on the fifty as a sort of godsend, and as he'd hearn tell of Old Nick's lookin like an angel of light, he didn't know how vicey-versey mightn't be the case, and that this chap might be a guardeen angel in awful ugly war paint.

Howsomever, next mornin to the courthouse he went, and sure enough, there was his handsome customer. His case come on, too, and a sweet one it was. The lawyer soon see it warn't no manner of use a-tryin to clear him, so he turned round to his man, handed him the fifty, and told him he couldn't do him no good.

"No you don't," says the beauty. "No *you* don't. I hired you a-purpose to lumber away for me, so you now just get up and lumber!"

Seein he couldn't help it, up jumped the lawyer, and begun. He went pretty much all over creation and talked about mighty nigh everything, except the case. He reckoned the less said about that, the better. When he got done, he were entirely stumped up to hear the jury bring in *Not Guilty* without even leavin their box.

But his wonderment didn't last long, for when he and his client went out to moisten up at the tavern, he asked him how on earth the jury could clear him?

"Why," says the chap, "eleven of them fellers has been indicted for cow-stealin and t'other will be afore court's over. I knowed they wouldn't fasten me, but I had to get somebody to make a show, and so I settled on you. To tell you the truth, I were a little afeared the old ones that knowed me wouldn't have nothin to do with it."

But them sort of fellers don't always get off so cheap, specially if they ain't got a pocketful of silver to pay all hands. I were travelin once, and met a feller I hadn't seen for a long time.

"Hello," says I. "Bill, where have you been this coon's age?"

"Why," says he, "I'll tell you just how it happened. I went out one day to kill a beef. Afore I'd fairly got the critter skinned, up rode a man that claimed the brand. I told him it was all a mistake, and that I wouldn't have killed it if I'd a-knowed he were so nigh.

"But this only made him madder yet, and so afore long the sheriff called on me and told me I were wanted very particlar up to court. Well I didn't like to disoblige, and so I went along with him. And when we got there, they made me set down, and pretty soon a feller got up and begun to talk about me in a way that warn't flatterin to my feelins. He seemed to have took a prejudice agin me.

"After he'd got done, the old feller that set on a high bench had his say, and, damn him, he'd got a prejudice agin me, too. When he got through, the jury had their turn, and hang my picture, if *they* hadn't got a prejudice agin me!

"After they'd all done, the sheriff and me went out into a sort of yard where there were a big tree, and I tell you—if *we* didn't have a hot time of it for a few minutes!

"Now, who'd a-looked for such treatment in a neck of the woods where no man ever eats his own beef unless he eats at a neighbor's? Well, after I explained this to the sheriff and he lay down and went to sleep, I thought it might hurt some people's feelins to see me agin, so I were took with a *leavin*! That's where I've been ever since."

But after all, I reckon the law is of some use. It gives a livin to them lawyer chaps. An old planter once said to me, when he met me inside of one of them perambuatin circuses and merry-jerries—he said:

"Uncle Billy, I ain't here because I've got any particlar likin for these things. But, you see, these chaps is bound to get a livin, and you know they won't work. I allow it's the cheapest way for us to *give* 'em a dollar apiece of our money now and then, than to have 'em to help theirselves."

1853

Sorry Coopering

ANONYMOUS

GENERAL PERKINS and Tom Marshall were canvassing the State in a hotly contested election. The General was a roaring Democrat and, by way of catching the lower flats of society, was fond of boasting that his father had been a cooper by trade in an obscure part of the State.

The great failing of General Perkins was his fondness for old whiskey. The more he drank, the more of a Democrat he became, and the prouder of being the son of a cooper. Of this fact he had been making the most, when Marshall, the Whig, arose to reply to his speech.

Looking at him with great contempt, Tom Marshall said, "Fellow citizens of Kentucky, this mighty military man's father may have been a very good cooper. I do not deny that. Honest toil and good handiwork is honorable. As I say, this man's father may, ordinarily, have been a good cooper. But, fellow citizens, this I must say:

"He put a mighty poor head"—pointing to Perkins—"*on that whiskey barrel!*"

1854

How Daddy Lovingood Played Hoss

GEORGE WASHINGTON HARRIS

OUR plow boss Tickytail was jist about next to the best hoss that ever shelled nubbins or toted jugs. But poor old Tickytail, starvation got him and he died. Thar we was, Dad and me and Mam and all the children, left in the woods alone, without airy a hoss to crop with.

Warn't that a devil's own mess of broth for a respectable white family to be sloshin around in? I'm durned if I didn't feel like stealing a hoss sometimes. I expect I'd a-done it, but the stealin streak in the Lovingoods all run to durn fool, and the unvirtuous streak all run to legs.

Well, we waited and wished and rested and planned and wished and waited agin till nigh onto strawberry time, hopin some stray hoss might come along. But, dog my cats, if any sich good luck ever comes within reach of whar Dad is, he's so dod-rotted mean and lazy and ugly and savage, and durn fool to boot.

One night he lay awake till cock-crowin, a-snortin and rollin and blowin and shufflin and scratchin hisself, and a whisperin at Mam a heap, and at breakfast I found what it meant.

Says he to me, "Sut, I'll tell you what we'll do. I'll be hoss my*self* and pull the plow whilst you drive me. Then the Old Quilt"—he meant that for Mam—"and the brats can plant and tend, or jist let it alone as they damn please. *I* ain't a-carin!"

So we went out in the pawpaw thicket and peeled a right smart chance of bark. Mam and me made harness-gears out of the bark for Dad, while he set on the fence lookin at us and a-studyin powerful. I afterwards found out he was studyin how to play the character of a hoss perfectly. He was rememberin jist how old Tickytail used to act and do.

Well, the bark gears become him mightily. Nothin would do him but he must have a bridle. So I got an umbrella brace—it's a little forked piece of square wire about a foot long, like a young pitchfork—and I twisted it sort of into a bridle bit, snaffle-shape. Dad wanted it made a curb bit, because a curb is for a mean, wild hoss, and Dad said he hadn't worked for a good while and said he might sort of feel his keepin and go to ravin and cavortin.

I twisted it curb, and when we got the bridle fixed onto Dad, don't you believe he set to chompin it jist like a real hoss and tried to bite me on the arm! He always was a most complicated durned old fool and Mam said so, when he warn't about.

I put on the gears, and while Mam was a-tyin the bellyband, a-strainin it powerful tight, Dad drapped onto his hands and said, *"Whay-a-ah!"* like a wild hoss would. Then I shouldered the gopher plow and tuck hold of the bridle. Dad he leaned back sulky, till I said, "Cluck!" with my tongue, and then he started. When we come to the fence, I let down the gap. It made Dad mad. He wanted to jump it on all fours, hoss-way. Oh, jimminy! What a durned old fool can come to when he gives up to the complaint!

Watchin him powerful close, I hitched him to the gopher plow, for I seed how quick he could drap on his hands and kick. And away we went, Dad leanin forward to his pullin. We made right peart plowin for to have a green hoss and bark gears. He went over the sprouts and bushes same as a real hoss, only he traveled on two legs. I felt mightily hoped up about corn, could almost see it comin up. But thar is a heap of whiskey spilt twixt the counter and the mouth, even if it ain't got but two foot to travel.

About the time Dad were beginnin to break sweat, we come to a sassafras bush. To keep his character as a hoss, he bulged square *into* it and *through* it. What he didn't see was a ball hornets' nest in that sassafras bush. It was about as big as a hosses' head and he tore it down. The whole tribe kivered him as quick as you could kiver a sick pup with a saddle blanket.

Dad he lit onto his hands agin and kicked straight up once, then he rared and fetched a squeal worse'n airy a stud hoss in Tennessee. He set into straight runnin jist as natural as you ever seed any other skeered hoss do.

I let go the line and hollered, "Whoa, Dad, whoa!" But you might jist as well say "Whoa" to a locomotive or "Suke cow" to a gal.

How he run! When he come to bushes, he'd clear the top of 'em with a squeal, gopher plow and all. Maybe he thought thar might be another settlement of ball hornets thar and it was safer to go over than through, and quicker done anyhow. Every now and then he'd fan the side of his head, first with one foreleg and then tother. Then he'd give his self a round-handed slap that sounded like a wagon whip. He was a-runnin all the time and a-carryin that plow jist about as fast and high from the earth as ever any plow was carried, I swear.

When he come to the fence, he jist tore through it, bustin and scatterin nigh onto seventeen panels with lots of broken rails. Right here he left the gopher plow—gears, singletree, every stitch of his clothes, and all, mixed up and not worth a damn.

The ball hornets, nigh onto a gallon of 'em, kept on with Dad. He seemed to run exactly as fast as a hornet could fly. It was the tightest race I ever seed, for one hoss to git all the whippin. Down through a sage field they all went, the hornets makin it look like thar was smoke round Dad's bald head, and him with nothin on the green earth about him in the way of clothes but the bridle and about a yard of plow line a-sailin behind with a tired-out hornet ridin on the end of it.

I seed he was aimin for the swimmin hole in the creek, whar the bluff is over twenty-five foot to the water and the water nigh ten foot deep.

To keep in his character of hoss, plumb through, when he got to the bluff he loped off, or rather he jist kept on a-runnin. Ker-*slunge*! Into the creek he went. I seed the water fly way above the bluff from whar I was.

Right thar he overdid the thing, if actin hoss to the letter were what he was after. For thar's nairy a hoss ever foalded durned fool enough to lope over any sich place. A mule might a-done it, but Dad warn't actin mule, though he ought to a-tuck that character—it's exactly suited to his disposition.

Anyhow, I crept up to the edge of the bluff and peeped over. Thar was Dad's bald head, for all the world like a peeled onion, a-bobbin up and down and around, and the hornets sailin round turkey buzzard-fashion, and every once in a while one, and sometimes ten, would take a dip at Dad's bald head. He kept up a right peart dodgin under, sometimes before they hit him, and sometimes afterwards, and the water was kivered with drowned hornets.

To look at him from the top of the bluff was powerful interestin. Dad couldn't see the funny part from whar he was, but it did seem to be interestin to him from the attention he was a-payin to divin and cussin.

Says I, "Dad, the hoss has drunk enough. Let's git back to our plowin. It will soon be mighty hot."

"Hot, hell!" says Dad. "It's hot right now!" He kept a-dippin and divin and thrashin and dippin, all out of breath. "Don't you see these cussed varmints after me?" He went on dippin and a-bustin under and blowin and cussin.

"What?" says I. "Them is hoss flies thar. That's natural, Dad. You ain't really afeared of 'em, are you?"

"Hoss flies hell and damnation!" says Dad, a-dippin and churnin the water and the hornets. "They're real cannibal ball hornets, you ignorant cuss!"

"Kick 'em, paw 'em, switch 'em with your tail, Dad," says I.

He was dippin, and a-splutterin, "Oh, sonny, sonny! How I'll sweeten your hide when these hornets leave here!"

"Well, Dad," says I, "you'll have to stay thar till night, and after they go to roost, you come home. I'll have your feed in the trough ready. You won't need any curryin tonight, will you?"

The hornets was takin a fresh interest and Dad was sousin up and down like a churn dasher. Says he, in between dives, "I wish I may never see tomorrow, Son Sut, if I don't make hamestrings out of your hide when I *do* git out of here!"

"Better say you wish you may never see another ball hornet if you ever play hoss again," says I.

Them words touched Dad to the heart, and I felt they must be my last words, knowin Dad's unmollified nature, so I broke from them parts.

When I got to the house, "Whar's your Dad?" says Mam.

"Oh," says I, "he turned durned fool and run away and busted everything all to smash, and is now in the swimmin hole a-divin for minners."

"Laws sake!" says Mam. "I knowed he couldn't act hoss for ten minutes without actin damn fool, to save his life!"

My health begun to bother me, so I stayed hid out till next afternoon, and I seed a feller a-travelin. Says I, "Howdy-do, Mister. What were goin on at the cabin this side of the creek when you passed thar?"

Says he, "Oh, nothin much. Only a powerful fat man was a-layin in the yard with no shirt on, and a woman was greasin of his shoulders and arms out of a gourd. An awful vicious and skeery lookin cuss he was, to be sure. His head is big as a-a—*wash* pot, and he ain't got the first sign of an eye—jist two black slits midst the puffin of flesh. Is thar much smallpox around here, young feller?"

"Smallpox?" says I. "No, sir."

"Been much fightin lately in this neighborhood?"

"None worth speakin of," says I.

"Nor French measles?"

"Not jist close."

"Well, do you know *what* ails that man back thar?"

"Jist gittin over a violent spell of damn fool," says I.

"Well, who is he, anyhow?"

I riz to my feet and stretched out my arm and, says I, "Stranger, that man is my Dad!"

He looked at my legs and personal features and, says he, "Yes, damned if he ain't!"

I ain't seed Dad since then, and I don't have much appetite to see him for some time to come. Well, luck to the durned old fool—and to the hornets, too.

1853

Miss Albina McLush

N. P. WILLIS

I HAVE a passion for fat women. If there is anything I hate in life it is what dainty people call a spirituelle. Motion—rapid motion—a smart, quick, squirrel-like step, a pert, voluble tone—in short, a lively girl—is my exquisite horror! I would as lief have a diable petit dancing his infernal hornpipe on my cerebellum as to be in the room with one. I have tried before now to school myself into liking these parched peas of humanity. I have followed them with my eyes, and attended to their rattle till I was as crazy as a fly in a drum. I have danced with them, and romped with them in the country, and periled the salvation of my "white tights" by sitting near them at supper. I swear off from this moment. I do. I won't—no—hang me if ever I show another small, lively, spry woman a civility.

Albina McLush is divine. She is like the description of the Persian beauty by Hafiz: "Her heart is full of passion and her eyes are full of sleep." She is the sister of Lurly McLush, my old college chum, who, as early as his sophomore year, was chosen president of the *Dolce far niente* Society—no member of which was ever known to be surprised at anything (the college law of rising before breakfast excepted). Lurly introduced me to his sister one day, as he was lying upon a heap of turnips, leaning on his elbow with his head in his hand, in a green lane in the suburbs. He had driven over a stump, and been tossed out of his gig, and I came up just as he was wondering how in the d—l's name he got there! Albina sat quietly in the gig, and when I was presented, requested me, with a delicious drawl, to say nothing about the adventure—it would be so troublesome to relate it to everybody! I loved her from that moment. Miss McLush was tall, and her shape, of its kind, was perfect. It was not a fleshy one exactly, but she was large and full. Her skin was clear, fine-grained and transparent; her temples and forehead perfectly rounded and polished, and her lips and chin swelling into a ripe and tempting pout like the cleft of a bursted apricot. And then her eyes—large, liquid and sleepy—they languished beneath their long black fringes as if they had no business with daylight—like two magnificent dreams, surprised in their jet embryos by some bird-nesting cherub. Oh! it was lovely to look into them!

She sat, usually, upon a fauteuil, with her large, full arm embedded in the cushion, sometimes for hours without stirring. I have seen the wind lift the masses of dark hair from her shoulders when it seemed like the coming to life of a marble Hebe—she had been motionless so long. She was a model for a goddess of sleep as she sat with her eyes half-closed, lifting up their superb lids slowly as you spoke to her, and dropping them again with the deliberate motion of a cloud, when she had murmured out her syllable of assent. Her figure, in a sitting posture, presented a gentle declivity from the curve of her neck to the instep of the small round foot lying on its side upon the ottoman. I remember a fellow's bringing her a plate of fruit one evening. He was one of your lively men—a horrid monster, all right angles and activity. Having never been accustomed to hold her own plate, she had not well extricated her whole fingers from her handkerchief before he set it down in her lap. As it began to slide slowly toward her feet, her hand relapsed into the muslin folds, and she fixed her eye upon it with a kind of indolent surprise, drooping her lids gradually till, as the fruit scattered over the ottoman, they closed entirely, and a liquid jet line was alone visible through the heavy lashes. There was an imperial indifference in it worthy of Juno.

Miss McLush rarely walks. When she does, it is with the deliberate majesty of a Dido. Her small, plump feet melt to the ground like snowflakes; and her figure sways to the indolent motion of her limbs with a glorious grace and yieldingness quite indescribable. She was idling slowly up the Mall one evening just at twilight, with a servant at a short distance behind her, who, to while away the time between his steps, was employing himself in throwing stones at the cows feeding upon the Common. A gentleman, with a natural admiration for splendid person, addressed her. He might have done a more eccentric thing. Without troubling herself to look at him, she turned to her servant and requested him, with a yawn of desperate ennui, to knock that fellow down! John obeyed his orders; and, as his mistress resumed her lounge, picked up a new handful of pebbles, and tossing one at the nearest cow, loitered lazily after.

Such supreme indolence was irresistible. I gave in—I—who never before could summon energy to sigh—I—to whom a declaration was but a synonym for perspiration—I—who had only thought of love as a nervous complaint, and of women but to pray for a good deliverance—I—yes—I —knocked under. Albina McLush! Thou were too exquisitely lazy. Human sensibilities cannot hold out forever.

I found her one morning sipping her coffee at twelve, with her eyes wide open. She was just from the bath, and her complexion had a soft, dewy transparency, like the cheek of Venus rising from the sea. It was the hour, Lurly had told me, when she would be at the trouble of thinking. She put away with her dimpled forefinger, as I entered, a cluster of rich curls that had fallen over her face, and nodded to me like a waterlily swaying to the wind when its cup is full of rain.

"Lady Albina," said I, in my softest tone, "how are you?"

"Bettina," said she, addressing her maid in a voice as clouded and rich as the south wind on an Aeolian, "how am I today?"

The conversation fell into short sentences. The dialogue became a monologue. I entered upon my declaration. With the assistance of Bettina, who supplied her mistress with cologne, I kept her attention alive through the incipient circumstances. Symptoms were soon told. I came to the avowal. Her hand lay reposing on the arm of the sofa half-buried in a muslin foulard. I took it up and pressed the cool soft fingers to my lips—unforbidden. I rose and looked into her eyes for confirmation. Delicious creature—she was asleep!

1853

The Deacon's Trout

HENRY WARD BEECHER

H E WAS a curious trout. I believe he knew Sunday just as well as Deacon Marble did. At any rate, the deacon thought the trout meant to aggravate him. The deacon, you know, is a little waggish. He often tells about that trout.

Says he, "One Sunday mornin, just as I got along by the willows, I I heard an awful splash. Not ten feet from shore I saw the trout, as long as my arm, just curving over like a bow, and goin down with somethin for breakfast.

" 'Gracious!' says I, and I almost jumped out of the wagon. But my wife Polly says, 'What on earth are you thinkin of, Deacon? It's Sabbath Day, and you're goin to meetin! It's a pretty business for a deacon!'

" 'That sort of cooled me off. But I do say that, for about a minute, I wished I wasn't a deacon. But 'twouldn't made any difference, for I came down next day to mill on purpose. I came down once or twice more, and nothin was to be seen, though I tried him with the most temptin bait.

"Well, next Sunday I came along again and, to save my life, I couldn't keep off worldly and wandering thoughts. I tried to be sayin my catechism, but I couldn't keep my eyes off the pond as we came up to the willows. I'd got along in the catechism, as smooth as the road, to the Fourth Commandment, and was saying it out loud for Polly, and just as I was sayin: 'What is required in the Fourth Commandment?' I heard a splash, and there was the trout, and before I could think, I said, 'Gracious, Polly, I must have that trout!'

"She almost riz right up. 'I knew you wan't sayin your catechism hearty! Is this the way you answer the question about keepin the Lord's Day?

202

'" I'm ashamed, Deacon Marble,' says she. 'You'd better change your road, and go to meetin on the road over the hill. If *I* was a deacon, I wouldn't let a fish's tail whisk the whole catechism out of my head!'

"And I had to go to meetin on the hill road all the rest of the summer."

1850's

A Piano in Arkansas

Thomas Bangs Thorpe

W E SHALL never forget the excitement which seized upon the inhabitants of the little village of Hardscrabble, as the report spread through the community that a real piano had actually arrived within its precincts.

Speculation was afloat as to its appearance and use. The name was familiar to everybody; but what it precisely meant, no one could tell. That it had legs was certain, but that was about all. So, public opinion was in favor of its being an animal, though a harmless one; for there had been a man through the village a few weeks previously, who distributed circulars of a "Female Academy," for the accomplishment of young ladies. These circulars distinctly stated "the use of the piano to be one dollar per month."

The owner of this strange instrument was a quiet and very respectable late merchant of a little town somewhere "North," who having failed at home, had emigrated into the new and hospitable country of Arkansas, for the purpose of bettering his fortune, and escaping the heartless sympathy of his neighbors who seemed to consider him a very degraded man because he had become honestly poor.

The newcomers were strangers, of course. The house in which they were setting up their furniture was too little arranged to admit of calls; and as the family seemed little disposed to court society, all prospects of immediately solving the mystery that hung about the piano seemed hopeless.

The depository of this strange thing was looked upon by passers-by with indefinable awe; and as noises unfamiliar sometimes reached the street, it was presumed the piano made them, and the excitement rose higher than ever.

In the midst of it, one or two old ladies, presuming upon their age and respectability, called upon the strangers and inquired after their health, and offered their services and friendship. Meantime, everything in the house was eyed with great intensity, but seeing nothing strange, a hint was given about the piano. One of the new family observed carelessly, "that it had been much injured by bringing out, that the damp had affected its tones, and that one of its legs was so injured that it would not stand up, and for the present it would not ornament the parlor."

Here was an explanation, indeed! "Poor thing!" ejaculated the old ladies with real sympathy, as they proceeded homeward. "Travelling has evidently fatigued it. The Mass-is-sip has given it a cold, poor thing!" And they wished to see it with increased curiosity.

The village agreed that if Mo Mercer was in town, they would have a description of the piano, and the uses to which it was put; and, fortunately, in the midst of the excitement, Mo arrived, he having been temporarily absent on a hunting expedition.

Moses Mercer was the only son of Old Mercer, who was, and had been, in the State Senate ever since Arkansas was admitted into the Union. Mo, from this fact, received great glory, of course. His father's greatness alone would have stamped him with superiority; but his having been twice in Little Rock, the Capital of the Wonder State, when the legislature was in session, stamped his claims to pre-eminence over all competitors.

Mo Mercer was the oracle of the village. Mo knew everything. He had all the consequence and complacency of a man who had never seen his equal, and never expected to. Mo bragged extensively on his having been to the Capital twice—of having seen the world. His return to town was therefore received with a shout. The arrival of the piano was announced to him, and *he alone* of all the community was not astonished at the news.

He treated the piano as a thing that he was used to, and went on, among other things, to say that he had seen more pianos in the Capital than he had ever seen woodchucks; and that it was not an animal, but a musical instrument, played upon by the ladies. He wound up his description by saying that the "way the dear critters could pull music out of it was a caution to hoarse owls."

The new turn given to the piano excitement in Hardscrabble by Mo Mercer, was like pouring oil on fire to extinguish it, for it blazed out with more vigor than ever. That it was a musical instrument made it a rarer thing in that wild country, than if it had been an animal, and people of all sizes, colors, and degrees were dying to see and hear it.

Jim Cash was Mo Mercer's righthand man, Mo's wheel-horse. Cash believed in Mo Mercer with abandonment. Mr. Cash was consumed to see the piano, and when he was alone with Mo, he expressed the desire that was gnawing his vitals.

"We'll go at once and see it," said Mercer.

"Strangers!" said the frightened Cash.

"Humbug! Do you think I've visited the Capital twice, and don't know how to treat fashionable society? Come along, at once, Cash."

Off the pair started, Mercer all confidence and Cash all fears, as to the propriety of the visit. A few minutes walk brought them to the house that contained the object of so much curiosity. The doors and windows were closed, and a suspicious look was on everything.

"Do they always keep a house closed up this way that has a piano in it?" asked Cash.

"Certainly," said Mercer. "The damp would destroy its tones."

Repeated knocks at the doors, and finally at the windows, satisfied Cash and Mercer that nobody was at home. In the midst of their disappointment, Cash discovered a singular machine at the end of the gallery, crossed by bars and rollers, and surmounted with an enormous crank. Cash approached it on tip-toe. He had a presentiment that he beheld the object of his curiosity, and as its intricate character unfolded itself, he gazed with distended eyes, and asked Mercer with breathless anxiety what the strange and incomprehensible box was?

Mercer turned to the thing as coolly as a North wind to an icicle, and said:

"That's *it*."

"That IT?" exclaimed Cash, opening his eyes still wider. Then, recovering himself, he asked to see the tones.

Mercer pointed to the cross-bars and rollers with trembling hands, with resolution that would have enabled a man to have been scalped without winking, Cash reached out a hand and seized the handle of the crank (Cash, at heart, was a brave and fearless man). He gave it a turn. The machinery grated harshly, and seemed to clamor for something to put in its maw.

"What delicious sounds!" said Cash.

"Beautiful," observed the complacent Mercer, at the same time taking Cash's arm and asking him to desist, for fear of breaking the instrument, or getting it out of tune.

The simple caution was sufficient. Cash, in the joy of the moment, at what he had done and seen, looked as conceited as Mo Mercer himself.

Busy, indeed, was Cash from this time forward, in explaining to gaping crowds the exact appearance of the piano, how he had actually taken hold of it, and, as his friend Mo Mercer observed, "pulled music out of it."

The curiosity of the village was thus allayed, and consequently died comparatively away. Cash, however, had risen to almost as much importance as Mo Mercer, for having seen and handled the thing.

Our Northern family knew little or nothing of all this. They received, meanwhile, the visits and congratulations of the villagers, and resolved to give a grand party to return some of the kindness. The piano was, for the first time, moved into the parlor. No invitation was neglected. Early at the post was every visitor, for it was rumored that Miss Patience Doolittle would, in the course of the evening, "perform on the piano."

The excitement was immense. The supper was passed over with contempt, rivalling that which is cast upon an excellent farce played preparatory to a dull tragedy, in which the *star* is to appear. The furniture was all critically examined, but nothing could be discovered answering Cash's description. An enormous thick-leafed table, with a spread upon it, attracted little attention, timber being so very cheap in a new country. Everybody expected soon to see the piano brought in.

Mercer, of course, was the hero of the evening. He talked much and loudly. Cash, as well as several young ladies, went into hysterics at his wit. Mercer, as the evening wore away, grew exceedingly knowing, even for him. He graciously asserted that the company present reminded him of his two visits to the Capital, and other associations, equally exclusive and peculiar.

The evening progressed apace, and still—no piano. That hope deferred which maketh the heart sick, was felt by some elderly ladies, and by a few younger ones. Mercer was solicited to ask Miss Patience Doolittle, to favor the company with the presence of the piano.

"Certainly," said Mercer, and with all grace, he called upon the lady to gratify all present with a little music, prefacing his request with the remark, that if she was fatigued, his friend Cash would give the machine a turn.

Miss Patience smiled, and looked at Cash.

Cash's knees trembled.

All eyes in the room turned upon him.

Cash trembled all over.

Miss Patience said she was gratified to hear that Mr. Cash was a musician; she admired people who had musical taste. Whereupon Cash fell into a chair, as he afterwards observed, "chawed up."

Oh, that Beau Brummel, or any of his admirers could have seen Mo Mercer all this while! Calm as a summer morning—complacent as a newly-painted sign—he smiled and patronized, and was the only unexcited person in the room.

Miss Patience rose. A sigh escaped from all present. The piano was evidently to be brought in. She approached the thick-leafed table, and removed the covering, throwing it carelessly and gracefully aside. She opened the instrument and presented the beautiful arrangement of dark and white keys.

Mo Mercer at this, for the first time in his life, looked confused. He was Cash's authority in his descriptions of the appearance of the piano. Cash, himself, began to recover the moment that he ceased to be an object of attention. Many a whisper now ran through the room as to the tones, and more particularly, the crank, as Cash, relying on Mo, had described them. None could see them.

Miss Patience took her seat, ran her fingers over a few octaves— and if *Moses in Egypt* was not perfectly executed, Moses in Hardscrabble *was*. The dulcet sound ceased.

"Miss," said Cash, the moment that he could express himself, so entranced was he by the music—"Miss Doolittle, what was that instrument Mo Mercer showed me in your gallery once, that went by a crank, and had rollers in it?"

It was now the time for Miss Patience to blush. She hesitated, stammered, and said, "If Mr. Cash must know, it was a-a-a—Yankee washing machine."

Mercer's knees trembled, the sweat started to his brow. Mo Mercer, who had visited the Capital twice—Mo Mercer, the great—the confident —the happy and self-possessed—surprising as it may seem, disappeared then and finally, and was never heard of again in Hardscrabble, Arkansas.

1854

Lightwood

ANONYMOUS

O F ALL the sounds that ever broke upon the cold, wet hungry traveller's ear during peregrinations through the Sunny South, where it rains three days every week, and is awful wet the remainder, there is one that is worst of all. Fancy my feelings on alighting at the City Hotel at Albany, Georgia, after riding the stage line all night, anxious to meet a blazing fire and knowing how soon from experience it would be created by lightwood, to hear Caesar, in reply to the landlord's order to fly round and get a fire, say in despairing tones:

"Massa, de lightwood am done gone, sir."

Gone, too, then is all chance for fire or food. For whoever heard of a Georgian, black or white, that could build a fire without lightwood?

Who that has ever partaken of a sumptuous supper in the Georgia pine woods, with a thousand dollar living ebony candlestick six feet high at either corner of the table, shedding light from four lightwood candles upon the feast—who that has ever luxuriated around the campfire of a Georgia hunt, that is not ready to swear that lightwood is one of the actual necessaries of life?

Talk to a Georgia cracker about the fertile soil of the West, or the rich gold mines of California and the fortunes awaiting him there, and he interrupts you with an unanswerable question as a clincher why he does not emigrate:

"Stranger, is lightwood tolerably handy there?"

Which, being answered in the negative, decides the case of emigration forever.

It is an historical fact that the greatest objection of the Seminole Indians against leaving Florida was that in the Arkansas country they would find no lightwood.

And what is lightwood? It is a name given to the old dry wood of the long-leaf pine which abounds in the lower part of all the southern states, and is so full of pitch that a splinter of it will burn like a candle—rather a smoky one, it is true. A more appropriate name would be *torchwood*, as it is the best article for that purpose that ever grew. It is equally valuable, and is considered in regions where it abounds as indispensable for kindling wood. To set a Negro to build a fire without lightwood is an act of oppression almost equal to those old task masters who ordered bricks made without straw.

A traveler came one day upon a most desolate-looking location in the sandy pine woods of Georgia. There was a small field of excessively small corn over which trunks of deadened trees stood sentry—a very black log cabin, with about half a chimney, doorless, floorless, windowless. Thrusting their long noses through a surrounding rail fence stood half a dozen miserable land-pike breed of hogs, looking anxiously on an equal number of half-starved, half-hound curs that were looking enviously at an equal number of white-headed, white-faced children who were disputing over half a supply of roasted sweet potatoes while the owner sat upon the fence looking the very picture of happy contentment.

The traveler said, "I'll thank you for a gourd of water."

"Got none. Spring's dry. Hogs have been in the brook."

"Why, I don't see how you live without water."

"All in getting used to it. Roast taters is better than biled. Have one."

"No, I thank you. . . . You have poor land here. Your corn is very small."

"Yes. Not worth planting."

"Is it good for potatoes?"

"No. Nor nothing else."

"Poor for hogs, I should think."

"Yes, till pine mast falls."

"Is your range good for stock, then?"

"Not worth a damn."

"How's game? That's good, I reckon?"

"No, 'tain't. Hunters have drove all the deer out of these parts."

"Well, then, I hope you have plenty of fish in that stream I crossed back there."

"What? In that stinking black swamp? None but mud fish and alligators, and a man must be sort of short of provisions before he eats such meat."

"Well, now, my friend, I see your land is miserably poor. You can raise nothing. You have no water to drink, and I don't see any sign of cows to give you milk. You have no range for cattle or hogs. You have neither game nor fish. This stinking swamp, as you call it, must make this location unhealthy. Now, will you tell me what in the world there is about to induce you to locate here or remain in such a place?"

The dignity of the man on the fence was offended to think anyone would be so stupid as to ask such a question. He lifted his long legs from the fence, looked over his field, so as to take in the whole view of dead pine, and waving his right hand in the same direction, replied in the most unanswerable manner:

"Sir! Don't you see that the lightwood is tolerably handy!"

1854

Broadway Theatrics, 1855

MORTIMER THOMPSON (Q. K. Philander Doesticks)

W E TOOK a stage and navigated up Broadway until we came opposite Bond Street, to the place where a big canvas sign marks the entrance to the headquarters of Modern Orpheus. Through a wedge-shaped green-baize door—down a crooked pair of stairs—under an overhanging arch—and we stood in the parquette.

Took a front seat—then proceeded to admire in detail the many beauties of this superb edifice, which, at first glance, reminded me of an overgrown steamboat cabin.

Looked for a long time at the indefinite Indian over the stage, trying to fix the gender to my satisfaction, and decide whether it is a squaw or a buck—hard to tell, for it has the face, form, and anatomical developments of the former, and the position and hunting implements of the latter—I concluded that it must be an original Woman's Rights female, who, in the lack of breeches, had taken possession of the traps of her lord and master, and, getting tired of the unusual playthings, had lain down to take a snooze.

Admired the easy and graceful drapery painted on the drop, which looks as if it was whittled from a pine shingle—took a perplexed view of the assorted landscape depicted thereon—endeavored to reconcile the Turkish ruins with the Swiss mountains, or the Gothic castle—wanted to harmonize the camels and other tropical quadrupeds on the right, with the frozen mill pond on the left—admired exceedingly the two rows of private boxes, which look like windows in a martin-house, but could not perceive the propriety of having them supported by plaster-of-Paris ladies, without any arms, and their bodies covered up in patent metallic burial-cases (I was informed that the artist calls them *Caryàtides*).

Was impressed with the admirable proportions of the stage; a hundred and eleven feet wide, by four feet ten inches deep—reminded me forcibly of an empty seidlitz-powder box, turned up edgeways—was much chagrined about a mistake I made concerning a picture on one of the proscenium flats, which I mistook for a Kentucky backwoods girl, with a bowie-knife in one hand and a glass of corn-whiskey in the other; but I was told that it represents the tragic muse, with the dagger and poison bowl.

Resolved not to be deceived about the match picture on the other side, and after an attentive scrutiny, I determined that it is either a female rag-picker with a scoop-shovel, or a Virginia wench with a hoe-cake in her hand; and I made up my mind that any one disposed to heathenism might safely worship the same, and transgress no scriptural command against graven images, for it certainly is a likeness of "nothing in the heavens above, the earth beneath, or the waters under the earth."

But now I perceived by the stir in front of the stage that the performance was about to commence.

The orchestra came out in a crowd—the big fiddle man took the emerald epidemis from off his high-shouldered instrument, and after a half hour preparatory tuning, and forty-one pages of excruciating overture, there was a creaking of pulleys, a trampling of feet, a rattling of ropes, and a noise like a full-grown thunderstorm—and the curtain went up.

Magnificent forest scene—two blue-looking trees on one side—a green baize carpet to represent grass—blue calico borders over head to suggest sky—a border so low the hero thrice knocked his hat off going under to see his lady love, and a mossy bank in one corner, made of canvas, stretched over a basswood plank, and painted mud color.

Audience all silent, waiting the coming of the lovelorn heroine of the piece—at length she comes—with a hop, step, and a jump, she blushingly alights in the middle of the stage—applause—she teeters—cheering—she teeters lower yet—prolonged clapping of hands—bouquet hits her on the head; she picks it up and teeters lower still—a dozen or so more fall at her feet, or are scattered indiscriminately over the fiddlers and the boys in the front row—somebody throws a laurel wreath—she again teeters to the very earth, so low that I think she will have to sit flat down and pick herself up by degrees at her leisure, but she ultimately comes up all right.

Villain comes on with a black dress and a blacker scowl—has some hard words with the heroine—she calls him a "cowardly wretch," a "vile *thing*," defies him to his teeth, tells him to do his worst, and finishes in an exhausted mutter, in which I could only distinguish disconnected words, such as "poison," "vengeance," "heaven," "justice," "blood," "true-love," and "death."

Despairingly lover appears in the background, remarkable principally for his spangled dress and dirty tights, at sight of whom the defiant maid immediately changes her tune, and prays powerful villain to spare her beloved Adolphus—villain scowls blacker, and turns up his lip—heroine gets more distracted than before—villain won't relent—suffering young lady piles on the agony, and implores him "to save my father from a dungeon, and take this wretched hand."

Powerful villain evidently going to do it, when heroic lover comes down on a run, throws one arm around his lady-love, draws his sword with the other, strikes a grand attitude, and makes a terrific face at villain, who disappears incontinently—lover drops his bloodthirsty weapon, slaps his hand on his breast, and the interesting pair poke their head over each other's shoulders, and embrace in the orthodox stage fashion. Scene closes.

Magnificent chamber, furnished with a square-legged table, two chairs, and carpets whose shortcomings are distinctly visible to the naked eye—triumphal march, long dose of trumpet, administered in a flourish—supposed to portend the advent of royalty.

Enter procession of badly scared "supes," with cork whiskers, wooden spears, pasteboard helmets, tin shields, and sandals of ingenious construction and variety—they march in single file, treading on each other's heels, keeping step with the majestic regularity of a crowd of frightened sheep, and form a line which looks like a rainbow with a broken back.

King swaggers in, looking very wild—distracted heroine enters all in tears, her hair down her back, her sleeves rolled up, and her general appearance expressive of great agony of mind.

She makes a tearing speech to the king, during which she rolls up her eyes, throws her arms about, wrings her hands, pitches about in an unreliable manner, like a galvanized frog—sinks on her knees, rumples her hair, yells, cries, whispers, screams, squirms, begs, entreats, dances, wriggles, shakes her fist at powerful villain—stretches forth her hand to heaven—throws her train around as if she was cracking a coach whip—slides about like a small boy on skates, and at length, when she has exerted herself till she is hoarse, she faints into the arms of heroic lover, who stands convenient; her body from the waist up being in a deep swoon, while her locomotive apparatus retains its usual action, and walks off without assistance, although the inanimate part of her is borne away in the careful arms of the enamored swain in the dirty tights.

Several scenes follow, in all of which the heroic lover, the dark villain, and the despairing maiden figure conspicuously, and the scenic resources of this magnificent establishment are displayed to the utmost advantage —the omnipresent square-legged table being equal to any emergency —being an ornament of elegant proportions in the palace, then an appropriate fixture in the lowly cot of the poor but honest parents of heroic lovers.

It is used by the king to sign a death-warrant on, and is then transferred to the kitchen, where it makes a convenient platform upon which the low-comedy servant dances a hornpipe—it then reappears in the country house of powerful villain, who uses it by night for a bedstead—and then makes its final apearance in the king's private library.

And the same two ubiquitous chairs go through every gradation of fortune, turn up in all sorts of unexpected places, are always forthcoming when we least expect to see them.

The end draws nigh—brigands begin to appear in every other scene— dark lanterns, long swords, and broad cloaks are in the ascendant. The plot thickens, so does the weather—terrible thunder-storm prevails—the dashing rain is imitated as closely as dried peas and No. 1 shot can be expected to do—the pendant sheet iron does its duty nobly, and the home-made thunder is a first-rate article.

Heroic lover is in a peck of troubles—has a clandestine moonlight, midnight meeting with injured damsel, and they resolve to kill themselves. Comic servant eats whole mince pies, drinks innumerable bottles of wine, and devours countless legs of mutton and plum-puddings at a sitting.

Villain is triumphant—blood and murder seem to be victorious over innocence and virtue—when suddenly "a change comes o'er the spirit of their dreams."

Heroic lover resolves not to die, but to distinguish himself—fights a single-handed combat with seven robbers—stabs three, kicks one in a mill pond, and throws the rest over a precipice—distressed maid is pursued by bandit chief—is rescued by lover, who catches her in his arms and jumps with her through trap-door over a picket fence.

Hero is unexpectedly discovered to be a Prince, which fact is made known to the world by his old nurse, who comes from some unknown region, and whose word everybody seems to set down as gospel.

Despairing lady proves to be a Princess—king summons all hands to appear before him—heroic lover plucks up courage, runs at villain with his sword—fight, with all the usual stamps by the combatants, and appropriate music by the orchestra.

Big villain is stabbed—falls with his head close to the wing—prompter slaps red paint in his left eye—looks very bloody—acts very malicious—spits at hero—squirms about a good deal—kicks his boots off—soils his stockings, and after a prolonged spasmodic flourish with both legs, his wig comes off, he subsides into an extensive calm, and dies all over the stage.

Everybody is reconciled to everybody else. King comes down from his throne to join the hands of the loving pair, and immediately abdicates in favor of the persevering lover—people all satisfied—young husband kisses his bride, leaving part of his painted moustache on her forehead, and she, in return, wipes the Venetian red from her cheeks upon his white satin scarf—Grand Tableau—triumph of virtue over vice—(big dead rascal.)

The appreciative audience cries "hooray"—curtain goes down.

1855

Parson Bullen's Lizards

GEORGE WASHINGTON HARRIS

LAST year I went to the big bresh-arbor revival meetin at Rattlesnake Springs. Thar was a friend of mine thar, and I found us a shady place a pieceway off from the camp ground into the huckleberry thicket whar we could be sort of quiet. I've heard my friend called handsome, but that *air* don't kiver the case. It's like callin good whiskey water when you are ten mile from a still, it a-rainin, and your flask empty.

Oh, I tell you! She shows among women like a sunflower among dog fennel. Her skin is white as the inside of a frogstool and her cheeks and lips as rosy as a perch's in dogwood time. She takes exactly fifteen inch of garter. She weighs one hundred and twenty-six in her petticoat-tail before breakfast, and she couldn't crawl through a whiskey barrel with both heads stove out nor set in a common-width arm cheer—but you could lock a dog collar round the huggin place. And sich a buzzim! Jist you think of two snow balls with a strawberry stuck butt-ended into both of 'em!

Oh, *durn* sich women! It's jist no use a-talkin!

So me and my friend was settin off in the huckleberry bushes thar behind the big meetin at Rattlesnake, jist a-doin nothin to nobody an makin no fuss, when the first thing I remember I was knocked into a trance by a hickory stick in the paw of old Parson Bullen.

He was standin astraddle of me, and a-preachin to me so you could a-heared him a mile. My poor friend were done gone, and I was glad of it, for I thought he meant to kill me right whar I lay, and I didn't want her to see me die. In between whackin of me, old Bullen said I was a livin proof of the hell-deservin nature of man, and that thar warn't grace enough in all that neighborhood to soften my outside rind. He said I was lost forty year before I was born, and the best thing they could do for the church was turn me out, and then hunt me down till I was shot.

217

But I managed to git in a quick twist and lunge out from under that hickory club. I bulged to my feet and got to pumpin of my long legs and— any damn fool knows that, besides bein full of foolery and whiskey, Sut Lovingood, when thar's a skeer into him, can make further-apart tracks than any critter ever bornded.

Well, I left the old pious tub of soap grease foamin and a-howlin, and that night a neighbor gal got an all-fired, overhanded stroppin from her mam with a stirrup leather, and old Parson Bullen had et supper thar, and what's worse nor all, that poor gal had done her level best a-cookin it for him. She begged him, tremblin and a-cryin, not to tell on her. *He et her cookin,* he promised her he'd keep dark—and then went straight and told her mam. That were *real,* lowdown, *wolf* mean!

But I paid that stinkin old ground hog up for it.

At the next meetin at Rattlesnake, I was thar, as solemn as an old hat. I had my face drawed into the shape of a tailor's sleeve board, pint down. I put on the convicted sinner so perfect that an old observin she-pillar of the church said to an old he-pillar, "Law sakes alive! If thar ain't that awful sinner Sut Lovingood, pierced plumb through!"

I needed to git nigh to old Bullen, so I tuck a seat on the side steps of the pulpit and kivered as much of my stretched face as I could with my hands, to prove I was in earnest. It tuck powerful. I heared a sort of thankful buzzin all over the congregation. Old Bullen hisself looked down on me over his old copper specks, and it said as plain as a look could, "Durn you, it's a good thing you did come!"

I sort of thought different from that, but didn't say it jist then.

Thar was a monstrous crowd in that grove, for the weather was fine and believers was plenty round about Rattlesnake Springs. Old Bullen lined out the hymn and they sung it, you know the one:

"Thar will be mournin, mournin here and thar,
"On that dreadful day to come."

Thinks I, "Old Hoss, can it be possible anybody has told you what's a-goin to happen?" And then I thought nobody knowed it but me, and I were comforted.

Old Bullen next tuck hisself a text powerfully mixed with brimstone and trimmed with blue flames, and then he opened.

He commenced onto the sinners. He threatened 'em awful, tried to skeer 'em with all the worst varmints he could think of, and after awhile he got onto the idea of hell-serpents and dwelt on it some. He told 'em how *cold* the old hell-serpents would crawl over their naked bodies, and how like unto pitch they'd *stick* to 'em as they crawled. And, oh! How they'd *wrop* their tails round their necks, a-chokin close, and *poke* their forked tongues up their noses and *hiss* in their ears.

He kept a-bellerin, but I got so busy jist then that I didn't listen to him much, for I seed my time for action had come.

Now, you see, I'd catched seven or eight big pot-bellied lizards and had 'em in a little narrow bag I'd had made a-purpose, with their tails all at the bottom and so crowded for room they couldn't turn around.

So when he was a-ravin on his tiptoes and a-poundin the pulpit with his fist, unbeknown to anybody, I untied my bag of rep-tyles, put the mouth of it under the bottom of his britches leg, and set into pinchin their tails. Quick as gunpowder, they tuck up his bare leg, makin a noise like squirrels a-climbin a shellbark hickory.

He stopped preachin right in the middle of the word damnation. He looked for a moment like he was listenin for somethin—sort of like the old sow does when she hears you whistlin for the dogs. The terrific shape of his features stopped the congregation shoutin and screamin. You could have heared a cricket chirp.

I give a long groan and held my head twixt my knees. He give hisself an awful slap with first one hand, then tother, then he fetched a vigorous rough rub agin the pulpit, then stomped one foot, then tother, then both at once. Then he run his hand twixt his waistband and his shirt and reached down and around with it. Then he spread his big legs and give his back a good rattlin rub agin the pulpit, like a hog scratches hisself agin a stump, a-leanin to it and twitchin and squirmin all over like he'd slept on a dog bed or a fire-ant hill.

About this time, one of my lizards, skeered and hurt by all this poundin and feelin and scratchin, popped his head from the parson's shirt collar and was a-lookin at the crowd, when Old Bullen struck at him and was jist too late, for he dodged back again.

The old rascal's speech now come back to him, and he says, "Pray for me, brethren and sistren, for I'm a-wrastlin with the *Great Enemy* right now!" And his voice was the most pitiful, tremblin thing I ever heared.

Some of the women fetched a painter-yell, while old Bullen's eyes stuck out like two buckeyes flung agin a mud wall, and he was a-cuttin up more shines than a cockroach in a hot skillet. Off went the clawhammer coat. He flung it behind him like he was a-goin into a fight. He had no jacket to take off, so he unbuttoned his galluses and flung the ends back over his head. He fetched his shirt off overhanded, and throwed it straight up into the air like he wanted it to keep on goin up forever, but it lodged onto a blackjack oak, and I seed one of my lizards, with his tail up, a-racin about all over the old dirty shirt, skeered too bad to jump.

Then old Bullen give a sort of shake and a stompin kind of twist, and he come out of his britches. He tuck 'em by the bottom of the legs and swung 'em round his head a time or two, then fetched 'em down, *kerwallop*, over the front of the pulpit. You could have heered the smash a quarter of a mile. Nigh onto fourteen shortened biscuits, a biled chicken with its legs crossed, a big double-bladed knife, a hunk of terbacker, a corncob pipe, lots of broken glass, a sprinkle of whiskey, and three lizards flew all over the meetin ground out of the upper end of them big flax britches.

Now Old Bullen had nothin left on him but a pair of heavy, low-quartered shoes, short woolen socks, and eel skin garters to keep off the cramp. His skeer had drove him plumb crazy, for he felt around in the air above his head like he was huntin somethin in the dark, and he bellered out, "Brethren, brethren, take keer of yourselves! The hell-serpents has got me!"

When this come out, you could of heared the screams to Halifax. He jist spit on his hands and loped over the front of the pulpit—*kerdiff!* He opened a perfectly clear track to the woods of every livin thing. He weighed three hundred and had a black hairy stripe down his back. Thar was cramp knots on his legs as big as walnuts and mottled splotches on his shins. Takin him all over, he minded me of a durned crazy old elephant, rared up on his hind end, and jist *gittin* from some imeejit danger or tribulation.

Oh, he did the loudest and skeeriest and *fussiest* runnin I ever seed— to be no faster than it were.

Well, he disappeared in the huckleberry thicket, jist a-bustin. And of all the noises you ever heared, were made thar on that camp ground.

Some women screamin—they was the scary ones. Some laughin—they was the wicked ones. Some a-cryin—they was the fool ones. Some tryin to git away with their faces red—they was the modest. Some lookin after Old Bullen—they was the curious ones. Some a-hangin close to their sweethearts—they was the sweet ones. Some on their knees with their eyes shut but facin the way the old mud turkle was a-runnin—they was the deceitful ones. Some doin nothin—they was the *waitin* ones, and the most dangerous of 'em all by a damned long sight!

I tuck a big skeer myself after a few rocks and sich spattered onto the pulpit nigh my head. And, as the Lovingoods knows how to ramble when they git a skeer into 'em, I jist put out for the swamp and the creek.

As I started, a black bottle of baldfaced likker smashed agin a tree beside me, after missin the top of my head about an inch. Some durned fool schoolmaster must of been in the congregation and done this. Nobody else would have that little sense. For I say that any man who'd waste a quart of even *mean* spirits, for the chance of knockin a poor ornery devil like me down with the bottle, is a bigger fool than Old Squire MacMullen, and *he* tried to shoot *his*self with an unloaded hoe handle.

Well, the congregation was onto me, but they never catched me. And Old Bullen never preached agin. He tried to, but he didn't have a sign of a congregation. No, sir, *they had seed too much of him.*

Melancholy Accident

GEORGE HORATIO DERBY (John Phoenix)

MR. MUDGE has just arrived in San Diego from Arkansas. He brings with him four yoke of oxen, seventeen cows, nine children, and Mrs. Mudge.

Mr. Mudge is about thirty-seven years of age. His hair is light, *yaller*; you can see some of it sticking out of the top of his hat. His costume is the national costume of Arkansas—coat, waistcoat, and pantaloons of home-spun cloth, dyed a brownish yellow with a decoction of the bitter-barked butternut. His countenance presents a determined, combined with a sanctimonious, expression, and in his eye we fancy a spark of poetic fervor may be distinguished.

Mr. Mudge called on us yesterday. We were eating watermelon. Perhaps the reader may have eaten watermelon. If so, he knows how difficult a thing it is to speak when the mouth is filled with the luscious fruit and the slippery seed and sweet though embarrassing juice is squizzling out all over the chin and shirt bosom. So, at first, we said nothing but waved with our case knife toward an unoccupied box, as who should say, "Sit down." Mr. Mudge accordingly seated himself and removed his hat, whereat all his hair sprang up straight like a jack-in-the-box.

"Take some melon, Mr. Mudge?" said we, as with a sudden bolt we recovered our speech and took another slice ourself.

"No, I thank you," replied Mr. Mudge. "I wouldn't choose any, now."

There was a solemnity in Mr. Mudge's manner that arrested our attention. We paused, listening to what he might have to say.

"Thar was a very serious accident happened to us," said Mr. Mudge, "as we was crossing the plains. 'Twas on the banks of the Pecos River. Thar was a young man named Jeems Hambrick along, and another young feller he got to fooling with his pistol and he shot Jeems. He was a good

223

young man and hadn't an enemy in the company. We buried him thar on the Pecos River. And as we went off, these lines sort of passed through my mind."

So saying, Mr. Mudge drew from his pocket a crumpled piece of paper, and handed it over. Then he wiped his eyes and blew his nose, and disappeared.

We publish Mr. Mudge's lines with the remark that anyone who says they have no poets or poetry in Arkansas would doubt the existence of Shakespeare:

Mr. Mudge had penned, "This is a epitaff which I think is short and would do to go over his grave,

"EPITAFF
"here lies the body of Jeems Hambrick
"who was accidentally shot
"on the bank of the pecos river
"by a young man

"he was accidentally shot with one of the large size colts revolver with no stopper for the cock to rest on it was one of the old fashion kind brass mounted and of such is the kingdom of heaven.

"truly yourn
"Orion W. Mudge, Esq."

1855

Prenticiana

GEORGE D. PRENTICE (In the *Louisville Journal*)

A DISHONEST critic, by severing passages from their context, may make the best book appear to condemn itself. A book, thus unfairly treated, may be compared to the laurel—there is honor in the leaves but poison in the extract.

Place confers no dignity upon such a man as the new Missouri senator. Like a balloon, the higher he rises, the smaller he looks.

The *Vermont Statesman* asks why we do not tickle the Democratic editors occasionally with the feather-end of our quill, instead of running them through with the point of it. We can give as good a reason as the sailor gave for stabbing with his sword a cross mastiff that had tried to bite him. "Why did you not strike him with the hilt of your sword?" inquired the owner. "So I would," said the sailor, "if the beast had run at me with that end of himself."

We see that a couple of fools in Virginia are talking about a duel on horseback. If they must fight, they should be compelled to fight on foot. They have no right to endanger the lives of their betters.

An Alabama editor says, in an ill-natured paragraph, that he is "very unlike the gentleman of the *Louisville Journal*." The latter replies that he is probably unlike *any* gentleman.

1855

San Diego

GEORGE HORATIO DERBY (John Phoenix)

OH MY what a trying thing it is for a feller
To git cooped up in this here little place
Where the mails dont run reglar nohow
Nor the females nuther, cause their aint none.
But by the mails I mean the post orifices
By which we git our letters and sufforth
From the Atlantic states and the British provinces.
But here there aint no kind of a chance
Except by the *Southerner* and the leaky *Fremont*
Which runs very seldom, and once in the latter
I come to this place, and wisht I was further.
The natives is all sorts complected
Some white, some black, & some kinder speckled,
And about fourteen rowdy vagabonds
That gits drunk and goes round licking every body,
And four sloons to every white human,
With a grand jury that's sitting forever
But don't never seem to indict nothing,
And if they do what comes of it?
The petty ones finds em not guilty
And then they go off much in likker
And hit the fust feller they come to.
All night long in this sweet little village
You hear the soft note of the pistol
With the pleasant screak of the victim
Who's been shot prehaps in his gizzard.
And all day hosses is running

With drunken greasers astraddle
A hollering and whooping like demons
And playing at billiards and monte
Till they've nary red cent to ante
Having busted up all the money
Which they borryed at awful percentage
On ranches which they haint no title
To, and the U.S. board of commission
Will be derned if they ever approve it.
While the Squire he goes round a walking
And sasses all respectable persons.
And persons fight duels.
Oh its awful this here little place is
And quick as my business is finished
I shall leave here you may depend on it
By the first leaky steamboat,
Or if they are all of em busted
I'll hire a mule from some feller
And—just—put out!

1855

Things in General

HENRY WHEELER SHAW (Josh Billings)

THE mule is half hoss and half jackass, and then comes to a full stop, nature discovering her mistake. You can trust them with anyone whose life ain't worth any more than the mule's. The only way to keep them into a pasture is to turn them into a meadow joining, and let them jump out. They never have no disease that a good club won't heal. They are like some men, very corrupt at heart. I've known them to be good mules for six months, just to get a good chance to kick somebody.

They can't hear any quicker nor further than the hoss, yet their ears are big enough for snowshoes. They are the strongest creature on earth, and heaviest, according to size. I heard tell of one that fell off the tow path on the Erie Canal, and sunk till he touched the bottom, but he kept right on towing the boat to the next station, breathing through his ears, which stuck out of the water about two feet six inches. I didn't see this did, but an auctioneer told me of it, and I never knew an auctioneer to lie unless it was absolutely convenient.

There is two things in this life for which we are never fully prepared, and that is twins.

A little learning is a dangerous thing. This is as true as it is common.

A Court Martial is where they try the misdemeanors of an officer so that he'll do to promote.

An insult to one man is an insult to all men.

We often hear of men who have come within an inch of dying, and I ain't any doubt there is some that everybody would like to hear had come within an inch of being born.

We don't question a person's right to be a fool, but if he claims wisdom, we compare it with our own.

The power of oratory lays more in the manner than in the matter. You can't reduce it to writing any more than you can play a streak of lightning on a hand organ.

Avarice eats up all the good things in a man, and then feeds on his vices.

It has been observed "that corporations ain't got any souls." There is exceptions to this rule, for I know several that have got the meanest kind of souls.

I argue this way—if a man is right, he can't be too radical. If he is wrong, he can't be too conservative.

It is a very delicate job to forgive a man, without lowering him in his own estimation, and yours too.

As a general thing, when a woman wears the pants in a family, she has a good right to them.

I haven't got as much money as some folks, but I have got as much impudence as any of them, and that is the next thing to money.

I am violently opposed to ardent spirits as a beverage, but for manufacturing purposes, I think a little of it tastes good.

After all is said and done, the grand secret of winning is to win.

After Joseph's brethren had beat him out of many colors, what did they do next? They pitied him!

There are a great multitude of individuals who are like blind mules, anxious enough to kick, but can't tell where.

My advice to them who are about to begin, in earnest, the journey of life, is to take their heart in one hand and a club in the other.

As men grow older, their opinions, like their diseases, grow chronic.

To bring up a child in the way he should go—travel that way yourself.

1850's-1865

Hezekiah Bedott

FRANCES MIRIAM WHICHER

HE WAS a wonderful hand to moralize, husband was, specially after he begun to enjoy poor health. He made an observation once, when he was in one of his poor turns, that I shall never forget the longest day I live.

He says to me one winter evenin as we was a-settin by the fire—I was a-knittin. I was always a great knitter—and he was smokin, though the doctor used to tell him he'd be better off to leave tobacco alone. When he was well, he used to take his pipe and smoke a spell after he'd got the chores done up, and when he warn't well, he used to smoke the biggest part of the time.

Well, he took his pipe out of his mouth and turned toward me, and I knowed somethin was comin, for he had a particular way of lookin round when he was a-goin to say anything uncommon. Well, he says to me, "Silly,"—my name was Prisilly, naturally, but he generally called me "Silly" because 'twas handier, you know—well, he says to me, "Silly," and he looked pretty solemn, I tell you! He had a solemn countenance, and after he got to be deacon 'twas more so, but since he'd lost his health he looked solemner than ever, and certainly you wouldn't wonder at it if you knew how much he underwent. He was troubled with a pain in his chest and mazin weakness in the spine of his back, besides the pleurisy in his side, and bein broke of his rest of nights because he was put to it for breath when he laid down. Why, it's an unaccountable fact that when that man died he hadn't seen a well day in fifteen year, though when he was married and for five or six year after, I shouldn't desire to see a ruggeder man than he was. But the time I'm a-speakin of, he'd been out of health nigh upon ten year, and, oh dear sakes! How he had altered since the first time I ever see him! That was to a quiltin to Squire Smith's

231

a spell before Sally was married. I'd no idea *then* that Sal Smith was a-goin to be married to Sam Pendergrass. She'd been keepin company with Mose Hewlitt for better'n a year, and everybody said *that* was a settled thing, and lo and behold! All of a sudden she up and took Sam Pendergrass. Well, that was the first time I ever see my husband, and if anybody'd a-told me then that I should ever marry him, I should a-said——

But lawful sakes! I was a-goin to tell you what he said to me that evenin, and when a body begins to tell a thing I believe in finishin on it some time or other. Some folks have a way of talkin round and round and round for evermore. Now there's Miss Jenkins, she that was Poll Bingham before she was married—but what husband said to me was this. He says to me, "Silly."

Says I, "What?" I didn't say, "What, Hezekiah?" for I didn't like his name. The first time I ever heard it I near killed myself a-laughin. "Hezekiah Bedott!" says I. "Well, I would give up if I had such a name!" But then, you know, I had no more idea of marryin the feller than you have this minute of marryin the governor. I suppose you think it's curious we should name our oldest son Hezekiah. Well, we done it to please Father and Mother Bedott. It's his name, and he and Mother Bedott both used to think that names had ought to go down from generation to generation. But we always called him Kiah, you know. That boy *is* a blessin! I ain't the only one that thinks so, I guess. Now, don't you ever tell anybody that I said so, but between you and me, I rather guess that if Kesiah Winkle thinks she's a-goin to catch Kiah Bedott, she is a *little* out of her reckonin!

Well, husband he says to me, "Silly." And says I, "What?" though I'd no idea what he was a-goin to say, didn't know but what it was somethin about his sufferins, though he warn't apt to complain, but used to say that he wouldn't wish his worst enemy to suffer one minute as he did all the time, but that can't be called grumblin—think it can? Why, I've seen him when you'd a-thought no mortal could a-helped grumblin, but *he* didn't. He and me went once in the dead of winter in a one-hoss sleigh out to see a sister of his. You know the snow is deep in this section of the country. Well, the hoss got stuck in one of them snow banks, and there we set, unable to stir, and to cap it all, husband was took with a dreadful crick in his back. Now that is what I call a predicament! Most men would a-swore, but husband didn't. We might a-been settin there to this day, far as *I* know, if there hadn't a-happened to come along a mess of men in a double team, and they pulled us out.

But husband says to me—I could see by the light of the fire, for there didn't happen to be any candle burnin, if I don't disremember, though my memory is sometimes rather forgetful, but I know we weren't apt to burn candles exceptin when we had company—I could see by the light of the fire that his mind was uncommon solemnized. Says he to me, "Silly."

I says to him, "What?"

He says to me, says he, "We're all poor creatures."

1855

Illustrated Newspapers

GEORGE HORATIO DERBY (John Phoenix)

A YEAR or two since, a weekly paper was started in London, called the *Illustrated News*. It was filled with tolerably executed wood cuts, representing scenes of popular interest, and though perhaps better calculated for the nursery than the reading room, it took very well in England, where few can read but all can understand pictures. It soon attained an immense circulation.

As when the inimitable London *Punch* attained its world-wide celebrity, supported by such writers as Thackeray, Jerrold, and Hood, would-be funny men on this side of the Atlantic attempted absurd imitations—the *Yankee Doodle*, the *John Donkey*, &c., which as a matter of course proved miserable failures—so did the success of this Illustrated affair inspire our money-loving publishers with hopes of dollars. There soon appeared from New York, Boston, and other places Pictorial and Illustrated Newspapers, teeming with execrable and silly effusions and filled with the most fearful wood engravings, "got up regardless of expense," or anything else; the contemplation of which was enough to make an artist tear his hair and rend his garments.

A Yankee named Gleason, of Boston, published the first, we believe, calling it *Gleason's Pictorial* (it should have been called *Gleason's Pickpocket) and Drawing Room Companion*. In this he presented to his unhappy subscribers views of his house in the country, and his garden, and for aught we know, of "his ox and his ass, and the stranger within his gates."

A detestable invention for tansferring Daguerreotypes to plates for engraving, having come into notice about this time, was eagerly seized upon by Gleason, for further embellishing his catch-penny publication. Duplicates and uncalled-for pictures were easily obtained, and many a man has gazed in horror-stricken astonishment on the likeness of a respected friend, as a "Portrait of Monroe Edwards," or that of his deceased grandmother in the character of "One of the Signers of the Declaration of Independence."

They love pictures in Yankeedom. Every tin peddler has one on his wagon, and an itinerant lecturer can always obtain an audience by sticking up a likeness of some unhappy female, with her ribs laid open in an impossible manner for public inspection. The factory girls of Lowell, Mass., and the Professors of Harvard all bought one. Gleason's speculation was crowned with success. He bought himself a new cooking stove and erected an outbuilding on his estate, with both of which he favored the public in a new wood cut immediately.

Inspired by his success, old Fiji-Mermaid-Tom-Thumb-Woolly-Horse-Barnum, forthwith, got out another illustrated weekly, with pictures far more extensive, letter-press still sillier, and engravings more miserable, if possible, than Yankee Gleason's. And then we were bored and buffeted by having incredible likenesses of Santa Anna, Queen Victoria, and poor old Webster thrust beneath our nose, to that degree that we wished the respected originals had never existed, or that the art of wood engraving had perished with that of painting on glass.

It was, therefore, with the most intense delight that we saw the other day a notice of the failure and stoppage of *Barnum's Illustrated News*. We rejoice thereat greatly, and we hope that it will never be revived, and that Gleason will also fail as soon as he conveniently can, and that his trashy *Pictorial* will perish with it.

It must not be supposed from the tenor of these remarks, that we are opposed to the publication of a properly conducted and creditably executed illustrated paper. On the contrary, quite the reverse. We are passionately fond of art ourselves, and we believe that nothing can have a stronger tendency to refinement in society than presenting to the public chaste and elaborate engravings, copies of works of high artistic merit, accompanied by graphic and well-written essays. At a vast expenditure of money, time, and labor, and after the most incredible and unheard-of exertion on our part, individually, and with all the pictorial resources of the *San Diego Herald* at our command, we are at length able to present to the public an illustrated publication of unprecedented merit. It contains engravings of exceeding costliness and rare beauty of design, got up at an expensive scale, which never has been attempted before in this or any other country.

We furnish our readers this week with the first number, merely premising that the immense expense attending its issue will require a correspond-

Army. The Prince is of German extraction, his father being a Dutchman and his mother a Duchess.

Mansion of John Phœnix, Esq., San Diego, California.

House in which Shakspere was born, in Stratford-on-Avon.

Abbotsford, the residence of Sir Walter Scott, author of Byron's Pilgrim's Progress, etc.

The Capitol at Washington.

Residence of Governor Bigler, at Benicia, California.

Battle of Lake Erie, (*see remarks*, p. 96.)

[Page 96.]

The Battle of Lake Erie, of which our Artist presents a spirited engraving, copied from the original painting, by Hannibal Carracci, in the possession of J. P. Haven, Esq., was fought in 1836, on Chesapeake Bay, between the U. S. Frigates Constitution and Guerriere and the British Troops, under General Putnam. Our glorious flag, there as every where was victorious, and "Long may it wave, o'er the land of the free, and the home of *the slave.*"

Fearful accident on the Camden and Amboy Railroad!! Terrible loss of life!!!

View of the City of San Diego, by Sir Benjamin West.

Interview between Mrs. Harriet Beecher Stowe and the Duchess of Sutherland, from a group of Statuary, by Clarke Mills.

Bank Account of J. Phœnix, Esq., at Adams and Co., Bankers, San Francisco, California.

Gas Works, San Diego Herald Office.

Steamer Goliah.

View of a California Ranch.—Landseer.

Shell of an Oyster once eaten by General Washington; showing the General's manner of opening Oysters.

ing liberality on the part of the Public to cause it to be continued:—

PHŒNIX'S PICTORIAL,

And Second Story Front Room Companion.

| Vol. 1.] | San Diego, Oct. 1, 1853. | [No. 1. |

Portrait of His Royal Highness Prince Albert.—
Prince Albert, the son of a gentleman named Coburg,
is the husband of Queen Victoria of England, and the
father of many of her children. He is the inventor
of the celebrated "Albert hat," which has been
lately introduced with great effect in the U. S.

There! This is but a specimen of what we can do if liberally sustained. We wait with anxiety to hear the verdict of the public, before proceeding to any further and greater outlays.

INDUCEMENTS FOR CLUBBING

Twenty copies furnished for one year for fifty cents. Address John Phoenix, Office of the *San Diego Herald.* Payments *invariably* in advance.

John Phoenix.

1853

Critique of the Plains, Ode Symphonie Par Jabez Tarbox

GEORGE HORATIO DERBY (John Phoenix)

THIS glorious composition was produced for the first time in this or any other country by a very full orchestra (the performance taking place immediately after supper) and a chorus composed of the entire Sauer Kraut Verein, the Wie Gehtes Association, and the Pike Harmonic Society, assisted by Messrs. John Smith and Joseph Brown who held their coats, fanned them, and furnished water during the more overpowering passages.

The Plains does not depend for its success upon its plot, its theme, its school, or its master, for it has very little if any of them, but upon its soul-subduing, all-absorbing, highfaluting effect upon the audience.

The symphony opens upon the wide and boundless plains, Longitude 115 W., Latitude 35° 21' 03" N., and about sixty miles from the west bank of the Pitt River. These data are beautifully and clearly expressed by a long-drawn note from an E-flat clairionet. The sandy nature of the soil, sparsely dotted with bunches of cactus and artemesia, the extended view, flat and unbroken to the horizon, save by the rising smoke in the extreme verge from a Piute village, are represented by the bass drum. A few notes on the piccolo call the attention to a solitary antelope picking up mescal beans in the foreground. The sun, having an altitude of 36° 27', blazes down upon the scene in indescribable majesty. Gradually the sounds roll forth in a song of rejoicing to the God of Day:

"Of thy intensity
"And great immensity

238

> "Now then we sing;
> "Beholding in gratitude
> "Thee in this latitude,
> "Curious thing."

Which swells out into, "Hey, Jim along, Jim along, Josey!" Then *decrescendo*, dies away, and dries up.

Suddenly we hear approaching a train from Pike County, consisting of seven families with forty-six wagons, each drawn by thirteen oxen. Each family consists of a man in butternut-colored clothing driving the oxen, a wife in butternut-colored clothing riding in the wagon holding a butternut baby, and seventeen butternut children running promiscuously about the establishment. All are barefooted, dusty, and smell unpleasantly.

All these circumstances are expressed by pretty rapid fiddling for some minutes, winding up with a puff from the orpheclide. It is impossible to misunderstand the description.

Now rises o'er the plains in mellifluous accents the grand Pike County Chorus:

> "Oh, we'll soon be thar
> "In the land of gold,
> "Through the forest old,
> "O'er the mounting cold,
> "With spirits bold—
> "Oh, we come, we come,
> "And we'll soon be thar.
> "Gee up, Bolly! Whoo up! Whoo haw!"

The train now encamps. The unpacking of the kettles and mess pans, the unyoking of the oxen, the gathering about the various camp fires, the frizzling of the pork, are so clearly expressed by the music that the most untutored savage could comprehend it. Indeed, so vivid and lifelike was the representation, that a lady sitting near us involuntarily exclaimed aloud, *"Thar! That pork's burning!"* And it was truly interesting to watch the gratified expression of her face when, by a few notes of the guitar, the pan was removed from the fire and the blazing pork extinguished.

This is followed by the beautiful *aria*:

> Oh, marm! I want a pancake!"

Then that touching *recitative*:

> "Shet up, or I will spank you!"

To which succeeds a grand *crescendo* movement representing the flight of the child with the pancake, the pusuit of the mother, and the final arrest and summary punishment of the former, represented by rapid and successive strokes of the castanet.

The turning in for the night follows, and the deep and stertorious breathing of the encampment is well given by the bassoon, while the sufferings and trials of an unhappy father with an unpleasant infant are touchingly set forth by the cornet.

The NIGHT ATTACK of the Piutes, the fearful cries of the demonic Indians, the shrieks of the females and children, the rapid and effective fire of the rifles, the stampede of the oxen, their recovery and the final repulse—the Piutes being routed after a loss of thirty-six killed and wounded, while the Pikes lose but one scalp, from an old fellow who wore a wig and lost it in the scuffle. All this is faithfully given and excites the most intense interest in the minds of the hearers.

Then follows the grand chorus:

"Oh, We give them fits,
"The Injun Piutes.
"With our six-shooters—
"We give 'em particular fits."

After which we have a charming *recitative* to a frightened infant, which is really one of the most charming gems in the performance:

"Now, dern your skin, *can't* you be easy!"

Morning succeeds. The sun rises magnificently (octavo flute)—breakfast is eaten in a rapid movement on three sharps—the oxen are caught and yoked up, with a small drum and triangle—the watches, purses, and other valuables of the conquered Piutes are stored away in a camp kettle, to a small movement on the piccolo.

The train moves on with a grand chorus:

"We'll soon be thar.
"Gee up, Bolly! Whoo hup! Whoo haw!
"Whup! Whoo haw!
"Gee!
"Whup! Whoo haw!
"Gee!"

The immense expense attending the production of this magnificent work, the length of time required to prepare the chorus, the incredible number of instruments destroyed at each rehearsal, have hitherto prevented Mr. Tarbox from placing it before the American public. It has remained for San Diego to show herself superior to her sister cities of the Union in musical taste and appreciation and in high-souled liberality by patronizing this immortal prodigy.

We trust every citizen of San Diego and Vallecetos will listen to it ere it is withdrawn. And if there yet lingers in San Francisco one spark of musical fervor or a remnant of taste for pure harmony, we can only say that the *Southerner* sails from that place to San Diego once a fortnight and that the passage money is but forty-five dollars.

1854

Minority Report

Jonathan F. Kelley

Of ALL the public lecturers of our time and place, none have attracted more attention from the press, and consequently the people, than Ralph Waldo Emerson.

Lecturing has become quite a fashionable science—and now, instead of using the old style phrases for illustrating facts, we call travelling preachers perambulating showmen, and floating politicians, lecturers.

As a lecturer, Ralph Waldo Emerson is extensively known around these parts; but whether his lectures come under the head of law, logic, politics, Scripture, or the show business, is a matter of much speculation; for our own part, the more we read or hear of Ralph, the more we don't know what it's all about.

Somebody has said, that to his singularity of style or expression, Carlyle and his works owe their great notoriety or fame—and many compare Ralph Waldo to old Carlyle. They cannot trace exactly any great affinity between these two great geniuses of the flash literary school. Carlyle writes vigorously, quaintly enough, but almost always speaks when he says something; on the contrary, our flighty friend Ralph speaks vigorously, yet says nothing!

Of all men that have ever stood and delivered in presence of a reporter, none surely ever led these indefatigable knights of the pen such a wild-goose chase over the verdant and flowery pastures of the King's English, as Ralph Waldo Emerson. In ordinary cases, a reporter well versed in his art, catches a sentence of a speaker, and goes on to fill it out upon the most correct impression of what was intended, or what is implied. But no such license follows the outpouring of Mr. Emerson; no thought can fathom his intentions, and quite as bottomless are even his finished sentences. We have known "old stagers," in the newspaporial line, veteran reporters, so dumbfounded and confounded by the first fire of Ralph, and his grand and lofty acrobating in elocution, that they up, seized their hat and paper, and sloped, horrified at the prospect of an attempt to "take down" Mr. Emerson.

If Roaring Ralph touches a homely mullen weed, on a donkey heath, straightway he makes it a full-blown rose, in the land of Ophir, shedding an odor balmy as the gales of Arabia; while with a facility the wonderful London auctioneer Robbins might envy, Ralph imparts to a lime-box, or pig-sty, a negro hovel, or an Irish shanty, all the romance, artistic elegance and finish of a first-class manor-house, or Swiss cottage, inlaid with alabaster and fresco, surrounded by elfin bowers, grand walks, bee hives, and honeysuckles.

Ralph don't group his metaphorical beauties, or dainties of Webster, Walker, &c., but rushes them out in torrents—rattles them down in cataracts and avalanches—bewildering, astounding, and incomprehensible. He hits you with a metaphor so unwieldy and original, that your breath is soon gone—and before it is recovered, he gives you another rhapsody on t'other side, and as you try to steady yourself, bim comes another, heavier than the first two, while a fourth batch of this sort of elocution fetches you a bang over the eyes, giving you a vertigo in the ribs of your bewildered senses, and before you can say "God bless us!" down he has you —cobim! with a deluge of high-heeled grammar and three-storied Anglo Saxon, settling your hash, and brings you to the ground as though you were struck by lightning, or got in the way of a 36-pounder! Ralph Waldo is death and an entire stud of pale horses on flowery expressions and japonica-domish flubdabs. He revels in all those knock-kneed, antique, or crooked and twisted words we used all of us to puzzle our brains over in the days of our youth and grammar lessons and rhetoric exercises. He has a penchant as strong as cheap boarding-house butter, for mystification, and a free delivery of hard words, perfectly and unequivocally wonderful.

We listened one long hour by the clock of Rumford Hall, one night, to an outpouring of argumentum ad hominem of Mr. Emerson's—at what? A boy under an apple tree! If ten persons out of the five hundred present were put upon their oaths, they could no more have deciphered, or translated Mr. Ralph's argumentation, than they could the hieroglyphics upon the walls of Thebes, or the sarcophagus of old King Pharaoh!

When Ralph Waldo opens, he may be as calm as a May morn—he may talk for five minutes, like a book—we mean a common-sensed, understandable book; but all of a sudden the fluid will strike him—up he goes —down he fetches them. He throws a double somerset backwards over Asia Minor—flip-flaps in Greece—wings Turkey—and skeets over Iceland; here he slips up with a flower garden—a torrent of gilt-edged metaphors, that would last a country parson's moderate demand a long lifetime, are whirled with the fury and fleetness of Jove's thunderbolts. After exhausting this floral elocution, he pauses four seconds, pointing to vacuum, over the heads of his audience, he asks, in an anxious tone, "Do you see that?" Of course the audience are not expected to be so unmannerly as to ask "What?" If they were, Ralph would not give them time to "go in," for after asking them if they see that, he continues—

"There! Mark! Note! It is a malaria prism! Now, then; here—there; see it! Note it! Watch it!"

During this time, half of the audience, especially the old women and the children, look around, fearful of the ceiling falling in, or big bugs lighting on them. But the pause is for a moment, and anxiety ceases when they learn it was only a false alarm, only—

"Egotism! The lame, the pestiferous exhalation or concrete malformation of society!"

You breathe freer, and Ralph goes in, gloves on.

"Egotism! A metaphysical, calcareous, oleraceous amentum of—society! The mental varioloid of this sublunary hemisphere! One of its worst feelings or features is, the craving of sympathy. It even loves sickness, because actual pain engenders signs of sympathy. All cultivated men are infected more or less with this dropsy. But they are still the leaders. The life of a few men is the life of every place. In Boston you hear and see a few, so in New York; then you may as well die. Life is very narrow. Bring a few men together, and under the spell of one calm genius, what frank, sad confessions will be made! Culture is the suggestion from a few best thoughts that a man should not be a charlatan, but temper and subdue life. Culture redresses his balance, and puts him among his equals. It is a poor compliment always to talk with a man upon his specialty, as if he were a cheese-mite, and was therefore strong on Cheshire and Stilton. Culture takes the grocer out of his molasses and makes him genial. We pay a heavy price for those fancy goods, Fine Arts and Philosophy. No performance is worth less of geniality. That unhappy man called of genius, is an unfortunate man. Nature always carries her point despite the means!"

If that don't convince you of Ralph's high-heeled, knock-kneed logic, or au fait dexterity in concocting flap-doodle mixtures, you're ahead of ordinary intellect as far as this famed lecturer is in advance of gin and bitters, or opium discourses on—delirium tremens!

In short, Ralph Waldo Emerson can wrap up a subject in more mystery and science of language than ever a defunct Egyptian received at the hands of the mummy manufacturers.

In person, Mr. Ralph is rather a pleasing sort of man; in manners frank and agreeable; about forty years of age, and a native of Massachusetts. As a lawyer, he would have been the horror of jurors and judges; as a lecturer, he is, as near as possible, what we have described him.

1856

How Congress Governs

WILLIAM WIRT HOWE

To the Erudite Abel Ben Hassan:

(Copy to that excellent journal, the *Evening Post*, of New York, a place of some importance in the American Republic.)

My well-beloved, magnanimous, and eminent friend, Keeper of the Green Seal, Superintendent of the Sacks of the Bosphorus, Antelope of my Affections—In the Name of the Prophet, Greetings! I have been to Washington, in my capacity of Rear Admiral of the Turkish Navy, and—ALLAH be praised! I have returned in safety to New York.

I ought to give you a full description of the Capital of the United States of America, but, really, I am at a loss for something to describe.

It has no topography—no commerce—no art—no manufactures—no physical characteristics of a city.

Perhaps it may best be described by saying that it is a large lodging house for the executive, legislative, and judicial representatives of the Sovereign People. While these representatives remain in their lodging house, it flourishes. When they depart, it is like the ruins of Palmyra, and the wild beast and the serpent might wander safely through its desolate halls.

But what you chiefly wish to know, O learned friend, is the manner in which the business of governing is done in Washington. Let me briefly unfold this to your mind.

The representatives of the Sovereign People of the United States are original in their theory, and aboriginal in their practice, of legislation. The theory is that the Best Government is that which governs least.

The Members of Congress convene, pledged to support that glorious doctrine. From all parts of the land they assemble, prepared to do as little as possible in the way of governing. They have been carefully selected from the members of those who know nothing about the business of governing. They have studiously avoided any preparation for the task of governing. They carefully shun any associations, affiliations, affinities that might possibly furnish them with any knowledge of the subject of governing. Having assembled in solemn conclave, fully imbued with this original theory, they commence its aboriginal practice.

Like the North American Indians, of whom you have read in history—they have a Big Talk.

Before the session has commenced, however, it is well known that the Territory of Kickapoo is the subject to be talked about, and every Senator and Representative is fully prepared to talk about Kickapoo. As to the material and moral welfare of Kickapoo, they know nothing and care nothing; but as a subject for a Big Talk, they understand it thoroughly, and soon the talk begins.

Mr. Spreadeagle, Republican Representative in the House from Pennsylvania, gives notice of a Bill to Extend the Free Soil Area by Organizing the Territory of Kickapoo. The Bill goes to the Committee on Territories, whose chairman is hostile to the measure. He combats it from motives of the purest patriotism. Is he not a Democrat, and will not the Territory of Kickapoo send to Congress a Republican delegate, and when she becomes a state, Republican Senators and Representatives? The chairman puts the bill in his pocket and employs his time in driving out with the lovely wife of the gentleman from Arkansas.

Just as the motion is finally about to be put, Mr. Spreadeagle rises to a question of privilege.

——His remarks have been distorted and misinterpreted by the *Metropolitan Tomahawk*—the most ignorant, contemptible, dirty newspaper——

The Member from New York, second cousin of the editor of the *Tomahawk*, expresses the opinion that the Gentleman from Pennsylvania is a villain.

Mr. Spreadeagle gives utterance to his conviction that the Gentleman from New York is a drunken liar.

Sensation! Flashing of bowie knives! A rush from different quarters of the chamber! A lull. The Member from Pennsylvania explains his language by saying that he intended no personal allusion to the Gentleman from New York. The Gentleman from New York avers that the Member from Pennsylvania is the most upright and honorable man on the floor, and that as his remark to the contrary was made under the excitement of sudden exasperation, he withdraws the same.

The question returns to the motion to instruct the Committee on Territories to report on Kickapoo. The motion is debated by twenty-five Members on either side, each speaking not less than three hours.

The Gentleman from Alabama moves as an amendment that the word "not" be inserted in the resolution under discussion, so that it shall read that the Committee on Territories be instructed *not* to report on Kickapoo.

The debate is renewed and continued for a fortnight; during which time the Gentleman from Missouri distinguishes himself by talking three days and a half—the longest speech ever made by any man from the beginning of the world to the date of this letter.

At the expiration of this fortnight, the Gentleman from Vermont moves an amendment that the words "Fejee Islands" be inserted in the resolution, in place and stead of the word "Kickapoo."

The Speaker rules that the amendment is out of order. An appeal is taken from his decision. The Speaker holds that the question of appeal cannot be discussed. Another appeal is taken, and decided against the Speaker.

The question of the first appeal is thereupon discussed for one week— during which period the Gentleman from Connecticut favors the House with an eloquent review of English Parliamentary Law and Jefferson's Manual.

At length, the decision of the Speaker is sustained—when a motion is made to strike out from the resolution everything after the word, "Resolved." More talk. The Gentleman from Wisconsin delivers a speech which fills ten columns of the *Great Western Prairie Hen*, and which, says the editor of that journal, "for profound research and classic elegance, is unequaled in the annals of debate."

As he concludes, and the vote on the last amendment is about to be taken, the Gentleman from Michigan moves that the House adjourn. As that motion is always in order, the vote is taken and the House adjourns.

The friends of the Bill are in despair. The Senate has just passed a Bill to organize the Territory of Kickapoo, with the proviso that no native of Congo or Switzerland shall ever be allowed to set foot upon its soil; and that no one shall vote who cannot with his revolver bring down six men in six seconds at the distance of sixty feet.

Sensation! The Senate produces the sensation. The measure is known as the Six Sixty Bill. It goes to the House, and, after an interesting discussion of four weeks, is referred to a Special Committee. With singular swiftness, the Commitee report it in six minutes, without amendment. Greater sensation!

The Lobby—mighty mystery—is too busy for the Special Committee, and when the Report comes in it is ordered to lie on the table. It lies there for one month, and is nearly forgotten; when Mr. Spreadeagle gives notice that he shall call up the Bill—the Senate Bill—next week in the House.

The Bill is called up. The Gentleman from Maine offers an amendment to the effect that all natives of Congo who are whitewashed once a month may enter the territory, and that the Six Sixty Revolvers shall be of the Colt patent.

Debate on this amendment exceeds in length any previous one, occupying six weeks, including the evening sessions. Six of the more prominent members speak two days, each. The Gentleman from Maryland denounces the Colt patent, and asserts that Colt, the patentee, spends all his winters in Washington, dining, wining, and winning the Representatives of the People.

The Gentleman from Florida reviews the Scriptural and Ethnological arguments in favor of refusing any residence to natives of the Congo, whitewashed or unwhitewashed, and proves clearly that they have no business to be natives of the Congo. Fifteen other Gentlemen obtain permission to print speeches, which they have never had a chance to deliver, and so the country is supplied with waste paper at a postal expense of $250,000.

At last the previous question is moved and carried, and the Bill, as amended by the House, is passed. It returns to the Senate, and, by way of instructive variety, is there debated. The Senate orders a Committee of Conference. The House does the same.

The Committee of Conference convene. After due deliberation, they report in favor of the House amendments, provided the House will vote an appropriation of $50,000,000 for the purpose of establishing a line of ferry boats from San Francisco to the Navigator Islands.

A majority of the House are in favor of this simple compromise—their system of legislation being, confessedly, a congeries of compromises—but, unfortunately, only six days of the session remain.

Twenty members of the Opposition speak against time, relieving each other like sentinels, and instructing the country with regard to the prospects of everybody in the next Presidential campaign.

The momentous hour of adjournment arrives. The clock strikes. The Speaker's hammer falls. Congress has adjourned. THE BILL IS KILLED. At the hour of adjournment, thirty members of the House are on the floor, in a technical sense, and twenty-five, in a literal sense. Spiteful observers say that the supine posture of the latter is to be attributed to the effect of stimulating drink.

But the sublime theory, of which I have spoken, has been realized in practice. The Legislature has disbanded without governing at all. Do you ask what they *have* done? Well—

They have worn a large number of well-cut garments.

They have driven a large number of elegant horses.

They have aided the cause of temperance by destroying a large quantity of alcoholic beverages.

They have played innumerable games of billiards.

They have argued some causes in the Supreme Court.

They have combatted, with more or less success, the great Washington Tiger—faro.

They have aided a deserving Lobby in the prosecution of its shrewd ·designs.

They have flooded the country with printed documents, which are useful for various purposes.

They have drawn their pay and mileage.

And, with this, I suppose that you and I must be content.

In wonder, Thine,
Mohammed.

1859

How Abe Received the News

CHARLES FARRAR BROWNE (Artemus Ward)

THERE are several reports afloat as to how Honest Old Abe received the news of his nomination, none of which are correct. We give the correct report.

The Official Committee arrived in Springfield at dewy eve, and went to Honest Old Abe's house. Honest Old Abe was not in. Mrs. Honest Old Abe said Honest Old Abe was out in the woods splitting rails. So the Official Committee went out into the woods, where sure enough they found Honest Old Abe splitting rails with his two boys. It was a grand, a magnificent spectacle. There stood Honest Old Abe in his shirt-sleeves, a pair of leather home-made suspenders holding up a pair of home-made pantaloons, the seat of which was neatly patched with substantial cloth of a different color.

"Mr. Lincoln, Sir, you've been nominated, Sir, for the highest office, Sir—."

"Oh, don't bother me," said Honest Old Abe; "I took a stent this mornin' to split three million rails afore night, and I don't want to be pestered with no stuff about no Conventions till I get my stent done. I've only got two hundred thousand rails to split before sundown. I kin do it if you'll let me alone."

And the great man went right on splitting rails, paying no attention to the Committee whatever. The Committee were lost in admiration for a few moments, when they recovered, and asked one of Honest Old Abe's boys whose boy he was?

"I'm my parent's boy," shouted the urchin, which burst of wit so convulsed the Committee that they came very near giving out completely. In a few moments Honest Old Abe finished his task, and received the news with perfect self-possession. He then asked them up to the house, where

he received them cordially. He said he split three million rails every day, although he was in very poor health.

Mr. Lincoln is a jovial man, and has a keen sense of the ludicrous. During the evening he asked Mr. Evarts, of New York, "Why Chicago was like a hen crossing the street?" Mr. Evarts gave it up. "Because," said Mr. Lincoln, "Old Grimes is dead, that good old man!" This exceedingly humorous thing created the most uproarious laughter.

1860

The Latest Improvements in Artillery

ROBERT H. NEWELL (Orpheus C. Kerr)

Washington, D. C., August —, 1861.

By invitation of a well-known official, I visited the Navy-Yard yesterday, and witnessed the trial of some newly-invented rifled cannon. The trial was of short duration, and the jury brought in a verdict of "innocent of any intent to kill."

The first gun tried was similar to those used in the Revolution, except that it had a larger touch-hole, and the carriage was painted green, instead of blue. This novel and ingenious weapon was pointed at a target about sixty yards distant. It didn't hit it, and as nobody saw any ball, there was much perplexity expressed. A midshipman did say that he thought the ball must have run out of the touch-hole when they loaded up—for which he was instantly expelled from the service. After a long search without finding the ball, there was some thought of summoning the Naval Retiring Board to decide on the matter, when somebody happened to look into the mouth of the cannon, and discovered that the ball hadn't gone out at all. The inventor said this would happen sometimes, especially if you didn't put a brick over the touch-hole when you fired the gun. The Government was so pleased with this explanation, that it ordered forty of the guns on the spot, at two hundred thousand dollars apiece. The guns to be furnished as soon as the war is over.

The next weapon tried was Jink's double back-action revolving cannon for ferry-boats. It consists of a heavy bronze tube, revolving on a pivot, with both ends open, and a touch-hole in the middle. While one gunner puts a load in at one end, another puts in a load at the other end, and one touch-hole serves for both. Upon applying the match, the gun is whirled swiftly round on a pivot, and both balls fly out in circles, causing

254

great slaughter on both sides. This terrible engine was aimed at the target with great accuracy; but as the gunner has a large family dependent on him for support, he refused to apply the match. The Government was satisfied without firing, and ordered six of the guns at a million dollars apiece. The guns to be furnished in time for our next war.

The last weapon subjected to trial was a mountain howitzer of a new pattern. The inventor explained that its great advantage was, that it required no powder. In battle it is placed on the top of a high mountain, and a ball slipped loosely into it. As the enemy passes the foot of the mountain, the gunner in charge tips over the howitzer, and the ball rolls down the side of the mountain into the midst of the doomed foe. The range of this terrible weapon depends greatly on the height of the mountain and the distance to its base. The Government ordered forty of these mountain howitzers at a hundred thousand dollars apiece, to be planted on the first mountains discovered in the enemy's country.

These are great times for gunsmiths, my boy; and if you find any old cannon around the junk-shops, just send them along.

There is much sensation in nautical circles arising from the immoral conduct of the rebel privateers; but public feeling has been somewhat easier since the invention of a craft for capturing the pirates, by an ingenious Connecticut chap. Yesterday he exhibited a small model of it at a cabinet meeting, and explained it thus:

"You will perceive," says he to the President, "that the machine itself will only be four times the size of the *Great Eastern*, and need not cost over a few millions of dollars. I have only got to discover one thing before I can make it perfect. You will observe that it has a steam-engine on board. This engine works a pair of immense iron clamps, which are let down into the water from the extreme end of a very lengthy horizontal spar. Upon approaching the pirate, the captain orders the engineer to put on steam. Instantly the clamps descend from the end of the spar and clutch the privateer athwartships. Then the engine is reversed, the privateer is lifted bodily out of the water, the spar swings around over the deck, and the pirate ship is let down into the hold by the run. Then shut your hatches, and you have ship and pirates safe and sound."

The President's gothic features lighted up beautifully at the words of the great inventor; but in a moment they assumed an expression of doubt, and says he:

"But how are you going to manage, if the privateer fires upon you while you are doing this?"

"My dear sir," says the inventor, "I told you I had only one thing to discover before I could make the machine perfect, and that's it."

So you see, my boy, there's a prospect of our doing something on the ocean next century, and there's only one thing in the way of our taking in pirates by the cargo.

Yours, pensively,

Orpheus C. Kerr.

1861

Special Order

ANONYMOUS

WHEN General Grant was a brigadier in Southeast Missouri, he commanded an expedition against the rebels under Jeff Thompson in Northeast Arkansas. The greater portion of the route lay through a wilderness. The imaginary suffering that our soldiers endured the first two days of their march was enormous. It was impossible to steal or confiscate uncultivated real estate, and not a hog or a chicken or an ear of corn was anywhere to be seen.

On the third day, however, affairs looked more hopeful, for a few small specks of ground, in a state of partial cultivation, were here and there visible. That day, Lieutenant Wickfield, of an Indiana cavalry regiment, commanded the advance guard, consisting of eight mounted men. About noon, he came upon a small farmhouse, from the outward appearance of which he judged that there might be something fit to eat inside.

He halted his company, dismounted, and with two second lieutenants entered the dwelling. He knew that Grant's fame had already gone out through all that country, and it occurred to him that by representing himself to be the general, he might obtain the best the house afforded. So, assuming a very imperative demeanor, he accosted the inmates of the house, and told them that he must have something for himself and staff to eat.

They desired to know who he was, and he told them that he was Brigadier-General Grant. At the sound of that name, they flew around with alarming alacrity, and served up about all they had in the house, taking great pains all the while to make loud professions of loyalty to the Union. The lieutenants ate as much as they could of the not oversumptuous meal, but which was, nevertheless, good for that country. They demanded what was to pay?

"Nothing!" And they went their way rejoicing.

In the meantime, General Grant, who had halted his army a few miles back for a brief resting spell, came in sight of, and was rather favorably impressed with, the appearance of this same house. Riding up to the fence in front of the door, he asked to know if they would cook him a meal?

"No," said a woman in a gruff voice. "General Grant and his staff have just been here and eaten everything in the house except one pumpkin pie."

"Hmmm," said Grant. "What is your name?"

"Selvidge," replied the woman.

Casting a half dollar in at the door, Grant asked if she would keep the pie till he sent an officer for it—to which she replied that she would.

That evening, after the camping ground had been selected, the various regiments were notified that there would be a grand parade at half-past six, for orders. Officers would see that all their men turned out, etc.

In five minutes the camp was in a perfect uproar, and filled with all sorts of rumors. Some thought the enemy were upon them, it being so unusual to have parades when on a march.

At half-past six the parade was formed, ten columns deep, and nearly a quarter of a mile in length. After the usual routine of ceremonies, the Acting Assistant Adjutant-General read the following order:

HEADQUARTERS, ARMY IN THE FIELD

Special Order No. ——.

Lieutenant Wickfield, of the —— Indiana Cavalry, having on this day eaten everything in Mrs. Selvidge's house, at the crossing of the Ironton and Pocahontas and Black River and Cape Girardeau Roads, except one Pumpkin pie, Lieutenant Wickfield is hereby ordered to return with an escort of one hundred cavalry and eat that pie also.

U. S. GRANT,
Brigadier-General Commanding.

1862

The Yankee of It

JAMES ROBERTS GILMORE (Edmund Kirke)

I NEVER knowed a Yankee but once, and he was about as smart as could be, for he sold Dad a clock. You see, Dad had nary a clock, and couldn't tell when the sun riz—he had a great respect for the sun, never got up afore it in all his life—so when a peddler come long with a whole wagonload of clocks, Dad was dreadful put to it to have one.

They was the eight-day kind, all painted up slick, and warranted to go till the end of time. The peddler asked ten dollars for 'em, and Dad hadn't but three. I had two dollars I'd been a-saving up, and Dad wanted to borrow them, but I wouldn't a-lent to him to save his soul, for I knowed he'd never pay in nothing but promises, and for his age Dad was the most promising man you ever knowed on.

Well, I buttoned up my pocket and Dad eyed the clocks. And, says he to the peddler, "Stranger, I'd like one of them mightily, but money's scarce just now. I hain't got only three dollars in the world."

"Hain't ye?" said the peddler. "Well, that's an all-fired pity. But being's you're a monstrous nice sort of man, and being's I always kind of took to such folks as you are, you can have the clock for your three dollars. But I wouldn't sell one to nary other man for that money."

So Dad took the clock and the peddler took the money and moseyed off.

Dad set dreadful high on that clock. He took on over it for all the world, just like a child with a new plaything. He got up earlier and set up later than I ever knowed him to afore, just to hear it strike, but after a few days it stopped striking and never struck again. Dad was sold—and sold, too, by a rantankerous Yankee, and Dad always accounted that a Yankee is a little the measliest critter in all creation.

Not more than a month after that, as Dad and I was a-working in the corn patch one day, who should come long the road but the Yankee peddler.

As soon as Dad seed him, he says to me, "Bullets and blisters, Tom! There's that outdacious Yankee! Now, if I don't strike better time on his noggin than his clocks ever struck in all their lives, I'll pike straight for Kingdom Come, if I have to go afoot!"

Biling with wrath, Dad made for the peddler. He hadn't got more than inside hearing afore the Yankee bawled out:

"I say, Mister, you've got a clock as belongs to me. It won't go, and I want to get it and give ye one as will go. I had just one bad un in the lot, and I've been searching for it among nigh onto a hundred folks I've sold clocks to, and hain't found it yet, so you must have took it."

That mellowed Dad to once. To own the truth, it give *me* a sort of good opinion of Yankees. Well, Dad and he swapped clocks and the peddler stayed to dinner. The old man wouldn't take a red cent for it, he was so taken with the Yankee.

As he was a-going to leave, the peddler opened the hind end of his wagon, and taking out a peck measure, heaping full of what peared to be the tallest oats that ever growed, he says to me, says he, "Tom, you and your father have been amazing clever to me. I never like to be obligated to nobody. So here's some of the finest planting oats you ever knowed on. Take them. They'll grow you a monstrous crop, as big as oak trees."

Now, you see, I had a four-year-old mare I'd raised up with my own hands. I set dreadful high on her, and she was dreadful anxious for oats. I'd been saving up them two dollars to buy seed to make a crop for her private eating. When I viewed them oats of the peddler's, they filled my eye, like the camel filled the eye of the needle in Scripture. He hadn't given me enough to go no distance in planting, but, being's he was so generous-like, I couldn't ask him to give more.

So I says to him "Stranger, wouldn't ye sell a bushel of them oats?"

"Well, Tom," he says, "being's it's you, and you and your father is such monstrous clever folk, I don't know but what I'd sell you the whole of 'em. The fact is, they're too *hearty* for my hoss. You see, the feller's got a sort of weak stomach and can't digest 'em. I guess there's nigh onto five bushel, and seeing's they're no use to me, you shall have 'em for that two dollars of yours."

I figgered on my fingers, and found that warn't more than forty cents a bushel. Oats, such as were raised in our diggings, and they warn't noway as nice as them, went for sixty cents, so you can reckon I took 'em, and you might believe it rained big blessings on that peddler about the time he drove off.

He'd altered my opinion of the Yanks completely. I told him he ought to travel the whole Southern country, just to show folk what the Yankees really is. I told him I knowed if he done that, our folk would swap their opinions of the Yankees just as I had.

After he was gone, I took the five bushel into the house. I kivered 'em up careful in the cockloft. But, feeling mighty generous-like, on account of my big bargain, I thought I'd kind of give the mare a dinner of the peck measure full. I put them afore her, and she smelled on 'em, ravenous mad for a minute. Then she turned up her nose and wouldn't look at 'em again.

She found them too hearty-like, I suppose. I reckon they would have been rather hard of digestion, for they was *shoe pegs!* Wooden shoe pegs! The damned Yankee had scoured the whole district and found nobody green enough to buy 'em but me. And the clock he'd swapped to Dad—it was worse than t'other. It never struck once.

It takes a smart one to get ahead of a Yankee, but he didn't get ahead of me. I was three dollars into him when I got shut of them oats. Ye see, I toted 'em to Pikeville. I sold 'em for what they really was—shoe pegs—and got five dollars for the lot. The Yankee peddler might have done it, if he could anyhow have brought his mind to be honest. But he'd rather cheat for half-price than trade for full pay.

And that's the sort of Yankee that's sent amongst us here in Tennessee. They've done a heap towards giving us the opinion we hold about the North and bringing on war between us.

1864

Honest Abe's Instances

ANONYMOUS

LINCOLN neither smoked nor drank, and once a visitor praised him on having no vices. "That's a compliment, but a doubtful one," the gaunt Illinois lawyer said. "It's been my experience that folks who have no vices, have plaguey few virtues."

Some years before Lincoln became President, a New York firm wrote him as to the financial condition of a neighbor in Springfield, Illinois. For some speculation or other, the man had applied to the Eastern firm for credit.

Lincoln replied, "Yours of the 10th instant received. I am well acquainted with Mr. Blank and know his circumstances. First of all, he has a wife and baby. Together, they ought to be worth $50,000 to any man. Secondly, he has an office in which there is a table worth $1.50, and three chairs worth, say, $1. Last of all, there is in one corner a large rat-hole which will bear looking into.

Respectfully yours
A. Lincoln."

As to his being a candidate for reelection in 1864, Lincoln said, "That reminds me of what old Jesse Dubois once said to an itinerant preacher. Jesse was State Auditor of Illinois and had charge of the State House at Springfield. The preacher asked use of the State House for a lecture.

" 'On what subjects?' said Jesse.

" 'On the second coming of Our Saviour, which is soon due,' answered the long-faced man.

" 'Oh, bosh!' said Uncle Jesse. 'If our Saviour had ever been to Springfield and had got away with his life, he'd be too everlastingly smart to think of coming here again.'

"And," said Lincoln, "that's very much the way I feel about a second term."

At another time, someone speaking about the coming election, remarked to Lincoln that nothing could defeat him short of Grant's capturing Richmond before the balloting. In that case, Grant, the hero of the hour, would probably be nominated at the Chicago Convention.

"Well," said the President, "about that, I feel very much like the man who didn't want to die particularly, but said, if he *had* to die, that was precisely the disease he would like to die of."

Defrees, the Government printer, who had charge of setting up the President's messages to Congress, was disturbed by Lincoln's use of the term "sugar-coated." He went to him and pointed out that a message to Congress was a different affair from a speech at a mass meeting in Illinois.

"You have used an undignified slang expression, Mr. President," said Defrees. "I suggest substitution of some more fitting expression. Remember, this message becomes a part of our history and should be written accordingly."

"Defrees," replied Lincoln, "that word expresses precisely my idea. I am not going to change it. The time will never come in this country when the people won't know exactly what *sugar-coated* means."

Franklin W. Smith, a Boston contractor, furnishing war supplies, was tried by court-martial and found guilty of shadily pocketing money out of a contract with the Navy Department. The report of the court-martial was sent to President Lincoln for his examination. He returned it with this characteristic endorsement:

Whereas, Franklin W. Smith had transactions with the United States Navy Department to a million and a quarter of dollars, and had the chance to steal a quarter of a million; and, *whereas*, he was charged with stealing only ten thousand dollars, and from the final revision of the testimony it is only claimed that he stole one hundred dollars, I don't believe he stole anything at all.

Therefore, the records of the court-martial, together with the finding and sentence, are disapproved, declared null and void, and the defendant is fully discharged.

A. LINCOLN.

The Chief Magistrate was besieged with citizens, of high and low degree, from near and far, who came to define the flaws in his war policies and offer him their own sure-fire remedies and general advice. In the procession at the White House one day was a Western clergyman.

The President shook hands with him, invited him to be seated, and resignedly sat down himself. Then, with a patient expression, Lincoln sighed, "I am now ready to hear what you have to say."

"Oh, bless you, sir!" said the clergyman. "I have nothing special to say. I merely called to pay my respects to you, and to assure you, as one of millions who feel as I do, of hearty sympathy and support."

"My dear sir!" gasped the President, rising quickly, his face showing instant relief. For the second time, and heartily, he grasped the visitor's hand. "My *dear* sir! I am *very* glad to see you! I thought you had come to preach to me!"

To ease the tension of the black news from the fronts, Lincoln asked Seward to take with him a brisk stroll down Pennsylvania Avenue. However, the gloom of the Secretary of State was too deep to be broken by mere exercise. Lincoln's attempts at conversation and anecdotal stories evoked only mumbles in response.

"A new shop," the President remarked in passing, gesturing to a freshly painted sign projecting out over the footway. "Hm-m, I haven't my spectacles, Seward. What is the owner's name?"

Seward glanced up, saying listlessly, "T. R. STRONG."

"But coffee are stronger," wickedly murmured the President.

It is said that Seward's startled and indignant groan alarmed the lobbiests in the Willard Bar, and that his subsequent roar of helpless laughter carried all the way back to the White House.

Rebel raiders, cutting telegraph lines and uprooting railway tracks, had made communications very difficult and slow. When finally the telegram from Cumberland Gap informed Lincoln that "firing had been heard in the direction of Knoxville," he said, "I'm glad of it."

Governor Sprague, who had the perils of Burnside's position in mind, could not see why Lincoln should be "glad of it," and so expressed himself.

"Why, you see, Governor," responded the President, "it reminds me of Mistress Sally Ward, a neighbor of mine in Illinois, who had a very large family. Occasionally one of her numerous children would be heard crying in some out-of-the-way place, and Mistress Sally would always say, 'Well, there's one of them that ain't dead yet.' "

After the death of Chief Justice Taney, a committee from the Philadelphia Union League came to Washington to urge Lincoln to appoint Salmon P. Chase to the vacancy on the Supreme Court bench. They took with them a memorial addressed to the President, signed by many citizens, and this was read to him by one of the committee.

After listening to it, Lincoln said in a deliberate manner, "Gentlemen, will you do me the favor to leave the paper with me? I want it so that, if I appoint Mr. Chase, I may show the friends of the other persons for whom the office is solicited, how powerful an influence and by what strong personal recommendations, the claims of Mr. Chase were supported."

The committee listened with great satisfaction. They were about to depart, thinking that Chase was sure of the appointment, when they perceived that the President had not finished what he intended to say.

"And I want the paper also," said he, after a pause, "in order that, if I should appoint any other person, I may show *his* friends how powerful an influence, and what strong recommendations, I was obliged to disregard in appointing him."

The committee departed as wise as they came.

"Why do men vote as they do?" said the President. "Well, that's sometimes hard to say. Senator Zack Chandler, of Michigan, delved into that a little last election, I believe.

"Uncle Zack, you know, likes to know what's what. During the voting, he took his stand near the polls, with a box containing a fat possum, just the right sort for roasting. He questioned three men as to how they intended voting, saying that he would give the possum to the one with the best reasons for the way he intended casting his ballot.

"The first man said, 'I aim to vote Republican, because my party has freed the slaves, is putting down the rebellion, and ain't never fired on the old flag.'

" 'Fine, fine!' said Uncle Zack.

" 'I'm voting Democrat,' said the second man, 'because I think the greenbacks and bonds will be repudiated, and because I think this cruel war should stop and we ought to make peace before there's any more bloodshed.'

"Uncle Zack scowled and put the lid on the box that held the possum. 'Now,' he said to the third man, 'how are you voting?'

" 'Republican, sir.'

" 'Why are you voting Republican?' said Uncle Zack, brightening a little.

" 'Because,' said the man, 'because—because I want that possum!' "

A gentleman called on Lincoln, and solicited a pass through the lines to Richmond, where he had relatives.

"Well," said the President, "I would be very happy to oblige you, if my passes were respected. But the fact is, sir, I have, within the last two years, given passes to two hundred and fifty thousand men to go to Richmond, and not one has got there yet."

1861-1890

A. Lincoln.

Shiloh

Anonymous

THEY say the Shiloh battle was a turning point, and I reckon, when all the returns come in, it will be found I turned it, all unbeknown to myself.

You see, on the second day of the fighting, early in the morning it was, with the outcome in the balances, Clem Acuff and me was stationed behind a big water oak on an advanced position. There's no better place to picket from than behind a big tree. It takes a siege-mortar shell hitting that tree square to distract you from your business.

Unless, naturally, there's a charge in force. Which I pretty soon saw there was.

Heard it, rather—heard the Yankees coming. It was just the skirmishers but I could hear the way they hit the ground with their feet, and I said to Clem, "Look around this here tree, Clem, and see how many's at hand."

"You look," says Clem. "Your neck's the longest."

I didn't like to hear that kind of talk from Clem, and I told him so and told him he ought to be ashamed. But Clem, to be blunt on it, he was always apt to be a *leetle* on the safe side, where fearlessness comes proper to me. So, feeling the responsibility of the whole Confederate army in the West on my shoulders, I made him do his duty. I'm bigger'n Clem, you know, and I gave him a heave and pushed him out to see what was coming?

That's when I found my trust had been mislaid in Clem Acuff. He never even bothered to look. He took a running start from my shove and made for the rear, while the pounding of them feet approaching the water oak tree sounded louder and dangerouser than ever.

Well, there was Clem out in the open a-running. It made my heart bleed. Maybe I ought not to have put the safety of one comrade before the thousands that depent on me that day, but flesh is weak. I couldn't help it. I left my musket where it was tilted against the tree and took after Clem, to see if I could shield my friend's rear in case of enemy volleys, you know, with my own body.

A thousand times I've told myself I was at fault. But right then, all I could think on was Clem's safety. Even if the Yankees I could listen to scampering behind us didn't plant a ball in his back, he might get lost in all them woods and get to feeling bad. Well, sir, not if I could help it! I aimed to ketch up with Clem, and lead the way for him so as he wouldn't find himself lost the first thing I knew.

Clem, I must say, didn't make it easy for me. If he'd gone a little milder and hadn't kept jumping so high over bushes, logs, trenches, and earthworks, I could have possibly eased down enough to turn around and get a reckoning on the size of the force that was crowding us. But not Clem—no sir! He went racketing through them Shiloh woods to where I could hardly keep abreast of him, and was hard put to draw ahead.

That's where the big run commenced. You see, the rest of the boys, knowing me for the fearless-charactered man I am, mistook my motions. It's true I tried to signal them as I went past, to let them know. I winked at a Mississippi rigiment—that's what I think that gray blur was—and I lept a Louisiana battery a little lower than I'd been leaping batteries, all a purpose to give them an idea that I was acting unusual, and there must be something back of it.

Misfortunately, none of it did any good. You see, it was famous among the boys how fearless I am, and they took the wrong notion. They said, "If a man as all-fired Yankee-eating brave as all that is making for California in two days on foot, then there ain't any use, boys, in us wasting any more time here. The whole blue-bellied horde must be upon us, and maybe the Redcoats, too!"

That's when General Johnston's boys took out. He'd passed on, and there was only Beauregard to try and stop them, and you know they wouldn't pay any attention to any little spruce feller from the Louisiana swamps. They never stopped the rout this side of Corinth, but I never knew about it till later, what a springtide of running I'd started.

You see, I'd caught my toe on the top branch of a small twenty or thirty year-old beech tree I was passing, and took a tumble. The army was two hours passing over my prostrate form before I could get to my feet.

When I did get erect, I heard that Yankee scampering noise still behind, just like had alarmed Clem Acuff way back at the big water oak tree. Twenty thousand feet, bare and shod, had made stepping stones of my spine-bones, and I wasn't all ready, right then, to pick up after poor Clem till I got my breath back.

I couldn't help it. I had to look back, for I now realized how the Confederate army had stampeded because of watching me trying to do an innocent, friendly deed for Clem Acuff.

Yes, I looked behind toward that scampering sound that was closing in on me—and I tell you! I never saw a handsomer pair of red milch-heifers gamboling through the woods in all my life.

1870's

Waifs and Strays from the Late Unpleasantness

ANONYMOUS

A SENTIMENTAL young lady in Northern Georgia indited the following to some of her admirers in a regiment of that State:

> 'Tis hard for you-ens to sleep in camp;
> 'Tis hard for you-ens to fight.
> 'Tis hard for you-ens through snow to tramp,
> In snow to sleep at night.
> But harder for we-ens from you-ens to part,
> Since you-ens have stolen we-ens' hearts.

Among the troops in Western Virginia, stories about the Philippa affair formed a staple of conversation. One of their favorites concerned a certain Indiana company. Almost worn out with marching, the men were straggling along with very little regard to order.

Hurrying up to his men, the Captain shouted, "Close up, boys! Damn you, close up! If the Rebs was to fire on you when you're straggling along like you are, they couldn't hit a damned one of you!"

A war correspondent of a New Orleans paper wrote from Jackson, Tennessee, "An officer of my acquaintance, who is inordinately fond of fritters, just dropped into a dwelling at Jackson a day or two since, where this delicacy was smoking hot on the table, and very politely asked to share the meal with the landlady. She complied graciously, and asked him to be seated.

" 'Will you take the *twinkley twinkle*,' she asked, 'or *on the dab?*'

"My friend was entirely ignorant of these terms, but at a venture chose the former. He was soon enlightened. The ancient female dipped her not over-clean fingers into a tumbler of molasses standing beside her, and allowing the drippings to fall on the delicacy, presented it to him as *twinkley twinkle. On the dab* was a spoonful of treacle upon the center of the fritter."

Stonewall Jackson did not conceal his contempt for incompetent fellow officers. At a council of generals early in the war, one remarked that Major ——— had been wounded, and would be unable to perform a task that it was proposed to assign him.

"Wounded!" said Jackson. "If it is really so, it must have been by an accidental discharge of his duty."

Congressman John M. Allen, of Mississippi, told the story of an officer who "was leading his regiment in one of the most gallant retreats that regiment ever engaged in. The Yankees were riding close behind and pressing the boys everywhere. There were some indiscreet men in his command who would turn around and fire at them occasionally. With hat off, from the head of his regiment, the officer turned and looked back and gave his command:

" 'Boys, stop that shooting. It just makes 'em madder.' "

One of our warships was just going into action against an armed, richly laden rebel blockade runner, when an officer noticed a sailor down on his knees praying vigorously.

"Afraid?" sneered the officer.

"No, not especially, sir."

"Then what are you praying for?"

"That the rebel shot will be distributed the same way as the prize money is—principally among the officers."

A letter that passed through the Louisville post office bore the following superscription:

> "Feds and Confeds, let this go free
> "Down to Nashville, Tennessee.
> "This three-cent stamp will pay the cost,
> "Until you find Sophia Yost.

"Postmasters North, or even South,
"May open it and find the truth.
"I merely say my wife's got well,
"And has a baby cross as hell."

When we arrived into Maryland, I saw around a Yankee lady a large crowd of Dixie soldiers. She was telling them she had expected to see the finest men of the South, clothed magnificently, but she was disappointed; she found them a set of ragamuffins, and asked why we did not wear good clothes?

One of our lieutenant-colonels says, "Madam, we do not put on our best things to kill dogs in. But," he continued, "madam, *we* expected to find the greater portion of your state to be secessionists, but I find them Yankees."

The lady replied, "Yes, but I understand that there are plenty of Yankees in Virginia, too."

An old Negro wagoner, getting upon his mule, says, "Yes, marm, I know it, kaze I seed 'em dar. Dey was dead-uns, though."

During the march of McClellan's army up the Peninsula from Yorktown, a tall Vermont soldier got separated from his regiment and was trudging along through the mud, endeavoring to overtake it. Finally coming to a crossing, he was puzzled as to which road he should take, but on seeing one of the natives, his countenance lighted up, and he inquired:

"Where does this road lead to?"

"To hell," was the Virginian's surly reply.

"Well," drawled the Vermonter, "judging by the lay of the land and the looks of the inhabitants, I calculate I'm most there."

Colonel Sol. Meredith, of Wayne County, commanded the Nineteenth Indiana on the Potomac. At the Lewinsville skirmish, the Colonel was at the head of his men as they were formed in line of battle under the fire of the enemy. As the shells exploded over them, his boys would involuntarily duck their heads. The Colonel saw their motions, and in a pleasant way exhorted them as he rode along the line, to hold up their heads and act like men.

He turned to speak to one of his officers, and at that moment an eighteen-pounder shell burst within a few yards of him, scattering the fragments in all directions. Instinctively he jerked his head almost to the saddle-bow, while his horse squatted in fear.

The Colonel raised up and reined his steed. "Boys," he said, "you MAY dodge the large ones."

After that, no more was said about the impropriety of dodging shells.

"After Stonewall Jackson was killed," said the rebel prisoner, "two angels were sent down to earth to carry him back with them. They searched all through the camp but couldn't find him. They went to the prayer-meeting, to the hospital, and every other place they thought he'd likely be. No sign of him anywhere. Finally they had to give up and return without him. What was their surprise to find that he'd executed another of his brilliant flank movements and got into heaven before them! Old Stonewall apologized and said it was just force of habit, he reckoned."

A political Brigadier was dozing under an oak, complaining of the noise, during the full fury of Antietam, when a stray bullet, which was somehow spending itself far to the rear, knocked him sideways.

"Are you hurt?" babbled an aide, rushing to him, as the portly military man staggered to his feet and glanced downward in horror.

"Hurt!" wheezed the warrior. "I'm a dead man! Don't you see? Shot through the bladder!" And he fainted dead away.

A glance showed that the Brigadier, from his standpoint, was even more seriously injured than he had supposed. The minié ball had pierced, not his flesh, but his canteen, draining off almost two pints of twenty year-old brandy.

Military necessity prevented two Massachusetts lovers from joining in marriage. The young soldier was repeatedly refused leave of absence, and the War Department would not permit the lady to go to the distant front to have the rite solemnized. At last, appeal was made to the heart of His Excellency the Governor of Massachusetts. He at once forwarded the lady's correspondence to Washington with, as it turned out, this most effective endorsement:

"*To the Hon. E. M. Stanton, Secretary of War:*

"This case appeals to all our sympathies as patriots and as gentlemen. I appeal to the chivalry of the Department of War, which presides over more heroes than Homer ever dreamed of. I pray that you may grant this request of my fair correspondent, and generations will rise up and call us blessed.

"J. A. Andrew."

An Arkansas Colonel, whose formal military training is not of the most extensive, has the following order for mounting his men:
First order—"Prepare for to git onto yore critters."
Second order—"GIT!"

Writing to her cousin, a prisoner at Camp Morton, Indianapolis, a Southern girl says: "I will be for Jeffdavise till the tenisee river freazes over, and then scratch on the ice,

> " 'Jeffdavise rides a white horse,
> " 'Lincoln rides a mule,
> " 'Jeffdavise is a gentleman,
> " 'And Lincoln is a fule.' "

In the vicinity of Culpepper, where both sides had been foraging, a correspondent talked to a farmer, asking him which side he took in the struggle?
"I'm a no-sider," said the old fellow, gloomily surveying the streaks in the soil where his fences and hog pens had once stood. "I hain't tuck no sides, but I'll be doggoned if both sides hain't tuck me."

Jake Mathis, of the 13th Georgia, was a good soldier, but when the Confederates were retreating from Gettysburg, Jake threw his musket on the ground, flopped at the roadside, and said, "Now, I'll be dogged if I walk another step! I kain't do it."
"Git up, you Jake there!" said the Captain. "Don't you know the Yankees is at our heels?"
"Kain't help that. I jest kain't march another step. I'm beat out."
The column trotted on, over a hill, and lost sight of Jake.
In a few moments, musket-fire broke out behind and shells commenced to crash. All at once, Jake streaked over the point of the hill, followed by clouds of dust. As he passed the column, his captain called:
"Thought you said you couldn't march, Jake?"
"Hell's afire!" Jake's voice faded back. "You don't call *this* marching, do you?"

A war-beaten veteran of Longstreet's corps was talking to a Northern officer. Said he, "I don't understand this. Lee won a big victory over Grant on the Rapidan, and told us so, and that night we retreated. Then he won another in the Wilderness, and told us so, and we retreated to Spottsylvania. Then Lee won another tree-*men*-jus victory, and I got tuck prisoner, but I reckon he's retreating agin.

"Now, when *we* used to lick 'em, the Yanks fell back and claimed a victory, and we understood it. Now, Lee claims victories, and keeps a-falling back, and I *can't understand it.*"

1861-1890's

Gain for Somebody

ANONYMOUS

A GENTLEMAN in Atlanta, Georgia, whom we will call Mack, mysteriously intimated to a freedman he had once owned that he had hidden his plate at the bottom of his well, to save it from the Yankees. He said that, as soon as it was safe, he intended to exhume the plate, and asked the freedman to hold the information in strictest confidence.

The upshot of the matter was that about one hundred Negroes soon knew that several thousands of dollars worth of silver, and an unknown quantity of gold, had been precipitated into this well, and had sunk among the trash and rubbish with which it had for some time been filled, rendering it useless.

Speedily the affair was brought to the ears of the Provost Marshal, and Mack one morning, on going to see about his well, found it guarded by a strong squad of soldiers who forbade anyone coming on the premises.

Mack protested against any such proceeding, and persisted that everything on the lot, in the well and out of it, was his property. The Assistant Provost Marshal ordered him off his own property, rebel that he was.

A strong posse of freedmen was sent down into the well to work. Bucketful after bucketful of rubbish and mud was drawn out, but no treasure as yet made its appearance. Occasionally the officer of the guard went down on a prospecting tour. In punching about with a bayonet, he would hit on something that had the true metallic ring. They had the treasure now, surely. Again the Negroes went to work, and after laboring some hours succeeding in bringing out an old tin plate, the top of a discarded stove, or something similar.

At last, the firm bottom of the well was reached, but no treasure. Mack said he thought it was about ten feet further down. Whatever may have been the Provost Marshal's opinion on the subject, he concluded he had not time to prosecute the search further, and withdrew his forces, leaving Mack in possession of a thoroughly cleansed well, and at liberty to hunt up the treasure if he wanted to.

Mack didn't want to.

1864

The Evidence in the Case

SAMUEL L. CLEMENS (Mark Twain)

I REPORTED this trial simply for my own amusement, one idle day last week—but I have seen the facts in the case so distorted and misrepresented in the daily papers that I feel it my duty to come forward and do what I can to set the plaintiff and defendant right before the public. This can best be done by submitting the plain, unembellished statements of the witnesses as given under oath before his honor Judge Sheperd, in the San Francisco Police Court. There is that nice sense of justice and that ability to discriminate between right and wrong among the masses, which will enable them, after carefully reading the testimony, to decide without hesitation in the remarkable case of Smith vs. Jones.

To such as are not used to visiting the Police Court, I will observe that there is nothing inviting about the place, there being no rich carpets, no mirrors, no pictures, no elegant sofa or armchairs to lounge in, no free lunch—and, in fact, nothing to make a man who has been there once desire to go again.

There is a pulpit at the head of the hall, occupied by a handsome gray-haired judge, with a faculty of appearing pleasant and impartial to the disinterested spectator, and prejudiced and frosty to the last degree to the prisoner at the bar. To the left of the pulpit is a long table for reporters; in front of the pulpit the clerks are stationed, and in the center of the hall a nest of lawyers. On the left again are pine benches behind a railing, occupied by seedy white men, negroes, Chinamen, Kanakas—in a word, by the seedy and dejected of all nations—and in a corner is a box where more can be had when they are wanted. On the right are more pine benches, for the use of prisoners, and their friends and witnesses.

An officer in a gray uniform, and with a star upon his breast, guards the door.

A holy calm pervades the scene.

The case of Smith vs. Jones being called, each of these parties, stepping out from among the other seedy ones, gave the court a particular circumstantial account of how the whole thing occurred, and then sat down.

The two narratives differed from each other.

In reality, I was half persuaded that these men were talking about two separate and distinct affairs altogether, inasmuch as no single circumstance mentioned by one was even remotely hinted at by the other.

Mr. Alfred Sowerby was then called to the witness stand, and testified, "I was in the saloon at the time, your Honor, and I see this man Smith come up all of a sudden to Jones, who warn't saying a word, and split him in the snoot."

LAWYER.—"Did what, sir?"

WITNESS.—"Busted him in the snoot."

LAWYER.—"What do you mean by such language as that? When you say that the plaintiff suddenly approached the defendent, who was silent at the time, and 'busted him in the snoot,' do you mean that the plaintiff struck the defendent?"

WITNESS.—"I'm swearing to that very circumstance. Yes, your Honor, that was just the way of it. Now, for instance, as if you was Jones and I was Smith. Well, I comes up all of a sudden and says to your Honor, says I, 'Damn your old tripe—'"

THE COURT.—"Order in the court! Witness, confine yourself to a plain statement of the facts in this case."

LAWYER.—"Take the witness. I have no further use for him."

The lawyer on the other side said he would endeavor to worry along without the assistance of Mr. Sowerby, and Mr. McWilliamson was next called, and deposed as follows:

"I was a-standing as close to Mr. Smith as I am to this pulpit, a-chaffing with one of the lager beer girls—Sophronia by name, being from somewheres in Germany, so she says, but as to that I—"

LAWYER.—"Never mind the nativity of the beer girl, but state as concisely as possible what you know of the assault and battery."

WITNESS.—"Well, German or no German—which I'll take my oath I don't believe she is, being red-headed, with long, bony fingers—"

LAWYER.—"Stick to the assault and battery. Go on with your story."

WITNESS.—"Well, sir, she—that is Jones—he sidled up and drawed his revolver and tried to shoot the top of Smith's head off, and Smith run, and Sophronia she walloped herself down in the sawdust and screamed twice, just as loud as she could yell. I never see a poor creature in such distress —and then she sung out: 'Oh, hell's fire! What are they up to now?' Saying which, she jerked another yell and fainted away as dead as a wax figger. Thinks I to myself, I'll be damned if this ain't getting rather dusty, and I'll—"

THE COURT.—"We have no desire to know what you thought. We only wish to know what you saw. Are you sure Mr. Jones tried to shoot the top of Mr. Smith's head off?"

WITNESS.—"Yes, your Honor."

THE COURT.—"How many times did he shoot?"

WITNESS.—"Well, sir, I can't say exactly as to the number—but I should think—well, say, seven or eight times—as many as that, anyway."

THE COURT.—"Be careful now, and remember you are under oath. What kind of pistol was it?"

WITNESS.—"It was a derringer, your Honor."

THE COURT.—"A derringer! You must not trifle here, sir. A derringer only shoots once. How could Jones have fired seven or eight times?"

The witness is evidently as stunned by that last proposition as if a brick had struck him. "Well, your Honor—he—that is, she—Jones, I mean— Soph—"

THE COURT.—"Are you sure he fired more than one shot? Are you sure he fired at all?"

WITNESS.—"I—I, well, perhaps he didn't—and—and, your Honor may be right. But, you see, that girl, with her dratted yowling—altogether, it might be that he did only shoot once."

LAWYER.—"And about his attempting to shoot the top of Smith's head off—didn't he aim at his body or legs? Come now."

WITNESS.—"Yes, sir—I think he did—I—I'm pretty certain of it. Yes, sir, he must a-fired at his legs."

Nothing was elicited on the cross examination, except that the weapon used by Mr. Jones was a bowie knife instead of a derringer, and that he made a number of desperate attempts to scalp the plaintiff. It also came out that Sophronia, of doubtful nativity, did not faint, and was not present during the affray, she having been discharged from her situation the previous evening.

Washington Billings, sworn, said: "I see the row, and it warn't in no saloon. It was in the street. Both of 'em was drunk, and one was a-coming up the street, and tother was a-going down. Both of 'em was close to the houses when they first see each other, and both of 'em made their calculations to miss each other, but the second time they tacked across the pavement—drifting-like, diagonal—they come together, down by the curb—al-mighty soggy, they did—which staggered 'em a moment, and then over they went into the gutter. Smith was up first, and he made a dive for a cobble and fell on Jones. Jones dug out and made a dive for a cobble, and slipped his hold and jammed his head into Smith's stomach. They each done that over again, twice more, just the same way. After that, neither of 'em could get up any more, and so they just laid there in the slush and clawed mud and cussed each other."

On the cross examination, the witness could not say whether the parties continued to fight afterward in the saloon or not—he only knew they began it in the gutter, and to the best of his knowledge and belief they were too drunk to get into a saloon, and too drunk to stay in it after they got there. As to weapons, he saw none used except the cobble stones, and to the best of his knowledge and belief, they missed fire every time while he was present.

Jeremiah Driscoll came forward, was sworn, and testified, "I saw the fight, your Honor, and it wasn't in a saloon nor in the street. It was up in the Square, and they fought with a pine bench and a cane—"

LAWYER.—"There, there, there—that will do—that—will—do! Take the witness."

The testimony on the cross examination went to show that during the fight one of the parties drew a sling-shot and cocked it and at the same time the other discharged a hand-grenade at his antagonist. He could not say, however, which drew the sling-shot or which threw the grenade. Upon questioning him further, and confronting him with the parties to the case before the court, it transpired that the faces of Jones and Smith were unknown to him, and that he had been talking about an entirely different fight all the time.

Other witnesses were examined, some of whom swore that Smith was the aggressor, and others that Jones began the row. Some said they fought with their fists, others that they fought with knives, others tomahawks, others revolvers, others clubs, others axes, others beer mugs and chairs, and others swore that there had been no fight at all. However, fight or no fight, the testimony was straightforward and uniform on one point, at any rate, and that was that the fuss was about two dollars and forty cents, which one party owed the other, but it was impossible to find out which was the debtor and which the creditor.

After the witnesses had all been heard, his honor, Judge Sheperd,

observed that the evidence in this case resembled the evidence before him
in some thirty-five cases every day, on an average. He then said he would
continue the case, to afford the parties an opportunity of procuring more
testimony.

I have been keeping an eye on the Police Court for the last few days,
and I have arrived at the conclusion that the office of Police Judge is a
profitable and comfortable thing to have, but then, it has its little draw-
backs. Hearing testimony must be worrying to a Police Judge sometimes,
when he is in his right mind. I would rather be secretary to a wealthy
mining company, and have nothing to do but advertise the assessments
and collect them in carefully, and go along quiet and upright, and be one
of the noblest works of God, and never gobble a dollar that didn't belong
to me—all just as those fellows do, you know. (Oh, I have no talent for
sarcasm, it isn't likely!) But I trespass.

Now, with every confidence in the instinctive candor and fair dealing
of my race, I leave the accused and the accuser in the case of Smith vs.
Jones before the bar of the world. Let their fate be pronounced. The
decision will be a holy and just one.

1864

Dehorning the Dilemma

ANONYMOUS

IN Norfolk there was a religious society called "Perfectionists," and some ten or twelve of them addressed a letter to the Commanding General of that department, setting forth their objections to swearing allegiance to any earthly government.

The subject was disposed of by Gen. Butler in the following characteristic manner:

HEADQUARTERS OF EIGHTEENTH ARMY CORPS,
FORT MONROE, VA., JANUARY 13, 1864.

J. F. Dozier, E. H. Beaseley, and others:

GENTLEMEN: I have read your petition to Gen. Barnes, setting forth your objections to swearing allegiance to any earthly government.

The first reason which you set forth is that "all human governments are a necessary evil, and are continued in existence only by the permission of Jehovah until the time arrives for the establishment of his kingdom, and in the establishment of which all others will be subdued unto it, thus fulfilling that declaration in the eighth of Daniel, fourteenth verse," &c.

You therein establish to your own satisfaction three points:

First. That government, although an evil, is a necessary one. Second. That for a time it is permitted to exist by the wisdom of Jehovah. Third. That the time at which a period is to be put to its existence is not come.

Therefore, you ought to swear allegiance to the government of the United States:

First. Because, though an evil, you admit it to be necessary. Second. Although an evil, you admit that it is permitted by the wisdom of Jehovah, and that it is not for his creatures to question the wisdom of his acts.

Third. You only claim to be excused when Jehovah's government is substituted, which period, you admit, has not yet arrived.

Your obedient servant,

Benj. F. Butler.

1864

Petroleum V. Nasby Attempts to Draw the Color Line

DAVID ROSS LOCKE

POST OFFIS, CONFEDRIT X ROADS
(wich is in the Stait uv Kentucky),
November 25, 1867.

I hev bin in the Apossel biznis more extensively than any man sence the time uv Paul. First I established a church uv Democrats in a little oasis I diskivered in the Abolition Stait of Ohio, to wit, at Wingert's Corners, where there wuz four saloons, but nary church or school house within four miles, and whose populashen wuz unanimously Democratic, the saloon-keepers havin mortgages on all the land around em—but alars! I wuz forced to leeve it after the election uv the Tyrant Linkin.

It come about this way. When the war come up and South Carliny and several other uv the trooly Democratic staits seceshed, it looked awful dim for sech of us Northern Democrats as had always bin troo-bloo. Why, I had voted for Andy Jaxon seven times and for every other Democratic candidate as many times each election as possible, in hopes uv bein rewarded with a post offis. No man has drunk more whiskey for the Party than I hev—none has done it more willin. So the Republicans and Abolitionists called us staunch Northren sons of Democracy "Copperheads" and drafted jest sech uv us as didn't hev ruptures in nine places and entirely enveloped with trusses, and varicose veins, corns and bunions, and unsound teeth and a palate that ain't exactly right—wich wuz my case—or didn't make for Canada where they'd be safe under the protectin tail uv the British Lion—wich wuz likewise my case.

But when I come back from Canada, thinkin that Stanton's order to draft wuz over, Nasby's name begun to shine in the list uv martyrs, for soldiers in bloo laid a heavy hand onto my shoulder and I wuz led out to camp and allowed to volunteer to fight against my convictions—against my brethren in Grey wich hed took up arms in a righteous cause, to wit, to keep the nigger down, wich is his place.

As soon as the rigiment hit Southern soil, one night I ran the guard and become a soldier uv the Democratic Confedricy. But I couldn't abide the food, wich consisted uv jest what you could lay your hands on, and usually you couldn't—or the pay, wich the Confedricy printed onto wall paper at every local printing press—or the style uv uniform, wich was a hole in the seat uv the pants with the ragged tail uv the shirt wavin gracefully therefrom.

Again I wuz forced to run the guard, this time the guard uv my Confedrit brethren. I knowed I wuz worse needed amongst my Northern Democratic brethren, sech as Saint Vallandigham, to keep the torch uv troo Democrisy (wich means post offises for the faithful) burnin bright. It was ornery and cussid sufferins I went through—more than enough to choke a new Book of Martyrs (wich I hev always bin) durin the years uv an unjest and unrighteous war. O, the eggins I endoored! How I wuz rid out of town upon rails!

I don't want to harrow up the public buzzum, but one night I wuz pulled out of bed. I wuz compelled to kneel onto my bare knees in the cold snow, and by a crowd uv laffin soldiers in hateful bloo, compelled to take the Oath of Allegiance—and drink a pint uv raw, undiluted water!

After many more tribilations, like the Wanderin Jew, I wended my weary way to Kentucky, where, at Confedrit X Roads, I hoped to spend the few remainin years uv my life. Here the glad noos come! The Tyrant Linkin had bin laid low—*halleloogy!* Saint Androo Johnson was elevated where he could reward the Democrisy, wich ever hed bin his troo love, Southern man that he wuz. I wuz happy and contented. Under the Administration uv President Johnson, upon whose head blessins! I wuz at last give the enjoyment uv that end of the hopes uv all Democrats—a post offis! The Post Offis at Confedrit X Roads (wich is in the Stait uv Kentucky) has four saloons within a stone's throw, and a distillery ornamentin the landscape only a quarter uv a mile from where I write these lines, with the ruins of a burnt nigger school house in sight uv my winder.

I wanted nothin more. I hoped to be allowed to live here and thus forever, and when Death should come, he would find me at Bascom's Saloon, enjoying the delightful company uv them wich I am proud to call my friends.

But, alars! It wuz not to be so. I am ever vigilant and have to tare myself loose from comforts and friends when the Democrisy is threatened.

There was trouble in one uv the Southren counties uv Ohio. In a reliably Democratic township in that county is a settlement uv niggers, who, in the old time, ran away from Kentucky, and settled there where they could hev what they earned, wich wuz jest so much swindled out uv Kentucky. Of course, comin from Kentucky, these niggers are, many uv em, as near white as they can be. One uv em who carried with him the name uv his master, and, as he says, *father*, Lett, is as near a white man as may be, and has married a wench who wuz a shade whiter than he. Ther children are jest a touch whiter than both uv em. Uv these he had three daughters, rangin from sixteen to twenty.

Now this Lett is a disturber. He hed a farm uv perhaps 200 akers, and wuz taxed heavy for school purposes, but his children wuzn't, uv course, allowed to attend the school. None uv the nigger children were. But Lett got the idea into his head that there wuzn't no propriety in his payin taxes without enjoyin the benefits arizin from em, and aided and abetted by other niggers, who were wicked enough to complain uv payin taxes to the support uv white schools, he sent his daughters to the school, directin em to present themselves boldly, take their seats quietly, and study per-severinly. They did so. The schoolmarm, who wuz a young huzzy from Noo Hampsheer, where they persecute the saints, gave em seats and put em into classes—think uv that!—with white children.

There wuz trouble in that township. I wuz sent for to-wunst, and gladly I come. I wuz never so gratified in my life. Hed smallpox broken out in that school, there wouldn't hev bin half the eggscitement in the township. It wuz the subjick uv universal talk everywhere, and the Democrisy was a bilin like a pot.

I met the trustees uv the township, and demanded if they intended tamely to submit to this outrage? I askt em if they intended to hev their children set side by side with the children uv Ham, who in the Bible wuz condemned to a position uv inferiority forever? Can you, I askt, so degrade yourselves, and so blast the self-respect uv your children?

And, bilin up with indignashen, they answered, "Never!" and yoonanimously requested me to accompany em to the school house, that they might expel these disgustin beins who hed obtrooded themselves among those uv superior race.

On the way to the school house, wich wuz perhaps a mile distant, I askt the Board if they knowed these girls by sight. No, they replied, they hed never seed em. "I hev bin told," said I, "that they are nearly white."

"They are," said one uv em. "Quite white."

"It matters not," said I. "There is somethin in the nigger at wich the instink of the white man absolootely rebels, and from wich it instinktively recoils. So much experience hev I had with em, that put me in a dark room with one uv em, no matter how little nigger there is in em, and that unerrin instink would betray em to me, wich, by the way, goes to prove that the dislike we hev to em is not the result of prejudis, but is part uv our very nacher, and one uv its highest and holiest attriboots."

Thus communin, we entered the school house. The schoolmarm wuz there, as bright and as crisp as a Janooary mornin. The scholars wuz ranged on the seats, a studyin as rapidly as possible.

"Miss," said I, "we are informed that three nigger wenches, daughters uv one Lett, a nigger, is in this school, a-minglin with our daughters as a ekal. Is it so?"

"The Misses Lett are in this school," said she, "and I am happy that they are among my best pupils."

"Miss," said I sternly, "pint em out to us!"

"Wherefore?" says she.

"That we may bundle em out!" said I.

"Bless me!" said she. "I reely couldn't do that. Why expel em?"

"Because," said I, "no nigger shel contaminate the white children uv this districk. No sech disgrace shel be put onto em."

"Well," said this aggravatin schoolmarm, wich was from Noo Hampsheer, "you put em out."

"But show me wich they are," said I.

"Can't you detect em, sir?" said she. "Don't their color betray em? If they are so near white that you can't detect em at a glance, it strikes me that it can't hurt very much to let em stay."

I wuz sorely puzzled. There wuzn't a girl in the room that looked at all niggery. But my reputashen wuz at stake. Noticin three girls settin together who wuz somewhat dark complected and whose black hair waved, I went for em and shoved em out.

Here the tragedy okkerred. At the door I met a man who rode four miles in his zeal to assist us. He had always hed an itchin to pitch into a nigger, and as he could do it now safely, he proposed not to lose the chance. I wuz a-putting the girls out, and hed jest dragged em to the door, when I met him enterin it.

"What is this?" he said, with a surprised look.

"We're puttin out these cussed wenches, who is contaminatin your children and mine," said I. "Ketch hold uv that disgustin one yonder!" said I.

"Wenches!" said he. "You damned scoundrel! Them are my girls!"

And without waitin for an explanashen, the infooriated monster sailed into me, the schoolmarm layin over one of the benches explodin in laughter. The three girls assisted their parent, and between em, in about four minutes, I wuz insensible. One uv the trustees, pityin my woes, took me to the nearest railroad station, and somehow, how I know not, I got home.

When the Almighty made niggers, he ought to hev made em so that mixin with the sooperior race would hev bin an impossibility. I write these lines propped up in bed at my boarding house, my face beaten to a jelly, and perfectly kivered with stickin plaster. My nose, always the beauty and glory uv my face, is enlarged to twice its fair proportions. My few remainin teeth hev been knockt down my throat. My lips resemble sausages. My left ear is forever no more, and what little hair was a-hangin around my venerable temples is gone—my head is as bald as a billiard ball, and twict its normal size.

I hev only to say that when I go on sech a trip again, I shel require as condishen precedent that the Afrikins to be put out shel hev enuff Afrikin into em to prevent sech mistakes. But, good Lord, what haven't I suffered in this cause?

PETROLEUM V. NASBY, P.M.
(wich is Postmaster).

1867

Advertising

P. T. Barnum

WE ALL depend, more or less, upon the public for our support. We all trade with the public—lawyers, doctors, shoemakers, artists, blacksmiths, showmen, opera singers, railroad presidents, and college professors. Few people can depend on chance custom. You all need to have your customers return and purchase again. A man said to me, "I have tried advertising, and did not succeed. Yet I have a good article."

I replied, "My friend, there may be exceptions to the general rule. How did you advertise?"

"I put it in a weekly paper three times, and paid a dollar and a half for it."

I replied, "Sir, advertising is like learning—a little is a dangerous thing. Your object in advertising is to make the public understand what you have got to sell. If you have not the pluck to keep advertising until you have imparted that information, all the money you have spent is lost.

"You are like the fellow," I said, "who told a gentleman that if he would give him ten cents it would save a dollar. 'How can I help you so much with so small a sum?' asked the gentleman in surprise. 'I started out this morning,' said the fellow, 'with the full determination to get drunk. I have spent my only dollar to accomplish the object, and it has not quite done it. Ten cents worth more of whiskey would just do it, and in this manner I should save the dollar already expended.'"

So a man who advertises at all must keep it up until the public know who and what he is, and what his business is.

Some men have a peculiar genius for writing a striking advertisement, one that will arrest the attention of the reader at first sight. Recently I observed a swing sign extending over the sidewalk in front of a store, on which was the inscription in plain letters:

DON'T READ THE OTHER SIDE.

Of course I did, and so did everybody else, and I learned that the man had made an independence by first attracting the public to his business in that way and then using his customers well, afterwards.

Genin the hatter bought the first Jenny Lind ticket at auction for two hundred and twenty-five dollars, because he knew it would be a good advertisement for him.

"Who is the bidder?" said the auctioneer, as he knocked down that ticket at Castle Garden.

"Genin the hatter," was the response.

Here were thousands of people from the Fifth Avenue and from distant cities, in the highest stations of life. "Who is Genin the hatter?" they exclaimed. They had never heard of him before. The next morning the newspapers and telegraph had circulated the facts from Maine to Texas, and from five to ten millions of people had read that the tickets sold at auction for Jenny Lind's first concert amounted to about twenty thousand dollars and that a single ticket was sold at two hundred and twenty-five dollars to Genin the hatter. Men throughout the country involuntarily took off their hats to see if they had a Genin hat on their heads. At a town in Iowa it was found that in the crowd around the post office there was one man who had a Genin hat, and he showed it in triumph, although it was worn out and not worth two cents.

"Why," one man exclaimed, "you have a real Genin hat! What a lucky fellow you are!"

Another man said, "Hang on to that hat. It will be a valuable heirloom in your family."

Still another man in the crowd, who seemed to envy the possessor of this good fortune, said, "Come, give us all a chance. Put it up at auction."

He did so, and it was sold as a keepsake for nine dollars and fifty cents.

What was the consequence to Mr. Genin? He sold ten thousand extra hats per annum, the first six years. Nine-tenths of the purchasers bought of him, probably, out of curiosity, and many of them, finding that he gave them an equivalent for their money, became his regular customers.

Now, I don't say that everybody should advertise as Mr. Genin did. But I say if a man has got goods for sale, and he don't advertise them in some way, the chances are that some day the sheriff will do it for him. Nor do I say that everybody must advertise in a newspaper, or, indeed, use printers' ink at all.

I thoroughly understand the art of advertising, not merely by means of printers' ink, which I have always used freely, but by turning every possible circumstance to my account. In my monomania to make Barnum's American Museum the town wonder and town talk, I often seized upon an opportunity by instinct, even before I had a very definite conception as to how it should be used. But it always seemed, somehow, to mature itself and serve my purpose.

One morning a stout, hearty-looking man came into my ticket office at the Museum and begged some money. I asked him why he did not work and earn his living? He replied that he could get nothing to do and that he would be glad of any job at a dollar a day. I handed him a quarter of a dollar, told him to go and get his breakfast and return, and I would employ him at light labor at a dollar and a half a day.

When he returned I gave him five common bricks.

"Now," said I, "go and lay a brick on the sidewalk at the corner of Broadway and Ann Street; another close by the Museum; a third diagonally across the way at the corner of Broadway and Vesey Street, by the Astor House; put down the fourth on the sidewalk in front of St. Paul's Church, opposite; then, with the fifth brick in hand, take up a rapid march from one point to the other, making the circuit, exchanging your brick at every point, and say nothing to anyone."

"What is the object of this?" inquired the man.

"No matter," I replied. "All you need to know is that it brings you fifteen cents wages per hour. It is a bit of my fun, and to assist me properly, you must seem to be deaf as a post, wear a serious countenance, answer no questions, pay no attention to anyone. But attend faithfully to the work and at the end of every hour, by St. Paul's clock, show this ticket at the Museum door, enter, walking solemnly through every hall in the building, pass out, and resume your work."

With the remark that it was "all one to him, so long as he could earn his living," the man placed his bricks and began his round.

Half an hour afterwards, at least five hundred people were watching his mysterious movements. He had assumed a military step and bearing, and looking sober as a judge, he made no response whatever to the constant inquiries as to the object of his singular conduct. At the end of the first hour, the sidewalks in the vicinity were packed with people, all anxious to solve the mystery.

The man, as directed, then went into the Museum, devoting fifteen minutes to a solemn survey of the halls, and afterwards returning to his round. This was repeated every hour till sundown, and whenever the man went into the Museum, a dozen or more persons would buy tickets, hoping to gratify their curiosity in regard to the purpose of his movements. This continued for several days—the curious people who followed the man into the Museum considerably more than paying his wages—till finally the policeman complained that the obstruction of the sidewalk by crowds had become so serious that I must call in my brick man. This trivial incident excited considerable talk; it advertised me; and it materially advanced my purpose of making a lively corner near the Museum.

For other, and not less effective, advertising, I kept a band of music on the front balcony and announced on large banners:

FREE MUSIC FOR THE MILLION!

People said, "Well, that Barnum is a liberal fellow to give us music for nothing," and they flocked down to hear my outdoor free concerts. But I took pains to select and maintain the poorest band I could find—one whose discordant notes would drive the crowd into the Museum, out of earshot of my outside orchestra. Of course the music was poor. When people expect to get something for nothing, they can be sure to be cheated, and generally deserve to be.

After various managers had failed in the New York Museum, a rival to mine, it was let to Henry Bennett, who reduced the entrance price to a shilling—a half price, which led me to characterize his concern in the newspapers as "cheap and nasty"—and he began a serious rivalry with my museum.

Bennett's main reliances were burlesques and caricatures of whatever novelties I was exhibiting. Thus, when I advertised an able company of vocalists, well-known as the Orphean Family, Bennett announced the Orphan Family. My Fejee Mermaid he offset with a figure made of a monkey and a codfish joined together and called the Fudg-ee Mermaid. These things created some laughter at my expense, but they also served to advertise my Museum.

When the novelty of this opposition died away, Bennett did a decidedly losing business. I used to send a man with a shilling to his place every night, and I knew exactly how much he was doing and what were his receipts. The holidays were coming and might tide him over a day or two, but he was at the very bottom, and I said to him one day:

"Bennett, if you can keep open one week after New Year's, I will give you a hundred dollars."

The day after New Year's, January 2, 1843, Bennett had to shut up shop, having lost his last dollar and even failing to secure the handsome premium I had offered him.

The entire collection fell into the hands of the landlord for arrearages of rent, and I privately purchased it for $7,000 cash, hired the building, and secretly engaged Bennett as my agent. For advertising purposes, we ran a very spirited opposition for a long time, and abused each other terribly in the public prints. While people were supposing we were rivals, Bennett said to me one day:

"Barnum, you and I are like a pair of shears. We seem to cut each other, but we only cut what comes between."

Once I almost over-reached myself in my readiness to turn every chance occurrance to my favor for advertising purposes. Mr. Louis Gaylord Clark, the editor of the *Knickerbocker*, which had given me some favorable publicity, came in breathless one day, and asked me if I had the club with which Captain Cook was killed in the Sandwich Islands?

As I had a lot of Indian war clubs in the collection of aboriginal curiosities, I told him I had the veritable club with documents which placed its identity beyond question, and I showed him the warlike weapon.

"Poor Cook! Poor Cook!" said Clark, musingly. "Well, Mr. Barnum," he continued with great gravity, at the same time extending his hand and giving mine a hearty shake, "I am really very much obliged to you for your kindness. I had an irrespressible desire to see the club that killed Captain Cook. I felt quite confident that you would accommodate me. I have been in half a dozen museums, and as they all have it, I felt sure that a large establishment like yours would not be without it."

1869

Tell and Kiss

Charles H. Smith (Bill Arp)

THEY used to have a kissing game up there in the mountains that they still keep up over in East Tennessee. This is the way they practiced it:

A lot of big-limbed, powerful young men and apple-cheeked, buxom girls gather and select one of their number as master of ceremonies. He takes his station in the center of the room, while the rest pair off and parade around him. Suddenly one young woman will throw up her hands and say:

"I'm a-pining."

The master of ceremonies takes it up and the following dialogue takes place:

"Miss Arabella Jane Apthorp says she's a-pining. What is Miss Arabella Jane Apthorp a-pining for?"

"I'm a-pining for a sweet kiss."

"Miss Arabella Jane Apthorp says she's a-pining for a sweet kiss. Who is Miss Arabella Jane Apthorp a-pining for a sweet kiss from?"

She blushes and giggles but forces herself to say, "I'm a-pining for a sweet kiss from Mr. William Arp."

Mr. William Arp now walks up manfully and relieves the fair Arabella's pining by a smack that sounds like a three-year old steer drawing his hoof out of the mud.

Then a young man will be taken with a sudden pining which, after the usual exchange of questions and answers, reveals the name of the maiden who causes the gnawing and pining. She coyly retreats outdoors, only to be chased, overtaken, captured, and forcibly compelled to relieve her captor's distress.

At one of these entertainments I attended, there was a remarkably beautiful young woman who had been married about a month. Her husband was present, a huge, beetle-browed, black-eyed young mountaineer, with a fist like a ham. The boys fought shy of the bride for fear of the anger of her hulking spouse.

The game went on for some time, when symptoms of anger developed in the giant. Striding into the middle of the room, he said:

"My wife is as purty an nice an sweet as any gal here. You-uns has knowed her all her life. This game has been a-goin on half an hour, an nobody has pined for her once. If somebody don't pine for her purty *soon*, boys, thar will be trouble!"

She was the belle of the ball after that. Everybody pined for her.

1870's

Newspaper Caustics

AMBROSE BIERCE

GIRLS daily sell themselves for gold and for bread in San Francisco's streets, and you do not try to rescue them."—Anna Dickenson. Yes we do; we buy them.

Our virtuous press professes grief at the discovery of another gigantic fraud upon the public treasury. We know better. A fraud is a thing your journalist dotes upon. He makes merry with it as a pig tosses a wisp of straw, and dallies with it as an elephant wraps his trunk lovingly about the loins of a sleek puppy. To breathe an atmosphere of gigantic fraud is an editor's heaven on earth. It affords him an opportunity to display his loftiest public virtues, to get rid of the withering sarcasm that is spoiling in stock, to platitudinize, to make a donkey of himself, and provoke a sublime indifference in the object of his attacks. It is very jolly to be an editor under such creditable circumstances, and see men go on year after year, robbing the public treasury under the very noses of a united and influential press.

Some German naturalist has written a book to prove Man's descent from the hog. We do not believe in any such retrogression. The hog is a lineal descendant of Man. And he's an honor to his parent.

"It is rumored in society circles that Mrs. William C. Ralston is about to contract a new matrimonial alliance."—*San Francisco Post*. Respected author of this paragraph, we crave a word with you. Sir, we venture to remind you that to "contract a new matrimonial alliance" is simply to "marry again." Will you kindly state the existing objections to the latter expression, and point out the merits of the former? The word "marry" is not, we hope, an immodest term. We find it in all the dictionaries, but in few of the newspapers—never in the one which your talent deigns to adorn. The ingenuity that you and the gentlemen who have the honor to labor in the same literary field display in the invention of circumlocutory equivalents for that word, is above and beyond all praise; but pardon us, we do not quite perceive the necessity. To "lead to the altar," to "join in the holy bonds of wedlock," to "contract a matrimonial alliance," these are all sweet and pleasing phrases. We accept them without persuasion, and admire them without comprehending. But as at present advised, and pending better instruction that will doubtless be your pleasure to impart, we like the meaner term, "to marry." But if you deem that objectionable, why don't you just say "nuptiate," you royal Bengal jackass?

A convention of colored editors have gravely resolved never to mention in their papers the name of the aspiring youth who shot President Garfield. Things have come to a pretty pass when a man can't keep his name out of the newspapers without shooting the chief magistrate of his beloved country.

"The most deplorable fact of our political life," says a contemporary, "is the national habit of making charges of corruption." Almost as deplorable is the national habit of being guilty of them.

Twenty pioneers, who have not seen "God's Country" since '49, have arranged to go east from California in June. We warn that section that a treat is in store for it. Each gentleman in question is six feet four in his moccasins and with a beard as long as your arm. Each carries three Colt's revolvers and a bowie-knife, and usually an exaggerated rifle. They all pack about with them habitually their picks and rockers, and one adobe house to four men. They are addicted to profanity and tobacco, hanging, chivalry, and weeping at the sight of babies. Every man of them carries about fifteen pounds of gold dust in a belt, and is accustomed to bestow it upon whomever will accept. Such, dear Eastern friends, are these '49ers as you yourselves have created them—such are the homely virtues to which they are indebted to your own lively fancy. If you find them a bevy of asthmatic old gentlemen in stove-pipe hats and clean shirts, mild-mannered to the point of inanity, and somewhat given to lying, you may justly decline to receive them; they are impostors, and you may keep the dinner warm until the genuine heroes appear.

A morning paper says three unclaimed gold watches are in the hands of the San Francisco police, and that it is not definitely known who stole them. It is definitely known who will steal them.

1869-1881

Matter of a Hat

ANONYMOUS

IN THE Gilded Age, when railroad promoters were generously contributing to the living expenses of Congressmen, one representative, accused of venality in the matter of accepting a hat, replied:

Mr. Speaker. I hope that you will just let me have a few moments time to place myself on the record—square on it. Mr. Abernathy has up and said that I've accepted a hat from a railroad president. He is hinting, in a way to gall a sensitive man, that I've sold myself for that twenty-dollar, broad-rimmed hat.

I'd like to know, Mr. Speaker, if there's anything in our wonderful Constitution that says a man can't accept a gift-hat? Sir, I say there ain't!

Mr. Speaker, I say that I am a present-taker. Always have been, always will be. As encouragement to them as contemplates giving me a little something, I want to say that my capacity for taking presents—though well-developed—hain't been over-taxed. I want to say, likewise, that a man that won't take a free hat and so save himself the expense of buying one. is sort of half fool and thief. Why, I'd think twice before I'd meet such a man in the woods of a dark night!

Now, I know of an affair in Pike County which illustrates the sort of man who won't take presents when they are give to him.

A black-bearded fellow named Dunlap went to work for old man Honeycutt, one of my rural constituents. So, this Dunlap feller made himself so useful to Honeycutt that Honeycutt, who does favor merit, went to him one day and says to him:

"Dunlap, there's never been a man I've met I thought more of than you."

"I thank you kindly," said Dunlap.

"I tell you what. I put so much store by you, Dunlap, that I'm determined you shall have the hand of my daughter, Polly, in marriage."

"I thank you, sir," said Dunlap, "but I'm not the man to accept presents."

Well, Mr. Speaker, this was the kind of man that wouldn't accept presents. And the next day, he ran off with Honeycutt's wife!

Ever since then, Mr. Speaker, to keep fair-minded men from suspicioning my motives, I have determined to refuse nothing.

1870's

Sam Snaffles—American Munchausen

WILLIAM GILMORE SIMMS

IT WAS about a dozen or fourteen years ago, when I was a young feller without much beard on my chin, though I was full grown and strong as a hoss if not quite so big as a buffalo. I was then just beginning my apprenticeship to the hunting business in the Carolina mountains, but I had a great deal to learn, and reckon I missed more bucks than I ever hit.

No, Sam Snaffles wasn't doing much among the bucks—just for the reason I was too hot on the scent after a certain doe. Of all the womankind in the mountains, Merry Ann Hopson was the very yaller flower of the forest, with the reddest rose cheeks you ever did see, and such a mouth and such bright curly hair, and so tall and so slender and so all-over pretty. She was the only daughter of Squire Jeff Hopson, and I was all the time on a hot trail after her, poor man though I was, just a squatter on the side of a little bit of a mountain.

I went to see her almost every night. Sometimes I carried a buck for the Squire and sometimes a doeskin for the girl. I do think I pretty much kept the family in deer meat through the whole winter.

Though Squire Hopson was glad enough to get my meat, he didn't affection me as I did his daughter. He was a sharp, close, money-loving old feller who was always considerate of the main chance. But 'twasn't so with my Merry Ann. She had the eyes for me from the beginning. We sometimes did get a chance, when old Jeff was gone from home, to come to a sort of understanding. The long and short of it was that Merry Ann confessed to me that she'd like nothing better than to be my wife. She told me how old John Grimstead, the old bachelor—a feller about forty years old, and the dear gal not yet twenty—how he was after her, and because he had a good farm and mules and hosses, how her daddy was a-giving him the open-mouth encouragment.

Then I says to Merry Ann, "I must out with it and ask your daddy at once."

I just went ahead, determined to have the figure straight, whether odd or even. I bolted into the house, as free and easy and bold as if I was the best customer that the old man wanted to see.

He was a-setting in his big square hidebottomed armchair, looking like a judge on the bench just about to send a poor feller to the gallows. As he seed me come in, his mouth put on a grin that showed all his grinders.

"Well, Sam Snaffles," he says, "how goes it?"

So I up and told him I was mighty fond of Merry Ann and she, I was a-thinking, of me, and that I come to ask if I might have Merry Ann for my wife.

Then he opened his eyes wide and says, "What! *You?*"

"Just so, Squire," I says. "If it pleases you to believe me and consider it reasonable."

He set quiet for a minute, then got up, knocked all the fire out of his pipe on the chimney, filled it, and lit it again. He came straight up to me where I was a-setting on the chair in front of him. Without a word, he took the collar of my coat betwixt the thumb and forefinger of his left hand, and he says:

"Get up, Sam Snaffles. Get up, if you please."

With that he led me right across the room to a big looking-glass that hung against the partition wall. There he stopped before the glass, facing it and holding me by the collar all the time. When we had stood there for a minute or so, he says, solemnlike:

"Look in the glass, Sam Snaffles. Look good. *Observe* well."

"Well," says I, "I'm a-looking with all my eyes. I only see you and myself."

"But you don't *observe*," says he. "Looking and seeing's one thing. *Observing's* another. Now, Sam Snaffles, now that you've had a fair look at yourself, just now answer me from your honest conscience if you honestly think you're the sort of person to have my daughter!"

I answered quick, "And why not, I'd like to know, Squire Hopson? I'm not the handsomest man in the world but I'm not the ugliest. I'm as good a man of my inches as ever stepped in shoe leather. Whatever you may think, Squire, Merry Ann has a way of thinking that I'm the very one that ought to have her."

"Merry Ann's thinking," says he, "don't run all-fours with her father's thinking. You see only the inches. You see that you have eyes and mouth and nose, and the arms and legs of a man. But that don't make a man."

"They don't?" says I. "What's wanting to make me a man?"

"*Capital!*" says he, and he lifted himself up and looked mighty grand.

"Capital?" says I. "And what's that?"

"There are many kinds of capital," says he. "Money's capital, for it can buy everything. Houses and land is capital. Cattle, hosses, and sheep, when there's enough of them, is capital. And when I observed you in the glass, Sam Snaffles, I saw that *capital* was the very thing you wanted to make a man of you. Now I don't mean that any daughter of mine shall marry a person that's not a *perfect* man. I observed you long ago and saw where you was wanting. I asked about you. I asked your hoss."

"Asked my hoss!" says I, pretty nigh dumbfoundered.

"Yes. Asked your hoss, and he said to me, 'Look at me. I hain't got an ounce of spare flesh on my bones. You can count all my ribs. You can lay the whole length of your arm betwixt any two of them and it'll lie there as snug as a black snake betwixt two poles of a log house.' Says the hoss. 'Sam's got *no capital.* He ain't got any time five bushels of corn in his crib, and he's such a monstrous feeder himself that he'll eat out four bushels and think it's mighty hard upon him to give *me* the other one.'

"There now was your hoss's testimony against you, Sam," says the Squire. "Then I asked about your cabin and your way of living. I was curious and went to see you one day when I knowed you was at home. You had but one chair which you give me to set on and you sot on the end of a barrel for yourself. You give me a rasher of bacon that hadn't a streak of fat in it. Your cabin had but one room and that you slept in and ate in, and the floor was six inches deep in dirt.

"Says I to myself, 'This poor feller's got no *capital.*' From that moment, Sam Snaffles, the more I observed you, the more I was certain you never could be a man if you was to live a thousand years."

After that long speechifying, you might have ground me up in a mill, biled me down in a pot, and scattered me over a manure heap, and I wouldn't have been able to say a word.

I didn't stop for any more. I catched up my hat and bolted, like a hot shot out of a shovel, and didn't know my own self or what steps I took till I met Merry Ann a-coming towards me.

I just wrapped her up in my arms and I told her all, from beginning to end. I told her there was some truth in what the old man said. But I said I would do better, would see to things, would put things right, get corn in the crib, get capital if I could, and make a good comfortable home for her.

"Look at me, Merry Ann," says I. "Merry Ann, do I look like a man?"

"You're all the man I want," says she.

"That's enough," says I. "You shall see what I can do and what I *will* do. That is, if you are true to me."

And she throwed herself on my buzzom and cried out, "I'll be true to you, Sam. I love nobody in the world so much as I love you."

"And you won't marry any other man, Merry Ann, no matter what your daddy says? You won't listen to this old bachelor feller, Grimstead, that's got the capital already, no matter how they spur you?"

"Never!" she says.

"Swear it, Merry Ann,'" I says. "Swear it and cuss him for my sake and to make it certain. Cuss that feller Grimstead."

"Oh, Sam, I can't cuss," she says. "I can't do that!"

"Cuss him on my account," I says, "to my credit."

"Oh," says she, "don't ask me. I can't do that."

Says I, "Merry Ann, if you don't cuss that feller some way, I do believe you will go over to him after all. Just you cuss him, now. Any small cuss, will do, if you are in earnest."

"Well," she says, "if that's your idea, then I say, 'Drot his skin' and drot my skin too if I ever marry anybody but Sam Snaffles!"

"That'll do, Merry Ann," says I. "Now I'm easy in my soul and conscience. And now, Merry Ann, I'm going off and do my best to get the capital. I'll get it, by all the holy hokies, if I can!"

And so, after squeezes and kisses, we parted.

But before I mounted my hoss to go to my cabin, I give him a dozen kicks in his ribs just for bearing his testimony against me and for telling the old squire that I hadn't capital enough for a corn crib.

Then I considered all about capital, and it growed on me. I was living no better than a three-year-old bear in a sort of cave, a-sleeping on shuck and straw, and never looking after tomorrow. I felt mean all over except now and then when I thought of dear Merry Ann and the cuss that she give to that dried-up old bachelor Grimstead.

At day-peep I woke, determined on good works and making a man out of myself. Took my rifle, called up my dog, mounted my hoss, and put out for the laurel hollows.

Well, I hunted all day. Just about sunset I come to a hollow of the hills that I had never see before. In the middle of it was a great pond of water, and it showed like so much purple glass in the sunset and 'twas just as smooth as the big looking-glass of Squire Hopson's. There wasn't a breath of wind stirring.

I was mighty tired, so I eased down from the mare, tied up the bridle and let her pick about, and laid myself down under a tree, just about twenty yards from the lake, and thought to rest myself.

I reckon I must have slept a good hour, for when I woke the dark had set in and I could only see one or two bright stars here and there, shooting out from the dark of the heavens. But if I seed nothing, I heard, and just such a sound and noise as I had never heard before.

There was a rushing and a roaring and screaming and a splashing in the air as made you think the universal world was coming to an end. I tell you, if there was one wild goose a-settling down in that lake there was one hundred thousand of them. I couldn't see the end of them. They come every minute, swarm after swarm, in tens and twenties and fifties and hundreds. And such a fuss they did make, such a gabbling, such a splashing, such a confusion.

You never seed beasts so happy. How they flapped their wings, how they gabbled to one another, how they swam here and there to the very middle of the lake and to the very edge of it, just a fifty yards from where I lay squat, never moving arm or leg. It was wonderful to see. I wondered how they could find room, for I reckon there were forty thousand of them, all scuffling in that little lake together.

Well, I said to myself, "Now, if a feller could only captivate all them wild geese—fresh from Canniday, I reckon—what would they bring in the market at Spartanburg and Greenville? Walker, I knowed, would buy them at fifty cents a head. Forty thousand geese at fifty cents a head. *There* was capital!

"What a haul," thought I, "if a man could only get them in one net! Cover them all at one fling!"

The idea worked like so much fire in my brain. How can it be done? That was the question. "Can it be done?" I asked myself. "It can!" I said to myself. "And I'm the very man to do it!"

In the morning I went to work. I rode off to Spartanburg and bought all the twine and cord and half the plowlines in town. I got a lot of great fish hooks, all to help make the tanglement perfect. I got lead for sinkers and I got corkwood for floaters. And I pushed for home as fast as my poor mare could streak it.

I was at work day and night for nigh a week making my net. When I was done, I borrowed a mule and cart from Dr. Columbus Mills. Off I drove with my great net and got to the lake about noonday.

The net I aimed to stretch across the lake just deep enough to do the tangling of every leg of the birds in the midst of their swimming and snorting and splashing and cavorting. When I had it all fixed fine and just as I wanted it, I brought the ends of my plowlines up to where I was a-going to hide myself. This was under a strong sapling. My calculation was, when I had got the beasts all hooked, forty thousand, more or less, why then I'd whip the line round the sapling, hitch it fast, and draw in my birds at my ease.

I hadn't long finished my fixing when the sun suddenly tumbled down the heights and the dark begun to creep in upon me, and a pretty cold dark it was. My teeth begun to chatter in my head, though I was a-boiling over to be captivating the birds.

Soon I heard them come, screaming far away, pouring just like so many white clouds, straight down, millions upon millions, till I was certain there was ready nigh on forty thousand in the lake.

Lord! How they played and splashed and screamed and dived! So I watched and waited until I begun, little by little, to haul my lines in. When, Lord love you, such a ripping and raging and bouncing and flouncing and flopping and splashing and kicking and screaming you never did hear in all your born days!

By this I knowed I'd captivated the captains of the host and a pretty smart chance, I reckoned, of the regular army. So, getting more and more hot and eager, and pulling and hauling, I made one big mistake. Instead of wrapping the ends of my lines around the sapling that was standing just behind me, what do I do but wrap them around my own thigh—the right thigh, you see—and some of the loops was hitched round my left arm at the same time.

All this come of my hurry and excitement, for it was burning like a hot fever in my brain and I didn't know when or how I tied myself up, till suddenly, with an all-fired scream, them forty thousand geese rose like a great white cloud in the air, all tied up, tangled up—hooked about the legs, hooked about the gills, hooked and fast in some way in the beautiful little twistings of my net.

As I'm a-living today, they rose up all together, as if they had consulted upon it, like a mighty thundercloud, and off they went, screaming and flouncing, meaning, I reckon, to take the back-track to Canniday.

Before I knowed where I was, I was twenty feet in the air, my right thigh up and my left arm and the other thigh and arm a-dangling useless. I pulled with all my might, but that was mighty little in the fix I was in. I just had to hold on and see where the infernal beasts would carry me. I couldn't loosen myself, and if I could I was by this time too far up in the air and daresn't do it, unless I was willing to have by brains dashed out and my whole body mashed to a mammock.

There I was dangling, like a dead weight, at the tail of that cloud of wild geese, head downward, and a-going the Lord knows where—to Canniday or Jericho or some other heathen territory beyond the Mississipp, and it might be over the great eternal ocean.

I thought over all my poor sinnings in a moment and I thought of my poor, dear Merry Ann, and I called out her name, loud as I could. I knowed that I was fast a-getting unsensible. It did seem to me that my hour was come and I was a-going to die—die by a rope dangling in the air a thousand miles from earth.

Just then I roused up. I felt something brush against me. Then my face was scratched. On a sudden, there was a stop put to my travels. The geese had stopped flying. They was in a mighty great conflusteration, flopping their wings and a-screaming with all the tongues in their jaws.

I was shook rough against something. I put out my right arm and catched ahold of a long limb of an almighty big tree. Then my legs catched betwixt two other branches and I recovered myself so as to set up a little and rest.

The geese was a-tumbling and a-flopping among the branches. The net was hooked here and there, and the birds was all about me, swinging and splurging but unable to break loose and get away.

By little and little, I come to my clear senses and begun to feel my situation. After some hard work I managed to unwrap the plowlines from my right thigh and my left arm. I had the sense this time to tie the ends pretty tight to a great branch of the tree. I had had a hard riding, that was certain, and I felt sore enough, but now I felt easy because I considered myself safe. With day-peep, I calculated to let myself down from the tree by my plowlines. And, there below, tied fast, wasn't there my forty thousand captivated geese?

"Hurrah!" I sings out. "Merry Ann, we'll have the capital now, I reckon!"

I drawed up my legs and shifted my body, so as to find an easier seat in the crutch of the tree, which was an almighty big chestnut oak, when—oh, Lord!

On a sudden the limb which I had been a-setting on give way under me. Down I went, my legs first, slipping down, not on the outside, but into a great holler of the tree, all the heart of it being eat out by the rot. Before I knowed where I was, I was some twenty foot down, I reckon, and by the time I touched bottom, I was up to my neck in honey.

It was an almighty big honey-tree, full of the sweet treacle, and the bees all gone and left it. And I in it up to my neck. I could smell it strong and taste it sweet, but I could see nothing.

Lord! Lord! From bad to worse, buried alive in a holler tree, with never a chance to get out. I would then have given all the world if I was only sailing away with them bloody wild geese to Canniday and Jericho, even across the sea! "Lord help and save me!" I cried out from the depths, and, "Oh, my Merry Ann, shall we never meet again no more?"

It was the very gall of bitterness we read of in the Holy Scriptures! Who would get them geese, gabbling and a-cackling outside, that had cost me so much to captivate? Who would inherit my capital? and who would have Merry Ann? And what would become of the mule and cart, fastened in the woods by the little lake?

I cussed. I couldn't help it. I cussed from the bottom of my heart when I ought to have been saying my prayers, there in that deep holler of a mountain oak, with my head just above the honey. If I backed it to look up, my long hair at the back of my neck almost stuck fast, so thick was the honey.

But I couldn't help looking up. The holler was a wide one at the top, and I could see when a star was passing over. I seed them come and go, and I cried out, "O, sweet spirits, blessed angels! Come down and ixtricate me from this fix! I've no chance of help from mortal man or woman! Hardly once a year does a human come this way!"

There wasn't a star passed over me that I didn't pray to soon as I saw them a-shining over the opening of the holler. I prayed faster and faster as I seed them passing away and getting out of sight.

Suddenly I heard a monstrous fluttering amongst my geese. Then I heard a great scraping and scratching on the outside of the tree, and, sudden, as I looked up, the mouth of the holler was shut up.

All was dark. The stars and sky was all gone. Something black covered the holler and, a minute after, I heard something slipping into the holler right on me.

I could hardly draw my breath. I begun to fear I was to be siffocated alive. As I heard the strange critter slipping down, I shoved out my hands and felt hair—coarse wool—and with one hand I catched hold of the hairy leg of a beast and with the other I catched hold of his tail.

'Twas a great bear, one of the biggest, come to git his honey. He knowed the tree, you see, and if any beast in the world loves honey, 'tis a bear beast. He'll go to his death on honey, though the hounds are tearing at his very haunches.

When once I knowed what he was, and once got a good grip on his hindquarters, I wasn't going to let go in a hurry. I knowed that was my only chance for getting out of the holler. There was no chance of him turning round on me. He pretty much filled up the holler. I laid my weight on him as if all life and eternity depended upon it.

Now, that bear, I reckon, was pretty much as scared as I was. He couldn't turn in his shoes, and with something fastened to his ankles, and as he thought, I reckon, some strange beast fastened to his tail, you never seed beast more eager to get away, and get upwards. He knowed the way, and stuck his claws in the rough sides of the holler just as a sailor pulls a rope, and up we went.

We had, howsomever, more than one slip back, but, Lord bless you! I never let go. Up we went, I say, and I stuck just as close to his haunches as death to the dead. I felt myself moving. My neck was out of the honey. My arms was free. I could feel the sticky thing slipping off from me, and after a good quarter of an hour, the bear was at the great mouth of the holler.

As I felt that, I let go his tail, still keeping fast hold of his leg, and with one hand I cotched hold of the outside rim of the holler. I held fast on to it. Just then the bear sot squat, just on the edge of the holler, taking a sort of rest after his labor.

I don't know what 'twas made me do it. I wasn't a-thinking at all. I was only feeling and drawing a long breath. But I give him a mighty push, strong as I could, and he lost his balance, and went over outside clear to the earth, and I could hear his neck crack almost as loud as a pistol.

I prayed a short prayer after that, and, a-feeling my way all the time so as to be sure against rotten branches, I got a safe seat amongst the limbs of the tree, and sot myself down, determined to wait till broad daylight before I took another step in the business. There I sot, with the geese spread before me, flopping now and then and trying to ixtricate themselves, but they couldn't come it. There they was, captivated, and so much capital for Sam Snaffles.

Well, I calculated.

There was forty thousand geese, and for every goose I could get from forty to sixty cents in all the villages of South Carolina. Then, there was the bear. Judging from his strength in pulling me up, and from his size and fat in filling up that holler tree, he couldn't weigh less than five hundred pounds. His hide, I knowed, was worth twenty dollars. Then, there was the fat and taller, and the biled marrer out of his bones, what they make bears' grease out of. Then, there was the meat, skinned, clean, and all; there couldn't be under four hundred and fifty pounds, and whether I sold him as fresh meat or cured, he'd bring me ten cents a pound at the least.

Says I, "There's capital!"

"Then," says I, "there's my honey tree. I reckon there's a matter of ten thousand gallons in this here same honey tree. If I can't get from fifty to seventy-five cents a gallon for it, there's no alligators in Floriday!"

By morning I had calculated all I had to do and all I had to make. When I seed the first signs of daylight and looked around me, what should I see but old Tryon Mountain, with his grey head a-lifting itself up in the east! And beyond I could see the house and farm of Dr. Columbus Mills. As I turned to look a little south of that, there was my own poor little log cabin.

"God bless!" I said. "I ain't two miles from home!"

Soon as I got down from that tree, I pushed off to get the mule and cart I'd borrowed from Dr. Columbus Mills. I brought them to my bee tree, tumbled the bear into the cart, wrung the necks of all the captivated geese that was there—and counted some twenty-seven hundred that I piled away atop the bear.

Well, next about the bear. Sold the hide and taller for a fine market price. Sold the meat—'twas most beautiful meat. Biled down the bones for the marrow, melted down the grease and sold fourteen pounds of it to the barbers and apothecaries—got a dollar a pound for it—and sold that hide for twenty dollars. Got cash for everything.

But I wasn't done. There was my bee tree. I didn't let on to a soul what I was a-doing. They asked me about the wild geese, but I sent them on a wild goose chase. 'Twasn't till after I'd sold off all the bear meat and the geese that I made ready to get at that honey. I reckon them bees must have been making that honey for a hundred years, and was then driv out by the bears.

Dr. Columbus Mills, good feller that he is, lent me his mule and cart. I bought up all the tight-bound barrels that ever brought whiskey to

Spartanburg and Greenville, where they have the taste for that article. Day by day, I went off carrying as many barrels as the cart would hold and the mule could draw. I tapped the old tree close to the bottom, and drawed off the beautiful treacle. I was more than sixteen days about it, and got something over two thousand gallons of the purest, sweetest, yallerest honey you ever did see. I could hardly get barrels and jimmyjohns enough to hold it. I sold it at seventy cents a gallon, which was mighty cheap.

All this time, though it went against the grain, I kept away from Merry Ann and the old Squire, her daddy. I kept away and said nothing and beat no drum.

Well, finally come the day when I was ready. I crossed the bald ridge to get to the Squire's farm, and who should meet me in the road but Merry Ann. I reckon the dear girl had been a-looking for me the whole eleven days in the week, counting in all the Sundays. In the mountains, you know, the weeks sometimes run into twelve and even fourteen days when you're on a long hunt.

Well, Merry Ann, she cried and laughed together, she was so glad to see me again.

"Oh, Sam!" says she. "I was afeard you had clean give me up. And there's that fusty old bachelor, Grimstead, he's a-coming here almost every day. And Daddy he swears that I shall marry nobody else. He's at me all the time, a-telling how fine a farm he's got, and what a nice carriage, and all that. But I can't bear to look at him!"

By this time I had got down off the mare, and give Merry Ann a long, strong hug and almost twenty or a dozen kisses. She marveled at my new clothes and wondered where and how I had got them, but I only said for her to get her things ready to marry, for to marry her this night I was determined.

"But I've no clothes fit for a girl to be married in!" she says.

"I'll marry you this very night, Merry Ann," says I, "though you hadn't a stitch of clothing at all."

When we got to the yard, I led in the mare, and Merry Ann she run away from me and dodged around the house. I hitched the mare to the post, took off the saddlebags, which was mighty heavy, and walked into the house, stiff enough, I tell you.

There sat the old Squire, smoking his pipe and reading his newspaper. He looked at me through his specs over the newspaper, and when he seed who 'twas, his mouth put on that same conceited sort of grin and smile that he generally had when he spoke to me.

"Well," he says, "so it's you, Sam Snaffles, is it?"

Then he seemed to discover my new clothes and boots, and he sings out, "Heigh! You're tiptoe fine today! What fool of a shopkeeper in Spartanburg have you took in this time, Sam?"

Says I, cool enough, "I'll answer all them questions after awhile, Squire, but would prefer to see to business first."

"Business!" says he. "And what business could you have with me?"

I laid my saddlebags down at my feet and took a chair at my ease. Says I, "Squire Hopson, you owe a certain amount of money, say three hundred and fifty dollars, with interest on it for now three years, to Dr. Columbus Mills."

At this, he squared around, looking me full in the face. Says he, "What the Old Harry is that to you?"

Says I, "You give Columbus Mills a mortgage on this farm for security."

"What's that to you?" says he.

"The mortgage is overdue by two years, Squire," says I.

"What the Old Harry's all that to do with you?" he fairly roared out.

"Well, nothing much, I reckon. The three hundred and fifty dollars, with three years' interest at seven per cent, making it now—I've calculated it all without compounding—something over four hundred and twenty-five dollars. Well, Squire, that's not much to *you*, with your large capital. But it's something to *me*."

"But I ask you again, sir," he says, "what is all this to you?"

"Just about what I tell you—say, four hundred and twenty-five dollars. And I've come here this morning, bright and early, in hope you'll be able to square up and satisfy the mortgage."

I says, "Here's the document." And I drawed the paper from my breast pocket.

"You tell me that Dr. Mills sent you here," he says, "to collect the money?"

"No. I come myself on my own hook."

"Well," says he, "you shall have your answer at once. Take that paper back to Dr. Mills, and tell him I'll take an early opportunity to call and arrange the business with him. You have your answer, sir," he says, quite grand, "and the sooner you make yourself scarce, the better."

"Much obliged to you, Squire, for your civility," says I, "but I ain't quite satisfied with that answer. I've come for the money due on this paper, and must have it, Squire, or there will be what the lawyers call four closures upon it."

"Enough! Tell Dr. Mills I will answer his demand in person."

"You needn't trouble yourself, Squire, for if you'll just look at the back of the paper and read the signment, you'll see that you've got to settle with Sam Snaffles, and not with Dr. Columbus Mills."

Then he snatches up the document, turns it over, and reads the regular signment, writ in Dr. Columbus Mills' own handwrite.

Then the Squire looks at me with a great stare, and he says, to himself like: "It's a *bonny fodder* signment."

"Yes," says I, "it's *bonny fodder*—regular in law—and the title's all made out complete to me, Sam Snaffles. Signed, sealed, and delivered, as the lawyers says it."

"And how the Old Harry come you by this paper?" says he.

I was determined this time to give my hook a pretty sharp jerk in his gills, so I says, "See, I've got my wedding breeches on. I'm to be married tonight. I want to take my wife to her own farm as soon as I can. Now, you see, Squire, I all along set my heart on this farm of yours, and I determined, if ever I could get the capital, to get hold of it. That was the idea I had when I bought the signment of the mortgage from Dr. Mills. So, you see, if you can't pay after three years, you never can pay, I reckon. If I don't get my money this day, why—I can't help it—the lawyers will have to see to the four closures tomorrow."

"Great God, sir!" says he, rising out of his chair and crossing the room up and down. "Do you coolly propose to turn me and my family headlong out of my house?"

"Well, now," says I, "Squire, that's not exactly the way to put it. You see, I must have it for my wife—"

"Your wife!" says he. "Who the Old Harry is she? You once pretended to have an affection for my daughter."

"So I had, but you didn't have the proper affection for your daughter that I had. You preferred money to her affections, and you driv me off to get capital. Well, I took your advice and I've got the capital."

"And where the Old Harry," said he, "did you get it?"

"Well, I made good terms with the old devil for a hundred years, and he found me in the money."

"It must have been so," said he. "You were not the man to get capital any other way."

Then he goes on, "But what becomes of your pretended affection for my daughter?"

"'Twasn't pretended, but you throwed yourself betwixt us with all your force. You broke the girl's heart and broke mine, and as I couldn't live without company, I had to look for myself and find a wife as I could. I tell you, I'm to be married tonight, and as I've swore a most eternal oath to have this farm, you'll have to raise the wind today and square off with me, or the lawyers will be at you tomorrow, bright and early."

"Dod dern you!" he cries out. "Do you want to drive me mad?"

"By no manner of means," says I, just about as cool and quiet as a cowcumber.

The old Squire fairly sweated, but he couldn't say much. "If you only *did* love Merry Ann!" he says. Then the old chap begun to cry, and as I seed that, I just kicked over my saddlebags lying at my feet, and the silver dollars rolled out—a bushel of them, I reckon—and, oh Lord! How the old feller jumped, staring with all his eyes at me and the dollars.

"It's money!" says he.

"Yes," says I, "just a few hundreds of thousands of my capital."

Then he turns to me and says, "Sam Snaffles, you're a most wonderful man. You're a mystery to me. Where, in the name of heaven, have you been? and what have you been doing? and where did you get all this power of capital?"

I just laughed and went to the door and called Merry Ann. She come mighty quick. I reckon she was a-watching and waiting.

Says I, "Merry Ann, that's money. Pick it up and put it back in the saddlebags, if you please."

Then, says I, turning to the old man, "That whole bushel of dollars are monstrous heavy. My old mare—ask her about her ribs now!—fairly squelched under the weight of me and that money. And I'm pretty heavy loaded myself. I must lighten, with your leave, Squire."

And I pulled out a doeskin bag of gold half-eagles from my righthand pocket and poured them upon the table. Then I emptied my lefthand pocket, then the side pockets of the coat, then the skirt pockets, and just spread the shiners out upon the table.

Merry Ann was fairly frightened and run out of the room. When she come back in, the Squire took her by the shoulder and said, "Just you look at that there!"

Then the poor old hypocritical scamp sinner turned round to me and flung his arms round my neck and said, "I always said you was the only right one for Merry Ann!"

Well, we was married that night, and have been comfortable ever since.

1872

A Very Friendly Horse

JAMES M. BAILEY

I DON'T really believe a yellow horse is any worse by nature than a bay horse, or a white horse, or a horse of any color or combination of colors; but our judgment of things in this world is often liable to be influenced by our prejudices. For this reason, perhaps, I cannot look upon a yellow horse with feelings of delight.

The other day a yellow horse was standing at the depot as I came down the road. Looking at the animal as he felt around casually with his hind foot for his owner's brains, my mind receded to the home of my childhood.

I remember quite distinctly the day my father brought home a yellow horse. In fact, I can without difficulty pick out any day of the eight which the animal passed in our society. He was a comely beast, with long limbs, a straight body, and eyes that would rival those of an eagle in looking hungry.

When he came into the yard we all went out to look at him. My father stood near the well holding the animal by a halter. We had a dog, a black and white, and if there ever was a dog who thought he had a head stowed full of knowledge it was that dog.

How plainly I can see him approach that yellow horse, to smell of his heels. He ought to have got more of a smell than he did, considering that he lost the greater part of one ear in the attempt. It was done so quick that it is possible we would not have known anything about it, had the dog not spoken of it himself. He never smelt of that yellow horse again. The flavor wasn't what he had been used to, I think.

Three days later when he was turning around, to speak to a flea near his tail, as is customary with dogs, that yellow horse unexpectedly reached down and took a mouthful of spinal joints from the dog's back and this preyed so heavily on the dog's mind that he died in a minute or two.

That evening mother interested father with an account of Caper's death while he was waiting for her to replace the collar the yellow horse that afternoon had snatched from his best coat.

And thus time passed. But the horse lost none of it. There wasn't a neighbor within a half mile of our house but bore some mark of that animal's friendship. Like death, he was no respecter of persons. He never stopped to inquire whether a man was worth a million dollars or ten cents when reaching for him. Finally people came to avoid him when they met him on the street. I don't think they did it purposely, but it seemed to come natural to them to rush through the first doorway or over the most convenient fence when they saw him approach. This inexplicable dread communicated itself to the very dogs on the street, but before they had come fairly to understand him, he had succeeded in reducing the price of sausage to almost a mere song. After that they looked up to him with the respect exacted by a Hindu god with two changes of underclothes, and no dog within three blocks of us would think of going to sleep at night without first coming over to see if that horse was locked up. It was instinct, probably.

My father never enjoyed a single day of the eight he was the sole possessor of the animal. He nipped away some portion of him every once in a while. There was only one person that had anything to do with the animal who came out unscathed. He was the hired man, and he owed his salvation to a misfortune. He was cross-eyed. He was a great source of misery to that yellow horse. The misinformation of his eyes was calculated to deceive even smarter beings. The beast kicked at him a few times when he was evidently looking the other way, but that was just the time he was bearing one eye strongly on him, and he missed. When he really was not looking was just the time the beast thought he was, and so it went throughout the entire eight days, both stomach and heels yearning for a taste of him, but never getting it.

I am sure there never was another such horse to kick and bite. He did it so unexpectedly, too. He would be looking a stranger square in the face, apparently about to communicate some information of value, and then suddenly lift his hind foot, and fetch the unsophisticated man a rap on the head that would make him see seventy-five dollars worth of fireworks in a minute.

He would bite at anything, whether he reached it or not; but in kicking, he rarely missed. He could use any leg with facility, but prided himself mainly on the extraordinary play of the left hind leg. The very air about our place was impregnated with camphor and the various new kinds of liniments. The neighbors came around after dark, and howled for the blood of that yellow horse like so many Indians. Matters commenced to assume a critical form. The people wanted the animal killed, and cut open so they could get back their things.

And so my father determined to shoot the beast, but at the last moment his heart failed him. Pity triumphed, and he sold him to a man from a distance, and it was such a great distance that none of us were able to attend his funeral two weeks later. He was struck just above the right temple, I believe.

1873

Hospital for Liars

ANONYMOUS

A FEW days ago I visited the fairly recently established infirmary for liars in a quiet location in upstate New York. Since it was known that a representative of the *Times* was due, I was met at the door by a pleasant-faced gentleman, who spoke with a slight German accent and introduced himself as the Assistant Superintendent.

"Will you kindly walk this way?" he said. After I had inscribed my name in the Visitors' Book, he began to explain the system under which the infirmary for the mendacious operates.

"It is very simple," he said. "The theory of the Institution is that the habit of mendacity, which in many cases becomes chronic, is a disease, like habitual inebriety. It can generally be cured. We take the liar who voluntarily submits himself to our treatment, and for six months we encourage him in lying. We surround him with liars, his equals and superiors in skill, and cram him with falsehood until he is saturated.

"By this time, the reaction has set in. The patient is usually starved for the truth. He is prepared to welcome the second course of treatment. For the next half year the opposite course is pursued. The satiated and disgusted liar is surrounded by truthful attendants, and by force of example and moral influence, brought to understand how much more creditable it is to say the thing which *is* than the thing which is *not*. Then we send him back into the world. I will show you how our patients live. We will go first, if you please, through the left wing of the hospital, where the saturating process may be observed."

He led the way across a hall into a large room, comfortably furnished and occupied by two dozen or more gentlemen who sat or stood in groups, engaged in animated talk. Near one group, I overheard parts of the conversation.

"My rod creaked and bent double," a stout, red-faced gentleman was saying, "and the birch spun like a teetotum. I tell you, if Pierre Chaveau hadn't had the presence of mind to grip the most convenient part of my trousers with the boat hook, I should have been dragged into the lake in two seconds or less. Well, sir, we fought sixty-nine minutes by actual time-taking, and when I had him in and had got him back to the hotel, he tipped the scale, the speckled beauty did, at thirty-seven pounds and eleven-sixteenths, whether you believe it or not."

"Nonsense," said a quiet little gentleman who sat opposite. "That is impossible."

The first speaker looked flattered at this and flushed with pleasure. "Nevertheless," he retorted, "it's a fact, on my honor as a sportsman. Why do you say it's impossible?"

"Because," said the other, calmly, "it is an ascertained scientific fact, as every true fisherman in this room knows perfectly well, that there are no trout in Lake Mooselemagunticook weighing under half a hundred pounds."

"Certainly not," put in a third speaker. "The bottom of the lake is of a sieve formation. All fish smaller than the fifty-pounders fall through."

"Why doesn't the water drop through, too?" asked the stout patient, in a triumphant tone.

"It used to," replied the quiet gentleman gravely, "until the Maine Legislature passed an act preventing it."

"These sportsmen liars," said my guide, as we crossed the room, "are among the mildest and most easily cured cases that come here. We send them away in from six to nine weeks' time, with the habit broken up, and pledged not to fish or hunt any more. The man who lies about the fish he has caught, or about the intelligence of his red setter dog, is often in all other respects a trustworthy citizen."

"What," I asked, "are the most obstinate cases?"

"Undoubtedly the travellers and politicians. The more benign cases, such as the fisherman liars, the society liars, the lady-killer or *bonnes fortunes* liars, the Rocky Mountain and frontier liars (excepting the Texas cases), the psychical-research liars, and the miscellaneous liars of various classes, we permit, during the first stage of treatment, to mingle freely with each other. The effect is good. But we keep the politicians strictly isolated."

He was about to conduct me out of the room, by a door opposite, when a detached phrase uttered by a pompous gentleman, arrested my attention.

"Scipio Africanus once remarked to me——"

"There couldn't be a better example," said my guide, as we passed out of the room, "of what we call the forcing system in the treatment of mendacity. That patient came to us about two months ago. The form of his disease is a common one. Perfectly truthful in all other respects, he cannot resist the temptation to claim personal acquaintance and even intimacy with distinguished individuals.

"His friends laughed at him so much for this weakness that, like a sensible man, he put himself under our care. He is doing splendidly. When he found that his reminiscences of Beaconsfield and Bismarck and Victor Hugo created no sensation here, but were, on the contrary, matched and capped by still more remarkable experiences narrated by other inmates, he was at first a little staggered.

"But the habit is so strong, and the vanity that craves admiration on this score is so exacting, that he began to extend his acquaintance back into the past. Soon we had him giving reminiscences of Tallyrand, of Thomas Jefferson, and of Lord Cornwallis. There happens to be in this Institution another patient with precisely the same trouble. Thus, not long ago, I heard our patient describing one of Heliogabalus' banquets, which he had attended as an honored guest. They are in active competition, driving through ancient history at the rate of about three centuries a week. Before long they will be matching reminiscences of the antediluvian patriarchs, and then they'll bring square up on Adam. They can't go any further than Adam. By that time, they will be ready for the truth-cure process. After a few weeks spent in an atmosphere of strict veracity, they'll go into the world again, perfectly cured."

On our way back to the reception room, we met a gentleman about forty-years old. "He is a well known society man," said the Assistant Superintendent, as he approached. "He was formerly the most politely insincere man in America. I am glad to have you see him, for he is a good example of a radical cure. We shall be ready to discharge him by the first of next week."

The cured liar was about to pass us, but the Assistant Superintendent stopped him. "Mr. Van Ransevoort," he said, "let me make you acquainted with this gentleman who has been inspecting our system."

"I am glad to meet you, Mr. Van Ransevoort," I said.

He raised his hat and made me an unexceptionable bow. "And I," he replied, with a smile of charming courtesy, "am neither glad nor sorry to meet you, sir. I simply don't care a damn."

I stammered something, then said, "I suppose you are looking forward to your release next week?"

"Yes, sir," he replied. "I shall be rather glad to get out again. But my wife will be sorry."

I looked at the Assistant Superintendent. He returned a glance full of professional pride.

"Well, goodbye, Mr. Van Ransevoort," I said. "Perhaps I shall have the pleasure of meeting you again."

"I hope not, sir. It's rather a bore," said he, shaking my hand most cordially, and giving the Assistant Superintendent a nod as he passed on.

1870's

The United States of Boston

CHARLES HEBER CLARK (Max Adeler)

WHILE I was helping one of my youngsters a night or two ago to master a tough little problem in his arithmetic, I picked up the history that he had been studying, and as he went off to bed, I looked through the volume. It was Goodrich's *History of the United States,* for the use of beginners; and it had a very familiar appearance. I gained my first glimpse of the past from this very book. Not only could I remember the text as I turned over the leaves, but the absurd pictures of General Washington and the surrender of Cornwallis, the impossible portraits of John Smith and Benjamin Franklin, and the unnatural illustration of the manner in which the Pilgrim Fathers landed, seemed like respectable old acquaintances whom I had known and admired in happier days.

When Mrs. Adeler descended, after tucking the weary scholars comfortably in bed, I directed her attention to some of the peculiarities of Goodrich's effort:

"This little book, Mrs. A., first unlocked for me the door of history. It is a history of the United States. As it was written by a man who lived in Boston and believed in Boston, in my childhood I obtained from the volume the impression that our beloved native land consisted chiefly of Boston. I do not wish to revile that city. It is in many respects a model municipality. It has greater intellectual force than any of our cities, and its citizens have a stronger and more determined civic pride. Every Boston man believes in the greatness of his city. That is an excellent condition of public sentiment, and we may pardon it even if it does sometimes produce results that are slightly ridiculous.

"Goodrich was what might be called an excessive Boston man, and his little history is very apt, unintentionally, to convey erroneous impressions to the infant mind. In my early boyhood, being completely saturated with

Goodrich, I entertained an indistinct idea that the eye of Columbus rested upon Boston long before any other object appeared over the horizon. Somehow I cherished a conviction that the natives who greeted him and bowed down at his feet were men who inhabited the Bunker Hill Monument and disported themselves perpetually among the chambers of Faneuil Hall.

"I never doubted that every important event in our annals, from the landing of those unpleasant old Puritans of the Mayflower down to the election of Andrew Jackson, occurred in Boston, and was attributable entirely to the superiority of the people of that city. I scoffed at the theory that John Smith was in Virginia at the time of his salvation by Pocahontas. I was even disposed to regard the account of the signing of the Declaration of Independence at Philadelphia as a sort of insignificant side show which should have been alluded to briefly in a footnote. I honestly believed that the one great mistake of George Washington's life was that he was born elsewhere than in Boston. I felt that, however hard such retribution might appear, he deserved to be considered a little less great on account of that error.

"As for the war of the Revolution, I could not doubt, while I maintained my faith in Goodrich, that it was begun by the high-spirited citizens of Boston in consequence of the wrongs inflicted upon them by that daring and impious monarch, George III. It was equally clear that the conflict was carried on only by the people of Boston, and that the victory was at last won because of the valor displayed by the citizens of that community.

"In my opinion, and apparently in the opinion of Goodrich, the leading event of the war was that related in Chapter Eighty-five. The story occupies the whole chapter. The historian evidently intended that the youthful mind, while meditating upon the most important episode of the dreadful struggle, should not be disturbed by minor matters.

"Chapter Eighty-five relates that certain British soldiers demolished snow hills upon Boston Common, a hallowed spot which Goodrich taught me to regard as the pivotal point of the universe. The boys determined to call upon General Gage, and to protest against this brutal outrage committed by the hireling butchers of a bloated despot. Now, listen while I read the acccount of that interview as it is given by Goodrich:

" *'General Gage asked why so many children had called upon him. "We come, sir," said the tallest boy, "to demand satisfaction." "What!" said the general. "Have your fathers been teaching you rebellion, and sent you to exhibit it here?" "Nobody sent us, sir," answered the boy, while his cheek reddened and his eye flashed. "We have never injured nor*

*insulted your troops; but they have trodden down our snow hills and
broken the ice on our skating ground. We complained and they called us
young rebels, and told us to help ourselves if we could. We told the
captain of this, and he laughed at us. Yesterday our works were destroyed
the third time, and we will bear it no longer."* General Gage looked at
them a moment in silent admiration, and then said to an officer at his side,
*"The very children here draw in a love of liberty with the air they
breathe.' "*

"The story of this event, which shaped the destinies of a great nation
and gave liberty to a continent, I learned by heart. Many and many a
night have I lain awake wishing that Philadelphians would organize
another war with Great Britain, so that British soldiers could come over
and batter down a snow hill that I would build in Independence Square.
I felt certain that I should go at once, in such an event, to the commanding general, and should overwhelm him with another outburst of fiery
indignation. It seemed rather hard that Philadelphia boys should never
have a chance to surpass the boys of Boston. But I still could not help
admiring those young braves and regarding them as the real authors of
American independence. I was well assured that if that 'tallest boy' had
not entered the general's room and flashed his eye at Gage, all would have
been lost; the country would have been ground beneath the iron heel of
the oppressor, and Americans would have been worse than slaves.

"Perhaps it did me no harm to believe all this; but it seems to me that
we might as well instruct children properly to begin with. Therefore, I
shall give our boy some private lessons in history to supplement the
wisdom of Goodrich."

1874

Jud Brownin Hears Ruby Play

George W. Bagby

"Jud, they say you heard Rubenstein play when you were in New York?"

"I did, for a fact."

"Well, tell us all about it."

"What! Me? I might's well tell you about the creation of the world."

"Come, now. No mock modesty. Go ahead."

Well, sir, he had the blamedest, biggest, catty-corneredest pianner you ever laid your eyes on—something like a distracted billiard table on three legs. The lid was heisted, and mighty well it was. If it hadn't, he'd a-tore the entire sides clean out, and scattered 'em to the four winds of heaven.

Played well? You bet he did. When he first sit down, he peered to care mighty little about playing, and wished he hadn't come. He tweedle-eedled a little on the treble, and twoodle-oodled some on the bass—just fooling and boxing the things jaws for being in his way.

I says to a man setting next to me, says I, "What sort of fool playing is that?" And he says, "Hesh!" But presently his hands commenced chasing one another up and down the keys, like a passel of rats scampering through a garret very swift. Parts of it was sweet, though, and reminded me of a sugar squirrel turning the wheel of a candy cage.

"Now," says I to my neighbor, "he's showing off. He ain't got no idea, no plan of nothing. If he'd play me a tune of some kind or other I'd——"

But my neighbor says, "Hesh!" very impatient.

I was just about to git up and go home, being tired of that foolishness, when I heard a little bird waking up away off in the woods, and calling sleepy-like, and I looked up and see Ruby was beginning to take some interest in his business, and I sit down again.

It was the peep of day. The light come faint from the east, the breezes blowed fresh, some more birds waked up in the orchard, then some more in the trees near the house, and all begun singing together. People begun to stir at the house, and the gal opened the shutters. Just then the first beam of the sun fell on the garden and it teched the roses on the bushes, and the next thing it was broad day. The sun fairly blazed. The birds sung like they'd split their throats. All the leaves was moving and flashing diamonds of dew, and the whole world was bright and happy as a king. Seemed to me like there was a good breakfast in every house in the land, and not a sick child or woman anywhere. It was a fine morning.

And I says to my neighbor, "That's fine music, that is."

But he glared at me like he'd like to cut my throat.

By and by, the wind turned. It begun to thicken up, and a kind of gray mist come over things. I got low spirited directly. Then a silver rain begun to fall. I could see the drops touch the ground, and flash up and roll away. I could smell the wet flowers in the meadow, but the sun didn't shine, nor the birds sing, and it was a foggy day, pretty but kind of melancholy.

Then the moonlight come, without any sunset, and shone on the grave-yards, where some few ghosts lifted their hands and went over the wall. And between the black, sharp-top trees, there was fine houses with ladies in the lit-up windows, and men that loved 'em, but could never git a-nigh 'em, who played on gittars under the trees, and made me that miserable I could a-cried, because I wanted to love somebody, I don't know who, better than the men with the gittars did.

Then the moon went down, it got dark, the wind moaned and wept like a lost child for its dead mother, and I could a-got up then and there and preached a better sermon than any I ever listened to. There wasn't a thing left in the world to live for, not a blame thing, and yet I didn't want the music to stop one bit. It was happier to be miserable. I hung my head and pulled out my handkerchief, and blowed my nose to keep from crying. My eyes is weak, anyway, and I didn't want anybody to be a-gazing at me a-sniveling. It's nobody's business what I do with my nose. It's mine. But some several glared at me mad as Tucker.

All of a sudden, old Ruby changed his tune. He ripped out and he rared, he tipped and he tared, he pranced and he charged like the grand entry at a circus. Peared to me that all the gaslights in the house was turned on at once, things got so bright, and I hilt up my head, ready to look any man in the face, and not afraid of nothing. It was a circus, and a brass band, and a big ball, all going on at the same time. He lit into them keys like a thousand of brick. He give 'em no rest, day or night. He set every living joint in me a-going, and not being able to stand it no longer, I jumped spang onto my seat, and jest hollered——

"Go it, my Rube!"

Every blamed man, woman, and child in the house riz on me, and shouted, "Put him out! put him out!"

"Put your great-grandmother's grizzly gray cat into the middle of next month!" I says. "Tech me if you dare. I paid my money, and you jest come a-nigh me!"

With that, some several policemen run up, and I had to simmer down. But I would a-fit any fool that laid hands on me, for I was bound to hear Ruby out or die.

He had changed his tune again. He hop-light ladies and tip-toed fine from end to end of the keyboard. He played soft and low and solemn. I heard the church bells over the hills. I saw the stars rise—then the music changed to water, full of feeling that couldn't be thought, and begun to drop—drip, drop—drip, drop, clear and sweet, falling into a lake of glory. It was too sweet. I tell you the audience cheered. Rubin, he kind of bowed, like he wanted to say, "Much oblige, but I'd rather you wouldn't interrupt me."

He stopped a moment or two to ketch breath. Then he got mad. He run his fingers through his hair, he shoved up his sleeve, he opened his coat tails a little further, he drug up his stool, he leaned over, and, sir, he jest went for that old pianner. He slapped her face, he boxed her jaws, he pulled her nose, he pinched her ears, and he scratched her cheeks until she fairly yelled. She bellered like a bull, she bleated like a calf, she howled like a hound, she squealed like a pig, she shrieked like a rat, and then he wouldn't let her up. He run a quarter stretch down the low grounds of the bass, till he got clean in the bowels of the earth, and you heard thunder galloping after thunder, through the hollows and caves of perdition. Then he fox-chased his right hand with his left till he got way out of the treble into the clouds, where the notes was finer than the points of cambric needles, and you couldn't hear nothing but the shadders of 'em.

And then he wouldn't let the old pianner go. He forward two'd, he crossed over first gentleman, he sashayed right and left, back to your places, he all hands'd round, ladies to the right, promenade all, here and there, back and forth, up and down, perpetual motion, double-twisted and turned and tacked and tangled into forty-eleven thousand double bow knots.

By jinks, it was a mixtery! He fetched up his right wing, he fetched up his left wing, he fetched up his center, he fetched up his reserves. He fired by file, by platoons, companies, regiments, brigades. He opened his cannon—round shot, shells, shrapnels, grape, canister, mines, and maga- zines—every living battery and bomb a-going at the same time. The house trembled, the lights danced, the walls shuck, the sky split, the ground rocked—heavens and earth, creation, sweet potatoes, Moses, ninepences, glory, ten penny nails, Sampson in a 'simmon tree—Bang!!! lang! perlang! p-r-r-r-r!! Bang!!!

With that bang! he lifted himself bodily into the air, and he come down with his knees, fingers, toes, elbows, and his nose, striking every single solitary key on the pianner at the same time.

The thing busted and went off into fifty-seven thousand five hundred and forty-two hemi-demi-semi quivers, and I knowed no more that evening.

1870's

A Jersey Centenarian

Francis Bret Harte

I HAVE seen her at last. She is a hundred and seven years old, and remembers George Washington quite distinctly. It is somewhat confusing, however, that she also remembers a contemporaneous Josiah W. Perkins, of Basking Ridge, N. J., and, I think, has the impression that Perkins was the better man. Perkins, at the close of the last century, paid her some little attention. There are a few things that a really noble woman of a hundred and seven years never forgets.

It was Perkins who said to her in 1795, in the streets of Philadelphia, "Shall I show thee General Washington?"

Then she said careless-like (for you know, child, at that time it wasn't what it is now to see General Washington), she said, "So do, Josiah, so do!" Then he pointed to a tall man who got out of a carriage and went into a house. He was larger than you be. He wore his own hair— not powdered; had a flowered chintz vest, with yellow breeches and blue stockings, and a broad-brimmed hat. In summer he wore a white straw hat, and at his farm at Basking Ridge he always wore it.

At this point, it is too evident that she was decribing the clothes of the all-fascinating Perkins. So I gently but firmly led her back to Washington. Then it appeared that she did not remember exactly what he wore. To assist her, I sketched the general historic dress of that period. She said she thought he was dressed like that. Emboldened by my success, I added a hat of Charles II, and pointed shoes of the eleventh century. She indorsed these with such cheerful alacrity that I dropped the subject.

The house upon which I had stumbled, or, rather, to which my horse —a Jersey hack, accustomed to historic research—had brought me, was low and quaint. Like most old houses it had the appearance of being encroached upon by the surrounding glebe, as if it were already half in the grave, with a sod or two in the shape of moss thrown on it. A wooden house, instead of acquiring dignity with age, is apt to lose its youth and respectability together. A porch with scant, sloping eaves, from which even the winter's snow must have slid uncomfortably, projected from a doorway that opened most unjustifiably into a small sitting room. There was no vestibule for the embarrassed or bashful visitor. He passed at once from the security of the public road into shameful privacy. And here in the mellow autumnal sunlight, that, streaming through the maples and sumach on the opposite bank, flickered and danced upon the floor, she sat and discoursed of George Washington and thought of Perkins. She was quite in keeping with the house and season, albeit a little in advance of both; her skin being of faded russet, and her hands so like dead November leaves that I fancied they rustled when she moved them.

For all that, she was quite bright and cheery; her faculties still quite vigorous, although performing irregularly and spasmodically. It was somewhat discomposing, I confess, to observe that at times her lower jaw would drop, leaving her speechless, until one of the family would notice it, and raise it smartly into place with a slight snap—an operation always performed in such an habitual, perfunctory manner, generally in passing to and fro in their household duties, that it was very trying to the spectator. It was still more embarrassing to observe that the dear old lady had evidently no knowledge of this, but believed that she was still talking, and that, on resuming her actual vocal utterance, she was often abrupt and incoherent, beginning in the middle of a sentence, and often in the middle of a word.

"Sometimes," said her daughter, a giddy, thoughtless young woman of eighty-five—"sometimes just moving her head sort of unhitches her jaw, and if we don't happen to see it, she'll go on talking for hours without ever making a sound."

Although I was convinced, after this, that during my interview I had lost several important revelations regarding George Washington through these lapses, I could not help reflecting how beneficent were these provisions of the Creator—how, if properly studied and applied, they might be fraught with happiness for mankind—how a slight jostle or jar at a dinner party might make the post-prandial eloquence of garrulous senility satisfactory to itself, yet harmless to others—how a more intimate knowledge of anatomy, introduced into the domestic circle might make a home tolerable at least, if not happy—how a long-suffering husband, under the pretence of a conjugal caress, might so unhook his wife's condyloid process as to allow the flow of expostulation, criticism, or denunciation to go on with gratification to her and perfect immunity to himself.

They had their financial panics even in Jersey in the old days. She remembered when Dr. White married your cousin Mary—or was it Susan? —Yes, it was Susan. She remembered that your Uncle Harry brought in an armful of bank notes—paper money, you know—and threw them in the corner, saying they were no good to anybody. She remembered playing with them, and giving them to your Aunt Anna—no, child, it was your own mother, bless your heart! Some of them was marked as high as a hundred dollars. Everybody kept gold and silver in a stocking, or in a china vase, like that. You never used money to buy anything. When Josiah went to Springfield to buy anything, he took a cartload of things with him to exchange. That yellow picture frame was paid for in greens. But then people knew just what they had. They didn't fritter their substance away in unchristian trifles, like your father, who doesn't know there is a God, who will smite him, hip and thigh; for vengeance is mine, and those that believe in me.

But here, singularly enough, her jaw dropped, and when she recovered her speech again, it appeared that she was complaining of the weather.

The sun, meanwhile, was sinking, and I could not help feeling that I must depart, with my wants unsatisfied. I had brought away no historic fragment. I absolutely knew little or nothing new regarding George Washington. I had been addressed variously by the names of different members of the family who were dead and forgotten. I had stood for an hour in the past; yet I had not added to my historical knowledge, nor the practical benefit of readers. I spoke once more of Washington and she replied with a reminiscence of Perkins.

Stand forth, O Josiah W. Perkins, of Basking Ridge, N. J.! You were of little account in your life, I warrant. You did not even feel the greatness of your day and time. You criticised your superiors; you were small and narrow in your ways. Your very name and grave are unknown and uncared for.

But you were once kind to a woman that survived you, and lo! Your name is again spoken of men, and, for a moment, lifted up above your betters.

1875

Woman Nature

ANONYMOUS

Y ES, gents, it's true," said the man from Buffalo Wallow in answer to the subdued query. Wiping his mustaches with his red flannel sleeve, he set down his empty glass on the bar, gave his worn leather *chaperajas* a hitch, settled his sagging holsters higher on his hips, and sighed, "Yes, gents, last month I lost my Fanny."

As every high-heeled boot was lowered from the rail, spurs jingled. Sombreros came off, uncovering matted heads that bowed in sympathy.

"Thanks, gents," said the little man in his rusty voice. "What is to be, will be. Dutch, pour me about six fingers more of that tarantula juice, and dose these gents out what they want. My treat. Gents, name it and drink it."

The sombreros returned to normal. Low tones indicated their owners' preferences.

"Kiss baby, gents," said the man from Buffalo Wallow.

"Kiss baby," breathed the men at the bar. Then all was silence save for a brief community gurgling, and the screak of polishing-cloth against glass behind the bar.

"Once more again, all around, Dutch," said the man from Buffalo Wallow. "Yes, gents, Fanny was took off and is laid to her rest at last. I won't say I would have it no different. I done my best for her while she lingered, and you gents know I done my best, but I wouldn't of wanted her to drag on, the fix she was in."

Dutch began to fill the rank of glasses. He asked reverentially, "You been married ten years, ain't you, Mr. Buck?"

"Ten long years, Dutch, that's a fact. Seems to me like all my life, sometimes. Kiss baby."

"Kiss baby," softly echoed the others.

The little man said, "Repeat it, Dutch. My treat. Yes, gents, I'll never be able to forget. It's curious to think back now. Ten years ago, I was about thirty, and, like you all know, had accumulated a little place of a few ten thousands of acres of grassland, and had the cattle to make beef off it. One day I looked myself in the face and said, 'Buck Birdsong, you ain't getting no younger.'

"It was a fact, gents, and I knowed it was a fact. The thing to do, the way I saw it, was get myself a wife for my bosom. When a man is out here in the middle of all this space, and gets so much age on him, he needs some quiet little loving female around the place. He needs to hear some little footsteps that will carry his name on.

"In those days, gents, women wasn't the easiest thing to find in these parts. There wasn't no railroad ripping through to pour women out. So, for a while, I just thought I'd maybe search me out some likely Injun gal, and do her and me both a favor. But then I thought Buck Birdsong didn't want some day to be brother-in-law to some Injun insurrection, so I dropped that idea.

"I got lonesomer and lonesomer, gents, the more I thought of a woman. By and by, I couldn't help it. I just turned the place over to the help and I camped myself down here by the old trail, watching the wagons pass by.

"You never saw more women in all your life than I looked at for a few weeks. The homesteaders and so on might be poorer than Job in everything else, but they swarmed in daughters. They was all sizes, shapes, and conditions, gents. I'd edge myself into where they was camped out for the night, and I'd fetch them a haunch of antelope or some beef, or something else neighborly, just for the chance to see what I could see. Some of the gals, I tell you, was a thing apart, taking one feature with another. I was tempted more times than once. But every last one of them had a shining flaw. They talked too much. It is woman nature, I guess. Anyhow, I turned all those gals down, without mentioning it. Everybody that knows me knows I'm a man spare with words. Never could stand just a whole heap of jawing around where I was.

"I was about to give up and dust, when along came the broken-downdest democrat wagon, without no single shred of a tarpoleon over it. Stowed into it was a sour-looking old man and woman, and five strapping gals, among a few sticks of busted furniture. They cracked an axle and camped. And when they commenced to unload themselves, I saw *six* gals. A little least body crept out behind all the chatter and complaint of her sisters and her ma, and set herself down on an old box and folded her hands.

"Anyhow, gents, you might never of noticed it, but I'm a little sawed-off. One of my requirements for a wife was, she couldn't be no bigger than me. This little piece couldn't of measured more'n up to my eyebrows. The first glimpse I had, I fired up. I smothered that camp in meat during the three days while the old man was mending his axle. For an hour at a time, I stood near that little, neat gal. She never said a word, just set on her box, and didn't seem to eat enough to keep a bird alive. She wasn't what you'd call pretty as a spotted pup, but she was a little bit of a thing, and kept her mouth shut while her sisters gabbled like a flock of blackbirds. I was took something awful with her.

"I put at the old feller and asked him if I could have her. He said he didn't see no reason why not. I told him my circumstances and how I was prospering, and he said it sounded suitable. He went to where the gal was setting on her box. He repeated what I'd told him, and said:

" 'Well?'

"She looked up at me and said, 'Beef ranch, did you say?'

" 'Yes, ma'am,' I said.

" 'All right, Fanny,' said the old man, 'What you got to say?'

" 'Un-hunh,' she said.

"It was settled, and I was so full of it, I just turned some somersets and almost fell in the fire. Then the old feller drawed me off to one side and mentioned he was in financial need of a little money. I run to my saddlebags and come back and dumped a hundred silver dollars in his hat, and thanked him to boot, I was so happy. He had his axle repaired, so he piled his family into the old democrat wagon, and that's the last I saw of any of them.

"Fanny and me rousted out the nearest parson and was hitched, and rode, her behind me, home.

"I'm hungry, Mr. Buck," says she, no sooner than we had got inside the house. "I'm mortal hungry."

"So she set down on the bed, and I went out and wrastled up a bait of ham and beefsteak and so forth and so on—to put on a show of my prosperity, I admit.

"Gents, I was hungry too, real sharp-set. But I mean to tell you, I never did know before what eating was. That little slim gal outeat any starved hand ever came to me and begged to be hired. Two solid hours she eat, while I just set there not knowing which from what, and when she was done, she took some bread and sopped up the leavings of juice that was left.

"Finally she was done, and then she said, 'That'll give me strength to do some real eating tomorrow.'

"Well, gents, then she begun talking. Maybe you've seen a sifter at a mill, wagging side to side, bolting the grist? That's the way my little Fanny's jaws worked, never tiring on beef nor talk, and most usually busy on both of 'em. She talked enough for both of us and for our family of ten children, if we'd had the children, which we never did, because from that first night she made me bunk on a hard pallet on the cold floor. Many's the time I've woke in the middle of the night and heard her going it still. Once she took a cold weather ailment and she lost her voice a few days. I recollect I couldn't hardly sleep down there on my pallet. It was like tree frogs. You get used to sleep by their singing, and go where there ain't no tree frogs, and blamed if you can settle down."

The man from Buffalo Wallow heaved a great sigh. "Dutch," he said to the bar-keeper, "the gents looks parched. Shower about three fingers of blessings into their glass all round. On me.

"Little Fanny's talking," he continued, "wasn't the only surprise I got out of her, gents. Eating three or four pounds of beef at a setting, three square times a day, and I don't know how many twixt-meals, she seemed like she begun to swell. Gents, you that knowed her can bear yourself witness that within two years little Fanny could easy have made two of me and then some. Before she was done, she was crowding at near about three hundred pounds. If she'd of ever let me have anything to say, I'd of sounded like some little fice-dog yapping round the stout lady in a circus. It got so, when my Fanny walked, it didn't seem like she used her feet at all. It was more like she just shook her fat and somehow that carried her over the ground, puffing out talk like a railroad engine puffs smoke and steam.

"Nine years, gents. Nine years it went along, her talking and eating, me keeping my peace till my mouth almost growed shut like the lips of a healing wound, and me raising beef critters for her to take her pick of to eat and driving the balance to market.

"Yes, gents, Fanny was a talker. She never let up till she took that stroke of hers last year. It hit her all on a sudden. One minute she was setting in her rocker with her hands folded and chewing on a strip of beef brisket and talking away like sixty, as always, about something or another.

"Next minute, the silence was like a thunderclap. It made my short hairs stand on end. I quit washing the supper dishes and looked round. There she set, seeming just as should be, with her jaw going, but no words coming out. I scouted round her, trying to make it out. She never moved, except her jaw. Gents, fact is, she had been hit by a mighty near complete paralysis.

"But for one time, just before she passed on, the only thing Fanny could ever do again was look at you and chew when you put some rare beef in her mouth. Never lost the use of her jaws, which is the reason, being able to eat hearty, she lingered on like she did. The pitiful thing was, all those hundreds of pounds she'd packed into herself was no better able to make a move than a sack of meal. Poor thing, I guess it come, for the doctor said as much, from her joy in digging her grave with her teeth.

"Gents, when I come to realize what ailed her, I just stood in front of her and the tears dripped down like candle-wax. In a way, she hadn't wifed me none too good, you might say, but I hated to see anything in the fix poor Fanny was in.

"'Buck,' the doctor—old Doc Hiram Slade, it was—he said to me, 'Buck, your wife will never pull out. She's just a matter of time. A week, a month, maybe a year. It'll come in the night like a thief, so be prepared whenever it does come. Just try to ease her last days, Buck, is all.'

"Gents, it gave me an awful unaccustomed feeling. I never was much of a hand at gentling nothing, beast or man. But I knowed, and I wanted to give that poor woman the benefit of anything I could fuddle up and do to make her last days in her calamity peaceable. Talking and eating had been her life, since she'd been with me. The eating part I could manage, for she could work her jaws as good as ever. The other half of her life had been talking. I said to myself, 'Since the Lord or whatever did it has took from her her speech, Buck Birdsong, the least thing you can do is try and crack up the silence for her. I will try,' I said to myself, 'and see if I can practice up and talk to satisfy what she's been used to from herself.'

"It wasn't none of the easiest, I can tell you. You will believe me, I was put to it. You can talk about the weather, about prospects for the grass this year and how many cattle it will support, and about politics and such matters. But that's give and take. Just go out and try to talk all the time, like a woman, and see where you find yourself winding up at. Fifteen minutes of it and you feel like you've pulled your stopper and run out for months to come.

"Gents, I was in a devil of a hobble. I practiced up on the hands, and talked at them till they got so they'd hide under a bush when they saw me riding up. It got so I had to ride into town and foller women round, just to see if I could get to hear the sleight-of-hand of what they talked about to each other. I got in a stew, gents, till one day I stumbled on the secret. The way to talk all the time is not to have nothing to say worth listening to. When you get into that streak, you can talk from who laid the chunk to who laughs the longest. You have hit on the whole middle core of woman nature, and can work wonders in the way of talk.

"So I got so I could talk any time and all the time and be half asleep while I flapped my tongue. Gents, I could chew the rag hours on end, just spilling out the words and never know no more than a billy-goat what I'd been saying to that poor stricken woman. It was a God's mercy, of course, and I was willing to do it, and I done it. From the first peep she opened her eyes in the morning till she was asleep at night, I took turns giving Fanny bites of the beef she loved and talking to her. Turned over the management of the place to my foreman, and never left the house. Most times I stayed right at her side, but when I did have to go into another room for something, you know I'd leave her door open and talk louder the further off I moved, so as she wouldn't have to be one minute without hearing some talking going on.

"Used to be, before her stroke, Fanny got a heap of pleasure out of getting me into an argument. It was usually over some little something like I wasn't handling the place right, or how low and vile all men are and how pure women are, or I paid too much wages to the cow hands, or my mustache was disgusting and I ought to shave it off, or how she was meant for better things than I'd given her, and like that.

"She would draw it out for days, sometimes. I always got the worst of it, because she wouldn't ever let me say nothing in the argument. You see, gents, she argued for both of us. She used whiny, fool-sounding tones when it was supposed to be me talking and her own voice when she came back at what she'd made like I'd been saying.

"Well, since she liked contentions and fussing so much, I'd every now and then spice up my general talking with those argument pieces, only now with me taking both sides. I tell you, I gave myself some unshedded hell in some of those arguments. Other times, without noticing what I was up to, I sort of fell into a way of letting myself come out pretty near even. One time, it turned out that I clean won out in a squabble over purity.

"But, gents, it finally came that one morning I saw my Fanny was sinking. She refused to eat her breakfast beef steak, a good rare one. So I knowed she was in her sad final stage. I rung an alarm on the big bell, and when a hand came whiptailing up from the bunkhouse, I told him to burn the wind after Doc Slade, even though I was satisfied my Fanny would be gone before the old man could get there.

"My Fanny was propped up on a bolster and her pillers in her bed, fading before my eyes. It was all I could do, gents, to gird myself up and keep on talking so she would be able to slip off the world to the tune of the chin-music she'd wove around her life.

"A miracle happened then, gents. I could see Fanny making a terrible strain of some kind, like she was concentrating together the very last little sparks of life left in all her three hundred pounds. And, gents, she managed to move a finger that hadn't moved in most a year. Yes, she gave it a crook for me to come nearer. I'm not ashamed to say that tears almost came in my eyes. The poor thing had some dying message for me. I knowed that, and I was right, as it turned out."

After a pause for refreshment, the man from Buffalo Wallow said, "Like I was telling you, gents, I was touched, and I went and leaned down over Fanny. I kept talking as steady as I knowed how, for it was my duty to her last breaths. She gave her finger another crook, and I bent down closer still, saying her last words for her as I figured she'd want 'em said.

"Then the last thing poor Fanny ever done in the world happened to me. She gave a tearing effort, she lunged up, and, gents, *she bit the living fool out of me!*"

1870's

The Frustrated Bluejays

SAMUEL L. CLEMENS (Mark Twain)

ANIMALS talk to each other, of course. There can be no question about that; but I suppose there are very few people who can understand them. I never knew but one man who could. I knew he could, however, because he told me so himself. He was a middle-aged, simple-hearted miner who had lived in a lonely corner of California, among the woods and mountains, a good many years, and had studied the ways of his only neighbors, the beasts and the birds, until he believed he could accurately translate any remark which they made. This was Jim Baker.

According to Jim Baker, some animals have only a limited education, and use only very simple words, and scarcely ever a comparison or a flowery figure; whereas, certain other animals have a large vocabulary, a fine command of language and a ready and fluent delivery; consequently these latter talk a great deal; they like it; they are conscious of their talent, and they enjoy "showing off." Baker said, that after long and careful observation, he had come to the conclusion that the bluejays were the best talkers he had found among birds and beasts. Said he:

"There's more *to* a bluejay than any other creature. He has got more moods, and more different kinds of feelings than other creatures; and, mind you, whatever a bluejay feels, he can put into language. And no mere commonplace language, either, but rattling, out-and-out book-talk— and bristling with metaphor, too—just bristling! And as for command of language—why *you* never see a bluejay get stuck for a word. No man ever did. They just boil out of him! And another thing: I've noticed a good deal, and there's no bird, or crow, or anything that uses as good grammar as a bluejay. You may say a cat uses good grammar. Well, a cat does—but you let a cat get excited once; you let a cat get to pulling fur with another cat on a shed, nights, and you'll hear grammar that will give you the lockjaw. Ignorant people thing it's the *noise* which fighting cats make that is so aggravating, but it ain't so; its the sickening grammar they use. Now I've never heard a jay use bad grammar but very seldom; and when they do, they are as ashamed as a human; they shut right down and leave.

"You may call a jay a bird. Well, so he is, in a measure—because he's got feathers on him, and don't belong to no church, perhaps; but otherwise he is just as much a human as you be. And I'll tell you for why. A jay's gifts, and instincts, and feelings, and interests, cover the whole ground. A jay hasn't got any more principle than a Congressman. A jay will lie, a jay will steal, a jay will deceive, a jay will betray; and four times out of five, a jay will go back on his solemnest promise. The sacredness of an obligation is a thing which you can't cram into no bluejay's head.

"Now, on top of all this, there's another thing; a jay can outswear any gentleman in the mines. You think a cat can swear. Well, a cat can; but you give a bluejay a subject that calls for his reserve-powers and where is your cat? Don't talk to me—I know too much about this thing. And there's yet another thing; in the one little particular of scolding— just good, clean, out-and-out scolding—a bluejay can lay over anything, human or divine. Yes, sir, a jay is everything that a man is. A jay can cry, a jay can laugh, a jay can feel shame, a jay can reason and plan and discuss, a jay likes gossip and scandal, a jay has got a sense of humor, a jay knows when he is an ass just as well as you do—maybe better. If a jay ain't human, he better take in his sign, that's all. Now I'm going to tell you a perfectly true fact about some bluejays.

"When I first begun to understand jay language correctly, there was a little incident happened here. Seven years ago, the last man in this region but me moved away. There stands his house—been empty ever since; a log house, with a plank roof—just one big room, and no more; no ceiling—nothing between the rafters and the floor. Well, one Sunday morning I was sitting out here in front of my cabin, with my cat, taking the sun, and looking at the blue hills, and listening to the leaves rustling so lonely in the trees, and thinking of the home away yonder in the states, that I hadn't heard from in thirteen years, when a bluejay lit on that house, with an acorn in his mouth, and says, 'Hello, I reckon I've struck something.' When he spoke, the acorn dropped out of his mouth and rolled down the roof, of course, but he didn't care; his mind was all on the thing he had struck.

"It was a knot-hole in the roof. He cocked his head to one side, shut one eye and put the other one to the hole, like a possum looking down a jug; then he glanced up with his bright eyes, gave a wink or two with his wings—which signifies gratification, you understand—and says, 'It looks like a hole, it's located like a hole—blamed if I don't believe it *is* a hole!'

"Then he cocked his head down and took another look; he glances up perfectly joyful, this time; winks his wings and his tail both, and says, Oh, no, this ain't no fat thing. I reckon! If I ain't in luck!—why it's a perfectly elegant hole!' So he flew down and got that acorn, and fetched it up and dropped it in, and was just tilting his head back, with the heavenliest smile on his face, when all of a sudden he was paralyzed into a listening attitude and that smile faded gradually out of his countenance like breath off'n a razor, and the queerest look of surprise took its place. Then he says, 'Why, I didn't hear it fall!' He cocked his eye at the hole again, and took a long look; raised up and shook his head; stepped around to the other side of the hole and took another look from that side; shook his head again. He studied a while, then he just went into the *details*— walked round and round the hole and spied into it from every point of the compass. No use. Now he took a thinking attitude on the comb of the roof and scratched the back of his head with his right foot a minute, and finally says, 'Well, it's too many for *me*, that's certain; must be a mighty long hole; however, I ain't got no time to fool around here, I got to 'tend to business; I reckon it's all right—chance it, anyway.'

"So he flew off and fetched another acorn and dropped it in, and tried to flirt his eye to the hole quick enough to see what become of it, but he was too late. He held his eye there as much as a minute; then he raised up and sighed, and says, 'Confound it, I don't seem to understand this thing, no way; however, I'll tackle her again.' He fetched another acorn, and done his level best to see what become of it, but he couldn't. He says, 'Well, I never struck no such a hole as this before; I'm of the opinion it's a totally new kind of a hole.'

"Then he begun to get mad. He held in for a spell, walking up and down the comb of the roof and shaking his head and muttering to himself; but his feelings got the upper hand of him, presently, and he broke loose and cussed himself black in the face. I never see a bird take on so about a little thing. When he got through he walks to the hole and looks in again for half a minute; then he says, 'Well, you're a long hole, and a deep hole, and a mighty singular hole altogether—but I've started in to fill you, and I'm d—d if I *don't* fill you, if it takes a hundred years!"

"And with that, away he went. You never see a bird work so since you was born. He laid into his work like a nigger, and the way he hove acorns into the hole for about two hours and a half was one of the most exciting and astonishing spectacles I ever struck. He never stopped to take a look any more—he just hove 'em in and went for more. Well, at last he could hardly flop his wings, he was so tuckered out. He comes a-drooping down, once more, sweating like an ice-pitcher, drops his acorn in and says, 'Now I guess I've got the bulge on you by this time!' So he bent down for a look. If you'll believe me, when his head come up again he was just pale with rage. He says, 'I've shoveled acorns enough in there to keep the family thirty years, and if I can see a sign of one of 'em I wish I may land in a museum with a belly full of sawdust in two minutes!'

"He just had strength enough to crawl up on to the comb and lean his back agin the chimbly, and then he collected his impressions and begun to free his mind. I see in a second that what I had mistook for profanity in the mines was only just the rudiments, as you may say.

"Another jay was going by, and heard him doing his devotions, and stops to inquire what was up. The sufferer told him the whole circumstance, and says, 'Now yonder's the hole, and if you don't believe me, go and look for yourself.' So this fellow went and looked, and comes back and says, 'How many did you say you put in there?' 'Not any less than two tons,' says the sufferer. The other jay went and looked again. He couldn't seem to make it out, so he raised a yell, and three more jays come. They all examined the hole, they all made the sufferer tell it over again, then they all discussed it, and got off as many leather-headed opinions about it as an average crowd of humans could have done.

"They called in more jays; then more and more, till pretty soon this whole region 'peared to have a blue flush about it. There must have been five thousand of them; and such another jawing and disputing and ripping and cussing, you never heard. Every jay in the whole lot put his eye to the hole and delivered a more chuckle-headed opinion about the mystery than the jay that went there before him. They examined the house all over, too. The door was standing half open, and at last one old jay happened to go and light on it and look in. Of course, that knocked the mystery galley-west in a second. There lay the acorns, scattered all over the floor. He flopped his wings and raised a whoop. 'Come here!' he says, 'Come here, everybody; hang'd if this fool hasn't been trying to fill up a house with acorns!' They all came a-swooping down like a blue cloud, and as each fellow lit on the door and took a glance, the whole absurdity of the contract hit him and he fell over backward suffocating with laughter, and the next jay took his place and done the same.

"Well, sir, they roosted around here on the housetop and the trees for an hour, and guffawed over that thing like human beings. It ain't any use to tell me a bluejay hasn't got a sense of humor, because I know better. And memory, too. They brought jays here from all over the United States to look down that hole, every summer for three years. Other birds, too. And they could all see the point, except an owl that come from Nova Scotia to visit the Yo Semite, and he took this thing in on his way back. He said he couldn't see anything funny in it. But then he was a good deal disappointed about Yo Semite, too."

1880

Brer Rabbit and Brer Fox

JOEL CHANDLER HARRIS

ONE evening, when the little boy had finished supper and hurried out to sit with Uncle Remus, he found the old man in great glee. Indeed, Uncle Remus was talking and laughing to himself at such a rate that the little boy was afraid he had company. The truth is, Uncle Remus had heard the child coming, and when he put his head in the door, was engaged in a monologue, the burden of which seemed to be—

"Ole Molly Har,
"What you doin dar,
"Settin in de cornder
"Smokin yo seegar?"

This vague allusion reminded the little boy of the fact that the wicked Fox was still in pursuit of the Rabbit, and he asked, "Uncle Remus, did the Rabbit have to go clean away when he got loose from the Tar Baby?"

"Bless gracious, honey, dat he didn't. Who? Him? You dunno nothin bout Brer Rabbit if dat's de way you puttin him down. What he gwine way for? He mouter stayed sorter close twel de pitch rub offn his har, but twarn't many days fore he was lopin up en down de neighborhood same as ever, en I dunno if he warn't mo sassier dan befo.

"Seem like de tale bout how he got mixed up wid de Tar Baby got round mongst de neighbors. Leastways, Miss Meadows en de gals got wind of it, en de next time Brer Rabbit paid em a visit Miss Meadows tackled him bout it, en de gals sot up a monstrous gigglement. Brer Rabbit he sot up des as cool as a cowcumber, he did, en let um run on."

"Who was Miss Meadows, Uncle Remus?" inquired the little boy.

"Don't ax me, honey. She was in de tale, Miss Meadows en de gals was, en de tale I give you like hit were gin to me. Brer Rabbit he sot dar, he did, sorter lamb-like, en den bimeby he cross his legs, he did, en wink his eye slow, en up en say, sezee:—

"'Ladies, Brer Fox was my daddy's ridin-hoss for thirty year, maybe mo —but thirty year dat I knows on,' sezee. En den he paid up his respects, en tip his beaver hat, en march off, he did, des as stiff en as stuck up as a fire-stick.

"Next day, Brer Fox come a-callin, en when he begun for to laugh bout Brer Rabbit, Miss Meadows en de gals dey ups en tells him bout what Brer Rabbit say. Den Brer Fox grit his tooth sho enough, he did, en he look mighty dumpy, but when he riz for to go he up en say, sezee:—

"'Ladies, I ain't disputin what you say, but I'll make Brer Rabbit chaw up his words, en spit um out right here whar you kin see him,' sezee, en wid dat off Brer Fox marched.

"En when he got in de big road, he shuck de dew offn his tail, en made a straight shoot for Brer Rabbit's house. When he got dar, Brer Rabbit was spectin him, en de do was shet fast. Brer Fox knock. Nobody ain't answer. Brer Fox knock. Nobody answer. Den he knock agin—blam! blam! Den Brer Rabbit holler out mighty weak;—

"'Is dat you, Brer Fox? I want you to run en fetch de doctor. Dat bait of parsley what I et dis mawnin is gitting way wid me. Do, please, Brer Fox, run quick,'" says Brer Rabbit, sezee.

"'I come atter you, Brer Rabbit,' says Brer Fox, sezee. 'Dar's gwine to be a party up at Miss Meadowses',' sezee. 'All de gals'll be dar, en I promise dat I'd fetch you. De gals dey 'lowed dat hit wouldn't be no party, ceppin I fotch you,' says Brer Fox, sezee.

"Den Brer Rabbit say he was too sick, en Brer Fox say he warn't, en dar dey had it up en down, disputing en contendin. Brer Rabbit say he can't walk. Brer Fox say he tote him. Brer Rabbit say how? Brer Fox say in his arms. Brer Rabbit say he drap him. Brer Fox 'low he won't. Bimeby Brer Rabbit say he go if Brer Fox tote him on his back. Brer Fox say he would. Brer Rabbit say he can't ride widout a saddle. Brer Fox say he git de saddle. Brer Rabbit say he can't set in de saddle less he have bridle for to hold by. Brer Fox say he git de bridle. Brer Rabbit say he can't ride widout a blind-bridle, kaze Brer Fox be shyin at stumps long de road en fling him off. Brer Fox say he git a blind-bridle. Den Brer Rabbit say he go. Den Brer Fox say he ride Brer Rabbit most up to Miss Meadowses', en den he could git down en walk de balance of de way. Brer Rabbit agreed, en den Brer Fox lipt out atter de saddle en de bridle.

"Course Brer Rabbit know de game dat Brer Fox was fixin for to play, en he determine for to outdo him, en by de time he comb his har en twist his mustache, en sorter rig up, here come Brer Fox, saddle en bridle on, en lookin as peart as a circus pony. He trot up to de do, en stand dar pawin de ground en chompin de bit same like sho enough hoss, en Brer Rabbit he mount, he did, en dey amble off. Brer Fox can't see behind wid de blind-bridle on, but bimeby he feel Brer Rabbit raise one of his foots.

" 'What you doin now, Brer Rabbit?' sezee.

" 'Shortnin de left stirrup, Brer Fox,' sezee.

"Bimeby Brer Rabbit raise up de udder foot.

" 'What you doin now, Brer Rabbit?' sezee.

" 'Pullin down my pants, Brer Fox,' sezee.

"All de time, bless gracious, honey, Brer Rabbit were putting on his spurrers, en when dey got close to Miss Meadowses' whar Brer Rabbit was to git off, en Brer Fox made a motion for to stand still, Brer Rabbit slap de spurrers into Brer Fox flanks, en you better believe he got over de ground. When dey got to de house, Miss Meadows en all de gals was settin on de piazza, en stead of stoppin at de gate, Brer Rabbit rid on by, he did, en den come gallopin down de road en up to de hoss-rack, which he hitch Brer Fox at, en den he santer into de house, he did, en shake hands wid de gals, en set dar, smokin his seegar same as a town man. Bimeby he draw in a long puff, en den let hit out in a cloud, en square hisself back en holler out, he did:—

" 'Ladies, ain't I done told you Brer Fox was de ridin hoss for our fambly? He sorter losing his gait now, but I spect I kin fetch him all right in a month or so,' sezee.

"En den Brer Rabbit sorter grin, he did, en de gals giggle, en Miss Meadows she praise up de pony, en dar was Brer Fox hitch fast to de rack, en couldn't hep hisself.

"Well, dar on Miss Meadowses' piazza dey talk, en sing, en dey play on de pianner, de gals did, twel bimeby hit come time for Brer Rabbit for to be gwine, en he tell um all goodbye, en strut out to de hoss-rack same's if he was de king, en den he mount Brer Fox en ride off.

"Brer Fox ain't sayin nothin tall. He des rack off, he did, en keep his mouth shet, en Brer Rabbit knowed dar was business cookin up for him, en he felt monstrous skittish. Brer Fox amble on twel he git in de long lane, outer sight of Miss Meadowses' house, en den he turn loose, he did. He rip en he rar, en he cuss en swar, he snort en he cavort."

"What was he doing that for, Uncle Remus?" the little boy inquired.

"He was trying for to fling Brer Rabbit offn his back, bless yo soul! But he des might as well wrastle wid his own shadder. Every time he hump hisself Brer Rabbit slap de spurrers in him, en dar dey had it, up en down. Brer Fox fairly tore up de ground, he did, en he jump so high en he jump so quick dat he mighty nigh snatch his own tail off.

"Dey kept on gwine on dis way twel bimeby Brer Fox lay down en roll over, he did, en dis sorter onsettle Brer Rabbit, but by de time Brer Fox git back on his footses agin, Brer Rabbit was gwine through de underbresh mo samer dan a race hoss.

"Brer Fox he lit out atter him, he did, en he push Brer Rabbit so close dat it was bout all he could do for to git in a holler tree. Hole too little for Brer Fox for to git in, en he had to lay down en rest en gather his mind together.

"While he was laying dar, Mr. Buzzard come floppin long, en seein Brer Fox stretch out on de ground, he lit en view de premises. Den Mr. Buzzard sorter shake his wing, en put his head on one side, en say to hisself-like, sezee:—

" 'Brer Fox dead, en I so sorry,' sezee.

" 'No, I ain't dead, neither,' says Brer Fox, sezee. 'I got old man Rabbit pent up in here,' sezee, 'en I'm a-gwinter git him dis time, if it take twel Christmas,' sezee.

"Den, atter some mo palaver, Brer Fox make a bargain dat Mr. Buzzard was to watch de hole, en keep Brer Rabbit dar whiles Brer Fox went atter his axe. Den Brer Fox he lope off, he did, en Mr. Buzzard he tuck his stand at de hole. Bimeby, when all git still, Brer Rabbit sorter scramble down close to de hole, he did, en holler out:—

" 'Brer Fox! Oh! Brer Fox!'

"Brer Fox done gone, en nobody say nothin. Den Brer Rabbit squall out like he was mad, sezee:—

" 'You needn't talk less you want to,' sezee. 'I knows you're dar, en I ain't keerin,' sezee. 'I des want to tell you dat I wish mighty bad Brer Tukkey Buzzard was here,' sezee.

"Den Mr. Buzzard try to talk like Brer Fox:—

" 'What you want with Mr. Buzzard?' sezee.

" 'Oh, nothin in particlar, cep dar's de fattest gray squirrel in here dat I ever see,' sezee, 'en if Brer Tukkey Buzzard was round he'd be mighty glad for to git him,' sezee.

" 'How Mr. Buzzard gwine to git him?' says de Buzzard, sezee.

" 'Well, dar's a little hole round on de udder side of de tree,' says Brer

Rabbit, sezee, 'en if Brer Tukkey Buzzard was here so he could take up his stand dar,' sezee, 'I'd drive dat squirrel out,' sezee.

" 'Drive him out, den,' says Mr. Buzzard, sezee, 'en I'll see dat Brer Tukkey Buzzard gits him,' sezee.

"Den Brer Rabbit kick up a racket, like he were drivin somethin out, en Mr. Buzzard he rush round for to ketch de squirrel, en Brer Rabbit he dash out, he did, en he des fly for home."

The little boy had brought some tea cakes in his pockets for the old man and had given them to him. At this point Uncle Remus took one of the tea cakes, held his head back, dropped the cake in with a sudden motion, looked at the little boy with an expression of astonishment, and then closed his eyes, and began to chew, mumbling as an accompaniment the plaintive tune of "Don't You Grieve atter Me."

The session was over; but, before the little boy went to the "big house," Uncle Remus laid his hand on the child's shoulder, and remarked confidentially:—

"Honey, you must git up soon Christmas mawnin en open de do. Kaze I'm gwine to bounce in on Marse John en Miss Sally, en holler *Christmas Gift* des like I use to durin de farmin days for de war, when old Miss was alive. I bound dey don't forgit de ole nigger. When you hear me callin de pigs, honey, you des hop up en onfasten de do. I lay I'll give Marse John one of dese here sprize parties."

1880

Change the Name of Arkansas?

Anonymous

W HEN some foolhardy Arkansas legislator, stung, perhaps, by perennial bumper crops of jokes at the expense of his State, proposed that its name should be changed to something more dignified, a colleague, supposedly named Cassius M. Johnson, arose and trumpeted:

Mr. Speaker! You yaller-bellied rascal! For the last thirty minutes I've been trying to get your attention. Every time I caught your eye, you've wormed and squirmed like a hound dog with a flea in his hide. Sir, I say damn you!

Fellow Gentlemen! You may go and tear down the honored pictures from the halls of the U.S. Senate, haul down the Stars and Stripes, desecrate the grave of George Washington and his Uncle Bushrod, curse the Goddess of Liberty, and knock down into the dust the Rights of Man —but your crimes would noway compare with what you propose to do when you would change the name of Arkansas!

Change the name of Arkansas? Hell fire no!

Compare the dog fennel to the flaming sunrise—the discordant croak of an old bullfrog to the melodious tones of the nightingale—the classic strains of a Mozart to the bray of a Mexican mule—the feeble arm of a New York dude to the muscles of a Roman gladiator! But *never* change the name of Arkansas! Hell, *no*!

Hide the stars in a lard can, put out the sky to soak in a gourd, hang the Mississippi River on a clothes line, unbuckle the belly band of Time, and turn out the sun and moon to pasture. But you will never change the name of Arkansas!

The world will again pause and wonder at the audacity of the crop-eared, whomper-jawed, half-breed, mean-born, whiskey-soaked hyena who has proposed to change the name of Arkansas! He has just started to climb the political banister and wants to knock the hayseeds out of his hair, pull the splinters out of his big feet, and push on up to the governorship. He may make it, may purely blunder like a blind bull to that high office, but——

Change the name of Arkansas? Hell, Sir, *no!*

1881

The Nature of Boys

Robert J. Burdette

YOUR boy is an animal that asks questions. The older he grows, the more he asks, the more perplexing his questions are, and the more unreasonable he is about wanting them answered to suit himself. He asks today pretty much the same questions, with heaven knows how many additional ones, that Adam's boy did. Every time he asks one that you don't know anything about, just as Adam told Cain fifty times a day, you say he will know all about it when he is a man. So the boy looks forward to the time when he will be a man and know everything.

And now, not entirely ceasing to ask questions, your boy begins to answer them, until you stand amazed at the breadth of his knowledge. He knows now where the first snowdrop lifts its head on the barren earth in spring. He knows where the last autumn pink flames in the brown autumn woods. His pockets are cabinets from which he drags curious fossils, monstrous and hideous beetles and bugs and things that you never saw before, and for which he has names of his own. He knows where there are three orioles' nests. So far back as you can remember, you never saw an oriole's nest in your life. He can tell you how to distinguish the good mushrooms from the poisonous ones; how he ever found out without eating both kinds is a mystery.

He has a formula which, repeated nine times a day while pointing his finger fixedly toward the sun, will knock warts off his hand. He has a formula by which anything that has been lost may be found. He has, above all things, a natural, infallible instinct for the woods and can no more be lost in them than a squirrel. He has one particular marble which he regards with about the same superstitious reverence that a pagan does his idol. Carnelian, crystal, bull's-eye, china, pottery, boly, or blood alley— whatever he may call it, there's luck in it. When he loses this marble, he sees panic and bankruptcy ahead of him and retires from business prudently before the crash comes.

He is getting on, is your boy. His voice develops rapidly and thoroughly. In the yard, on the housetop, down the street, around the corner, wherever there is a patch of ice big enough for him to break his neck on or a pond of water deep enough to drown in, the voice of your boy is heard. He whispers in a shout and converses, in ordinary confidential moments, in a shriek. He exchanges bits of back-fence gossip about his family's domestic affairs with the boy living in the next block, to which interesting revelations the intermediate neighborhood listens with intense satisfaction and the two home circles in helpless dismay.

For a year or two, his feet never touch the stairway in his descent. His habit of polishing the stair rail by using it as a passenger tramway soon breaks the other members of the family of the careless habit of setting the hall lamp or the water pitcher on the baluster post.

Now he wears the same size boot as his father, and on the driest, dustiest days in the year always manages to bring in some mud for the carpets. He carefully steps over the door mat and, until he is about seventeen, actually never knew there was a scraper on the front porch.

About this time, he asks with great regularity for a new hat. He wears his hats on the ground and in the air far more than he does on his head. He never hangs a hat up that he doesn't pull the hook through the crown, unless the hook breaks off or the hat-rack pulls over.

You send your boy on an errand. There are three ladies in the parlor. You have waited as long as you can, in all courtesy, for them to go. They have developed alarming symptoms of staying to tea. You know there aren't half enough strawberries to go around. It is only three minutes' walk to the grocery, however, and Tom sets off like a rocket. You are so pleased with his celerity and ready good nature that you want to run after him and kiss him.

He is gone a long time. Ten minutes become fifteen, fifteen grow into twenty, the twenty swell into the half hour. Your guests exchange very significant glances as the half becomes three-quarters.

Your boy returns at last. Apprehension is in his downcast eyes, humility in his laggard step, penitence in the slouch of his battered hat, and a pound and a half of shingle nails in his hands.

"Mother," he says, "what else was it you told me to get besides the nails?" And while you are counting your scanty store of berries to make them go round, you hear Tom out in the back yard whistling and hammering away, building a dog house with the nails.

Poor Tom, he loves at this age as ardently as he makes mischief and is repulsed quite as ardently as he makes love. If he hugs his sister, he musses her ruffle and gets cuffed for it. Two hours later, another boy, not more than twenty-two or twenty-three years older than Tom, will come in and just make the most hopeless and chaotic wreck of that ruffle. And the only reproach *he* gets is the reproachful murmur, "Must you go so soon?" He doesn't make a movement to go until he hears the alarm clock go off upstairs and the old gentleman up there banging around and loudly wondering if young Mr. Bostwick is going to stay to breakfast?

Tom is at this age set in deadly enmity against company. He regards it as a mortal foe that always stays to dinner, invariably crowds him to the second table, and never leaves him any of the pie. In fact, he is a miniature Ishmaelite at this period. His hand is against every man, and about every man's hand and almost every woman's hand is against him, off and on. Often, and then the iron enters his soul, the hand that is against him holds the slipper. This is all wrong. It spreads the slipper and discourages the boy. It gives a bias to his moral ideas, sours his temper, but it sharpens his wits.

It is an historical fact that no boy is ever whipped twice for precisely the same offense. He varies and improves a little on every repetition until at last he reaches a point where detection is almost impossible.

By easy stages, he passes into the uncomfortable period of boyhood. His jacket develops into a tailcoat. Tom is slow, however, to realize the grandeur of that tailcoat on its trial trip. How different it feels from his good, snug-fitting, comfortable old jacket. It fits him too much in every direction, he feels. He sidles along as close to the fence as he can scrape, with a wary eye in every direction for other boys. When he forgets the school, he is half-tempted to feel proud of his toga, but when he thinks of the boys and the reception that awaits him, his heart sinks and he is tempted to go back home, sneak up the stairs, and rescue his worn old jacket from the rag bag. He notices with horror his distorted shadow on the fence and is convinced that it is a faithful outline of his figure.

He tries various methods of buttoning his coat to make it conform more harmoniously with his structure. He buttons just the lower button, and immediately it flies all abroad at the shoulders. Then he fastens just the top button, and the tails flap and flutter like a clothes line. As he reaches the last friendly corner that shields him from the pitiless gaze of the boys he can hear shrieking and howling before the school, he pauses to give final adjustment to the manly raiment. It is bigger and looser, flappier and wrinklier than ever. New and startling folds and unexpected wrinkles and bulges develop themselves just where the effect will be most demoralizing.

At this trying and awful juncture, a new horror discloses itself. He wants to lie down on the sidewalk and try to die. For the first time he notices the color of his coat. Hideous! He has been duped, swindled, betrayed . . . made a monstrous idiot by this coat that has been palmed off on him! A coat that the most sweetly enthusiastic and terribly misinformed women's missionary society would hesitate to offer a wild Hottentot and which the most benighted, old-fashioned Hottentot would certainly blush to wear in the dark.

Oh, madness! The color is no color. It is all colors. It is a brindle—a veritable, undeniable brindle. There must have been a fabulous amount of brindle cloth made up into boys' first tailcoats, sixteen or eighteen or nineteen years ago. Out of 894 boys I knew in the first tailcoat period, 893 came to school in brindle coats. And the other one—the 894th boy— made his wretched debut in a bottle-green coat, with dreadful, glaring brass buttons. He left school suddenly and was never again seen.

But Tom, shivering and faint with mortification over this new horror, gives one last despairing scrootch of his shoulders, to make the coat look shorter, and with a frantic tug at the tails, to make it appear longer, steps out from the protecting corner. He is stunned with a vocal hurricane of :—

"Oh, what a coat!" and his cup of misery is full.

Passing into the tailcoat period, Tom awakens to the knowledge of the broad physical truth that he has hands. At times he is ready to swear to an even two. Again, when cruel fate and the non-appearance of an escort compels him to accompany his sister to a church sociable, and he sits bolt upright in the grimmest of straight-backed chairs plastered right up against the wall—as the sociable custom is or used to be—and he tries to find enough unoccupied pockets in which to sequester all his hands, he vaguely wonders, if he has only five pair of regularly ordained hands, where this odd hand came from?

And: His mother never cuts his hair again. Never. His hair will be trimmed and clipped but she will not be accessory before the fact. She may sometimes long to have her boy kneel before her while she gnaws around his terrified locks with a pair of scissors that were sharpened when they were made and have since cut yards of calico, furlongs of lamp wick, punched holes in skate straps, opened oyster and fruit cans, and pried up carpet tacks. Many a time and oft they have gone toilsomely around Tom's head and made him an object of terror to the children in the street. When Tom assumes the manly tailcoat, she has looked her last upon his head with trimming ideas.

So a boy's world is ending, a world open to no one but a boy. You never revisit it, much as you may dream of it. You lose the marvelous instinct for the woods, you can't tell a pig nut tree from a pecan, you can't make friends with strange dogs, you can't make the terrific noises with your mouth, you can't invent the inimitable signals and catchwords of boyhood. After you get into a tailcoat and tight boots, you never again set foot in this realm of enchantment.

One day it dawns on the youth's deepening intelligence with the strength and unquestioned truth of a new revelation, that man's upper lip was designed by nature for a mustache. With what exquisite caution and delicacy are his first investigations conducted! In his microscopic researches it appears to him that the down on his upper lip is certainly more determined, more pronounced, more individual fuzz than that upon his cheeks. He makes cautious explorations with the tip of his tenderest finger, delicately backing up the grade the wrong way, going always against the grain, the more readily to detect the slightest symptom of velvety resistance. Day by day he is more convinced that there is in his lip the promise of glory.

In the first consciousness that the mustache is there, like the vote, and only needs to be brought out, how often Tom walks down to the barber shop, gazes longingly in at the window, and walks past. And how often, when he musters up sufficient courage to go in and climbs into the chair and is just on the point of huskily whispering to the barber that he would like a shave, the entrance of a man with a beard like Frederick Barbarossa frightens away his resolution, and he has his hair cut again. The third time that week.

Naturally, driven from the barber chair, Tom casts longing eyes upon the ancestral shaving machinery at home. And who shall say by what means he at length obtains possession of the paternal razor? No one. Nobody knows. Nobody ever did know. Even the searching investigation that always follows the father's demand for the immediate extradition of whoever opened a fruit can with that razor, which follows Tom's first shave, is ever and will ever be barren of results.

All that we know about it is that Tom holds the razor in his hand about a minute, wondering what to do with it, before the blade falls across his fingers and cuts every one of them. Then he straps the razor furiously. Or, rather, he razors the strap. He slashes and cuts that passive instrument in as many directions as he can make motions with the razor. He would cut it oftener if the strap lasted longer. Then he nicks the razor against the side of the mug. Then he drops it on the floor and steps on it and nicks it again. They are small nicks, not so large by half as a saw tooth, and he flatters himself his father will never see them.

He soaks the razor in hot water, as he has seen his father do. Then he makes a variety of indescribable grimaces and labial contortions in an effort to get his upper lip into approachable shape. At last, the first offer he makes at his embryo mustache, he slashes his nose with a vicious upper cut. He gashes the corners of his mouth, and wherever those nicks touch his cheek they leave a scratch apiece, and he learns what a good nick in a razor is for. When he lays the blood-stained weapon down, his gory lip looks as though it had just come out of a long, stubborn, and exciting contest with a straw-cutter.

But he learns to shave, after a while—just before he cuts his lip clear off.

Now, Tom's mustache has taken a start. The world begins to take notice of the newcomer. Tom patiently endures dark hints from other members of the family about his face being dirty. He loftily ignores his experienced father's suggestions about a spoonful of cream and the family cat. When his sisters, in meekly dissembled ignorance, inquire, "Tom, what *have* you on your upper lip?" he is austere, as becomes a man annoyed by the frivolous small talk of women.

The mustache grows. It comes on apace, very short in the middle, no longer at the ends, and blond all round. When you see such a mustache, do not laugh at it, do not point at it the slow, unmoving finger of scorn. Encourage it, speak kindly of it, affect admiration for it, pray for it—for it is a first.

When, in the fullness of time, it has developed so far it can be pulled, there is all the agony of making it take color. It is worse and more obstinate and more deliberate than a meerschaum. The sun that tans Tom's face and blisters his nose only bleaches his mustache. Nothing ever hastens its color.

Now, if ever, and generally now, he buys things to make it take color. He buys a wonderful dye, warranted to "produce a beautiful, glossy black or brown at one application, without stain or injury to the skin." Buys it at a little shabby, round the corner, obscure drug store, because he is not known there. And he tells the assassin who sells it to him that he is buying it for a sister. Of course, the assassin knows that he lies.

In the guilty silence and solitude of his room, with the curtains drawn and the door locked, Tom tries the virtues of the magic dye. It gets on his fingers and turns them black to the elbow. He applies it to his silky mustache, very cautiously and very tenderly. It turns his lip so black that it makes the room dark. Out of the sable splotches that pall everything else, that mustache smiles out, gleaming, unstained, unshaded: A natural, incorruptible blond.

That is the last time anybody fools Tom on hair dye.

During his time, the final, conclusive sign that momentous change is at hand is called loudly and repeatedly to the family's attention. He develops a stern and critical eye for immaculate linen and faultless collars. How it amazes his mother and sisters to learn that there isn't a shirt in the house fit for a pig to wear and that he wouldn't wear the best collar in his room to be hanged in.

Certain it is, there is one thing Tom will do just about this period of his existence. He will fall in love.

1880's

Genesis of a Ward-Heeler

RUFUS E. SHAPLEY

MICHAEL MULHOOLY owed nothing of his greatness to high birth or early advantages. On the contrary, the ancestral halls of the Mulhoolys, situated among the bogs of County Tyrone, Ireland, consisted of a cabin of the style of architecture then fashionable in that section of the country, containing a single apartment, inhabited at the moment of his birth by his parents, ten rapidly-maturing pledges of their love, and two pigs, which, encouraged by the example of the elder Mulhoolys, annually contributed somewhat more than their share towards the common wealth. These humble, but faithful, dependents of the family joined their voices to the general welcome which greeted the arrival of the future statesman, and as soon as he was able to crawl upon the cabin floor, treated him as a foster brother to their own latest addition to the family circle. Thus his infancy, like that of so many of his countrymen who have become leaders of men in our free and happy country, was spent in a condition not apparently conducive to exceptional mental growth, but which is, nevertheless, as experience has demonstrated, especially calculated to develop a genius for leadership in American politics.

Education, such as is derived from books, he did not acquire as he advanced towards manhood. The Mulhoolys had not learned to regard it as a disgrace that no member of the family of their acquaintance had ever learned to read or write. Had such a view of the case been suggested to them, they would, doubtless, have pointed proudly to that long line of Irish kings, from whom they, and all of their countrymen, are descended, not one of whom had ever troubled himself to acquire such useless accomplishments.

When Michael was eighteen years of age, Dennis Mulhooly, a distant cousin, while on a visit to the tombs of his ancestors, conceived the idea of taking the boy back with him to America, and putting him to work in

368

his saloon, known as the "Tenth Precinct House, by Mr. Dennis Mulhooly." So Michael, not unwillingly, yet not without many tears, bade farewell to that beautiful green isle which all of his countrymen from time immemorial have sworn, and until time shall be no more will continue to swear, is the finest spot of green earth on this large globe; but which, nevertheless, so many of them leave at the first opportunity, and to which so few of them ever return in the flesh; owing, probably, to the surprising dearth of native talent for statesmanship which they discover here as soon as they land upon our hospitable shores.

Upon his arrival, he began at the very foot of the ladder. The "Tenth Precinct House, by Mr. Dennis Mulhooly," was not situated in what certain people would call a fashionable neighborhood. There were safer places in the world for a man to fall asleep in if he wished to retain his watch or pocket book. An oyster counter, a bar, three or four chairs, and a stove comprised all the furniture of the one low room where Mr. Dennis Mulhooly catered to the appetites of the public. Two men were all the assistants he required, prior to the arrival of Michael, who was immediately installed in the responsible but unremunerative post of boy-of-all-work. He scrubbed the floor, carried out oyster shells, made fires, ran errands, and occasionally lent a hand behind the oyster bar and counter. But he was happy. For the first time in his life he knew the luxury of having enough to eat, a warm place in which to sleep when it was cold, and clothing enough to cover his entire body at one and the same time.

But this humble bar room was the school room in which his first lessons in life were learned, and where was revealed to his young ambition the shining ladder, like that which Jacob saw in a dream, leading up to the political Olympus upon which he was destined one day to stand and talk with the gods.

Here the party workers of the precinct were wont to congregate to discuss the affairs of the nation. And here, prior to party conventions, occasionally came the leaders of the ward, and, sometimes, those greater statesmen whose comprehensive minds ward-limits could not confine, to make those preliminary political arrangements for the good of the country, which they call "getting in their work."

Why continue to talk of the free school on the hillside as the hope of the Republic, when every day, under your very eyes, you see the indubitable proof that the despised grog shop is the birthplace of statesmanship, and the maligned gin mill the very cradle in which shall be rocked into manhood the coming American politician?

It is not surprising that the visits of these great men gave to the young

Irish lad glimpses of a world that seemed very far above him, and in which he hardly yet dared hope some day to live and move. It is not surprising that the fluency of their conversation about politics, sporting matters, and the women of their acquaintance; the richness and elegance of their clothing; the massiveness of their watch chains; the size of their seal rings; the brilliancy of their diamonds; their lavish expenditure of money; and the lordly grace with which they smoked the fragrant "Reina Victoria" cigars, and ordered the bar-keeper to "set 'em up agin," or "open another bot.," dazzled his young imagination and fired his soul.

As he approached the age of manhood, his eyes were opened to his want of education and the advantages which he might derive from being able to read and write. He set to work under the instruction of Pat, the bar-keeper, in his leisure moments, to master these accomplishments. Michael had industry, perseverence, and ambition, and, though great was his labor, great also was his reward. When he became able to spell out in the *Police Record* and *Sporting Man's Own* the chaste and graphic accounts of the latest prize fight, he felt something of that mental exaltation with which more fortunate school boys read of the days and deeds of chivalry. And as he read of these exhibitions of science and courage, he longed to be some day spoken of as a Heenan, a Morrissey, a Mace, or a Sayers. He lost no opportunity to perfect himself in the manly art, and, as opportunities for practice were not wanting in his neighborhood, before he had reached the age of manhood he had won the reputation of being the hardest hitter and most scientific sparrer in that end of the ward.

Before he came of age, Michael had commended himself to the party workers who frequented the saloon by acting as the representative at the polls in his precinct of a gentlemanly young clerk who had registered to vote. When the young clerk had offered to vote in person, he was surprised to learn that he had already voted at an hour when he could have sworn he was perfecting his toilet. He was rudely hustled from the polls, glad enough to escape being beaten, and afterwards arrested on the charge of attempting to violate the sanctity of the ballot.

At the age of twenty-one, Michael Mulhooly was duly naturalized. It is true that by the ordinary methods of computing time he had only spent two years in this country; but as the records of the court showed that two highly respectable citizens, known to and approved by the court, had made solemn oath that they had personally known the applicant for upwards of five years, during which time he had actually resided in this country, and that he was well-disposed to the Government and familiar with its Constitution, it was evident that the stringent naturalization laws of the United States had not been abused.

He was now clothed in the full panoply of American citizenship. There was no office of election or appointment, from constable to United States Senator, to which he might not lawfully and hopefully aspire. Only the office of President of the United States was hopelessly beyond his reach.

It is scarcely necessary to record the fact that Michael Mulhooly did not neglect to vote at the election immediately following his naturalization. Indeed, from his own statements, made that night while celebrating his political second birth, so great was his fear that his vote might not be properly counted in his own precinct, that he took the precaution to deposit another constitutional expression of his will in an adjoining precinct; and, to still further protect his newly acquired rights of citizenship, he repeated this precaution against fraud in two other precincts more remote from his home. The wisdom of this course was highly commended by all his hearers. Some of them, with prophetic eye, even looked forward to the time when the country would be proud of its newly-adopted child.

Owing to a misfortune which befell Pat about this time, resulting in his temporary withdrawal from the active labors of life by reason of his mistaking the ownership of a watch, which he said had been dropped upon the floor by a belated individual who had lost his bearings and wandered into the saloon very late one night, Michael was promoted to the post of regular bar-keeper, with a salary nominally fixed, but virtually to be determined by himself. This promotion enlarged his opportunities for prosecuting his political studies. It placed him at once upon terms of easy familiarity with the statesmen of his acquaintance who dropped in for that inspiriting morning drink, called by some a "cocktail" but which other authorities insist should be called an "eye-opener." It initiated him into that mystic brotherhood—that ancient, honorable, and well-dressed order which has, in every age, exercised such a powerful influence over its politicians and legislators. No wonder that the poet said, "Let me mix a nation's cocktails and I care not who make its laws."

Michael had by this time learned how to improve his natural personal advantages by those arts of dress that gentlemen of his class so well understand. He sauntered along the fashionable thoroughfares on Saturday afternoons when he was off duty, clad in light plaid breeches, tight at the knee and thence curving gracefully until nearly the whole foot was hidden, cut-away coat of darker plaid pattern, trim at the waist, and with shoulders projecting like the eaves of a Swiss chalet, red silk cravat, Derby hat, yellow kid gloves, and a fancy-headed cane. It was not strange, therefore, that he won the regard of a woman some years his senior, whose house, situated within a square of the saloon, was frequented by most of the political leaders of his acquaintance. In her society, and that which she drew around her, his manners rapidly acquired much of that polish which he had formerly so much admired in his exemplars, and which afterwards contributed so largely to his own popularity and success in life.

In return for the many delicate services which she received from him, she gave him a plentiful supply of pocket money, many articles of jewelry indispensable to a gentleman in his station; a diamond shirt stud; and, when Dennis concluded to purchase a larger saloon in another portion of the city, she furnished the necessary capital to buy out the old one, repaint, and refit it, and commence business for himself. That was a proud night for Michael, when, standing for the first time in front of his own bar, while the radiance of his diamond almost blinded his new bar-keeper, he invited up a number of his political friends who had assembled to offer him their congratulations, and himself gave the order he had so often obeyed, to "set 'em up all round."

At the next election Michael took another forward step in his political studies. Six brand-new American citizens from a neighboring city were so anxious to prove their gratitude to the government for adopting them, and so determined to put down its enemies, that, dropping all business at home, they hurried over to this city and placed their services at the disposal of the Hon. Hugh McCann, a member of the State Legislature, to whom the City Committee had given $1,000 to place where it would do the most good. These public-spirited men were provided with lodgings over the "Tenth Precinct House," and to Michael was intrusted the duty of guiding them to the precincts in which the committee had decided they could best serve their country.

One of these gentlemen had the misfortune to resemble a well-known kleptomaniac whom the police authorities of his own city were anxious to persuade to return in the hope of curing him of his malady by keeping him from temptation. This resemblance struck a police officer near the polls so forcibly that he insisted upon taking him, along with Michael, to the nearest station house for identification.

To this unconstitutional interference with a voter while in the exercise of the elective franchise, Michael objected, and commenced to discuss the constitutional questions involved with so much spirit and force that the officer, overcome by his arguments, twice lay down upon the pavement.

A squad of policemen under the command of a sergeant came up, and mistaking the meaning of Michael's gestures, captured him, and, not without some difficulty, at last got him inside the station house, where they preferred against him charges of assault and battery, resisting an officer, and vouching for a repeater.

Michael's detention, however, lasted for only a few minutes, until Hon. Hugh McCann, who had heard of the misunderstanding, came to hunt him up, entered bail for his appearance, and assured him that early in the morning he would himself see the Boss, who would see Judge Coke and have the whole thing "squared."

Michael had not yet reached that clause in the Constitution which referred to the office of Boss. Therefore, he failed to understand as clearly as he would have done a few years later, the nature of this office and the process of getting such matters squared.

Squared they were, for his record warranted it: He had voted once before he was of age. He had voted four times at the election immediately succeeding his naturalization. At the following election, he had led to the polls six citizens whose votes, it was known, would be challenged and had succeeded in persuading the election officers to receive five of them. He had twice knocked down a police officer who interfered with him while he was discharging this delicate and important public duty. Such talents are well known to be more valuable in politics than familiarity with the writings of Adam Smith. Such men never fail to receive that recognition from the party leaders to which such invaluable party services entitle them.

Accordingly, Michael Mulhooly was immediately placed upon his Ward Committee. At the next election, he was appointed by the court an election officer to fill a vacancy, at the instance of one of the ward leaders who was a candidate for constable.

This duty he discharged so successfully that when the returns were made up by the election officers, it was found that his candidate for constable had received nearly a hundred more votes than those who kept the lists could account for or believed had been cast. Thus, Michael commenced to comprehend those *unknown* quantities in politics which so materially affect results.

Michael Mulhooly had now won his political spurs. He had proved himself worthy of citizenship. He had given unmistakable evidences of possessing talents by which, with proper training, he could not fail to make his mark upon the political history of his country.

1881

The Kill-Ma-Roo

MELVILLE D. LANDON (Eli Perkins)

IN THE Blaine Presidential campaign, the Democrats were continually saying that he would be a radical President.

"He'll get up a war with Germany about Samoa," they said, "or get us into an embroglio with France on account of the Suez Canal."

"Yes," said Blaine, "the Democrats always have some trouble ahead. The Republicans are going to wreck the republic by high tariff one day, and bankrupt the nation through the pension office the next.

"The Democrats remind me of a story of the man who was carrying something across Fulton Ferry in a closed box. Every now and then he would open the box, peep in, and then close the lid mysteriously. His actions soon excited the curiosity of a man who sat on the seat by him. The man touched him on the shoulder and said:

" 'I beg pardon, sir, but I'm curious to know what you have in that box. What is it?'

" 'Oh, I don't want to tell. It will get all over the boat.'

" 'Is it a savage animal?'

" 'Yes—kills everything.' Then the man peeped in again.

"Still growing more curious, his neighbor begged him to tell the animal's name?

" 'It's a kill-ma-roo—a very savage beast.'

" 'And what do you feed it on?'

" 'Snakes, sir—plain snakes.'

" 'Where do you get snakes enough to feed such a monster?'

" 'Well, sir, my brother in Brooklyn drinks a good deal, has delirium tremens, and when he sees snakes, we just catch 'em and—"

" 'But those are imaginary snakes!'

" 'Why, the fact is,' said the man with the box, confidentially, 'the fact is, sir, but don't say a word about it, that this is an imaginary kill-ma-roo.' "

1880's

Texas Climate

A. E. SWEET

WHEN the pious old Spanish padres first came to Western Texas to convert the Indians, they noticed the extreme balminess of the atmosphere, the superior quality of the climate. They were surprised that the Creator should waste so much good climate on the wicked heathen. Back where they came from, they couldn't raise as much climate per annum as they could harvest in Western Texas in one short week.

In the early days of the Republic of Texas, and even after annexation, many who came from all parts of the United States had strongly sanitary reasons for preferring a change of climate. To be more explicit, the most of the invalids had been threatened with throat disease. So sudden and dangerous is this disease that the slightest delay in moving to a new and milder climate is apt to be fatal, the sufferer dying of dislocation of the spinal vertebra at the end of a few minutes and a rope.

A great many men, as soon as they heard of Western Texas, left their homes in Arkansas, Indiana, and other States—left immediately, between two days—the necessity for their departure being so urgent that they were obliged to borrow the horses they rode to Texas on. All these invalids recovered on reaching Austin. In fact, they began to feel better, and considered themselves out of danger, as soon as they crossed the Brazos River.

Some of those who would not have lived twenty-four hours longer if they had not left their own homes, reach a green old age in Western Texas. By carefully avoiding the causes that led to their former troubles, they are never again in any danger of the bronchial affection already referred to.

As soon as it was discovered that the climate of Western Texas was favorable towards invalids, a large number of that class of unfortunates came to Austin. Many well authenticated cases or recoveries are recorded. Men have been known to come to Austin, far-gone, and so recover as to be able to run for office within a year, and to be defeated by a large and respectable majority—all owing to the climate and the popularity of the other candidate.

Such is a short synopsis of the Texas climate.

1882

A Resign

EDGAR WILSON NYE (Bill Nye)

POSTOFFICE DIVAN, LARAMIE CITY, W. T., Oct. 1, 1883.

TO THE PRESIDENT OF THE UNITED STATES:

SIR.—I beg leave at this time to officially tender my resignation as postmaster at this place, and in due form to deliver the great seal and the key to the front door of the office. The safe combination is set on the numbers 33, 66 and 99, though I do not remember at this moment which comes first, or how many times you revolve the knob, or which direction you should turn it at first in order to make it operate.

There is some mining stock in my private drawer in the safe, which I have not yet removed. This stock you may have, if you desire it. It is a luxury, but you may have it. I have decided to keep a horse instead of this mining stock. The horse may not be so pretty, but it will cost less to keep him.

You will find the postal cards that have not been used under the distributing table, and the coal down in the cellar. If the stove draws too hard, close the damper in the pipe and shut the general delivery window.

Looking over my stormy and eventful administration as postmaster here, I find abundant cause for thanksgiving. At the time I entered upon the duties of my office the department was not yet on a paying basis. It was not even self-sustaining. Since that time, with the active co-operation of the chief executive and the heads of the department, I have been able to make our postal system a paying one, and on top of that I am now able to reduce the tariff on average-sized letters from three cents to two.

Through all the vicissitudes of a tempestuous term of office I have safely passed. I am able to turn over the office to-day in a highly improved condition, and to present a purified and renovated institution to my successor.

Acting under the advice of Gen. Hatton, a year ago, I removed the feather bed with which my predecessor, Deacon Hayford, had bolstered up his administration by stuffing the window, and substituted glass. Finding nothing in the book of instructions to postmasters which made the feather bed a part of my official duties, I filed it away in an obscure place and burned it in effigy, also in the gloaming. This act maddened my predecessor to such a degree, that he then and there became a candidate for justice of the peace on the Democratic ticket. The Democratic party was able, however, with what aid it secured from the Republicans, to plow the old man under to a great degree.

It was not long after I had taken my official oath before an era of unexampled prosperity opened for the American people. The price of beef rose to a remarkable altitude, and other vegetables commanded a good figure and a ready market. We then began to make active preparations for the introduction of the strawberry-roan two-cent stamps and the black-and-tan postal note. One reform has crowded upon the heels of another, until the country is to-day upon the foam-crested wave of permanent prosperity.

Mr. President, I cannot close this letter without thanking yourself and the heads of departments at Washington for your active, cheery and prompt co-operation in these matters. I need not say that I herewith transmit my resignation with great sorrow and genuine regret. We have toiled on together month after month, asking for no reward except the innate consciousness of rectitude and the salary as fixed by law. Now we are to separate. Here the roads seem to fork, as it were, and you and I, and the cabinet, must leave each other at this point.

You will find the key under the door-mat, and you had better turn the cat out at night when you close the office. If she does not go readily, you can make it clearer to her mind by throwing the cancelling stamp at her.

If Deacon Hayford does not pay up his box-rent, you might as well put his mail in the general delivery, and when Bob Head gets drunk and insists on a letter from one of his wives every day in the week, you can salute him through the box delivery with an old Queen Anne tomahawk, which you will find near the Etruscan water-pail. This will not in any manner surprise either of these parties.

Tears are unavailing. I once more become a private citizen, clothed only with the right to read such postal cards as may be addressed to me personally, and to curse the inefficiency of the postoffice department. I believe the voting class to be divided into two parties, viz: Those who are in the postal service, and those who are mad because they cannot receive a registered letter every fifteen minutes of each day, including Sunday.

Mr. President, as an official of this Government I now retire. My term of office would not expire until 1886. I must, therefore, beg pardon for my eccentricity in resigning. It will be best, perhaps, to keep the heart-breaking news from the ears of European powers until the dangers of a financial panic are fully past. Then hurl it broadcast with a sickening thud.

1883

Abram Jasper's Parable

ATTRIBUTED TO HENRY WATTERSON

SHORTLY before election, a colored political barbecue was held near Louisville and old Abram Jasper was asked to speak.

"Feller freemen," said he, "you all knows me. I is a Republican from way back. When dar has been any work to do, I has done it. When dar's been any votin to do, I has been in de thick of it. I is old line an tax-paid. I has seed many changes, too. I has seed de Republicans up. I has seed de Democrats up. But I is *yit* to see de nigger up.

"De other night I had a dream. Dremp I died and went to heaven. When I got to de Pearly Gate, old Saint Peter he say:

" 'Who dar?' says he.

" 'Abram Jasper,' says I.

" 'Is you mounted or is you afoot?' says he.

" 'I is afoot,' says I.

" 'Well, you kain't git in here,' says he. 'Nobody lowed in here cept dem as comes mounted,' says he.

" 'Dat's hard on me,' says I, 'atter comin all dat distance.' But he never say nothin mo, an so I starts back, an about halfway down de hill, who does I meet but Charles Sumner an dat good old Horace Greeley!

" 'Whar you gwine, Mr. Greeley?' says I.

" 'I is gwine to heaven wid Mr. Sumner,' says he.

" 'Mr. Greeley,' says I, ' 'tain't no use. I is jes been up dar, an nobody's lowed to git in cept dey comes mounted, and you is afoot.'

" 'Is dat a fack?' says he.

"Mr. Greeley sorter scratch his head, an atter awhile he says, says he, 'Abram, I tell you what less do. Supposin you gits down on all fours an Sumner an me will mount an ride you in, and in dat way we kin all git in.'

" 'Gentlemen,' says I, 'do you think you kin work it?'

380

" 'I *know* I kin,' says bof of dem.

"So down I gits on all fours, an Greeley an Sumner gits astraddle, and we ambles up de hill agin, an prances up to de Gate, and old Saint Peter say:

" 'Who dar?'

" 'We is, Charles Sumner an Horace Greeley,' says Mr. Greeley.

" 'Is you bof mounted or is you afoot?' says Peter.

" 'We is bof mounted,' says Mr. Greeley.

" 'All right,' says Peter. 'All right,' says he, 'jes hitch yo hoss outside, gentlemen, an come right in.' "

1880's

Unkindest Cut

ANONYMOUS

AFTER nearly three decades of out-maneuvering the best that the U.S. Army could send into the field, Sitting Bull was caught and held at the Red Cloud agency, where he was interviewed by the Quaker Indian Commissioners. They wanted to know if the old Sioux warrior had any special grievance to report to them?

Sitting Bull nodded grimly. "A white man has lied about me," he said. "He lied and put in newspaper for all world to read."

"Who was it?" asked the Commissioners.

"Indian don't know name. But Indian been told what man write in newspaper. Indian sensitive man. He no like being lied about." And here he gave vent to an accomplished burst of bi-lingual profanity.

"But what did the man write about you, Chief?"

"If Indian ever find him, he'll scalp the son-bitch say Sitting Bull graduated at West Point!"

1890

Notes on the Authors

"In editing this collection I have taken note of the lives and reputations of the writers, attempting wherever possible to identify them specifically. In some cases biographical material has proven exceedingly scanty and in others unrelated to my present purpose. Herewith, in alphabetical order, are some brief notes on a number of individuals who have made their contribution to the heritage of American humor.

J.R.A.

GEORGE W. BAGBY (1828-1883). Born in Buckingham County, Virginia, Bagby became a master of the bucolic vernacular of his section. During the Civil War, he was a clerical worker in Confederate Headquarters at Richmond and spare-time correspondent for Southern newspapers. In the affection of postwar Southerners, he was second only to Bill Arp. His master creation, Jud Brownin—half chawbacon cutup, half lachrymose poet, aware of his own nature and playing it for all it was worth—struck closer to the heart of the character of his people than Bagby may have realized.

JAMES M. BAILEY (1841-1894). Born in Albany, New York, he worked as a carpenter, went into the Union Army, and after the war settled in Danbury, Connecticut, where he edited the *News*. His good-natured columns on life in Danbury, interlarded with recollections of his youth and childhood, were published in several volumes which had large sales. His writing, which is much like that of Robert J. Burdette, belongs to the late nineteenth century, or house-broken, stage of American humor.

JOSEPH GLOVER BALDWIN (1815-1864). Born near Winchester, Virginia, Baldwin clerked in a store, studied law in his uncle's office, and edited a newspaper when he was seventeen. In 1836 he joined the land-rush to the Mississippi and Alabama territories where he practiced law and rode circuit court until 1854. His *Flush Times in Alabama and Mississippi*, published in 1853, is a rich account of the enormous vitality and chaos of the new settlements. But the section became too tame for Judge Baldwin. He packed off to California, where he became an associate justice of the state supreme court, later going into private practice. Despite its rollicking basic humor, his writing is spoiled for modern readers by his affectation of profuse Latin quotations and other stylistic arabesques. In the two selections chosen for *Native American Humor*, drastic weeding has been done.

P. T. BARNUM (1810-1891). The prince of bunko-steerers, appropriately from Connecticut—the Nutmeg State—said that a sucker was born every minute, and proved it with his exhibitions of magnificent frauds and curiosities. A Sam Slick and Simon Suggs rolled in one, on the grand scale, Barnum got his grounding in human credulity as a village storekeeper and newspaper editor. The Greatest Show on Earth was embryonic in his promotion of such wonders as Joice Heth, spurious nurse of George Washington; General Tom Thumb, dwarfish enough, but not so microscopic as Barnum advertised; and the genuine songbird, Jenny Lind— with whom Barnum didn't get along, naturally. His autobiography was republished by him periodically, "completely revised," which meant a footnote or a paragraph added to the end of a chapter here and there. It sold more than a million copies. Largely a rumbling display of Barnum's public virtues and argument to prove that he was humanity's benefactor, the weird book contains patches of hardheaded Yankee humor reminiscent of Ben Franklin.

HENRY WARD BEECHER (1813-1887). Born in Litchfield, Connecticut, this warmhearted Presbyterian minister was one of the towering figures of his day. Brought up "to put my hand to anything," he was at home in the pulpit, the lecture platform, in editing, and at writing articles for newspapers and magazines. Unlike many of his contemporary divines, Beecher preferred to illustrate his sermons with parables from everyday life, often humorous, rather than with allusions to lakes of boiling pitch and references to fiendish tortures to come for those who strayed from the path of righteousness, moral or political.

AMBROSE BIERCE (1842-1914). Born in Meigs County, Ohio, he served with the Union Army during the Civil War, was twice badly wounded, and was mustered out as a major. At loose ends, he flipped a coin to decide that he would go to California, where he wrote for San Francisco newspapers and West Coast magazines. Later he was Washington correspondent for the Hearst papers and on the staff of *Cosmopolitan Magazine*. In his newspaper columns as well as in his *Devil's Dictionary* and most of his fiction, Bierce demonstrated his belief that the human race was damning itself by its own stupidity. One of the basic faults, he felt, was its sloppy use of words. If words were dishonest, how, then, could thought be otherwise? At the age of seventy-one, he disappeared on some mysterious mission to Mexico.

HUGH HENRY BRACKENRIDGE (1748-1816). Scotch-born, he was brought to America as a child and had his education at Princeton. His whetted comments on life in the young republic were drawn from experience as tutor, headmaster of a Maryland academy, editor, patriot propagandist, chaplain in the Continental Army, lawyer, circuit judge, and state supreme court justice in Pennsylvania.

CHARLES FARRAR BROWNE—Artemus Ward—(1834-1867). Born in Waterford, Maine, he was a tall, shambling crane of a man with walrus mustaches, mournful eyes, and a platform pose of shy befuddlement which endeared him to millions much in the manner of Will Rogers, three-quarters of a century later. An apprentice typesetter in his early teens, he followed the trade from Skowhegan to New York, then meandered west into Ohio. In 1858, the *Cleveland Plain Dealer* hired him to write local news. He never became a "good reporter." Fact always appeared to him as through a wavy, sun-warmed windowpane, brightly. In addition to facetious accounts of doings in Cleveland, he concocted sketches purporting to come from a Barnumlike showman, *Artemus Ward*, owner of a traveling exhibit of "three moral bares—moral wax figgers of G. Washington, &c. &c." In a matter of weeks, Artemus Ward was a household term, synonym for cheerful lunacy. Charles Browne was showered with blushing honors, lecturing to packed houses in most of the states and territories. His repertory included *My Seven Grandmothers, Babes in the Woods*, and so on. The titles weren't important. The chief feature of his lectures, he said, was "that they contain so many things that don't have anything to do with the subject." He interrupted one of his tours for three hazy weeks in Virginia City, Nevada. Here he spent considerable time with a floundering young reporter on the *Enterprise*. He and Sam Clemens are said to have been arrested at midnight while trying to walk, barefooted, up the outside wall of a three-story saloon. Lionized and a universal favorite, in 1867 he sailed for England where he had an immense success. His tour ended in collapse. For years he had been tubercular. He died, aged thirty-two, in Southampton. Judging from his printed lectures, a later generation may find Artemus Ward's reputation puzzling. What he said wasn't so hilarious—it was the way he said it. His newspaper skits wear better. They were written for printing, not oral delivery. Artemus Ward's influence on the great humorists who immediately followed him rested on their love for the man.

ROBERT J. BURDETTE (1844-1914). Born in Greensburgh, Pennsylvania, he wrote gentle humor of domestic situations and lectured from his own sketches in the 80's and 90's. He was associate-editor of the Burlington, Iowa, *Hawkeye*. Previously, he had been a volunteer in the Civil War, had worked for a railroad, had been an unsuccessful newspaper publisher in Peoria, and had a Methodist license to preach. *The Nature of Boys* in this volume is abridged from Burdette's lecture, *The Rise and Fall of the Mustache*.

T. A. BURKE. He wrote and collected humorous sketches before the Civil War and edited a boys' magazine published in Macon, Georgia, in the late 1860's. No other data is available, except a surmise that he may have been author of *Lightwood*.

J. F. H. CLAIBORNE (1809-1884). Born in Natchez, Mississippi, he studied law in Virginia where he was admitted to the bar. Returning to Mississippi, he shuttled between law practice and politics, and, as lawyers seemed able to do so readily then, edited and wrote for newspapers. Speculation in timber made him wealthy. He retired to write magazine pieces and to compile historical sketches of his state.

CHARLES HEBER CLARK—Max Adler—(1847-1915). This Philadelphia banker's facetious accounts of suburban life were even more popular in England than in the United States.

SAMUEL L. CLEMENS—Mark Twain—(1835-1910). Mark Twain's career is too familiar for repetition. However, his debt to the older humor isn't commonly known. Like most of the writers appearing in this collection, he tried many callings before he found what he wanted to do. As a young man, he was for half a dozen years a printer, setting in type hundreds of the contemporary humorous sketches. "Exchanges," clipped and filed, came in handily to pad newspaper columns when local events went slack. The outlook and methods of these writers were etched in Sam Clemens' mind. In the course of time he dredged them up for his own use. Those wonderful hornswogglers, the King and the Duke, are kindred spirits to Johnson J. Hooper's Simon Suggs by considerably more than coincidence. Often in Mark Twain's sketches the ribald laughter of Sut Lovingood echoes. In the case of Simon Suggs, especially, if you didn't know the Shifty Man for Hooper's creation, you would swear it was Mark Twain's—and Mark Twain at his best.

DAVID CROCKETT (1786-1836). Born in Greene County, Tennessee, son of Irish immigrants, he was a mighty frontiersman and bear-hunter who entered politics in the train of Andrew Jackson and served in the state legislature and Congress. Falling out with Jackson over the latter's harsh Indian policy, Crockett struck out independently, with varying success. He dictated the first book of his *Autobiography* for circulation during a campaign in 1835, in which he was defeated. Two later books are fraudulent, scribbled out to take political advantage of Crockett's popularity. After his defeat in Tennessee, he told the voters in his district that "they could go to hell and I will go to Texas!" He did, fighting in the opening skirmishes of the Texan War and dying at the Alamo. The genuine part of his *Autobiography* is one of the raciest and most eccentric pieces of humor in the American vernacular. The Davy Crockett almanacs in vogue after his death, and which present-day professional folklorists collect with cackles of delight, are dreary conceits of hackwriters—about on a par with today's comic books.

JOSEPH DENNIE (1768-1812). Born in Boston, Dennie was a Harvard law student who became a lay preacher. He quickly gave up moralizing and fell into his proper niche as essayist and editor of several publications, including the *Farmer's Weekly Museum* and, finally, the Philadelphia *Port Folio*. Although he often wrote in the orotund style of his day, he was author of enough straight-faced parody to earn for himself the title of "The American Addison."

GEORGE HORATIO DERBY—John Phoenix—(1823-1861). In the mid-1840's, some Washington official of the United States Topographical Engineers sent a query to a young lieutenant detailed to a survey of the Florida coast: "How far does the so-and-so river run up?" Brevet Lieutenant George Horatio Derby is supposed to have answered: "The so-and-so river don't run up." The story may be apochryphal, but it is of a piece with the rambunctious field reports which kept Derby—an honor graduate of West Point who distinguished himself in the Mexican War and was severely wounded—from promotion until a year before his death. Born in Dedham, Massachusetts, he was the son of an eccentric writer for New England newspapers. After the Mexican War he was, in effect, banished to California. If the War Department had hoped he would desert to the gold fields, it was disappointed. He stuck, leading three expeditions to map the Colorado River and plodding the treadmill of army post routine. To pass time, he wrote burlesque letters to the *San Diego Herald*, signing them *John Phoenix* or *Squibob*. When the Presidential campaign between General Winfield Scott and Franklin Pierce was at its peak, the editor of the *Herald* was called on business to San Francisco. He left his hotly Democratic sheet in Derby's charge. Overnight the *Herald* was bellowing for the Whigs. Derby's subsequent interview with the editor he reported thus:

> We rose, and with an unfaltering voice said, "Well, Judge, how do you do?" He made no reply, but commenced taking off his coat. . . .
> The sixth and last round is described by the pressmen and compositors as having been fearfully scientific. We held the Judge down over the press by our nose (which we had inserted between his teeth for that purpose), and while our hair was employed in holding one of his hands, we held the other in our left . . .
> We write this while sitting without clothing, except our left stocking and the rim of our hat encircling our neck like a ruff of the Elizabethan era. . . .

A fellow West Pointer, William Tecumseh Sherman, in California as agent for a St. Louis bank, brought Derby's extravaganzas to the attention of an Eastern publisher who put out a best-selling collection of them. Suddenly a man of distinction, Derby was recalled from California in

1856, and three years later was promoted to captain. Shortly afterward, he suffered a stroke. He died insane in New York City during the first year of the Civil War. Mark Twain enthusiastically imitated his calm way of taking gigantic liberties with fact, his total disrespect for hallowed respectabilities. Derby was the grandfather of Western humor as we know it. Few of his literary progeny have measured up to him.

STEPHEN A. DOUGLAS (1813-1861). Born in New England, the "Little Giant" moved to Illinois at the age of twenty. There he practiced law, from which it was a natural step into a political career. An accomplished orator and teller of tales, Douglas might have gone on to the presidency had he not met his master on both scores in Abraham Lincoln.

EDWARD EVERETT (1794-1865). Born in Dorchester, Massachusetts, Everett graduated from Harvard and studied for the ministry. A year in the pulpit was enough. He resigned to teach Greek literature and, when that palled, he studied in Europe. He edited the *North American Review*, abandoning it for a political career. Serving in the House of Representatives for ten years, Everett was elected governor of Massachusetts in 1835. Six years later he was appointed United States minister to Great Britain. From 1846 to 1849 he was president of Harvard College. He succeeded his friend Daniel Webster as secretary of state in 1852. His versatile writings ran from sober biography to polished humorous essays.

HENRY S. FOOTE (1804-1880). This Virginia-born Mississippi lawyer and politician served as governor of the state, and as United States and Confederate congressman. His outspoken advocacy of compromise between the sundering North and South kept him in hot water. He fought four duels and roared into any number of canings and fist fights—one with Jefferson Davis. Like most moderates, he tended to see the life of his era humorously, and demonstrated that viewpoint in his *Bench and Bar of the South and Southwest*, published four years before his death.

JAMES ROBERTS GILMORE—Edmund Kirke—(1822-1903). Born in Boston, Massachusetts, Gilmore became a New York shipper, with much of his business in the South. After his retirement in 1857, he wrote voluminously of his trips below the Mason-Dixon line, particularly of his experiences as a correspondent with the Union armies. Because he was widely known and liked in the South, in 1864, he went as Lincoln's unofficial peace emissary to Jefferson Davis. He founded the *Continental Monthly* and wrote for the *Atlantic Monthly* and other magazines.

THOMAS CHANDLER HALIBURTON (1796-1865). Born in Windsor, Nova Scotia, he was a distinguished jurist and political figure in his native province and later in England, where he served in Parliament. His sketches of Sam Slick, the artful New England clock peddler, were originally written to jog Nova Scotians out of what he considered to be their lack of enterprise. By highlighting Yankee cunning in the person of Sam Slick, he hoped to bestir his people. However, the clock peddler became a comic figure of international popularity. His exploits were translated into many languages. Judge Haliburton capitalized on this tangent his brain child had taken by editing several excellent collections of United States backwoods humor.

BAYNARD RUST HALL (1798-1863). A graduate of Princeton Seminary, Hall was a pioneer Presbyterian minister in the Middle West. In addition to works on education and religion, he wrote graphic accounts of frontier life, including some of the best pictures of camp meetings during the Great Revival.

WILLIAM HALL. I have been able to find nothing about Hall, aside from the fact that his Mike Hooter sketches appeared first in the *New Orleans Delta* and were reprinted during the 1840's in the *Spirit of the Times* and other periodicals and newspapers. Each was subtitled: *A Yazoo Sketch.*

SAMUEL A. HAMMETT—Philip Paxton—(1816-1865). A Connecticut Yankee, Sam Hammett was on the loose in Texas for more than ten years and wrote sketches of frontier life as he knew it there. As Bernard DeVoto has pointed out, one of his accounts of a backwoods murder should rank with the greatest American short stories. His humorous sketches are of like quality.

GEORGE WASHINGTON HARRIS (1814-1869). Born in Alleghany City, Pennsylvania, Harris was reared in Knoxville, Tennessee. He had little schooling but read omniverously while apprenticed to a jeweler in the town. In his spare time he studied mechanics and wrote for local papers. At twenty-one he became captain of a steamboat and helped in the removal of the Cherokee from East Tennessee and Georgia. By the time he was thirty, Harris was a prosperous metal smith, jeweler, copper and wood engraver, and had several steam engine inventions to his credit. He wrote technical articles for the *Scientific American*, Whig editorials for Southern newspapers, and had begun contributing uproarious mountain sketches to newspapers and the *New York Spirit of the Times*. His Sut Lovingood yarns, the pranks and escapades of a whitetrash Tyll Eulenspiegel, were like nothing else ever written in this country—wild upheavals of gamey extravagance, seldom equaled since Rabelais. Harris used two popular literary techniques of his time which have deprived modern readers of his writing. He misspelled elaborately. He wrapped his tales in long passages of superfluous introduction and wind-up comment. I have translated the dialect, leaving enough phonetic spelling and idiom to localize the pieces. The envelopes of fancy writing have been cut.

JOEL CHANDLER HARRIS (1848-1908). Born near Eatonton, Georgia, Harris worked in the fields with slaves and came to love and understand them. Uncle Remus, a compendium of the wise old Negroes he had known, was already taking form in his mind when he chose journalism as his profession. In 1876, the *Atlanta Constitution* published the first Uncle Remus sketch. Four years later, *Uncle Remus, His Songs and Sayings* came out and became a best seller. It was followed by other sympathetic delineations of Georgia Negro and white folkways. To Harris goes the distinction of having recognized and lifted into the realm of art the mass of oral literature that had been neglected for generations under the noses of Southerners. With all his warm humanity, Uncle Remus has fallen into neglect today. I have been depressed to find well-read persons who have only foggy recollections of the Tar Baby story. One Western couple I know—versed in Tolstoy, Thomas Mann, Steinbeck, Saroyan, and so on—had never even heard of Uncle Remus, much less read him. The heavy dialect is a deterrant, I suppose, to those who haven't a familiar ear for it. Another road-block has been the dogma expounded by some of our literati: that only Negroes have any business writing about Negroes. Which, of course, is as absurd as its reverse would be.

FRANCIS BRET HARTE (1836-1902). Born in Albany, New York, he is now chiefly known for his sentimental poems and short stories about California during Gold Rush days. However, he wrote a variety of sketches after his return East in 1871. One of the best is *A Jersey Centenarian*, reprinted in this book.

JOHNSON J. HOOPER (1815-1862). Born in Wilmington, North Carolina, Hooper began newspaper work in Charleston at the age of fifteen. He roamed from job to job through the Gulf states until 1840 when he began studying law under his brother in Lafayette, Alabama. During the next six years, along with some law practice, he edited the *Dadeville Banner*, the *Wetumpka Whig*, and the *Montgomery Journal*, meanwhile placing miscellaneous sketches in national magazines. It was in this period that Simon Suggs, the cunningest backwoods rogue unhung, took form under his pen. Suggs was drawn from the life so faithfully that several Alabama worthies thought they had been pilloried in print and threatened variously to pound, horsewhip, and shoot Hooper on sight. True to the character of Suggs, all were careful that no encounter with Johnson Hooper should take place. The devious adventures of Suggs and other of Hooper's pieces, reprinted in newspapers North and South, were known also in Britain. Thackeray believed Hooper to be the most promising American writer of his day. Johnson Hooper could give only off-moments to Suggs. Defeated for office after four years as solicitor for the Ninth Alabama District, in 1849 he established the *Montgomery Mail*, editing it until 1861, when he was appointed secretary of the provisional Confederate Congress. When Congress moved to Richmond, Hooper went with it, throwing himself headlong into the Southern cause.

The last year of his life was embittered by the fact that his reputation as a humorist had become so firmly established that no matter how seriously he advanced an opinion, it was greeted with laughter.

WILLIAM WIRT HOWE (1833-1909). Born in Canandaigua, New York, Howe was a jurist, teacher, writer, and soldier. *How Congress Governs* is one of a succession of letters on local and national affairs which he contributed anonymously, under the running title *The Pasha Papers*, to the New York *Evening Post* in the winter and spring of 1859.

WASHINGTON IRVING (1783-1859) and JAMES KIRKE PAULDING (1778-1860). Irving, pre-eminent American writer of his day, and Paulding were linked by marriage—Paulding married Irving's sister—and by their collaboration, with William Irving in 1807-1808 on the *Salmagundi Papers*, a splatterdash about odd Gotham customs and characters appearing serially. Most of the piece abstracted for *Native American Humor* has a strong Washington Irving flavor. However, Paulding's writings were similar in style to Irving's. The only part of *Family Portraits from Cockloft Hall* known definitely as Paulding's is the Uncle John vignette. Of some literary reputation on his own account, Paulding wrote several historical novels. During Van Buren's administration he was secretary of the navy.

JONATHAN KELLEY (1818-1845). Born in Philadelphia, he wrote short humorous and adventure sketches for newspapers and periodicals, and became publisher of the *New York Arena* and the *Boston Traveller*. Some of his pieces appeared under the pseudonym, "Falconbridge."

MELVILLE D. LANDON—Eli Perkins—(1839-1910). Born in Eaton, New York, Landon was comic lecturer during the latter part of the nineteenth century. He was not so much a humorist as a collector of anecdotes of his prominent contemporaries—the Bennett Cerf of his day.

HENRY CLAY LEWIS—Madison Tensas. Little is known about the author of *My First Call is the Swamp*. In a random way he indicates that at the age of ten or eleven he ran away from Vicksburg, Mississippi, and was a scullion, cook, cabin-boy, gin-operator, plowboy, and cotton-picker. When he was sixteen, he went to work for a doctor living somewhere in Mississippi and, casual times that those were, struck out after a few years as a full-fledged, practicing physician in the fever-country of Lousiana.

DAVID ROSS LOCKE (1833-1888). Abraham Lincoln was once fifteen minutes late keeping an appointment with the British ambassador in order to read the latest eruption of Petroleum V. Nasby, the tomato-nosed apostle of bigotry created by Locke, who edited the Toledo, Ohio, *Blade*. The President is supposed to have said, "Nasby's worth a full division of infantry to the Union cause." To Charles Sumner he declared, "For the genius to write these things, I would gladly give up my office!" Some critics between the time of Nasby and our present curse of Bilbos, Rankins, and Talmadges thought Locke's caricature was reckless. Today we have too many Nasbys in the flesh and in full voice to agree with that judgment. A crusading editor, if there ever was one, Locke persisted in his fight for racial justice and, toward the end of his life, was to the forefront in the campaigns for equal rights for women.

AUGUSTUS BALDWIN LONGSTREET (1790-1870). Born in Augusta, Georgia, he graduated from Yale Law School, was admitted to the bar, was in the thick of state politics, edited (with William Tappan Thompson) the *State Rights Sentinel*, wrote on religious and political topics, turned out humorous sketches, became judge of the state supreme court, was ordained in the Methodist ministry, got involved in real estate deals, and was appointed in succession president of Emory College, Centenary College, the University of Mississippi, and the University of South Carolina. His *Georgia Scenes*, written during the early 1830's, depicted the backwoods in terms of salty realism. They were published anonymously. Later, Longstreet tried to suppress them as beneath the dignity of an eminent and godly man. That failing, he refused to have anything to do with the book when *Harper's* republished it at popular demand.

DAN MARBLE (1810-1849). A barnstorming actor of Yankee roles, born in Windsor, Connecticut, Marble was nearly as noted throughout the country as "Yankee" Hill. He occasionally wrote short pieces in character for sporting and theatrical magazines.

CORNELIUS MATHEWS (1817-1889). Born in Port Chester, New York, Mathews wrote waggish verse and political satire. He edited several magazines, including the short-lived comic *Yankee-Doodle* and the New York *Dramatic Mirror*. One of Dickens' American friends, he also knew and admired Elizabeth Barrett Browning and helped introduce her poems to this country.

ROBERT H. NEWELL—Orpheus C. Kerr—(1836-1901). Born in New York City, Newell's fame as a humorist was largely confined to the elaborately pompous newsletters he wrote from Washington, D. C., during the Civil War. They purported to come from a New York politician and "office seeker" who was looking out for the safety and comfort of boys from his ward while trying to clinch an easy, remunerative berth for himself. Orpheus C. Kerr's accounts of the idiocies of wartime bureaucracy are by no means dated.

EDGAR WILSON NYE—Bill Nye—(1850-1896). Born in Shirley, Maine, of a poverty-stricken family, Nye was a failure at everything he attempted —and he tried anything from odd jobs and teaching school in Wisconsin, to law practice in Laramie, Wyoming—until he began submitting

humorous scraps to the *Cheyenne Sun* and the *Denver Tribune*, hoping
to make a few dollars for groceries. The dry, sardonic sketches caught on
and were picked up by newspapers from coast to coast. The "delightful
parsimony of fact" under the byline *Bill Nye* became the most popular
newspaper column in America and soon spread to British journals. For a
time, Nye was postmaster and ran a newspaper, the *Laramie Boomerang*,
with offices of one loft room above a local livery stable. However, he
moved East to continue his column nearer the circuits of highly profitable
lecture tours, made with the treacley James Whitcomb Riley. At the
height of his fame, he died of tuberculosis.

ALBERT PIKE (1809-1891). A Bostonian who settled in Arkansas, Pike
was a lawyer, Whig politician, duelist, poet, Confederate Indian com-
missioner and later a brigadier general commanding Indian troops at the
battle of Pea Ridge. Among his legal anecdotes were many dealing with
the primitive back-country bar.

EDGAR ALLAN POE (1809-1849). Born in Boston, Massachusetts, of a
theatrical family, he was poet, critic, and pioneer in the short story form.
It would be superfluous to rehash his vital statistics. Suffice it to say, Poe
was enough an American of his times to have flings at humorous writing
—which, however, seeped out of his dark mind smelling of the charnel
house.

GEORGE D. PRENTICE (1802-1870). Born in Preston, Connecticut, Pren-
tice worked for several New England newspapers before he migrated to
Louisville, Kentucky, and rose to be the razor-penned editor of the
Journal. A Whig in politics, Prentice was feared because of his barbed
paragraphing, a technique in which he trained his successor, "Marse"
Henry Watterson.

H. H. RILEY (1813-1888). Born in Great Barrington, Massachusetts, he
was lawyer, editor, and writer of humorous pieces.

RUFUS E. SHAPLEY (1840-1906). A prominent member of the Philadelphia bar, Shapley was active in political reform, although he never ran
for office. His *Solid for Mulhooley*, published in 1881, bitingly satirized
the Irish-dominated machine politics of his city.

HENRY WHEELER SHAW—Josh Billings—(1818-1885). Born in Lanes-
borough, Massachusetts, son of a congressman, Shaw was too restless to
finish his education at Hamilton College or to accept an offer as John
Quincy Adams' secretary. He knocked about in Mexico, returned to become a steamboat pilot, shifted to school teaching, dropped that to run a
country store, tried his hand at cattle dealing, and finally turned up as an
auctioneer at Poughkeepsie. Dissatisfied with making his living at such
jabberwocky, he tried a series of pungent sayings, signed *Josh Billings*,

on a local newspaper. They attracted little notice. "I concluded," he said, "that I was boring with a pretty poor gimlet." For a year he abandoned writing, then tried again in a different style, "slewing the spelling round." His first misspelled effort, *Essa on the Muel*, an instant success, was copied by newspapers all over the country. From then on, Josh Billings had unflagging popularity as writer of cracker-barrel aphorisms and as a humorous lecturer. He was decried by the practitioners of New England belles-lettres. They feared that his influence would transform the American language into a kind of "joshbillingsgate."

WILLIAM GILMORE SIMMS (1806-1870). Born in Charleston, South Carolina, he was a prime example of genius flogging itself to frenzies of creation, evoking at best a sort of contemptuous tolerance from his people. His spate of historical novels and sketches have the faults of too voluminous writing, but they are shot through with an astounding richness. A more fortunate writer could have built a famous reputation on the themes and characterizations which Simms tossed into his potboilers for good measure. The Sam Snaffles yarn, with its mixture of lyrical moonshine and backwoods horse sense, is a good example of what William Gilmore Simms could do when he was enjoying himself.

CHARLES H. SMITH—Bill Arp—(1826-1903). Born in Lawrenceville, Georgia, this storekeeper, lawyer, politician, genial raconteur, lecturer, and contributor to newspapers and magazines shrewdly portrays rustic zanies and cracker-barrel garrulity. After the Civil War, he was one of the first Southerners to urge his people to accept defeat without rancor. Typically he replied to a reporter who asked details of his career in the Confederate Army: "Well, I reckon I'll have to give you the gory facts. I killed nearly as many Yankees as—they did of me."

SEBA SMITH (1792-1868). Born in Buckfield, Maine, Smith was editor of the *Portland Courier* and one of the first writers to use the ordinary American and his vernacular for purposes of humor. His Major Jack Downing series, beginning in 1830, was avidly read for a decade. The Major hid his Down East acuteness behind assumed countrified simplicity. He became the mythical confidant and adviser of Andrew Jackson—a device later used by David Ross Locke who made his Petroleum V. Nasby the familiar of Andrew Johnson, and by Will Rogers as Coolidge's crony. Today, the political issues on which most of Jack Downing was based are too remote for the humor to come through. However, the Yankee cunning of early Downing adventures can still bring us chuckles.

SOL SMITH (1801-1869). Born in Norwich, New York, he ran off from his father's farm with a roving troupe of actors and barnstormed through the upper Mississippi valley. Between trips, he learned the printer's trade in Louisville, studied law in Cincinnati, and worked as foreman of a composing room in Vincennes. He became partner in the theatrical firm of Ludlow & Smith, and conducted road companies through the South and Middle West. Meanwhile, he found time to practice law, teach singing schools, edit and write for newspapers, practice medicine, and organize volunteer fire companies. With a fortune made from land speculation, Sol Smith retired from the stage, settling in St. Louis where he wrote his theatrical reminiscences, was admitted to the bar, and became a leader in city and state politics.

A. E. SWEET (1841-1901). Born in St. Johns, New Brunswick, Canada, he was taken to San Antonio at the age of eight and grew up a thorough Texan. After a hitch in the Confederate Army, he practiced law ineffectually, then drifted into newswriting. His columns of broad humor attracted many readers, enabling him to found his own comic paper, *Texas Siftings*.

MORTIMER THOMPSON—"Q.K. Philander Doesticks"—(1831-1875). Born in Riga, New York, he was a newspaperman, traveling salesman, actor, writer of parody verse—with *Plu-Ri-Bus-Tah* he irreverently took Longfellow's *Hiawatha* over the hurdles—and author of "unpremeditated extravagances" about life in New York and the upper reaches of the Mississippi. His sketches, consistently of a sprightly debunking impudence, appeared in the New York *Tribune*.

WILLIAM TAPPAN THOMPSON (1812-1882). Born in Ravenna, Ohio, Thompson was by turns an apprentice reporter in Philadelphia, federal job holder in Florida, lawyer, and Georgia newspaper editor. With Augustus Baldwin Longstreet he edited the Augusta *States' Rights Sentinel*. Later he founded and edited the Savannah *Morning News*, one of the most vigorous of Southern newspapers. His popular Major Jones series, letters describing the misadventures of a love-sick Georgia swain, appeared during the 40's.

THOMAS BANGS THORPE (1815-1878). Called the father of the "Big Bear" school of Southern humor, Thorpe was a frail New Englander who went South for his health. In Louisiana, he edited newspapers, painted portraits, and penned many sketches of the mid-south frontier. Chief among them was *The Big Bear of Arkansas* from which *The Finishing-Up Country* in this book has been taken. He edited several anthologies of the humorous trend he set off. After serving in the Union Army, Thorpe took a government post in New York, holding it until his death.

HENRY WATTERSON—Marse Henry—(1840-1921). Long-time editor of the *Louisville Courier-Journal* and World War I interventionist, he was born in Washington, D. C., and wrote for several newspapers before he was trained on the old *Journal* by George D. Prentice. An officer in the Confederate Army, he was nevertheless an outspoken champion of reconciliation after the war. His editorials combined verbal bludgeoning and snapping wit. He was as noted as a raconteur as for his writing. In his dotage (1919), he resigned from the *Courier-Journal* because it advocated United States participation in the League of Nations.

FRANCES MIRIAM WHICHER (1811-1852). Born Frances Berry in Whitesboro, New York, she amused America during the 1840's with her Widder Bedott and Aunt Maguire portrayals of village life which appeared anonymously in *Neal's Saturday Gazette* and *Godey's Lady's Book*. For some time she persisted in hiding her identity and would give her publishers only this bit of self-description:

> Hands and feet
>   Of respectable size,
> Mud-colored hair,
>   And dubious eyes.

Finally she consented to publication of her name. Acclaim from the outside was fulsome, but at home her neighbors were scandalized that the Reverend Whicher's wife had been depicting their foibles with such sharp fidelity. Shunned, the subject of gossip, she left her husband whose parish was in Elmira, and spent the last three years of her life with her family at Whitesboro.

N. P. WILLIS (1806-1867). Born in Portland, Maine, Willis lightly satirized urban manners and customs. He was the most highly paid humorist of his day, a stand-by in such magazines as *Godey's* and *Graham's*. As editor of the New York *Evening Mirror*, he hired Edgar Allen Poe, and remained his stanch friend and defender.

Set in Linotype Fairfield
Format by A. W. Rushmore
Manufactured by The Haddon Craftsmen
Published by HARPER & BROTHERS
New York and London